Mediation and Facilitation Training Manual

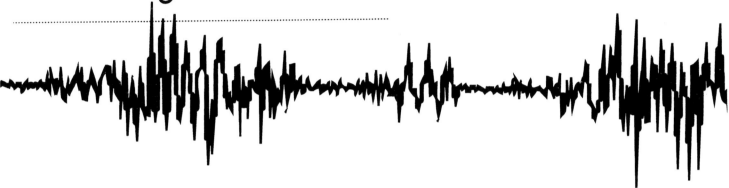

**Foundations and Skills for
Constructive Conflict Transformation**

Fourth Edition
Carolyn Schrock-Shenk, editor

Mennonite Conciliation Service
Akron, Pennsylvania
2000

Editor:	Carolyn Schrock-Shenk
Assistant Editor:	Kristin Reimer
Editorial Consultant:	Alice M. Price
Project Coordinator:	Phil Brubaker

Mennonite Conciliation Service

a program of Mennonite Central Committee U.S.
PO Box 500, Akron PA 17501-0500
717-859-3889; 717-859-3875 fax
mcs@mccus.org; www.mcc.org/mcs.html

MCS publishes this manual so that it will be used. We strive to maintain a responsible balance between sharing our material and retaining the rights to it. If you find this manual useful and would like to reprint or copy portions of it, please observe the considerations at the back of the manual.

Use of material from this manual does not constitute recognition or designation as an MCS trainer. MCS is not responsible for how material from this manual is used.

Table of Contents

Chapter 3 — Interpersonal Communication and Problem-Solving

Chapter 4 — Interpersonal Mediation: One Model

Chapter 5 — Groups: Process, Conflict, Systemic Change

Part 1 – Healthy Group Process

Part 2 – Conflict and Systemic Change

Chapter 6 — Standards and Ethics for Practice

Chapter 7 — Pedagogy

Foreword

Do not remember the former things, or consider the things of old. I am about to do a new thing; now it springs forth, do you not perceive it? I will make a way in the wilderness and rivers in the desert.

–Isaiah 43:18-19

"Transformation": to change markedly the appearance, form, nature, function or condition; to convert. Transformation is all around us. From cellular biology, math, and linguistics, to the current lingo of education and corporate management. It is in the changing of the season as I look outside my study window. And in the painstaking and often painful process in which many Mennonites have been involved in recent years: creating a new denomination out of two. As one pundit quipped early on: when you try to blend two into one, you end up with at least three!

"Transformation" is also a spiritual word. Those of us who work with peace and justice issues—all across the spectrum from international to neighborhood and family settings—are occasionally privileged to witness it: that sacred moment when the old makes way for new. Often it is as fragile as a pine seedling growing sideways out of a tiny cavity in a rocky mountainside; or a weed pushing up through a crack in an urban sidewalk. Occasionally it soars on eagles' wings over a wide landscape of change.

This manual is itself a parable of transformation—telling some of the change-story of MCS and of the broader mediation field. At the first MCS Summer Training Institute in 1985, we participants were each given a slim manila folder in which to collect the week's hand-outs. Copied on blue paper and pre-dating high-class word-processing and copying equipment, their somewhat ragged look is still precious to me—like the new teeth of a young child. Ron Kraybill's early distillation on paper of so many key concepts confirmed my own growth and invited me onward—both spiritually and intellectually. By the time I joined the staff in 1988, Dave Brubaker had organized 40 or so pages into loose-leaf binders for the now popular and oft-repeated training institutes. But Ron's bulging black "trainer's notebook," the mounting stack of *Conciliation Quarterly* newsletters, and John Paul Lederach's arrival were daily reminders of the burgeoning field and foreshadowed the rich editorial work that lay ahead. 1989 and 1992 each brought published training manuals, both editions a bit weightier in pages—and hopefully in diversity of voices and collective wisdom—than the last. In the 1995 third edition, editors Jim Stutzman and Carolyn Schrock-Shenk added much depth to issues of power, justice and diversity.

Each edition also continued to radiate farther and farther beyond those first 20 institute participants reading their blue study sheets in the Mennonite Central Committee chapel—into universities, community centers, church basements, and groups of people gathered here and there to ponder peace under the welcome shade of a tree. Now this change process has taken yet another step with this 2000 edition for the on-going benefit and growth of us all: trainers and students alike.

"Transformation." The term began to emerge in various writings in the field in the late 1980s and first appeared in the title of the MCS training manual in 1992. In the 2000 edition, it is as ubiquitous throughout the manual's varied authors and chapters as it is in our North American lingo at-large. While some efforts have been made to "capture" the term, to give it a prescriptive definition—as in "transformative mediation"—like the concept itself, it cannot really be "fixed." For it—and we—and those whom we serve with these "foundations and skills for constructive conflict transformation"—need always to be poised, ready to "do a new thing."

Do you not perceive it?

–Alice M. Price
La Jara, Colorado, April 30, 2000

Acknowledgments

Where does one begin to acknowledge all those who have been a part of bringing this fourth edition to fruition? The history of this manual, helpfully described by Alice Price in the Foreword, is many-layered and complex. I am grateful to all who have given parts of their work and experience to make this edition possible.

I am particularly grateful to Phil Brubaker who gave countless hours and carried the day with this project, from organizing details to formatting to giving editorial suggestions. Special thanks also to Kristin Reimer, my editorial assistant, who was equally creative, long-suffering and good-humored, and to Alice Price, my predecessor and constant source of wisdom for MCS, who again provided invaluable editorial assistance. Thanks to Suelda Hurst and Sharon Martin for keying in materials and other secretarial work, and to Bob VanDale and Ardell Stauffer for their excellent proofreading.

A particularly useful part of this project was inviting experienced members of the broader MCS network to give us editorial feedback on specific aspects of the third edition and to offer suggestions for improvements. Their comments, not all of which we were able to incorporate, have enhanced this edition considerably. Specifically, we are grateful to the following:

Elaine Enns and Dalton Reimer — Chapter 1
Pat Hostetter Martin and John Paul Lederach — Chapter 2
David Dyck — Chapter 3
Sandi Adams — Chapter 4
David Brubaker — Chapter 5
Michelle Armster and Nancy Ferrell— Chapter 6
Kirsten Zerger — Chapter 7
Roberto Chené and Beth Roy — Cultural issues
Julianna Birkhoff — Power issues

Finally there are the writers. While not every contributor is acknowledged below, we thank all the organizations and individuals who have so generously given permission to reprint their work here. A special note of thanks to Ron Kraybill whose wisdom and clear articulation has graced many pages of each edition of this manual, including some new material in this one. To give you an idea of the breadth of our authors, what follows are brief sketches of some of those most closely associated with MCS and this manual project.

And now, this project goes to print. With it goes my deep gratitude for the contributions of so many and my sincere hope that this manual will enrich your work and life.

–Carolyn Schrock-Shenk
Editor

Contributors

Sandi Adams   Instructor at the University of North Carolina, Wilmington. Sandi is also in private practice providing intervention and training services. She is the former director of Woodbury College Mediation Program and former staff of Friends Conflict Resolution Services.

Hizkias Assefa   Professor of conflict studies in the Conflict Transformation Program of Eastern Mennonite University (Harrisonburg, Va.) and coordinator of the African Peacebuilding and Reconciliation Network (Nairobi, Kenya). Based in Kenya, Hizkias is also a distinguished fellow at the Institute of Conflict Analysis and Resolution, George Mason University (Fairfax, Va.).

David Brubaker	Partner in Cooperative By Design, An Arizona Peacebuilding Consortium. Dave has been active in the conflict transformation field since he was associate director of MCS (1986-1988).
Roberto Chené	Director of the Southwest Center for Intercultural Leadership (Albuquerque, N.M.). Roberto has traveled throughout the United States and in South Africa and Mexico doing facilitation, consultation and training, focusing on intercultural leadership and conflict resolution.
Mark Chupp	Project manager at the Center for Neighborhood Development at Levin College of Urban Affairs, Cleveland State University. Mark previously worked in conflict transformation with Mennonite Central Committee in Central America.
Ron Claassen	Co-director of the Center for Conflict Studies and Peacemaking at Fresno Pacific University and co-director of the conflict and peacemaking master of arts degree program. Ron was the founder and director (1982-1999) of the Fresno Victim Offender Reconciliation Program.
Larry Dunn	Ph.D. candidate in social science at Syracuse University (N.Y.), affiliated with the Program on the Analysis of Resolution of Conflicts, and associate of the Center for Peacemaking and Conflict Studies at Fresno Pacific University (Fresno, Cal.). Larry has worked in conflict transformation for 15 years, most recently in Labrador, Canada.
David Dyck	Private practitioner in conflict resolution (Maritime region of Canada). Dave previously worked with Mediation Services of Winnipeg (Man.) and remains an associate. He lives in Halifax, Nova Scotia.
Elaine Enns	Associate of the Center for Peacemaking and Conflict Studies at Fresno Pacific University (Fresno, Cal.). Elaine is also the program director of the Los Angeles Victim Offender Reconciliation Program.
Larry Hoover	Mediation trainer in the Virginia area and member of a state-wide mediation group called McCammon. Larry also has a private law practice and teaches negotiation and mediation classes at Washington and Lee Law School.
Ron Kraybill	Associate professor in the Conflict Transformation Program of Eastern Mennonite University (Harrisonburg, Va.). Ron was the founding director of MCS (1979-1988) and director of training at the Centre for Conflict Resolution, Cape Town, R.S.A. (1989-1995).
John Paul Lederach	Professor of sociology and conflict studies in the Conflict Transformation Program of Eastern Mennonite University (Harrisonburg, Va.). John Paul maintains active involvement in numerous conciliation and training efforts in North America and beyond.
Diane LeResche	Independent consultant working collaboratively with tribes and nonprofit organizations to promote and prepare people to use sacred justice methods.
Dean Peachey	Administrator and conflict resolution studies professor at Menno Simons College in Winnipeg, Man.
Alice M. Price	Private mediator, trainer and director of the San Luis Valley Victim Offender Reconciliation Program (Colo.). Alice served as director of MCS in the early 1990s and edited the first editions of this manual.
Beth Roy	Mediator and mentor in private practice (San Francisco Bay Area). Beth is a sociologist exploring social conflict.

Dalton Reimer	Faculty member of Fresno Pacific University (Fresno, Cal.) since 1960, serving as academic dean for 18 years of that time. Dalton is currently the co-director of the university's Center for Peacemaking and Conflict Studies.
Duane Ruth-Heffelbower	Attorney, mediator and ordained Mennonite minister. Duane is associate director of the Center for Peacemaking and Conflict Studies at Fresno Pacific University (Fresno, Cal.).
Lisa Schirch	Assistant professor of conflict studies at Eastern Mennonite University (Harrisonburg, Va.). She has conducted research on and worked internationally in nonviolent interpositioning and on Native American issues.
Carolyn Schrock-Shenk	Associate professor of peace, justice and conflict studies at Goshen College (Goshen, Ind.). Carolyn worked at Mennonite Conciliation Service (Akron, Pa.) from 1992-2000 and served as director from 1996-2000.
Marcus G. Smucker	Certified pastoral counselor and congregational consultant from Bird-in-Hand, Pa. Until recently he was a professor at Associated Mennonite Biblical Seminary (Elkhart, Ind.) and is currently teaching part time for Eastern Mennonite Seminary (Harrisonburg, Va.) in the areas of spirituality, counseling and managing congregational conflict.
Jim Stutzman	Elementary school teacher in Lancaster, Pa. Jim was director of MCS from 1992-1996, having worked previously in victim-offender mediation.
Howard Zehr	Professor of sociology and restorative justice in the Conflict Transformation Program of Eastern Mennonite University (Harrisonburg, Va.). Howard previously served as director of the Office on Crime and Justice of Mennonite Central Committee U.S. (1977-1996).
Kirsten Zerger	Senior training associate for the Kansas Institute for Peace and Conflict Resolution at Bethel College (North Newton, Kan.). Kirsten is a former practicing attorney and was the director of a community mediation program.

Chapter 1

Conflict Transformation and Faith

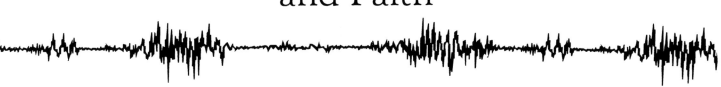

The higher goal of spiritual living is not to amass a wealth of information, but to face sacred moments.

-Rabbi Abraham Heschel

Introduction

Human activity consists of action and reflection: it is transformation of the world....
And as praxis, it requires theory to illuminate it. Human activity is theory and
practice; it is reflection and action. It cannot be reduced to either verbalism or
activism.

–Paulo Freire, *Pedagogy of the Oppressed*

This is a reflective chapter, one that examines the theological foundation of who we are and what we do as peacemakers. In one sense, a theology of peacemaking provides a comprehensive understanding of our relationship to conflict and violence as followers of Christ. As the opening articles note clearly, peacemaking in the Anabaptist tradition is central to the gospel, not simply an optional activity or secular notion.

On the other hand, to suggest that our theological task/activity is confined to this chapter is woefully inadequate. Faith is both orthodoxy (right belief) and orthopraxis (right action). In that sense, each section of this manual presents our theology of peacemaking. Each skill and process presented, each issue discussed, reflects and emerges from a theology of conflict and peacemaking.

This theology does not emerge only from a few selective biblical texts, such as the call to a "ministry of reconciliation" (2 Cor. 5:17). Rather, our theology centers on the whole of Christ's life and death and the meaning it gives to the entire biblical witness. With this as our starting point, the challenge of this first chapter is to articulate some of our theological assumptions which underlie all the material found in the following chapters.

We have organized the chapter loosely around the following themes:

- Who we are as peacemakers—roots and identity

- Why we do what we do—our call to peacemaking

- How we do what we do—our spiritual rootedness

- How we relate to each other—our commitment to right relationships

Though these themes are overlapping and interconnected, they helped provide structure and meaning for us as we compiled this chapter. We found ourselves moved and challenged by the lives, insights and commitment of many writers in the circle of Christian peacemakers. May it serve as a reflective resource in your life and faith as well.

–Larry Dunn and Carolyn Schrock-Shenk
© MCS 1995

Beatitudes of Reconciliation

*Blessed are those who are willing to enter
into the process of being healed,
for they will become healers.
Blessed are those who recognize their
own inner violence,
for they will come to know nonviolence.
Blessed are those who can forgive self,
for they will become forgivers.
Blessed are those who are willing to let go
of selfishness and self-centeredness,
for they will become a healing presence.
Blessed are those who listen with compassion,
for they will become compassionate.
Blessed are those who are willing to enter into conflict,
for they will find transformation.
Blessed are those who know their
interdependence with all of creation,
for they will become unifiers.
Blessed are those who live a contemplative life stance,
for they will find God in all things.
Blessed are those who strive to live these beatitudes,
for they will be reconcilers.*

–Sisters of St. Joseph of Concordia
© Sisters of St. Joseph, Concordia, Kansas. Used by permission.

Prayers of the People

Leader: O God, help us to face conflicts in our relationships with one another. Give us courage that we might by careful labor and loving encounter move beyond our disagreements to find true reconciliation.

People: O God, make us the instruments of your peace.

Leader: Encourage us to keep our own struggles and needs in perspective, so that we do not overpower others with our disappointments and our hurt.

People: O God, make us the instruments of your peace.

Leader: Enable us to do careful listening that gives understanding. Let us set aside our own needs long enough to respond to the needs of others.

People: O God, make us the instruments of your peace.

Leader: Save us from the preoccupations and busyness that cause us to lose touch with one another. Help us to follow one another's lives so that we can support when there is failure and celebrate when there is success.

People: O God, make us the instruments of your peace.

Leader: Lead us to understand that we are all your children—made in your image and carrying your promise. Help us to celebrate the uniqueness of each person and to see the differences among us as sources of strength and vitality.

People: O God, make us the instruments of your peace.

Leader: When there are dark moments in our relationships, teach us to recognize the pathway that you light for us. Let us see the peacemaking opportunities you create and help us to reach out to one another, to speak the loving word, and to do justice in our households.

People: O God, make us the instruments of your peace. Amen.

–George D. Parsons
© Presbyterian Peacemaking Program, from *Peacemaking Through Worship: Peacemaking: The Believer's Calling*

Anabaptist Peacemaking and Conflict Transformation

Recently, a number of authors who have reflected on the history of the broader "conflict resolution" movement have acknowledged the work of Mennonites as significant within its religious stream. The roots of Mennonite peacemaking can be traced back through a 400-year-old tradition, beginning with the leaders of the 16th century Anabaptist movement. While the inspiration for Mennonite Conciliation Service (MCS) occurred 25 short years ago, its practical focus on mediation can be viewed as one recent expression of that longer peacemaking tradition. It stands alongside other recent expressions such as the active, nonviolent presence in situations of conflict provided by the Christian Peacemakers Teams. It is the mediation stream which is the central object of this historical and theological reflection.

History and Background

For the early Anabaptists, to follow Christ was to be called to a life reconciled to God and all persons, including one's enemies. As part of the 16th century radical reformation movement, Mennonites lived this life of discipleship in a context of intense conflict and, at times, deadly persecution. Emphasizing the separation of church and state, these European believers spoke of "defenselessness," a term which came to mean both the refusal of violent self-defense and the rejection of military service. Termed "nonresistance" in the early 20th century, this belief was embodied in the conscientious objection stance during both world wars.

Contemporary Anabaptist peacemaking involves a new appropriation of the resources of biblical faith, and its activism is energized by an increasing concern for justice issues. Founded on the theological understanding of reconciliation as central to Christ's life and teachings, the call to peacemaking is extended to all who claim to be children of God (Mt. 5:9). In 1975, that call began to take a new shape in the establishment of MCS.

MCS was envisioned as a ministry of Mennonite Central Committee (MCC) U.S. Peace Section, offering a range of services for preventing and responding to conflict and intervening to reduce violence and destruction. Alongside MCS, the Office on Crime and Justice of MCC helped initiate a specialized form of mediation known as the Victim Offender Reconciliation Program (VORP) as a means for encouraging reconciliation between victims and offenders.

Anabaptist Theology and Peacemaking Practice Today

In the book entitled *The Promise of Mediation*, Robert Baruch Bush and Joseph Folger identify four different "stories" of mediation within the alternative dispute resolution (ADR) movement. Though not a theological model, their discussion of mediation in the U.S. provides a useful framework for reflecting theologically on the Anabaptist Peacemaking Story and the present MCS approaches to conflict transformation.

The first account is the "Satisfaction Story," which Bush and Folger believe presently dominates (U.S.) mediation practice. The Satisfaction Story is focused on creative problem solving and stresses "win-win" outcomes. The second account, the "Social Justice Story," sees mediation as a vehicle for organizing individuals and groups against exploitation, promoting equality and greater justice. Interestingly, the "Oppression Story" describes mediation as a dangerous instrument for neutralizing the social justice gains achieved by many social movements. Mediation, as a private, informal process, it says, produces unjust outcomes which favor the powerful and take advantage of the weak. Finally, Bush and Folger offer the "Transformation Story," the picture of mediation as they think it should be: a process which transforms the moral character of individual disputants and eventually society as a whole.

Transformation has become a buzzword within conflict resolution circles. Many practitioners have simply substituted transformation for other terms used in the past (such as "management," "reduction," and "resolution") without a real change in meaning. If we merely adopt the term without clearly defining its meaning for us, we are likely to do the same.

I believe transformation is a meaningful and accurate term for describing the work of MCS. This includes mediation as well as a range of other approaches to conflict. The reason should be obvious—the church has a similar term of great significance: conversion. Conversion (or, turning around) is a rich word, an important (and necessary) aspect of Christ's work of salvation.

MCS director Carolyn Schrock-Shenk suggests that it is salvation which connects conversion to peacemaking. Biblical salvation involves reconciliation between God and people, between the earth and people, and between and within ourselves. It is both "vertical" and "horizontal," personal and social, individual and corporate. And like Christ's transformation of our lives (see Rom. 12:2; 2 Cor. 3:18) the transformation of conflict is not of our own doing but received as a gift from God.

Bush and Folger's notion of transformative mediation involves empowerment of the individual and recognition of the other person's condition, their place in life and its conflicts. The call for empowerment and recognition is well grounded in the Biblical Story which is our own. Both are crucial to our life together, especially in times of conflict.

In the church we recognize the active role of the Holy Spirit for empowering followers of Christ (Rom. 8). The commitment to train peacemakers in practical skills is a form of empowerment which reflects a view of peacemaking as not just a profession but a way of life. As such, we accept the call to transform conflict as mediators and trainers, as parents and members of the church, and in other roles through fair and participatory processes which seek to include a diversity of voices in pursuit of justice and peace.

Recognition of the other is only possible through a Spirit-centered sense of humility, grounded in mutual confession and based on Christ's call to love even our enemies (though we must be careful about whom we label as the "enemy"). This does not mean sacrificing the gospel for religious relativism or ignoring our deepest convictions. But it does mean living by the "fruit of the Spirit" (Gal. 5:22-23) and refusing to play God by pretending that we grasp the entirety of God's revealed truth in all matters (Rom. 11:33-34). If we claim to have been delegated the final authority for deciding who's "in" and who's "out," we have mistaken the church for the Kingdom (see Rom. 2:1-4). In essence, we humbly recognize our own sinful condition as one with that of others before God.

But Christ's call to peacemaking requires an even more radical, all-encompassing kind of transfor-

mation than Bush and Folger describe. It also involves consideration of the Social Justice and Oppression Stories, which present both a challenge and a warning for the peacemaking work of the church.

In spite of conventional wisdom which suggests that we are becoming an increasingly litigious society, the voices which emerge from the Oppression Story have raised questions about the effect that certain forms of peacemaking, such as mediation, are having on society at large. Many claim that we have become a "harmony" society, suppressing the realities of class, gender, and racial antagonisms which surround us. A few have laid the responsibility for this ideology of harmony at the church's doorstep. Discomfort with conflict in Mennonite denominations, which arises from our often negative experience of it and its effects, has led us to view disagreement and controversy as dysfunctional and threatening to the life of the church community. No wonder, then, our concern for "resolution."

The church clearly has something to learn from the Oppression Story for its peacemaking work. In the present climate of concern over homosexuality and other divisive issues, the warning that mediation may be used to manipulate, silence, and exert coercive pressure is one we must not overlook. This kind of "peace" works against those who are already disadvantaged by encouraging conformity and acquiescence when more radical solutions may be called for. Conflict transformation constantly seeks to balance the ongoing tension between mediation and nonviolent advocacy as compatible, interdependent approaches.

"No justice, no peace!" This is not just the cry of protestors angry over the turn of recent events. Rather, this is a cry from the ages, from God's prophets of old. The prophet Jeremiah cried out against the false prophets who say, "Peace, peace," when there is no peace (Jer. 6:14; 8:11). While some claim that peacemaking is not about pursuing social justice, the biblical warning against oppression reminds us that we cannot have shalom without it. Justice is a matter of right relationships. And peace is the fruit of righteousness and justice (Is. 32:17).

Contemporary usage suggests a kind of quid pro quo, which holds out on the offer of peace as it waits for justice to be done. But peace is not peace at all in the absence of justice. One cannot be exchanged for the other. The biblical concern for social justice involves advocacy on behalf of the marginalized and oppressed (the crowd Jesus was accused of hanging out with) in an effort to redress imbalances of power. This is central to the peacemaking task. Perhaps this is in part what Jesus meant by that most difficult of statements, "I have not come to bring peace, but a sword" (Mt. 10:34).

Harmony can be essential for community well-being, because too much conflict—a constant state of chaos—can distract us from our mission as the church and put the survival of the group and its individual members at risk. For mediators and other types of peacemakers, helping to satisfy the needs of people entangled in the web of conflict may be an important, if not central, accomplishment. But focusing solely on the settlement of issues (which are often symptoms of underlying conflict) detracts from the transformative moments along the way. After all, conversion is not merely an isolated, one-time event; it is a life-long process experienced within community!

Although Bush and Folger deny that aspects of the four stories can be integrated (at least in a mediation model), I believe that the gospel demands a commitment to a kind of transformative peacemaking that neglects none of them. Mediation is no panacea. But the gospel is! And a biblical approach to transforming conflict affirms the value of different responses to brokenness and injustice—

–Larry Dunn
©MCS 1995

even those which choose to create or escalate conflict with the ultimate hope of establishing a new relationship of justice and peace.

It has been said in the past that Mennonites have a comprehensive peace theology without an equally comprehensive approach to peacemaking. As we approach the next century we are confronted with new and increasingly difficult challenges—of professionalism and pluralism, alienation and power imbalances, and the seemingly endless escalation of violence of all kinds. The implication for peacemakers is that we must resist the temptation of assuming that every conflict is the same and therefore in need of immediate resolution.

An old saying applies well to working as a mediator: "When the only tool you have is a hammer, everything looks like a nail." All conflicts are different, involve multiple factors, and are expressed in a variety of ways. How we understand a particular conflict will influence the "tool" we select to deal with it. A transformative approach recognizes the limits of any given strategy and seeks to determine the most appropriate response or combination of responses. It calls us to make decisions about when to stand between and when to stand alongside, when to forgive and when to hold back, when to pursue harmony and when to confront with conflict. As followers of the Prince of Peace, we need go no further than the gospel to find our way.

Shalom: The Road Taken

I love climbing to the top of a hill where I can see for miles in all directions. A highway turnout above a valley or a tall building will also do. In these high places, I am drawn to pick out the places below where I and my fellow travelers have been and point out where we will yet be going.

This new year-decade-century-millennium is a good time to look back at our lives and history and ahead to our future. We have just ended what has been arguably the most violent century in human history. More than 100 million persons lost their lives last century as a result of war alone. And murder, in the view of criminologist Colin Wilson, did "not really come into its own until the twentieth century." Today, even the children kill.

From the beginning, God has had a vision of shalom—of peace—for the world. Throughout Scripture, there are references to God's desire to establish his shalom on earth. As servants of God, we journey towards this shalom community. But how do we as Christians respond to violence and conflict today? What does God's vision of peace give us for the present and the future?

To get our bearings, I know of no better place to look than the Bible. What does it teach us about violence, conflict and peacemaking? Like the hill and mountain tops, the Bible gives us the larger view from a high place.

In the Beginning

As we look at where we have been, we see in the far distant past the start of our journey. "In the beginning God created the heavens and the earth," the book of Genesis boldly begins (Gen. 1:1). And God's creation was "good." Seven times, as an artist stepping back to examine his developing masterpiece, God viewed what he was making and proclaimed it to be "good"—indeed, the seventh time as "very good" (Gen. 1:4, 10, 12, 18, 21, 25, 31).

But the goodness of God's creation was soon marred by sin. Eve and Adam disobeyed God, and the shalom—the peace—of the idyllic garden of Eden God had created and placed them in was destroyed.

Shalom, a Hebrew word, is often translated into English as "peace," but it means much more than the simple absence of tension. In *Shalom, The Bible's Word for Salvation, Justice and Peace*, Perry

Yoder identifies three dominant meanings of shalom in the Old Testament. Shalom sometimes means "material well-being and prosperity" (Gen. 37:14, Ps. 38:3, Jer. 33:6-9), sometimes just and right relationships (1 Kings 5:12, Isa. 32:16-17) and sometimes "straightforwardness" as in speaking truth (Ps. 34:14).

Overall, shalom describes a state of goodness, where all is right, just, truthful, whole, complete and harmonious. It is the condition of Eden before the fall—and God's vision for his broken world after the fall.

How, then, is God's vision of shalom realized in a post-Eden, broken world? By looking back over the biblical landscape, we can find some answers to that question.

Signpost 1: I Am My Brother's Keeper

The first part of our post-Eden human journey was a long detour into violence, beginning with Cain's murder of his brother Abel (Gen.4:1-16) and ending with the flood (Gen. 6-9).

God clearly was not pleased. "We must not be like Cain," the New Testament affirms (1 John 3:12). We, too, must say no to violence, the destroyer of shalom.

But we must also say yes to Cain's defensive question, "Am I my brother's keeper?" (Gen. 4:9). Cain's implied answer to his question was no, but God's answer was a clear yes. Beginning with those closest to us—our brothers and sisters and family—we are each other's keeper. Joseph, in the final story of Genesis, models best the meaning of being a "keeper." He forgave his brothers and cared for them, even though they had done him great harm (Gen. 50:15-21).

"I am my brother's keeper" is our first signpost on our journey toward the recovery of God's shalom in a post-Eden world.

Signpost 2: Love God & Your Neighbor

The second signpost grows out of our life together in community. In our historical journey, God determined to begin anew after the flood by creating for himself a special people through whom all the families of the earth would be blessed—that is, a world where shalom might be realized. So God called Abraham and Sarah to parent this special people (Gen. 12:1-3).

All peoples of the earth require an ethic—or rule—to live by. Usually, some form of a "constitutional convention" is called. In the case of ancient Israel, God spared them the convention and simply gave them a law.

This law, though elaborately detailed, was anchored in two fundamental principles: "You shall love the Lord your God with all your heart and with all your soul and with all your might" (Deut. 6:5) and "you shall love your neighbor as yourself" (Lev. 19:18).

"And who is my neighbor?" a lawyer defensively asked Jesus one day (Luke 10:29). Like Cain, the lawyer, too, followed his human instinct to draw boundaries. He should have known better. The law he supposedly practiced made it clear that neighbor included more than his own kind, and that he was also to love the alien and the stranger in the land as himself (Lev. 19:33-34; Deut. 10:17-19). But Jesus patiently responded with the telling tale of a despised Samaritan who modeled being a neighbor to the lawyer's kind, who were of a different ethnic and religious persuasion (Luke 10:25-37). Being a neighbor is to know no boundaries.

Love God and love your neighbor are written large on the second signpost in our journey towards God's shalom.

Signpost 3: Lay Down the Sword, Take Up Your Cross

A fork in a road forces us to choose. Shall we go right or left? Our third signpost has to do with such a choice.

As we look back, we see that ancient Israel repeatedly failed to realize God's shalom. God's judgment for their failure was severe, but he did not leave them without hope. He promised them a Messiah who, among other things, would be "a Prince of Shalom" (Isa. 9:1-7). But when Jesus came, people found his version of the Messiah confusing.

Within ancient Israel itself, competing visions of how God would establish his shalom community on earth had developed over time. The Exodus experience provided one model. God, who had condemned the family violence of brothers in Genesis, interestingly chose violence as the means of liberating his people from slavery in Egypt.

Furthermore, God then pursued a strategy of military conquest to provide a home for them in the land he had promised. Indeed, the Exodus model portrayed God as a triumphant warrior (Exod. 15). With God in the lead, ancient Israel marched to the tune of holy war. Holy war was the prevailing pattern in the Israel of conquerors, judges and kings.

In the Israel of the later prophets, however, a contrasting vision began to emerge. We find this vision articulated most clearly by the prophet Isaiah. In this vision the recovery of God's shalom is seen as coming not through a conquering king, but a suffering servant (Isa. 53). A suffering servant and a conquering king are strikingly different.

These differences over the means to establish God's shalom community caused first century Jews to be confused by Jesus. He did not fully match their expectations of the Messiah. They hoped that he would once again be their liberator as in ancient Israel.

So, when Jesus began to share his understanding of messiahship in the servant terms of suffering, death and resurrection, Peter quickly took him aside and rebuked him (Matt. 16:13-28; Mark 8:27—9:1; Luke 9:18-27). Jesus, in return, most strongly rebuked Peter: "Get behind me, Satan! For you are setting your mind not on divine things but on human things" (Matt. 16:23, Mark 8:33).

This dramatic exchange set the direction for all that followed. At this fork in the road, Jesus chose the narrow way of the cross over the broad way of the sword. And, as the poet Robert Frost has said about such choices, "that has made all the difference."

Peter, however, was a slow learner. So when he took his sword in the spirit of holy war and cut off the ear of the high priest's servant at the time of the arrest of Jesus in the garden, Jesus made it very clear: "Put your sword back into its place; for all who take the sword will perish by the sword" (Matt. 26:52). Furthermore, Jesus said he could call on an army of twelve legions—72,000—of angels if he chose, but that was not his way (Matt. 5:53-54).

The cross is the way to God's shalom. Its reach is cosmic. Through Christ "God was pleased to reconcile to himself all things, whether on earth or in heaven, by making peace through the blood of his cross" (Col. 1:19-20).

Jesus, furthermore, challenged his followers to also choose the way of the cross. "If any want to become my followers, let them deny themselves and take up their cross and follow me" (Matt. 16:24; Mark 8:34: Luke 9:23). In *The Cost of Discipleship*, Dietrich Bonhoeffer said that when Christ calls us, he bids us come and die.

The cross stands tall at the fork in the road. The new way to God's shalom begins at the cross.

Signpost 4: Walk in His Way

A new way requires a new ethic or rule, and the teachings of Jesus set forth this new rule.

Nowhere is this new rule stated more concisely than in Jesus' sermon from a mountain (Matt. 507). Jesus made it clear that he did not come to dismiss the old, but to "fulfill" the old (Matt. 5:17). The Old Testament's first lessons of love for God, brothers and sisters, and neighbors were foundational for Jesus. He built on them. But he also did not hesitate to reshape that which was old into something that was new.

Reconciliation emphasized. Jesus elevated family life to a new level. Killing a brother clearly had been prohibited from the beginning, and that was affirmed. But Jesus went on to say that nursing anger or hating a brother or sister was akin to murder. He called for quick reconciliation between brothers and sisters (Matt. 5:21-26). The meaning of adultery as a physical act was expanded to include the disposition of the heart and mind (Matt. 5:27-30). And easy divorce was curbed (Matt. 5:31-32).

Hate, adultery and easy divorce in the family are destroyers of shalom. Reconciliation is the creator of shalom.

Integrity the norm. Relationships with others, Jesus said, are to be marked by a new standard of truth-speaking. In place of swearing to attest to one's truth, one's "yes" should simply be "yes" and one's "no," "no." One should be so trustworthy and credible that no more is required (Matt. 5:33-37).

Overcome evil with good. Justice rooted in the old equivalency principle of "an eye for an eye and a tooth for a tooth" was radically transformed by Jesus (Matt. 5:38-42). "Do not resist an evildoer," he said, "but if someone hits you on the right cheek, turn also the other; if someone demands your outer garment, give him also the inner; or if someone forces you to go one mile, go a second."

Such a strategy is anything but passive. It calls for seizing the initiative in the face of oppression, but with a strategy of goodness rather than vengeance and violence. "Do not be overcome by evil, but overcome evil with good," was the Apostle Paul's later summary of the principle (Rom. 12:21).

Love's Embrace Enlarged

Finally Jesus extended the embrace of love by drawing in even the enemy (Matt. 5:43-45).

Brothers and sisters are important, but Jesus said, "if you greet only your brothers and sisters, what more are you doing than others?" (Matt. 5:47). And the received tradition that "you shall love your neighbor and hate your enemy" simply does not reflect the nature of God, who "makes his sun rise on the evil and on the good, and sends rain on the righteous and on the unrighteous." Like God, who shares his goodness with all, Jesus challenged his followers to "love your enemies and pray for those who persecute you, so that you may be children of your Father in heaven" (Matt. 5:44-45). For "there must be no limit to your goodness, as your heavenly father's goodness knows no bounds" (Matt. 5:48 REB).

In teachings like these Jesus set forth a new way to God's shalom on earth. Angels had associated his birth with the coming of "peace on earth" (Luke 2:14), and through his death, resurrection and teachings he showed the way.

The Road Ahead

God's shalom movement will yet someday be climaxed by new heavens and a new earth. The old will be made new, and goodness will again prevail. In the vision of the Apostle Peter, "we wait for new heavens and a new earth, where righteousness is at home" (2 Pet. 3:13). That is our hope.

But our waiting cannot be passive. God has called us to the continuing ministry of reconciliation in this broken, post-Eden world (2 Cor. 5:16-21). Though centuries change, God's vision for the journey remains the same. As always, he calls his people to build places along the way where his shalom is "at home."

–Dalton Reimer
© Dalton Reimer 2000, from *Christian Leader*, January 2000. Used by permission.

70 x 7: A Theology of Reconciliation

Matthew 18:15-17 is well known in some Christian settings as a text that summarizes a process for handling conflict within the church or between church members.[1] These verses, however, are too often interpreted in isolation. When understood in the context of the entire chapter, we see an unfolding reflection upon power, offense and forgiveness. This narrative exhorts individuals to be reconcilers, and the church as a whole to be a reconciling community as an alternative to the spiral of retribution found in the dominant society.

Jesus's Challenge to Hierarchical Systems of Power (vv. 1-5)

Matthew 18 begins with a question of power. We need not be shocked at the disciples' query concerning "greatness" (v. 1). In fact, their aspirations for power reflect concerns common to all of us. The hierarchical institutions and social structures in which we live and work generate anxieties in everyone concerning status, prestige and professional advancement. Jesus presents a child and answers, "Whoever becomes humble like this child is the greatest" (v. 4). Jesus is not referring to an attitude of innocence here, but to social standing. In first-century Palestine, children were at the bottom of the social scale, had no rights and were the property of their parents. Whereas the disciples aspire upwards, Jesus invites them to solidarity downwards.

Exhortation and Consequences to Potential Offenders (vv.6-10)

In verses 6-10 Jesus further dramatizes the issues of power and vulnerability with a series of exhortations warning the disciples not to "scandalize" (take advantage of) those with less power. While the disciples are concerned about being the "biggest," Jesus is concerned with not taking advantage of the "little one" (literally the "tiniest"). Whether our exercise of power is redemptive or abusive will be determined by our treatment of and relationship to the weak and marginalized.

Our church communities are organic bodies in which we are all dependent on each other. When persons abuse their power someone is violated, damaged or left out. Jesus begins his exhortation warning potential offenders to be vigilant against

dominating action (v. 6). Jesus is not naive: He acknowledges that injustice and violation will occur in this world as a result of the abuse of power (v. 7). But the church is called to embody an alternative model in which such abuse is abnormal and unacceptable.

This is followed by a warning to Christians not to use hurtful behavior (hand, foot and eye were considered the symbols of agency in antiquity). Verses 8-9 state emphatically that it is far better to deprive ourselves of something than to get it at someone else's expense. Jesus exhorts us to not be "thoughtless" towards marginalized people, as if they were dispensable and without value (v. 10).

Central Parable Regarding the Least/ Lost as the Foundation of the Community (vv. 12-14)

The central parable of the lost sheep (vv. 12-14) can be read as referring back to the offender (vv. 6-9) or forward to the victim (vv. 15-35). Both those who abuse power and those who are marginalized by the abuse of power can be the "lost" ones in our church communities. In either case we are to seek out and restore to community the excluded or the alienated. Jesus' parable of the lost sheep suggests an alternative view of how power is distributed in the community. The health and the wholeness of the community are not determined by the influential few or even by the majority, but by the welfare of the weakest members.

Exhortation and Consequences to Potential Victims (vv. 15-22)

Process of Confrontation, Accountability, Restoration (vv. 15-17)

In verses 15-17, Jesus describes a demanding process for bringing offenders back into community. The moral authority, and thus the initiative, resides with the violated party. There is first an attempt to help the offender save face through a private approach by the victim (v. 15). But it is the victim who determines whether s/he has been heard and whether justice has been done. If the victim does not feel heard by the offender, the victim invites the support of one or two "witnesses," as was common rabbinic practice. "Every word" of both victim and offender's testimony is confirmed. The supporters may also help determine consequence and impact.

If this process does not lead to healing and justice, the next step is to consult the broader community. It is significant that there is no mention of an intermediary institution such as a prosecutor, judge or jury. The church community seeks to be an advocate for both offender and victim in its demand for accountability, repentance, justice and forgiveness. If the offender continues to refuse to cooperate, the church treats the offender as an outsider—that is, someone who needs to hear the good news and be redeemed (v. 17)! This is not a strategy of punishment but rather a change in the community's approach to the offender.

Community Conferencing and Unlimited Forgiveness (vv. 18-22)

Verses 18-20 seem to indicate that the church community, inclusive of the victim and offender, represent an alternative to the adjudication of justice by civil authority. This is akin to the process of Community Justice Conferencing where restitution and reconciliation are agreed upon consensually. Matthean scholar J. Andrew Overman writes, "Binding and loosing refer to the political and juridical power to punish or excuse, to imprison or set free. . . . They constitute both a challenge and a substitute for those processes already established in the civil realm outside of the community."[2] If the church can facilitate the victim, offender and supportive others arriving together at a decision that is reasonable and restorative, then the church is cooperating with the grace of God (2 Cor. 5:18-6:1). Whenever the church takes this community process of transforming conflict seriously, Jesus is profoundly present (v. 20).

But all of us have deep preconceptions about the ultimately retributive nature of "justice." This is reflected in the disciples' question about limits to forgiveness (vv. 21-22). We understand that we need to forgive sometimes, but surely there are some things that cannot be forgiven! Jesus' answer that we must forgive "70 times seven" seeks to reverse Lamech's curse in Gen 4:24. Christians must no longer cooperate with the spiral of violence and retribution begun by Cain's fratricide

and intensified by Lamech. If we refuse to forgive and thus "bind" God's grace, we are consigning ourselves to the logic of the retributive system. The cruelty of this system is described in the closing parable in verses 23-35.

Consequences of Limited Forgiveness: Retribution and Hierarchy Prevail (vv. 23-35)

The story compares forgiveness with the releasing of people from economic debt. As William Herzog has shown, this parable describes the dysfunctional system of patron-client relationships that characterized the ancient royal court.[3] A high-ranking servant owes his king the exorbitant sum of ten thousand talents (one talent was worth more than 15 years wages, v. 24). The king orders the slave and his family to be sold (v. 25). When the servant begs him, the King grants him amnesty thus making an exception to his own rules (vv. 26-27). But the servant turns around and exacts payment from his underling (v. 28). Because everyone is socialized into the system of indebtedness, one gesture of grace alone is not enough to transform the system. Thus the king violently reasserts the rule of retribution (v. 34).

This disturbing tale serves as a warning to us about the consequences of giving in to the logic of retribution. Only by experimenting with the truth of God's unlimited grace in concrete circumstances of conflict can the church offer an alternative to the world's spiral of violence.

Matthew 18 provides important theological grounding for contemporary church involvement in conflict transformation and restorative justice. The church needs to practice this in its own life and then be a model for the wider society.

[1] See for example Marlin Jeshke, *Discipling in the Church: Recovering a Ministry of the Gospel.* Scottdale, PA: Herald Press, 1988.
[2] J. Andrew Overman, *Matthew's Gospel and Formative Judaism: The Social World of the Matthean Community.* Minneapolis, MN: Fortress Press, 1990. p.160.
[3] William R. Herzog II, *Parables of Subversive Speech: Jesus as Pedagogue of the Oppressed.* Louisville, KY: Westminster John Knox, 1994.

–Elaine Enns
© MCS 2000

Selected Conflict-Related Themes in the Bible

The Bible is full of diversity, conflict, directives for attitudes, actions and processes in conflict, stories about positively transformed conflict and stories of conflict that are full of violence. Following are several conflict-related themes found in the Bible, many of which are foundational for those of us doing conflict transformation work.

It is important to note that this list is simply a starting point and not comprehensive in any way. These are themes that have been compelling to various members of the MCS network, including myself. It is also important to note that the very process of selecting themes reflects a particular cultural orientation. If the list were to be compiled by someone from another context or cultural group, it would undoubtably look different.

Conflict is an inevitable part of life for all people, in and out of the church.
- Genesis 1-3—God created very diverse humans who have the freedom of choice and the power to be co-creators, all of which produce conflict.
- Acts 6 & 15, I Corinthians 1, Galatians 2, Philippians 3—Conflicts in the early church.
- Romans 14:1-7—Differences around food and holy days.

The Bible provides guidance for both attitude and process in conflict.
- Genesis 33:1-11—Be prepared to both ask for forgiveness and grant forgiveness.
- Genesis 31:54—Symbols, such as sharing a meal, can be powerful reconciliation tools.
- Proverbs 18:13, John 7:51, James 1:19—Listen first to the concerns of the other. See the other's point of view.
- Matthew 7:1-5, Romans 14—Be nonjudgmental. Take responsibility for your part of the conflict or sin.
- Matthew 18:15-20—Deal with the situation directly. Use others to help. Use the church. Continue to seek reconciliation in spite of the distancing. God is present with us.
- Acts 6 & 15—Come together as people of God. Recognize the conflict. Develop a process to deal with it. Hear each other. Problem-solve. Work for consensus. Implement the decision.
- Romans 14:17, Ephesians 4:1-6—Remember our common bonds, what and who ties us together.
- I Corinthians 13:4-7—Love is fundamental. Be constructive in conflict. We have only part of the truth.
- Galatians 6:1-5, I Peter 3:8, 16—Be humble, gentle, respectful.
- Ephesians 4:15, 25-32—Speak the truth. Be constructive in attitude and action. Be kind. Forgive.

Conflict can be an arena for God's revelation. It can be a venue for learning, growth and change.
- Acts 6:1-7—A conflict that resulted in the appointment of deacons.
- Acts 15:1-12—A serious conflict through which fundamental truth emerged about inclusivity in the kingdom.
- Acts 15:36-41—A conflict ending with a division but God's work continues.

Conflict becomes sinful when our responses to it are destructive, hurtful or violent.
- Genesis 4:3-7, 37:5, 18-28—Anger turns to hate and murderous acts.
- I Corinthians 6:1-8—The folly of taking another to court.
- Ephesians 4:25-27, 29—Don't let anger result in sin. Don't use destructive language.

Reconciliation is central to Christ's mission on earth. It is both our mission and our distinguishing characteristic as followers of Christ.
- II Corinthians 5:17-20—Our call to be reconcilers with Christ.
- Ephesians 2:13-17—Christ breaks down the wall of hostility between us.
- Colossians 1:19-22—Our reconciliation to God through Christ.
- Colossians 3:10-11—Our "new nature" removes divisions.

Forgiveness is key in the restoration of right relationships.
- Gen 33:1-11, 45:4-6, 10-15—Forgiveness between brothers.
- Matthew 6:14-15, 18:21-22, Ephesians 4:32, Colossians 3:12-15—Forgive and you will be forgiven . . . 70 times seven . . . as the Lord has forgiven you.
- Luke 15:11-32—Prodigal Son/Forgiving Father.

We are commanded to love our enemies.
- Matthew 5:38-48, Luke 6:27-36—Love those who do not love you.
- Luke 22:47-51—Jesus models love for enemies.
- Romans 12:14-21—Bless your persecutors; feed and clothe your enemies.

We seek the presence of shalom, a peace based on justice.
- Isaiah 58—Justice is rewarded by God.
- Amos 5:21-24—Nothing matters if justice and righteousness are not present.
- Micah 6:6-8—Not sacrifice but justice, kindness and a humble walk with God.
- Matthew 23:23-24—Justice, mercy and faith are the weightiest laws.
- Luke 4:18-19—Jesus' mission of good news, liberty and justice.

–compiled by Carolyn Schrock-Shenk with thanks to many friends of MCS
© MCS 1995

Agreeing and Disagreeing in Love

"Making every effort to maintain the unity of the Spirit in the bond of peace," (Eph. 4:3) as both individual members and the body of Christ, we pledge that we shall:

In Thought

Accept conflict

1. Acknowledge together that conflict is a normal part of our life in the church. (Rom. 14:1-8, 10-12, 17-19, 15:1-7)

Affirm hope

2. Affirm that as God walks with us in conflict we can work through to growth. (Eph. 4:15-16)

Commit to prayer

3. Admit our needs and commit ourselves to pray for a mutually satisfactory solution (no prayers for my success or for the other to change but to find a joint way). (James 5:16)

In Action

Go to the other. . .

4. Go directly to those with whom we disagree; avoid behind-the-back criticism. (Matt. 5:23-24, 18:15-20) (Go directly if you are European-North American; in other cultures disagreements are often addressed through a trusted go-between.)

. . . In the spirit of humility

5. Go in gentleness, patience and humility. Place the problem between us at neither doorstep and own our part in the conflict instead of pointing out the others'. (Gal. 6:1-5)

Be quick to listen

6. Listen carefully, summarize and check out what is heard before responding. Seek as much to understand as to be understood. (James 1:19; Prov. 18:13)

Be slow to judge

7. Suspend judgements, avoid labeling, end name calling, discard threats, and act in a nondefensive, nonreactive way. (Rom. 2:1-4; Gal. 5:22-26)

Be willing to negotiate

8. Work through the disagreements constructively. (Acts 15; Phil. 2:1-11)
   - Identify issues, interests, and needs of both (rather than take positions).
   - Generate a variety of options for meeting both parties' needs (rather than defending one's own way).
   - Evaluate options by how they meet the needs and satisfy the interests of all sides (not one side's values).
   - Collaborate in working out a joint solution (so both sides gain, both grow and win).
   - Cooperate with the emerging agreement (accept the possible, not demand your ideal).
   - Reward each other for each step forward, toward agreement (celebrate mutuality).

In Life

Be steadfast in love

9. Be firm in our commitment to seek a mutual solution; be stubborn in holding to our common foundation in Christ; be steadfast in love. (Col. 3:12-15)

Be open to mediation

10. Be open to accept skilled help. If we cannot reach agreement among ourselves, we will use those with gifts and training in mediation in the larger church. (Phil. 4:1-3)

Trust the community

11. We will trust the community and if we cannot reach agreement or experience reconciliation, we will turn the decision over to others in the congregation or from the broader church. (Acts 15)
    - In one-to-one or small group disputes, this may mean allowing others to arbitrate.
    - In congregational, conference, district or denominational disputes, this may mean allowing others to arbitrate or implementing constitutional decision-making processes, insuring that they are done in the spirit of these guidelines, and abiding by whatever decision is made.

Be the Body of Christ

12. Believe in and rely on the solidarity of the Body of Christ and its commitment to peace and justice, rather than resort to the courts of law. (I Cor. 6:1-6)

–Mennonite Church and General Conference Mennonite Church
© Mennonite Church and General Conference Mennonite Church 1995

Spirituality: The Fertile Soil of Peacemaking

You are the people of God. God loved you and chose you. So then, you must clothe yourselves with compassion, kindness, humility, gentleness and patience. And to all these qualities add love which binds all things together in perfect unity. The peace that Christ gives is to guide you in the decisions you make, for it is to this peace that God has called you together in one body. Always be thankful.

–Colossians 3:12,14-15

The longer I am involved in this peacemaking work, the more I am aware of the Spirit's presence, of the many ways that God is at work in and through people's conflicts. Even in times when sin and evil are clearly present, I find the Spirit breaking through in amazing ways. Indeed I am finding that the rocky soil of conflict is fertile soil.

–Carolyn Schrock-Shenk, *Conciliation Quarterly* (Summer 1993)

As a follower of Christ, my call is precisely here, toiling in conflict's rocky soil. In the midst of conflict, crises, violence and injustice, I am called to both see the rocks and see beyond them, to see the possible in the seemingly impossible. I am called to the deeply spiritual tasks of peacemaking and reconciliation. Responding to this call brings me back to the very center of myself. It touches me at the core of who I am as person lovingly created in the very image of God.

This is a spirituality that transcends problem solving and agreements. The connection of human spirits through deep listening, dialogue and entering into the experience of another, the healing and restoration of a relationship, the emergence of new trust and commitment, the retrieval of justice, all call to, and emerge from, the deepest part of us. They connect us in new ways to the mystery of life, to the power of the Transcendent. They demand and produce vulnerability and risk. They awaken and enliven us.

This is a spirituality that facilitates problem solving and agreement. The spiritual nature of this work does not replace appropriate techniques and tools, well-honed skills and collaborative processes. Rather it is the fertile soil out of which they grow. It is the essence that gives them meaning and renders them powerful.

This is a spirituality that demands nurturing. Neither tending my own spiritual nourishment nor setting the context for transformation in each of my interactions come easily or naturally. Both must be intentional and ongoing.

Nurturing Our Own Spirituality

I am speaking of a sacramental view of life in which our outer lives are lived signs of inward spiritual groundedness. When we take the time to reflect, to ground ourselves in silence, we are given the gift of Grace. We are called to live grace-full lives. We must attend to our spiritual work in order to be faithful to our calling as ministers of reconciliation.

–Pat Washburn, *Conciliation Quarterly* (Winter 1989)

It is in solitude that we discover that being is more important than having and that we are worth more than the results of our efforts. In solitude we discover that our life is not a possession to be defended, but a gift to be shared.

–Henri Nouwen

What I didn't expect was to have some of that holiness seep up through the soles of my feet and begin to transform me as the intervenor. A woman approached me recently after my work with a congregation and said, "The thing I appreciated most was that I could feel the Spirit through you all the time—even when you couldn't, or

when you weren't sure what to do next." It is that very uncertainty that forces me to come again and again to God with humility and almost embarrassing need. I am learning to depend in new ways on the resources and power of the Spirit. That awareness of my own inadequacy that compels me to depend on God as well as witnessing the Spirit's work in the lives of others is transforming me. My confidence in the availability of God's power is growing and enabling me to take more risks.
–Carolyn Schrock-Shenk, *Conciliation Quarterly* (Summer 1993)

This is a spirituality of being rather than doing. It is modeling that which I teach and foster in others. This does not mean that the call of a practitioner is a kind of syrupy perfection—a robot lit up with holy lights. Rather the call to "being" and "modeling" is a call to sincerity and transparency. It means being in touch with my emotions, embracing them and seeking to understand their source and their meaning. It means recognizing my inadequacies, doubts and fears, and being honest about them. It means being ready to admit when I've "blown" it and then picking myself up with grace and humility. It means being able to laugh at myself.

It is also a call to reverence deeply the personhood of the other, their gifts, needs and vulnerabilities. It means that I try to listen deeply and seek to find "that of God" in the other, even in those who lash out with ferocity or seem completely unlovable.

This is a spirituality that must transform me from the inside out. Until I can deal with the anger, fear and violence within me, I will continue to act out of my unresolved struggles. So I must work at my own internal conflict transformation—and it must be interwoven with my external work. The exciting part is that these are naturally intertwined. Conflict transformation and peacemaking work is brimming with opportunities for personal reflection, awareness, growth and change.

How does it happen? In a myriad of ways. One way it happens for me is when I can tune into my own center as I work. What are the feelings and issues being raised for me during this intervention? How did that off-the-cuff response of my co-trainer affect me? And what about the tears of the man who reminded me of my father? Why am I uncomfortable when a particular subject is addressed? What are my fears, needs and vulnerabilities as I stand in front of these people?

Being in tune to my own feelings and responses is the very critical first step. How I deal with and learn from them is the next. Naming them to the group, journaling, searching for relevant biblical texts, addressing them with a mentor or colleague or support group, praying and meditating are all ways that I have found helpful.

It is true, as some maintain, that this work can be draining. But it can also be very life-giving. Perhaps it is draining to the extent that I focus on "doing" rather than "being." In other words, perhaps the more I can abandon my need to control, to be the expert, and to fix others, the less drained I will be. The more that I can replace those with a quiet confidence that "in my weakness, God will be made strong," the more energized I will be.

Creating Space for the Spirit's Work

The spiritual aspects of mediation also affect our role as mediators. Conflict transformation requires the use of the most effective mediation strategies and techniques, but ultimately requires something beyond technique—an inner centeredness of the mediator. Once we see ourselves as providers of a safe and trusting presence, and not simply as mediation technicians, we will be more comfortable inviting people to get close to their pain, to reflect on their inner struggles, values and learnings.
–Mark Chupp, *Conciliation Quarterly* (Summer 1993)

To be present in these moments of grace is a precious and timeless gift that carries me through many vexing and disappointing experiences as a mediator. They are impossible to orchestrate or control. As mediator I know that I have contributed to

their occurrence, but I never feel that I caused or earned them. . . .The mediator must be willing to let go of safety, control, predictability. If the mediator models letting go of the known order to allow the unknown to break in, the parties will often follow.
–Ron Kraybill, *Conciliation Quarterly* (Fall 1986)

Training participants and parties in conflict are people of choice. I as an intervenor and trainer cannot bring about their healing or transformation or reconciliation, nor even their growth or learning. This is a difficult truth for many of us to internalize. We long to have our fingers on the control buttons. We *know* what they need to do—if only we could make them do it.

The more I hold onto the belief that I know exactly what they need, the less I can set a context for the Spirit to work. And setting the context is a sacred task to which I am called. I have both the power and the responsibility to set an atmosphere that invites people to choose truth, that prepares the way for transformation. This includes a host of things—from my attitude and demeanor, to the atmosphere of the room, to the kind of process I lead throughout.

I have found that personal preparation before a training or intervention calms my anxiety, centers me and opens me up. Solitude, mixed with singing an invocation kind of song has helped most often. I have also found that prayer through imagining shalom, transformation, healing and growth in the lives of those involved has been powerful. Some practitioners find personal reflection empowering, such as thinking about past transformative experiences or remembering the encouragement and affirmation from a colleague. Others look for ways to "lighten up" and free their minds and hearts through humor, laughter or playfulness.

Preparing the space where the intervention or training will take place is also important. Chair and/or table arrangements are important considerations. Rather than being bound by convention, I try to think about what would be most re-creative and life-giving. That may mean even sitting on the floor or meeting outside.

Symbols and artifacts can be useful. When working with congregations, I have sometimes burned a candle or kept one chair intentionally empty to remind all of us of the Spirit's presence. I have used decorative fabric, pictures, flowers, branches and pine cones to help set a healing, restorative atmosphere. I have used rituals and music and meditative silence at various points in both interventions and trainings.

Sensitivity to the Spirit throughout the process is a discipline that takes careful listening—both to the hearts of the participants, and to my own heart as the practitioner. It involves listening for, and seizing, opportunities to address issues and emotions that delve deeper than simply reaching an agreement or learning a particular skill. I have found, for example, that ending a mediation with a time for reflection or additional comments has produced some wonderfully healing and deeply spiritual interactions.

Just as there are a host of ways to nurture my own spirituality, there are a host of ways to help set the context for transformation. What is important in terms of nurturing both of these is, once again, "being" more than "doing." The specific means of nurturing are much less important than the simple, yet profound, experience of bringing my whole self, and those with whom I am working, into the awareness of the Spirit's presence. That awareness opens us up to all the power and potential of that Presence. Then, truly, the rocky soil will become fertile.

–Carolyn Schrock-Shenk
© MCS 1995

From Head to Heart: The Cycle of Reconciliation

"I know I should forgive him," she said. "I want to forgive him. I can't carry this around for the rest of my life. But I just *can't*." Her eyes darkened as she emphasized the last word. Exasperation with herself? Stubbornness about her anger? I wasn't sure.

"If I have offended anyone here, I ask your forgiveness. I want to be reconciled with all my brothers and sisters." The words seemed appropriate enough. But there was not freedom in them. The speaker looked more angry than contrite. Others kept their eyes on their floor. No one moved till he sat down again.

They insisted they had forgiven each other. Yes, they wanted to be at peace. No, there wasn't really anything they needed to talk about. Their words said one thing, but their stiff bodies, tight gestures, and narrow eye movements said something else. "We are angry. . . . We want to fight," was the message I heard.

People in conflict frequently wage an internal battle between head and heart. By *"head"* I mean their values and conscience; by *"heart"* I mean their emotions. People think they *ought* to be reconciled with others, but their hearts are not ready. Bystanders often ignore this internal split or do things that make it worse. Religious settings are especially hazardous. Well-meaning friends, pastors, even mediators respond in ways that strengthen the "head" message, but ignore or disparage the cries of the heart.

I spend a great deal of time in religious settings mediating the conflicts that result between people who say they have already forgiven each other. But their voices and bodies say otherwise. These people have engaged in "head" reconciliation, but their hearts—key actors in most conflicts—were left behind. The consequence is often further damage. From field theory we know that if we amplify a restraining force in this case the "head" message without reducing a driving force (in this case the "heart" message) eventually the driving force gets even stronger and overwhelms the restraining force. In other words, through guilt you can get people to apologize. But if their hearts are not yet ready, resentment will remain and grow stronger over time.

The key to enabling heart reconciliation is the knowledge that it is a process with a rhythm and dynamic of its own. To the brain's concern with what *ought* to be, the heart responds with what is. The head functions like light in space—touch a switch and it's there. The heart functions like a radiator hearing a room—it takes *time* to get the job done. The head *can* set direction for the heart, but the heart must arrive at its own pace. Heart reconciliation is a cycle with stages along the way. Every time we experience alienation and restoration we go through this cycle, whether the offense is large or small. With experience and maturity we can move through the cycle more quickly. But there are no shortcuts. Efforts to bypass any stage simply halt us at that point.

The cycle of reconciliation begins with relationship:

1. **Open relationship.** The key to healthy relationships is *risk*. Information about self is shared and received with little anxiety. Promises are made and accepted with little second thought. No guarantees are demanded that information or promises be handled responsibly; parties assume this. Risk is continually present. If expectations are met, each risk results in higher trust.

2. **Injury.** At some point in all relationships, expectations are *not* met. A risk is taken and instead of a good outcome and higher trust, injury results.

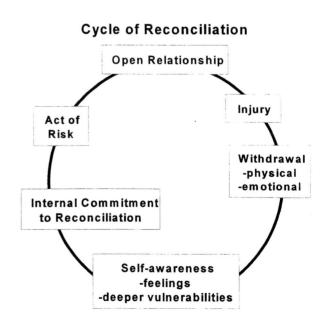

Cycle of Reconciliation

Open Relationship

Injury

Withdrawal -physical -emotional

Self-awareness -feelings -deeper vulnerabilities

Internal Commitment to Reconciliation

Act of Risk

3. **Withdrawal.** Withdrawal follows injury. Sometimes people withdraw physically. They turn their back, leave the room, avoid each other. Even when withdrawal is not physical, emotional withdrawal always takes place. People pull back into themselves to assess the situation. The withdrawal may be a second or a decade. But it is a necessary and healthy response to injury. Survival mechanisms cause any healthy person to get away from a situation that causes injury in order to determine next steps.

What happens at this stage is pivotal for the outcome. After a time of withdrawal, people frequently attempt "head" reconciliation. They want to return to open relationship, they think they ought not be withdrawn and alienated. With their heads and sometimes pushed by well-meaning individuals, they "will" themselves into reconciliation. They speak words from their heads to each other. This satisfies the demand of the head to do what is "right."

But the relationship they return to is not open. Willingness to risk is gone. Caution, distance and coldness creep in. If there is laughter, it is from the head and the throat; never from the belly, which is close to the heart.

Worst of all, heart reconciliation becomes difficult. "We already forgave each other," people say. "Forgiveness means it's over and done. Yet the other side still treats us coldly. They have serious problems! But don't look to us for further involvement!"

4. **Self-awareness.** Self-awareness is needed to move beyond withdrawal. The first level is being aware of and accepting one's emotions. Admitting to oneself, "I am angry, I am hurt, I am confused" begins the process of moving beyond withdrawal. Being able to name one's emotion to others, without self-deprecation, is better yet. The people most likely to get stuck at this stage are those who insist, "I'm not angry, I'm just concerned."

The second level of self-awareness is that deeper vulnerabilities inevitably get tapped in painful conflicts. Below the surface in every bruising encounter are memories of old injuries. Whenever any particular person or incident in the present proves especially capable of arousing deep resentment or feelings of helplessness, introspection is called for. We think we are fighting a neighbor,

spouse, or pastor. Often the real emotion comes from a trauma far removed in time!

An insightful question is: when have I felt this way before? Often the first thought delivered up by the mind seems questionable. What is the connection between my sixth grade teacher and *this* conflict?

Telling the story that came to mind or writing it out in journal form often elicits further memories and the connection becomes apparent.

The goal is not to go back and reopen old battles. The goal is self-awareness. Past traumas lose their power to control our responses in the present if we are conscious of them. Deep hurts are worth some concerted effort to escape. The field of "Re-evaluation Counseling" has discovered that a powerful technique for release of old hurts is repetition. Find a supportive friend who can listen nonjudgmentally. Tell the story, describing in detail the grief, anger, fear, or embarrassment experienced. When finished, start at the beginning and tell the story again. Continue re-telling the story, over and over, until it becomes boring. When you begin yawning at your own account, the trauma has lost its power to rule the present.

The third level of self-awareness is acknowledging one's own power in the conflict. Most people in conflict feel that they are the victims and that they have little power to inflict injury of any consequence on others. Self-awareness calls for acknowledging the impact of one's own responses on the other party.

5. **Internal Commitment to Reconciliation.** This is often an act of the head, a conscious choice that "I will put forth effort to be reconciled." This internal choice is difficult and may take time to reach. It is a decision to enter into risk again and deserves careful thought. What risk am I prepared to take in order to find restoration?

6. **Act of Risk.** Once the internal choice has been made, opportunities to take a risk are usually not hard to find. It is important to choose a risk one can afford to have rejected.

Rejection by the other party is a distinct possibility. It helps to cope if one knows that reconciliation is a process and that some people move through the stages much faster than others. An overture rejected today may be reciprocated in three months.

I used the Cycle of Reconciliation in several ways in a group I worked with recently. Although there was a lot of pressure for people to be reconciled, I could tell some were not yet ready. This pressure kept them stuck at the withdrawal stage. Others pointed to this behavior as evidence of childishness: *"See how stubborn and standoffish they are!"*

In describing the cycle for the group, I stressed that each stage is necessary and healthy and that each person moves through at his or her own pace. This gave "permission" to the feelings and behavior of the withdrawn group. I urged them to trust themselves and follow their hearts. Members of the withdrawn group were able to admit they *were* stuck. Having admitted it, they paradoxically became unstuck.

At the stage of Internal Commitment, trust was the hardest struggle. Individuals repeated over and over, *"I just don't trust that other group anymore, especially their leader."* I helped them to see that the question was not trust, but willingness to risk. They didn't need trust to move on. They needed willingness to risk again, a moderate risk that they themselves must choose.

Some people had made an Internal Commitment to reconciliation but were unsure about how to proceed. I set the stage to move to an Act of Risk by providing time in a meeting for statements to the group. I listed five kinds of statements on the board: statements that acknowledged hurt or concern; statements of desire to be restored; statements of apology or confession; statements acknowledging good intentions on the part of others (even if the outcome was painful); and statements of what one would do differently if one had a second chance. I invited those who were ready to take a risk by making statements of this nature to the group.

Finally, I helped the whole group to see that they will go through this cycle again many times. Healthy relationships always involve risk and occasionally trust will be broken. If they are prepared for this reality and allow each person to move at his or her own pace through the stages of reconciliation, they will find future conflicts less threatening and disruptive.

True healing involves a unity of head and heart. The head sets the goal and keeps things "on track." The heart provides the content of the emotions. Given a chance, the two will converge in common purpose. What makes the difference is a process which values and gives space to both.

–Ron Kraybill
© MCS 1988, from *Conciliation Quarterly*, Vol. 7 No. 4

Responses to Injury

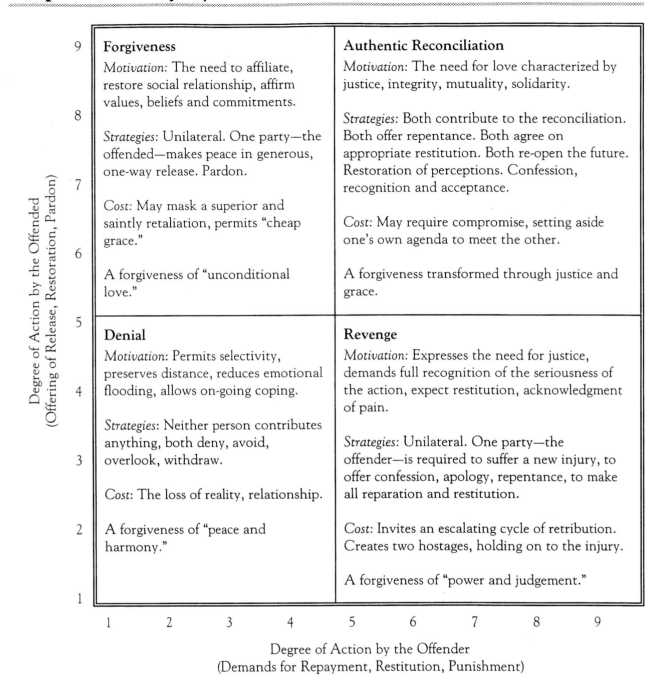

Degree of Action by the Offended
(Offering of Release, Restoration, Pardon)

9 — Forgiveness *Motivation:* The need to affiliate, restore social relationship, affirm values, beliefs and commitments. *Strategies:* Unilateral. One party—the offended—makes peace in generous, one-way release. Pardon. *Cost:* May mask a superior and saintly retaliation, permits "cheap grace." A forgiveness of "unconditional love."	**Authentic Reconciliation** *Motivation:* The need for love characterized by justice, integrity, mutuality, solidarity. *Strategies:* Both contribute to the reconciliation. Both offer repentance. Both agree on appropriate restitution. Both re-open the future. Restoration of perceptions. Confession, recognition and acceptance. *Cost:* May require compromise, setting aside one's own agenda to meet the other. A forgiveness transformed through justice and grace.
Denial *Motivation:* Permits selectivity, preserves distance, reduces emotional flooding, allows on-going coping. *Strategies:* Neither person contributes anything, both deny, avoid, overlook, withdraw. *Cost:* The loss of reality, relationship. A forgiveness of "peace and harmony."	**Revenge** *Motivation:* Expresses the need for justice, demands full recognition of the seriousness of the action, expect restitution, acknowledgment of pain. *Strategies:* Unilateral. One party—the offender—is required to suffer a new injury, to offer confession, apology, repentance, to make all reparation and restitution. *Cost:* Invites an escalating cycle of retribution. Creates two hostages, holding on to the injury. A forgiveness of "power and judgement."

Vertical scale marks: 9, 8, 7, 6, 5, 4, 3, 2, 1
Horizontal scale marks: 1 2 3 4 5 6 7 8 9

Degree of Action by the Offender
(Demands for Repayment, Restitution, Punishment)

Concluding Comments: Augsburger's model challenges us to go beyond a strictly individual and unilateral view of forgiveness, instead emphasizing the interdependence between the offender and the offended. Both need each other, if genuine reconciliation is to occur. There are two mistakes we make in thinking about this relationship: that forgiveness is the sole responsibility of one person (the offended), or that it is always shared equally by both. Because of this inevitable asymmetry, genuine reconciliation is not always possible, particularly in cases of significant power imbalance or when one or both parties is unavailable or unwilling to be present. In such cases we accept what is possible for two persons, not what is absolute or ideal. Short of this, each searches out the partial healing which is interiorly possible and grieves for what is not.

–Larry Dunn
1995, chart adapted with permission from David Augsburger, *Helping People Forgive* (Westminster/John Knox, 1996)

Forgiveness and Reconciliation

Introduction

Forgiveness. Reconciliation. Important concepts and experiences in our Christian walk. And difficult areas for those who have suffered violence at the hands of family members.

Forgiveness is a regular part of our corporate worship. In liturgy, hymn, prayer, Scripture, and sermon, we are reminded of and called to participate in God's forgiveness of us. We confess our sins and receive assurance of pardon. We are urged to follow Jesus who asked God to forgive his offenders.

Our human journey is guided by our understanding of how Jesus lived. When we are violated, we experience anger and bitterness. We struggle with letting go of hurts and forgiving. The more extreme the offense, the deeper the wound, the more difficulty we have in praying with Jesus, "Father, forgive them for they know not what they do."

Reconciliation is an equally significant Christian concept. In 2 Corinthians 5:18-19, Paul writes,

> God . . . reconciled us to himself through Christ, and gave us the ministry of reconciliation; that is, in Christ God was reconciling the world to himself, not counting their trespasses against them, and entrusting the message to us.

We experience reconciliation with God and yearn for that in our human relationships, particularly when those relationships have been fractured by conflict.

Myths to Consider

But we need to rethink our understandings of forgiveness and reconciliation. For some of our misunderstandings clutter the path to healing. Let's consider some commonly held myths.

Myth 1—Forgiving means forgetting.
But the survivors of domestic violence testify to the permanence of the effect of such violence. Healing is available—and it comes by remembering the offense, not by forgetting.

Myth 2—Forgiving means accepting the offense.
But the wrongs can never be justified or acceptable. All forms of abuse—physical, emotional, and sexual—have no place in any family.

Myth 3—Forgiving is automatic.
But our first tendency as humans is to respond to violence with violence. If you hurt me, I want to hurt you back. Reflection is often required before we relinquish that instinctual urge to inflict pain in response to injury.

Myth 4—Forgiving is a quick, one-time event.
But most people experience forgiveness as a process. It may occur quickly for a few individuals. However, generally it occurs over a longer period of time.

Myth 5—Forgiving means the relationship is reconciled.
But forgiveness is different from reconciliation. Forgiveness means the survivor has been able to let go of the resentment. It does not mean that the relationship is reconcilable, that the parent-child union can be restored, that the marriage can be resumed.

Reworking the Myths

By reworking the myths, we construct some principles for helpful understandings of forgiveness and reconciliation.

1. We acknowledge that remembering is essential for forgiveness.

The catchy phrase "forgive and forget" is not based on reality. Perhaps it is based on our discomfort with pain, our difficulty acknowledging the emotions of anger and hatred, and the denial that is a common response to great injustice. Too often survivors are silenced with the remark, "Forgive and forget," which actually says the speaker is unwilling to listen to the survivor.

Those of us who wish to be helpful must examine our own motives for hurrying through the excruciating process of recovery. We must learn to stay with pain. "Forgive and forget" is never appropriate counsel for survivors of family violence. Their healing depends on remembering.

We must support survivors as they learn to live with the memories of their experiences.

Offenders too must remember. Their recovery is dependent on their being willing to recall and take responsibility for their actions, and recognize the effect of their abuse on their victims.

2. We acknowledge that naming the abuse as sinful and unacceptable is essential to forgiveness.

The survivor must acknowledge that she has been injured before she can let go of the resentment she experiences in relationship to that offense. As witnesses, we must state our conviction that the abuse of power is unacceptable in Christian families. We must hold out a distinction between forgiveness and accepting or justifying the offense.

3. We acknowledge that anger, hatred and bitterness follow naturally from the abuse of power in family relationships.

Survivors have a right to experience such feelings and a right to express their pain. We place responsibility for the violation on the offender.

4. We acknowledge that forgiveness is a process.

Healing is a lengthy process and forgiveness, also a lengthy process, is only one part of the healing. (Reflect on the "Cycle of Reconciliation" by Ron Kraybill, pages 29-31). There are conditions which make forgiveness possible. The church community plays a valuable role in the provision of such conditions, which take time and effort.

The survivor needs to experience justice as a part of the healing process. This happens when the survivor's story of abuse is listened to and believed, when opportunity is provided to heal, and when the offender is called to accountability.

Restitution is one extremely valuable step in justice-making. Restitution generally involves a financial payment by the offender to the victim. It is a concrete symbol of the offender's willingness to acknowledge responsibility for the harm done. While this occurs infrequently in domestic abuse, it is one step churches can promote as they attempt to make justice.

5. We acknowledge the distinction between forgiveness and reconciliation.

Forgiveness precedes reconciliation. Reconciliation may or may not follow forgiveness. Reconciliation—the restoration to just and caring family relationships—may not be possible or healthy.

Our acts of forgiveness occur in the context of time and space. We cannot turn back the clock and give the child an abuse-free childhood; the chance for that parent to tenderly care for that child is gone. The battered wife may have endured too many years of abuse to permit her to move back into a marital relationship with her spouse, even if he has changed his ways. Either the offender or the survivor may have died or be unavailable for the relationship.

God Heals in Different Ways

Many survivors choose a time of separation from their offenders and discover that this separation is an essential condition for their healing. We need to walk alongside survivors as they determine the appropriate level of relationship with their offender.

A survivor may forgive his or her offender, but the offender's refusal to acknowledge wrongdoing prohibits harmony from developing. The survivor may then experience internal reconciliation without experiencing relationship reconciliation.

An offender may experience God's forgiveness and may be able to forgive herself. But her victim may still be working through the hurt and the hate and not be able to open himself to a relationship. The offender may then find internal reconciliation, hoping for the day when her victim can consider relating to her. Offenders who acknowledge their wrongdoing and demonstrate their willingness to turn from their sin pave the way for reconciliation.

At all times it is important to remember that it is the violence that has destroyed the covenant. The victim should not be blamed.

On some occasions, both survivors and offenders may be ready to be reconciled. When this occurs we thank God for the demonstration of healing grace. We do not assume that this is what must happen in all situations and push ourselves and others toward it. Rather, by submitting to a process of healing, we accept God's gracious touch wherever we receive it.

–Melissa A. Miller
© Herald Press 1994, adapted from *Family Violence: The Compassionate Church Responds*. Used by permission.

Truth and Mercy, Justice and Peace

For a number of years in the 1980s I worked under the auspices of Mennonite Central Committee throughout Central America as a resource person conducting workshops on conflict resolution and mediation. As an outgrowth of those efforts, I had the opportunity to serve as an adviser to a religiously-based conciliation team that mediated negotiations between the Sandinista government and the indigenous movement of the Nicaraguan East Coast, known as Yatama.

As part of its overall role the conciliation team accompanied returning exiled Yatama leaders back to their home area and villages to explain the agreement that had been reached with the Sandinistas. Given the context of war and the deep-rooted animosities that persisted, these were intense meetings. At the opening of each village meeting, the Nicaraguan conciliators would read Psalm 85, in which the Psalmist refers to the return of people to their land and the opportunity for peace. In two short lines at the heart of the text (85:10), the Spanish version reads (in translation), "Truth and mercy have met together; peace and justice have kissed."

Hearing these powerful images representing two paradoxes time and again across the East Coast, in the context of a deeply divided society, I became curious as to how the conciliators understood the text and the concepts. At a training workshop with local and regional peace commissions some time later, I had the opportunity to explore this in more detail. We first identified the four major concepts in the phrase: Truth, Mercy, Justice and Peace. I then asked the participants to discuss each concept as if it were a person, describing the images it brought to mind and what each would have to say about conflict.

When discussing the images of Truth, they suggested honesty, revelation, clarity, open accountability, and vulnerability. "We see each other as we are," one participant commented. "Without the person of Truth, conflict will never be resolved. Yet Truth alone leaves us naked, vulnerable, and unworthy."

On Mercy, images emerged of compassion, forgiveness, acceptance, and a new start. This is the idea of grace. Without the person of Mercy,

healthy relationships would not be possible. Without compassion and forgiveness, healing and restoration would be out of the question. Yet, Mercy alone is superficial. It covers up. It moves on too quickly.

Justice raised powerful images of making things right, creating equal opportunity, rectifying the wrong, and restitution. "Without justice," one person commented, "the brokenness continues and festers."

With Peace came images of harmony, unity, well-being. It is the feeling and prevalence of respect and security. But, it was mentioned, peace is not just for a few, and if it is preserved for the benefit of some and not others, it represents a farce.

As a conclusion we put the four concepts on paper on the wall, as depicted in the diagram. When I asked the participants what we should call the place where Truth and Mercy, Justice and Peace meet, one of them immediately said, "That *place* is reconciliation."

What was so striking about this conceptualization of reconciliation was the idea that it represents a *social space*. Reconciliation is a *locus*, a place where people and things come together.

Let's think for a moment of how the core concepts in the Psalmist's paradoxes might be formulated in terms of contemporary conflict. *Truth* is the longing for acknowledgment of wrong and the validation of painful loss and experiences, but it is coupled with *Mercy*, which articulates the need for acceptance, letting go, and a new beginning. *Justice* represents the search for individual and group rights, for social restructuring, and restitution, but it is linked with *Peace* which underscores the need for interdependence, well-being and security. Curiously, these concepts are played out in the political arena.

These elements lie at the heart of the challenge facing us in contemporary conflict. While enormous pain and deep-rooted animosity accompany any war, we have suggested that the nature of contemporary settings of armed conflict, where neighbor fears neighbor—and sometimes family member fears family member—and blood is shed by each, the emotive, perceptual, social-psychological, and spiritual dimensions are core not peripheral concerns. The immediacy of hatred and prejudice, of racism and xenophobia, as primary factors and motivators of the conflict require approaches to its transformation rooted in social-psychological and spiritual dimensions that traditionally have been seen as either irrelevant or outside the competency of international diplomacy. Reconciliation, seen as a process of encounter and as a social space, points us in that direction.

Reconciliation can be thus understood as both a *focus* and a *locus*. As a perspective it is built on and oriented toward the relational aspects of a conflict. As a social phenomenon, reconciliation represents a space, a place or location of encounter, where parties to a conflict meet. Reconciliation must be proactive in seeking to create an encounter where people can focus on their relationship and share their perceptions, feelings, and experiences with one another, with the goal of creating new perceptions and a new shared experience.

In more specific terms, we could suggest that reconciliation deals with three specific paradoxes. First, in an overall sense reconciliation promotes an encounter between the open expression of the painful past *and* the search for the articulation of a long-term, interdependent future. Second, reconciliation provides a place for truth and mercy to meet, where concern for exposing what has happened *and* letting go in favor of renewed relationship are validated and embraced. Third, it further recognizes the need to give time and place to both justice and peace, where redressing the wrong is held together with the envisioning of a common, connected future. The basic paradigm of reconciliation, therefore, is one that embraces paradox. It suggests, for example, that a focus on relationship will provide new ways to address the impasse on issues; or that providing space for grieving the past permits a reorientation toward the future, and, inversely, that envisioning a common future creates new lenses for dealing with the past.

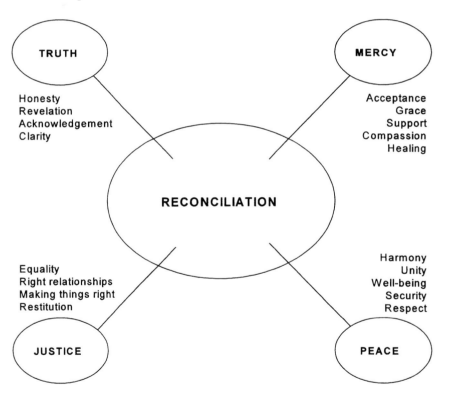

TRUTH

Honesty
Revelation
Acknowledgement
Clarity

MERCY

Acceptance
Grace
Support
Compassion
Healing

RECONCILIATION

Equality
Right relationships
Making things right
Restitution

Harmony
Unity
Well-being
Security
Respect

JUSTICE

PEACE

–John Paul Lederach

The Path to Justice: Retribution or Restoration?

Every day when I pick up my newspaper I read about crime—assaults, domestic violence, political bribes, corporate swindles and organized crime. Naturally, in the midst of what some consider a "crime wave," proposals for the best way to deal with the problem have become a topic of social and political debate.

What strikes me as tragic in these debates is that the solutions being proposed are simply more of the same: bigger threats and more punishment. Few people, inside or outside government, ask more basic questions about whether punishment ought to be our main concern. Even fewer seem genuinely concerned about victims and what they need.

Meanwhile, prisons are massively crowded, the death penalty is back with a vengeance and the costs of the "criminal-justice system" to us taxpayers keep soaring.

A Faulty Definition of Crime

The fact that the present criminal-justice system ignores victims and focuses instead on more pun-ishment for offenders is an important clue to un-derstanding what is wrong with the system. Both of these problems arise from inadequate definitions of what constitutes crime and what justice entails.

Legally, the essence of the crime lies in breaking a law rather than the actual damage done to a person. The official victim is the state, not an individual. It is no accident, then, that victims and their needs are so often forgotten: they are not even part of the equation, not part of the definition of the offense!

When a crime occurs, the state as victim decides what must be done, and the process of deciding focuses primarily on two questions: "Is the person guilty? If so, how much punishment does he or she deserve?" Our society's definition of crime and justice, then, might be summarized like this:

- Crime is a violation of the state and its laws.
- Justice establishes blame. . .
- and administers pain. . .
- through a contest between offender and state.

This way of viewing crime might be called "retributive justice." It has little place for victims, and uses what some scholars have called a "battle model" for settling things. Because it is centered so heavily on establishing blame, it looks primarily to the past rather than the future, and it assumes that punishment or pain, usually in the form of a prison term, is the normal outcome.

The Biblical Alternative: Restoration

But what is the alternative? How should we understand crime and justice? The Bible offers some suggestions.

First, the Bible defines crime as broken relationships. When people live in right relationship to each other—materially, socially, spiritually—they experience shalom.

The essence of crime is that it upsets shalom, making right relationships impossible. Crime, in the biblical view, is a wound that needs healing. That is why restitution, making things right, is found so often there. In fact, the word for making things right is the root word for shalom.

While restoration was the ultimate goal of justice in the Bible, God's people were not always open to that possibility. Clarence Jordan of the Koinonia community in Georgia has pointed out that in the Bible there is a kind of progression, an unfolding of understanding on this issue.

Genesis begins with a recognition that unlimited retaliation is a normal response to wrongdoing: the "law of Lamech," it is called, and in Genesis it is graphically characterized as "seventy times seven" (Gen. 4:24)—retribution almost without end.

But very soon revenge is limited: an eye for an eye *only*, God tells the Israelites (Ex. 21:22). Rightly understood, this passage is not intended as a command to do vengeance, but as a limitation on vengeance: "Do this much, but only this much."

Following that comes another limitation on retaliation: "Do not seek revenge or bear a grudge against one of your people, but love your neighbor as yourself" (Lev. 19:18).

Christ continues this direction. Love not only your neighbor but your enemy, he says; do good to those who harm you. Instead of unlimited retaliation or even limited retaliation, he calls for unlimited love (Matt. 5:38-48), and it is no accident that he graphically calls for forgiveness to seventy times seven (Matt. 18:22).

Second, an important clue to Old Testament justice is found in how God responds to wrongdoing. When confronted by sin, God is described as angry, full of wrath, with words that connote heat and heavy breathing; like crime victims, God is understood to be angry (e.g., Gen. 6:6).

But the real story is that in spite of Israel's wrongdoing, and in spite of the resulting anger, God never gives up. God expresses anger in the face of wrongdoing but does not remain there: God moves through wrath to restoration, as in Gen. 8:21 after the flood. Restoration, not retribution, is the thrust of biblical justice.

Christ's focus on forgiveness, restoration and reconciliation rather than retribution is thus quite logical, and not a rejection of the overall thrust of the Old Testament.

Justice Means Repairing Relationships

The biblical view of crime as a violation of shalom suggests a way of viewing crime that is closer to the way we actually experience it. Crime is a violation of people and of their relationships. Justice, then, ought to seek first of all to repair relationships, to make them right.

An alternate understanding of crime and justice might look something like this:

- Crime is a violation of people.
- Justice identifies needs and obligations. . .
- so that things can be made right. . .
- through a process that encourages dialogue and involves both victims and offenders.

A restorative approach to justice understands that the essence of crime is a violation of people and of harmonious relations between people. Instead of asking first of all, "Who 'done' it? What should they get?" (and rarely going beyond this), a restorative approach to justice would ask: "Who has been hurt? What can we do to make things right, and whose responsibility is it?" True justice would have as its goals restoration, reconciliation and responsibility rather than retribution.

Restorative justice would aim to be personal. Insofar as possible, it would seek to empower victims and offenders to be involved in their own cases, and, in the process, to learn something about one another. As in the Victim Offender Reconciliation Programs (VORP), which operate in many communities in the U.S. and Canada, when circumstances permit, justice would offer victims and offenders an opportunity to meet in order to exchange information and decide what is to be done. Important goals would be to create understanding between the victim and offender, acceptance of responsibility, healing of injuries and empowerment of participants.

Is the restorative approach practical? Can it work? The experience of the VORPs suggests that while there are limitations and pitfalls, restoration and reconciliation can happen, even in some tough cases.

Moreover, our own history points in this direction. Through most of Western history, most crimes were understood to be harms people did to other people. Such wrongs created obligations to make right, and the normal process was to negotiate some sort of restitution agreement. Only in the past several centuries did our present retributive understanding displace this more reparative approach.

If our ancestors could view crime and justice this way, why can't we?

–Howard Zehr

© Howard Zehr, first published in "Goshen College Bulletin," March 1990. Used by permission.

Additional resources on restorative justice can be found in Chapter Two and on page 127.

Conflict Creation

When I feed the hungry they call me a saint; when I ask why people are hungry they call me a communist.

–Dom Helder Camara

In the field of religion we like to suggest that authentic religion is a two-edged sword. On the one hand, religion has the duty to "comfort the afflicted" while on the other hand, religion must "afflict the comfortable." Those who comfort the afflicted are regarded as "saints" because of their charity, their compassion, and their ability to sacrifice their own comforts (and life, if necessary) to care for the poor and the socially ostracized. But these good people are only "half" religious. If they do not also challenge the cultural, social, economic, and religious systems that created economically disenfranchised and socially neglected people, they may, ironically, be contributing to the very crisis they are trying to cure.

Rich people like charitable people, and politicians love volunteers precisely because they patch the boat instead of rocking it. But few like the boat rockers because they are troublemakers. The troublemakers are people and organizations that hold justice to be the basis of peace and social transformation (rather than social reform), the only truly effective means to cure social ills.

Just as in the field of religion, people in the peace movement (activists, educators, researchers), have a dual mission: to resolve conflict but also to create conflict. Because of the woefully inadequate social, legal, and economic systems that dominate our lives, it is inevitable that abundant conflict will exist. Because we almost universally undervalue the human person and fail to recognize innate human rights, we will continue to have "wars and rumors of wars" for many years to come.

Internationally, the many crises following the end of the Cold War have dramatically increased the conflict in our world. Hence, conflict resolution is becoming the major growth field in peace studies, especially since it is far easier in education circles to talk about conflict resolution than conflict creation!

There are several reasons, however, why conflict resolution is only half the task of the peacemaker. First, conflict resolution can all too easily end up being reactive rather than proactive. The agenda and strategy of the conflict resolver is essentially dictated by those who have created the conflict in the first place. Hence, conflict resolvers must react to situations that have been created by those who have an interest in provoking any given crisis. In the last 50 years the peace movement has been reactive or—in Johan Galtung's terminology—has pursued "negative" peace by focusing primarily on antiwar and antinuclear activities.

Second, conflict resolution can fall victim to a shortsighted theory of human nature that holds that harmony is the ideal for which we should strive. People, it is argued, are meant to get along and be calm and quiet in their personal and social relations. Discord, disagreement, and anger should be minimized in human relations. Hence, it's thought that conflicts are resolvable and that, in fact, the ideal human state is one in which conflict does not exist at all. ("Will there be conflict in heaven?" asked the penitent. "If there is, I'll sure as hell put a stop to it," said the priest).

Third, conflict resolution can be reductive in its approach to peacemaking. We must resist the temptation of seeing conflict resolution as the essence of peacemaking. Conflict resolution is primarily a skill, or a weapon in the arsenal of the peacemaker, but it should not be equated with peace itself.

Instead, creating conflict is the central mission of the peacemaker. This is because authentic peacemaking is essentially a proactive or positive activity, because peacemaking is at heart a philosophy or way of life, because conflict is a natural and positive part of the human condition, because nonviolent force is an essential element in human affairs, and most important because there can be no authentic peace without social justice as its foundation.

In 1963, Martin Luther King shocked many who knew little about peacemaking when he defended "force," "tension," "direct action," and "crisis" creation as legitimate activities in the movement for a more just society. In a letter he wrote from his jail cell in Birmingham, he stated:

> Nonviolent direct action seeks to create such a crisis and foster such a tension that a community which has constantly refused to negotiate is forced to confront the issue. . . . My citing the creation of tension as part of the work of the nonviolent-resister may sound rather shocking. . . but there is a type of constructive, nonviolent tension which is necessary for growth.

King helped many—even those in the peace movement—to realize that force and conflict creation are as essential to peacemaking as are the traditional goals of harmony and reconciliation. In fact, there can be no authentic harmony or reconciliation without justice, and justice will almost never be secured without struggle since, in King's words, "freedom is never voluntarily given by the oppressor." History tells us that oppressors will ignore the oppressed unless they recognize in the oppressed some viable power for change.

Hence, conflict or crisis creation rests on the following postulates: First, conflict is essentially a positive force in human affairs. The human animal is problem centered and learns best when confronted with a conflict that must be addressed. Conflict stimulates our creative energies so that we are forced to seek novel solutions to ancient problems. Conflict can, of course, be destructive, but it is only such when managed badly (as it often is). Too many people—including some in the peace movement—regard conflict as unnatural or evil. The reality is far different.

Second, conflict creation is based on the quest for social justice. Authentic peace can never be based on anything but justice as its secure foundation. Philosophically, justice means to render to another her or his due as a human person (*suum quique tradere*), while biblically justice means the salvation or wholeness or integrity of the person (body and spirit) and society. Authentic justice is never minimal (as in minimum wage); rather it is always maximal in its desire to recognize, develop, and promote the rights of all creation.

Third, conflict creation uses nonviolent force or sanctions to produce a peaceful society. Among his many contributions to peace studies, Gene Sharp has challenged the field to recognize that sanctions are essential in human affairs and are most often used by people who are neither pacifists nor well educated in the methods of nonviolent action. Since there are some people and social systems that will never do justice voluntarily, it will always be necessary to use force to coerce them into doing what is right.

Fourth, conflict creation seizes the initiative in struggling for justice. In the past half century, the peace movement has spent most of its energy reacting to wars, arms races, massacres, human and animal rights abuses, and so forth. (When the war in Indochina ended, for example, I remember being surprised when a peace activist friend said to me: "Good, now we can turn to the true task of the peacemaker: disarmament). Conflict creation is essentially proactive since it chooses the struggle, defines the conflict's parameters, and selects the nonviolent weapons to be used in confronting it.

The peace movement has many questions to ask about peace, hunger, human rights, and a host of other issues in the years ahead. But asking is not enough. We must give answers as well, and here is the great promise of a proactive peace movement. We have an opportunity to pursue, for example, things such as democratic socialism as an alternative to capitalism, a federated world rather than one dominated by sovereign nation states, and the restoration of our globe to the garden it was intended to be. To achieve these goals, however, many conflicts must be created so that the tension that results from this healthy debate will produce positive contributions to a dramatically more just society and world.

–Joseph J. Fahey

Taking Sides

We live today in a world of conflict: between governments and peace movements, between trade unions and employers, between feminists and male-dominated institutions. There may be differences of opinion about the nature of a particular conflict, whether it is a racial conflict or a class conflict, or whether the conflict might be resolved by peaceful negotiation rather than the use of force. But for many people in the world the fact of a conflict, which may encompass every aspect of their lives, can hardly be doubted.

Taking Sides

This poses very important questions for us as Christians. What should be our attitude to the conflicts in which we find ourselves and which we see around us? Should we take sides or must we always remain neutral?

It is as well to make it clear from the start that these questions are distinct from the questions of using or not using violence. We are not in this article discussing the question of whether or not there are occasions when the use of violence in pursuit of justice is justified. In countries like El Salvador, Guatemala and South Africa it is often almost impossible to disentangle the question of taking sides and the question of violence, but it is nonetheless a separate question and one that has to be talked about quite separately in the light of the gospel.

To many of us it is pretty obvious that there are some conflicts in which we ought to take sides. But what about the Christian belief in reconciliation, forgiveness and peace? How can you take sides if you love everybody, including your enemies? And how do we account for the widespread belief that in any conflict a Christian should be a peacemaker who avoids taking sides and tries to bring about reconciliation between the opposing forces?

This belief rests on a mistaken understanding of reconciliation. We have all heard people say: "We must be fair;" "We must listen to both sides of the story;" "There is always right and wrong on both sides. If we could only get people to talk to one another, to sort out their misunderstandings and misconceptions of one another, the conflict could be resolved." On the face of it this sounds very Christian. It sounds like a genuine concern for fairness and justice.

Three Common Mistakes

So what is wrong with this argument?

In the first place it makes reconciliation an *absolute principle* that must be applied in *all* cases of conflict. The model or example that it envisages is that of what one might call the "private quarrel" between two people who are being argumentative and not trying to understand one another and whose differences are based on misunderstandings. *But not all conflicts are like this.* In some conflicts one side is right and the other wrong, one side is being unjust and oppressive and the other is suffering injustice and oppression. In such cases a policy of seeking consensus and not taking sides would be quite wrong. Christians are not supposed to try to reconcile good and evil, justice and injustice; we are supposed to do away with evil, injustice and sin.

The first mistake, then, is the assumption that all conflicts are based upon misunderstandings and that there is always blame on both sides. There is no evidence for believing that this is always the case, either in conflicts between individuals or in conflicts between groups in society. It is an unfounded assumption that has nothing whatsoever to do with Christianity. It is an assumption that could only be made by people who do not suffer under injustice and oppression or who do not really appreciate the sinfulness and evil of what is happening.

The second mistake in this argument is that it assumes that a person can be neutral in all cases of conflict. In fact, neutrality is not always possible, and in cases of conflict due to injustice and oppression, neutrality is totally impossible. If we do not take sides with the oppressed, then we are, albeit unintentionally, taking sides with the oppressor, because it enables the status quo to be maintained; it hides the true nature of the conflict, keeps the oppressed quiet and passive and it brings about a kind of pseudo-reconciliation without justice. The injustice continues and everybody is made to feel that the injustice doesn't matter because the tension and conflict have been reduced.

This brings us to the third mistake. The commonly held view that Christians should always seek harmony and a "middle way" in every dispute assumes that tension and conflict are worse evils than injustice and oppression. This again is a false supposition based upon a lack of compassion for those who suffer under oppression. Those who are afraid of conflict or confrontation, even when it is nonviolent, are usually those who are not convinced of the need for change. Their caution hides an un-Christian pessimism about the future, a lack of hope. Or they use the Christian concern for reconciliation to justify a form of escapism from the realities of injustice and conflict.

All in all, these mistakes about Christian reconciliation are not simply a matter of misunderstandings, but come from a lack of real love and compassion for those who are suffering, or from a lack of appreciation of what is really happening in a grave conflict. In the final analysis, the insistent pursuit of an illusory neutrality in every conflict is a way of siding with the oppressor.

True Reconciliation

What then is the true meaning of reconciliation? What does reconciliation mean in the Bible?

"Do you suppose that I am here to bring peace on earth?" (The question is interesting. It seems to suggest that there were people who *did* "suppose" that Jesus had come to bring peace on earth). "No, I tell you, but rather dissension. For from now on a household will be divided: three against two, and two against three; the father divided against the son, son against father, mother against daughter, daughter against mother; mother-in-law against daughter-in-law, daughter-in-law against mother-in-law." (Lk. 12:51-53; Mt. 10:34-36).

Most of this is a quotation from the prophet Micah (7:6), who was deploring the conflict between parents and children. Jesus used the quote to say that this is just the kind of conflict and dissension that he will bring. And of course this is exactly what he did do. Not because he wanted to bring dissension and conflict for their own sake, but because his uncompromising stance inevitably divided the people into those who were for him and those who were against him.

Moreover, in the already existing conflict between Pharisees and the so-called "sinners," he sided with the sinners, prostitutes and tax collectors against the Pharisees. And in the conflict between the rich and the poor he sided with the poor. Jesus did not treat each side as equally right or equally wrong, or only needing to overcome their misunderstandings about one another. He condemns the Pharisees and the rich in no uncertain terms, and he forgives the sinners and blesses the poor. In fact he enters right into the conflict with the Pharisees and the rich to such an extent that they set out to discredit him, arrest him, charge him and execute him. Jesus makes no attempt to compromise with the authorities for the sake of a false peace or reconciliation or unity.

On the other hand there are times when Jesus does try to reconcile people who have been in conflict with one another; e.g., Jews and Samaritans, Zealots and tax-collectors, some individual Pharisees and sinners or the poor, etc. And it was probably for this reason that he was known as a man of peace.

But how is one to reconcile these two apparently contradictory approaches to conflict?

Jesus made a distinction between the peace that God wants and the peace that the world wants (Jn. 14:27). The peace that God wants is a peace that is based on truth, justice and love. The peace that the world offers us is a superficial peace and unity that compromises the truth, that covers over the injustices and that is usually settled on for thoroughly selfish purposes. Jesus destroys this false peace and even highlights the conflicts in order to promote a true and lasting peace. There is no question of preserving peace and unity at all costs, even at the cost of truth and justice. Rather it is a matter of promoting truth and justice at all costs, even at the cost of creating conflict and dissension along the way.

Different Kinds of Conflict

We noted before that there are different kinds of conflict. We must analyze each situation and respond accordingly. If one side is right, we must recognize this and side with them. If the other side is wrong and in power, we must oppose them and dethrone them from power.

On the other hand we may discover that both sides are basically right, that both sides are working for justice. In such cases, reconciliation is very important in order to create a cooperative solidarity in the struggle against injustice. And if we discover that both sides are wrong and that both are part of the oppression, then both must be confronted. And then, obviously, we don't try to reconcile them in their differences about the most effective way to oppress others.

Structural Conflict

It is important to realize that to get to the real root of many conflicts, we have to begin to think in structural terms—in other words, that not just individuals may be right or wrong, but the way societies are structured may itself be right or wrong. In some cases there is a *structural* conflict between the oppressor and the oppressed, between the rich and the poor. It is not a personal squabble. In these cases we cannot and should not impute guilt to the individuals concerned, nor should we treat everyone on the one side as blameless and everyone on the other side as guilty. Structurally, the cause of the poor and the oppressed is right and just, no matter what individual poor people may be like in their personal and private lives. And the cause of the rich and oppressor is wrong no matter how honest and sincere and unaware they may be.

Thus in the Magnificat or Song of Mary in the gospel of Luke, Mary says that it is God who "pulls down the mighty from their thrones and exalts the lowly, who fills the hungry with good things and sends the rich away empty." (Lk. 1:52-53). This does not mean that God hates the rich and powerful and that God wants to destroy them as people. It simply means that God wants to pull the rich and powerful from their thrones, from their position in society, because the structures of that society are unjust and oppressive.

This is the sense in which we must be on the side of the poor if we want to be on God's side. We must take an option for the poor, for the sake of both the poor and the rich as individual people. In fact, within this situation of structural conflict, the only way to love everyone is to side with the poor and the oppressed. Anything else is simply a way of siding with oppression and injustice.

Loving Our Enemies

This brings us to the question of loving our enemies. Here we must first point out that the commandment to love one's enemies only makes sense once we recognize that we do have enemies, and that they are really and truly our enemies. When people hate you and curse you and oppress you, Jesus does not say that you must pretend that they are not your enemies. They are. And when he says you must love them despite of this, he does not mean that you must avoid conflict or confrontation with them.

Confrontation and conflict do not, and need not necessarily, entail *hatred*. Class conflict and class struggle, which Christians have traditionally been reluctant to acknowledge, do not necessarily entail hatred. Such struggles may in fact be the only effective way of pulling down the mighty from their thrones.

Those who maintain an unjust distribution of wealth and power and those who prop up their thrones are in fact our enemies. They are everybody's enemies; they are even the enemies of their own humanity. As a group or class, they will never come down from their thrones willingly or voluntarily. A few individuals here and there may do so, but there will always be others to replace them. The ruling class as a whole cannot step down: we will have to pull them down from their thrones. Not in order to sit on those thrones ourselves, or to put others on them, but in order to destroy thrones.

The temptation for a Christian is to think that the most loving thing to do is to convert one by one those who sit on the thrones of injustice and thus to destroy the system. But change does not happen that way, because as long as the throne remains, it will always be filled by others and the oppression will remain. The only effective way of loving our enemies is to engage in action that will destroy the system that makes them our enemies. In other words, for the sake of love and for the sake of true peace, we must side with the poor and the oppressed and confront the rich and powerful and join the conflict or struggle against them, or rather against what they stand for and what they are defending.

In countries marked by grave injustice, joining the conflict, not judging it from a distance, is the only effective way of bringing about the peace that God wants. To take an example closer to home: in countries possessing nuclear weapons, there may be no shortcut around conflict with governments if the world is to progress toward disarmament. It is not possible to "balance" or "reconcile" the needs of the forty million people who die from starvation each year in the Third World with the needs of arms manufacturers and military strategists or the demands of a few wealthy nations to be able to destroy any potential attacker many times over. Decisions have to be made; one has to "take sides."

–Albert Nolan, OP
© Quixote Center (Hyattsville, MD) 1985, from "Rocinante" (newsletter). Used by permission.

Resources for Further Study on Faith and Conflict Transformation

Augsburger, David W. *Helping People Forgive*. Louisville, KY: Westminster/John Knox Press, 1996.
An exploration of the complicated issues of Christian forgiveness, reconciliation and their real-world applications.

Buzzard, Lynn, Juanita Eck and Laurence Eck. *Readiness for Reconciliation: A Biblical Guide*. Merrifield, VA: Christian Legal Society, 1988.
Seven biblical studies to help persons assess their readiness for reconciliation when disputes arise. Workbook format.

Driedger, Leo, and Donald B. Kraybill. *Mennonite Peacemaking: From Quietism to Activism*. Scottdale, PA: Herald Press, 1994.
Documents the shift among Mennonites from passive nonresistance to active participation in the political order and examines the ties between Mennonite peacemaking attitudes and social and theological forces.

Krieder, Robert, and Rachel Waltner Goossen. *When Good People Quarrel: Studies of Conflict Resolution*. Scottdale, PA: Herald Press, 1989.
Modern and biblical case studies (full of suspense and strong feelings) that invite one to play peacemaking roles. Useful for group study. Scripture passages and discussion questions included with each case study.

Lederach, John Paul. *Journey to Reconciliation*. Waterloo, ON: Herald Press, 1999.
Help for conflicted families, communities and nations to encounter themselves, each other and God.

Mouw, Richard J. *Uncommon Decency: Christian Civility in an Uncivil World*. Downers Grove, IL: Intervarsity Press, 1992.
A reflection on the ways in which Christians deal with controversial issues of the times.

Qualben, James. *Peace in the Parish*. San Antonio, TX: Langmarc Publishing, 1991.
Addressed to clergy and lay people who care deeply about their church and are frustrated with its inability to deal constructively with conflict. Lays out a "conflict redemption" approach based on biblical principles.

Sampson, Cynthia, and Douglas Johnston. *Religion: The Missing Dimension of Statecraft*. New York: Oxford University Press, 1994.
A collection of case studies and theoretical pieces looking at religion's role in international diplomacy.

Sande, Ken. *The Peacemaker: A Biblical Guide to Resolving Personal Conflict*. Grand Rapids, MI: Baker Book House, 1991.
Offers biblical principles for resolving conflict in the home, workplace, church and neighborhood. Includes numerous helpful illustrations.

Schreiter, Robert J. *The Ministry of Reconciliation: Spirituality and Strategies*. New York, Orbis Books, 1998.
Biblical and theological study of reconciliation in settings of structural conflict. Proposes that reconciliation begins with victims and their restoration. Deeply informed by narrative theory; attentive to symbol and ritual.

Schrock-Shenk, Carolyn, and Lawrence Ressler (eds). *Making Peace with Conflict: Practical Skills for Conflict Transformation*. Scottdale, PA: Herald Press, 1999.
A practical guide to understanding and transforming conflict based on biblical and Anabaptist principles.

Thomas, Marlin E. *Resolving Disputes in Christian Groups*. Winnipeg, MB: Windflower Communications, 1994. Articulates in very practical terms a biblical approach to interpersonal and group relations, facilitation and problem-solving.

Willimon, William. *Preaching About Conflict in the Local Church*. Philadelphia: Westminster Press, 1987. Focuses primarily on the issue of substantive conflict and how it can be addressed in sermons. Asserts that preaching is a valid pastoral response in the midst of conflict and provides strategies toward that end.

Wink, Walter. *Engaging the Powers: Discernment and Resistance in a World of Dominations*, Vol. 3 of *The Powers*. Minneapolis: Augsburg Fortress Publishers, 1992.

Yoder, Perry. *Shalom. . . The Bible's Word for Salvation, Justice and Peace*. Newton, KS: Faith & Life Press, 1987. A biblical study of the ways in which shalom is connected with other core aspects of biblical faith such as justice and salvation. Written with the context of the Two-thirds World in mind.

Zehr, Howard. *Changing Lenses: A New Focus for Crime and Justice*. Scottdale, PA: Herald Press, 1990. Examines our "retributive" assumptions about crime and justice, then proposes a "restorative" model based on the needs of victims and offenders, on past ways of responding to crime, on recent experiments, and on biblical principles.

Chapter 2

Understanding Conflict
and Transformation

The central core of conflict theory is not conflict at all, but power.

-J. T. Duke

Introduction

Conflict transformation represents a comprehensive set of lenses for describing the way conflict emerges from, evolves in, and brings about changes in the personal, relational, structural and cultural dimensions, and for intervening to promote peaceful change at those levels through nonviolent mechanisms.

–John Paul Lederach

Conflict and transformation—both are huge topics about which many books and articles have been written. In this chapter we pull together an eclectic set of articles from a collection of writers in the MCS network to provide a theoretical foundation for the rest of the manual and for the work we do as peacemakers and practitioners. We have chosen to organize this rather lengthy chapter around the interdependent dimensions that John Paul Lederach describes in more depth on the following page:

Personal (page 53 and following)—The effects of conflict and transformation within the individual including the spiritual, emotional, physical, and perceptual aspects.

Relational (page 70)—The effects of conflict and transformation upon the relationship including such aspects as communication, interdependence and relational patterns.

Structural (page 78)—Includes the root causes of conflict, the social conditions, the patterns of decision-making, the rules, roles and rituals that give rise to conflict and that are affected by conflict's transformation.

Culture (page 99)—Refers to the effect of conflict and conflict transformation on the cultural patterns of a group as well as the way these shared patterns affect people, their understanding of and response to conflict.

In reality, these dimensions are interdependent and overlapping. So, also, are the articles that we have placed within each section; some articles fit clearly into one section, other articles are more cross-cutting and their placement a bit arbitrary. We hope you find the organization of this rich writing useful.

–**Carolyn Schrock-Shenk**
© MCS 2000

Conflict Transformation: A Working Definition

At essence transformation refers to change. Transformation as change can be understood in two fundamental ways. **Descriptively**, transformation refers to the empirical impact of conflict, the *effects* that social conflict produces; it describes the general changes social conflict creates and the patterns it typically follows. **Prescriptively**, transformation implies deliberate intervention to effect change; it refers to the *goals* we have as intervenors as we work with conflict. At both levels, transformation is operative in four interdependent dimensions.

Dimension	Perspective	
	Descriptive	Prescriptive
Personal The changes effected in and desired for the individual. This involves emotional, perceptual and spiritual aspects of conflict.	Suggests that individuals are affected by conflict, in both negative and positive ways, for example, in terms of physical well-being, self-esteem, emotional stability, capacity to perceive accurately and spiritual integrity.	Represents deliberate intervention to *minimize* the destructive effects of social conflict and *maximize* its potentialities for growth in the person as an individual human being, at physical, emotional and spiritual levels.
Relational Depicts the changes effected in, and desired for the relationship. Here we take into consideration the areas of relational affectivity and interdependence, and the expressive, communicative and interactive aspects of conflict.	Refers to how the relational patterns of communication and interaction are affected by conflict. It looks beyond the tension around visible issues to the underlying changes produced by conflict in the patterns of how people perceive, and what they desire and pursue in their relationship: how close or distant, or how interdependent they wish to be, what they perceive the other wants, how reactive or proactive they become in the relationship, etc.	Represents intentional intervention that minimizes poorly functioning communication and maximizes mutual understanding, and that surfaces in an explicit manner the relational fears, hopes and goals of the people involved in terms of affectivity and interdependence.
Structural Highlights underlying causes of conflict and the patterns and changes it brings about in the social structures. At times understood as the "content" or "substance," structural dimensions focus attention on the areas related to basic needs, access to resources, and institutional decision-making patterns.	Refers to the analysis of social conditions that give rise to conflict and the way that conflict affects change in existing structures and patterns of making decisions.	Represents the intervention to provide insight into underlying causes and social conditions that create and foster *violent expressions* of conflict, and openly promotes *nonviolent mechanisms* that reduce adversarial confrontation, minimize and ultimately eliminate violence, and foster structures that meet basic human needs (substantive justice) and maximize participation of people in decisions that affect them (procedural justice).
Cultural Refers to the changes produced by conflict in the cultural patterns of a group, and the ways culture affects the development and handling of conflict.	Interested in how conflict affects and changes cultural patterns of a group, and how those accumulated and shared patterns affect the way people in that setting understand and respond to conflict.	Seeks to understand explicitly the cultural patterns that contribute to the rise of violent expressions of conflict, and to identify, promote, and build on the resources and mechanisms within a cultural setting for constructively responding to and handling conflict.

In summary, conflict transformation represents a comprehensive set of lenses for *describing* the way conflict emerges from, evolves in, and brings about changes in the personal, relational, structural and cultural dimensions, and for *intervening* to promote peaceful change at those levels through nonviolent mechanisms.

–John Paul Lederach
© 1995. Used by permission.

We don't see things as they are; we see things as we are.

–Anais Nin

Feelings in Conflict

Those tears shining on Mama's face were falling for me. When the bus started down the street, I wanted to run back and say something to Mama. I didn't know what. I thought, maybe, I woulda said, "Mama, I didn't mean what I said, 'cause I really do care." No, I wouldn'a said that. I woulda said, "Mama, button up your coat. It's cold out here." Yeah, that's what I forgot to say to Mama.

–Claude Brown, *Manchild in the Promised Land*

To say "feelings are not *bad*—they just *are*," is inadequate. The capacity to feel, and the feelings themselves, are wonderful and deeply spiritual. It is not anger or hate or loneliness that signifies the dying of my spirit or of a relationship: These mean I continue to be engaged and connected. Rather it is apathy that spells death. When I no longer feel, when my capacity to be touched at a heart level has drained away, I am spiritually dead. To feel—even the "negative" feelings—is to be truly alive.

The Challenge

- Be aware of my feelings.
- Be comfortable with my feelings.
- Separate my feelings from my actions/responses.
- Deal with the roots of my feelings.
- Express my feelings in constructive ways.
- Lessen and heal the negative feelings.
- Affirm and build on the positive feelings.

Myths/Unhelpful Assumptions About Emotions In Conflict

- Emotions are bad, irrational and irritating obstacles.
- Emotions are irrelevant in conflict, "substance" is what counts.
- If I ignore or repress feelings, they'll eventually go away.
- The feelings behind a destructive action are as wrong as the action.

Helpful Assumptions About Emotions in Conflict

- Feelings are an important part of every human interaction, every conflict.
- Emotions/feelings and behavior/action are very different.
- If I don't talk out my feelings, I'll act them out.
- To the degree that I am not aware of my feelings, my behavior is apt to be random. To the degree I am aware of them, I can choose my response.
- Belligerent, hurtful or intimidating behavior is rooted in one's woundedness and insecurity.
- Feelings often intensify until they have been acknowledged and validated.
- We have different skill and comfort levels in dealing with feelings.
- Each culture has its own ways of viewing and expressing emotions.

–Carolyn Schrock-Shenk
© MCS 1995

For many people, the bottom line in conflict is individual discomfort. When an individual reaches the end of his or her tolerance zone nothing in the world will stop a defensive action or reaction from occurring. So it is essential to know something about how emotions work.

There are two advantages in coming to understand our own emotions and the emotions of others. First, we will be able to negotiate differences better without taking things as personally as we otherwise might. Second, we will not get upset so quickly at others.

The only successful method I know for avoiding bad emotional consequences in our relationships is to know how each type of feeling or emotion works and what its early warning signs are. Our emotions are produced by the tension or relaxation of skin, muscles and organs, the secretion of hormones and the illness or health of the various parts of our body. Those feelings or emotions, whether pleasant or protective, cause us to act and react in certain ways as we attend to the needs of our bodies and spirits.

That is why neither theology nor Bible verses can stem the tide of strong feelings. Only training and commitment to deeply held principles can guard and guide us in the most extreme emotional situations.

Six Basic Emotions

We all recognize there are many individual emotions. However, most of those feelings can be grouped around six basic emotions in two categories.[1] All other emotions are complex configurations of those basic six. The three "pleasant" emotions are happiness, excitement, and tenderness. The three "protective" emotions are sadness, scare and anger.

Happiness is the sensation of fulfillment. When happiness is sustained it turns into joy. Its biblical equivalent is *shalom*, a concept which speaks of everything in life being just right. There are no losses, no fears and no insults or attacks. But there is one important catch. Happiness is always defined by our own individual standards. It is our own comfort zone that is at peace. The same set of circumstances that bring us satisfaction may leave another person very uncomfortable and unhappy.

Sadness is defined as the emotion of loss. When things which make us content disappear or do not even materialize, our lives become empty. We cry because the structures of our body contract to fill the (emotional) void. As we cry that inner tension is relieved to some degree. Children cry easily because they have not yet learned to stifle their emotions. Adults refuse to allow their emotions full expression, because it hampers their work and makes them appear to be inefficient and unable to deal with life.

Excitement is the emotion of positive action. Any event or activity which we perceive as good for us calls for the secretion of huge amounts of adrenaline. That produces high levels of energy, which we can use to accomplish the activity or event with which we are absorbed.

Scare or startle is the emotion of protection from events or activities which may hurt us. It causes us to pull back, flee, fight, react verbally, or engage in other activities designed to protect us from harm. In this case also huge amounts of adrenaline are secreted into the body system. This gives us extra energy and strength to provide for our own physical and emotional protection.

Tenderness is the sensation of closeness and togetherness in a trusting environment. It gives us the feeling that there is no threat of loss or fear of danger. We feel free to allow our emotions a full and free range of expression, expecting to be fully accepted and understood. Sustained tenderness usually turns into emotional love. It is deepened without fear until our own comfort zone or the comfort zone of the other is stretched to its limit. Then, as it seeks to move even further into the recesses of the heart, it can be offended as we or the other suddenly draw back, fearing too much intimacy or self-exposure.

Anger is the emotion of offense. It occurs when another assaults our integrity, our reputation, or our abilities. It also can occur when another moves in too close to our personal tender spots, pulls back too soon, or does not continue to honor our vulnerability. The resulting reaction may include insults or assaults as we attempt to punish the offender. Or it may result in flight as we seek to get as far away from the offender as possible. While tenderness/openness is the deepest and most intense of all emotions, anger is the most volatile.

Early Warning Signs

One of the most important things we can do when conflict begins is to pay attention to the early warning signs of the protective emotions. They are present in all three cases (sadness, scare and anger), but they escalate more rapidly in each successive wave of emotion, becoming more intense and tending to last longer.

There are at least four physical "early warning signs" as the body prepares for the danger it perceives to be present. Some are more intense and manifest themselves in different kinds of ways. While they function to prepare the body to protect itself, they are also helpful in alerting us to the danger of potential sin. Thus we can beware that we do not act out our feelings inappropriately.

The early warning signs include an accelerated heartbeat, rapid breathing, muscle tension (in preparation for physically defensive actions) and the escalation of energy produced by the secretion of adrenaline. As all four of these physical functions combine to fend off the perceived danger, the body feels flushed and invigorated. Fists can fly, words can tumble out of the mouth and feet and legs can go into instant action. It is important, therefore, that we are prepared to direct our energies into the right paths so that our actions do not cause additional offenses. We can learn to be more aware of early warning signs in ourselves and others, to better understand what is going on, and make choices about our actions and responses.

Comfort Zones

Another element of emotion is that everyone is most comfortable in her or his own emotional environment. Many persons who grew up in a hostile setting learned either to implode (keep feelings to themselves) or explode. A person who grew up in a nurturing, caring environment may greatly fear a hostile person, for he or she did not learn to function well in the face of intense explosions. Thus the explosive person may interpret quietness as timidity or as accommodation, while the gentler person may interpret explosiveness as hostility when it is not meant that way at all. Different emotional environments can cause persons to speak past each other. The other is the levels of energy which each is willing to expend in order to actually relate to the other.

Emotional Pain

Whatever personality test or inventory we consult in an attempt to understand ourselves and others better, one very important personality factor is usually left out—the impact of emotional trauma and pain upon otherwise well-rounded personality types.

Emotional pain can come from a variety of sources. These may include deep disappointments in life, traumatic loss of friends and family members, a variety of abuses and a host of obsessions.

[1] Morris, Dixie, and Frank Morris, *Therapeutic Feelings: A Companion for Adventurers*. Arlington Heights, IL: Liberation Psychology Training Center, 1988.

–**Marlin Thomas**
© Windflower Communications 1994, excerpted from *Resolving Disputes in Christian Groups*. Used by permission.

Powerlessness

Recently a mediator friend commented that she feels like a powerful person. This seems odd, she added, for she possesses neither the wealth nor the position usually associated with power. Upon further reflection she realized that much of her sense of power came from another source—her mastery of interpersonal skills. "Very rarely," she mused, "do I any longer feel like there is nothing I can do if difficulties come up with other people. Even when others have more institutional or political power than I, I am able to respond constructively. Often this influences others."

Feeling powerful (that is, able to significantly influence situations affecting one personally) is a prerequisite to constructive conflict management. This contradicts the popular belief that people get feisty because they feel *too* powerful. In fact, just as a cornered rat fights the dirtiest, so too do humans.

Where there is dirty fighting, someone is feeling powerless. This is hard to remember. Cornered people are often intimidating and can inflict serious injury. Worse, they mask their powerlessness—from themselves as well as others. Nothing suppresses a whimper better than a snarl! As a consequence, the root of the problem often lies hidden. Anyone close enough to hear the whimper is likely to get snarled at. Or bitten.

People experience powerlessness at various levels, each more debilitating than the previous:

1. Outcome. When one's preference is overruled. This form of powerlessness disappoints but doesn't embitter. People empowered in other ways know that no one always wins and tolerate such losses.

2. Process. When one doesn't just lose, but is not even seriously consulted. Or when the process for arriving at a decision is too hasty, exclusive or unclear for one to feel included. Process powerlessness is far more serious than outcome powerlessness. When people complain about outcomes, it is usually because they believe the process was unfair.

3. Social Esteem. When one is not only excluded from fair decision-making, but is also not valued or respected as a person. If the functions of a group or society diminish the value of certain persons, they will feel powerless and react destructively.

4. Self-Esteem. When one feels worthless, regardless of what others may think. These people believe they have no ability to influence who they become and no options for constructive response to problems.

5. Existential Issues. When one feels the inevitability of death and feels no connection of meaning or personal continuity to the eternal. As a result, such a person feels fundamentally powerless and inconsequential in the face of ultimate reality.

These levels function hierarchically, like a pyramid. Existential issues influence people's feelings of empowerment the most, outcome issues the least. The more empowered people feel at lower levels, the greater their capacity to respond appropriately to incidents of disempowerment at the upper levels.

If I know that I am loved eternally in the universe, I possess greater tolerance if my neighbor or colleague communicates disrespectfully with me. If I truly respect myself, I am less likely to feel threatened by a bad decision-making process. Not that I will be indifferent or acquiescent to violations by others. Rather, I possess the inner strength and calmness to respond with constructive assertiveness, not with frantic aggressiveness.

When responding to people in conflict, in most cases we have no choice but to begin at the top of the hierarchy and work downwards. The deeper we go, the greater the trust required to work openly on what is happening. For example, empowerment at the level of process and social esteem often enables persons to find empowerment at deeper levels. Efforts to crash quickly towards issues of existential empowerment in most cases only heighten resistance to genuine self-scrutiny at any level.

This hierarchy enables us to recognize several critical truths regarding conflict. One is that people who appear intimidating are often in reality deeply frightened human beings, and they themselves may not even be aware of this. Thus, in responding to them, we must look for strategies that avoid intimidating them further. This often calls for doing exactly the *opposite* of what we feel like doing.

Secondly, peacemaking is at its roots a profoundly *spiritual discipline*. This does not mean that all peacemaking strategies are "spiritual" in nature. On the contrary, the majority of what mediators, for example, spend their time on is mundane and practical. But we do well to know that underneath the practical strategies lie deeper issues which follow all humans like shadows that grow larger as the night approaches.

No mediator can disperse another person's shadows. But we can make sure we are able to recognize shadows when they are present. More important, we can make sure that we have found for ourselves the Light which illumines the darkness.

–Ron Kraybill
© MCS 1987, from *Conciliation Quarterly*, Vol. 6 No. 3

"Fessing Up" to Power

I am a powerful person. I am a white, middle-class, educated, North American woman with a strong community of friends, a supportive church and a stable, well-paying job. These are a few of my sources of power in this society. There are others. And it is critical that I look at these things squarely and "fess up" to them.

But it is hard.

I suspect few things make us church folk more skittish than talking about power. Most of us are more comfortable talking about servanthood, brotherhood or sisterhood. Talking about power is as difficult as talking about sex, race or money.

We need to talk about how power is distributed in our congregations, agencies and in society—who has most of it, who has least, why the disparity and what difference that disparity makes. And that reflection needs to start with ourselves. We who are committed to justice and right relationships need to become aware of and acknowledge the ways we are powerful as individuals and as groups.

Honesty about power is critical for at least three reasons:

1. *I want to avoid abusing my power.* Power is ambiguous, slippery and intoxicating, and will control me if I am not conscious of its role in my life. I cannot control or manage something I deny having. Declaring myself as only a servant among people with less power than I have is not honest. And it is dangerous. Denying my power is a small step away from abusing it. Unless the rules and structure of my organization or society provide fair boundaries, I am not held accountable for how I use my power.

2. *I want to use my power responsibly.* Power—the ability to get things done or to influence outcomes —is not intrinsically negative, or even neutral. I have been leading workshops on power for several years in order to address abuses of power, and I am only recently understanding that power is inherently positive. All of us need power to exist, to do good, to transform conflict and violence and evil.

What is problematic is the tendency for the disparity between the powerful and the powerless to produce oppression and injustice. In situations where I have more power than those around me by virtue of my role or ethnicity or class or gender, I can hang on to my power and impose control, subtly or overtly. Or, I can find ways to share power, to make decisions *with* others rather than *for* others, to provide opportunities for empowering the less powerful, to refuse the privilege my power gives me.

3. *I want to build right relationships in my family, community, church, place of employment and society.* We have become so accustomed to power inequities that many of us accept them as inevitable. A small percentage of people control a large percent of the world's resources, for example. African Americans face the death penalty much more frequently than Anglos for the same crimes. Women get paid less than men for the same tasks.

These and similar inequities are not inevitable. As I read in the Bible about justice, and the life and mission of Jesus, I realize inequities are not part of "God's will on earth as it is in Heaven." Systemic evils must be named, addressed and changed. We are God's hands and feet on earth and we are called to this task.

Become God's Instruments

If we want to cause fundamental change in our own relationships and in society more broadly, we can only do so if we understand our own power in relationship to others and understand how that reality is a microcosm of broader society.

Those of us who are relatively powerful people must both acknowledge our own power and understand these power dynamics to become effective instruments of God's peace and God's justice. Just as importantly, those who are relatively powerless due to ethnicity or gender or class are called to respond to that injustice.

Truly this is the message of the kingdom: the first shall be last, the greatest shall be the least, a little child shall lead them, the captives shall be released. May we embrace the difficulty, the complexity and the wonder of that message.

–Carolyn Schrock-Shenk

Ten Principles of Identity for Peacebuilders

1. People have a human need to define themselves. We need ways of saying "this is who I am."

2. People create a sense of who they are through their relationships with others. We define ourselves by our interactions with those around us.

3. Individuals define themselves in multiple ways based on the social or cultural groups that influence and/or shape them (Diagram 1). In order to understand any identity component, one must look at the interactions between that identity component and the others held by that individual or group. To describe a person as "white" says very little about her identity. To describe someone as a "white, middle-class, well-educated, Protestant, professional, Californian, mother" enriches the description of a person, but it still does not define all her characteristics and qualities.

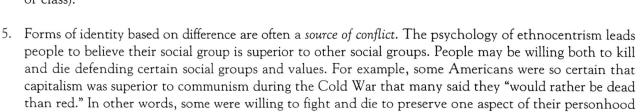

Diagram 1

4. People gain a sense of self through their relationships with people who are the same as they are and/or those who are different. Forms of identity based on *sameness* use positive comparisons with others: I know who I am because of my positive association with others like me. For example, adopted children may belong to an association of other adopted children in order to find social support. Identities based on *difference* use negative comparisons with others: I know who I am by knowing who I am not. People distinguish themselves from others through biological differences (such as gender, skin color or age) or socially constructed differences (such as religion, ideology or class).

5. Forms of identity based on difference are often a *source of conflict*. The psychology of ethnocentrism leads people to believe their social group is superior to other social groups. People may be willing both to kill and die defending certain social groups and values. For example, some Americans were so certain that capitalism was superior to communism during the Cold War that many said they "would rather be dead than red." In other words, some were willing to fight and die to preserve one aspect of their personhood based on the economic ideology of their country.

6. Forms of identity based on difference may also *result from conflict*. Conflict plays a role in creating "in-groups" or allies and "out-groups" or enemies. Conflict strengthens perceptions of who is good and who is bad, allowing people to create simplified ways of understanding the world. For example, many early European settlers to the "New World" peacefully coexisted with First Nations peoples, sharing a sense of common humanity and friendship. When struggles for land and resources increased between settlers and First Nations peoples, the group identities of "white" and "native" took on new importance. In these conflicts, each group set out to dehumanize and often do away with the "other."

7. The way an individual identifies himself or herself differs in conflict and nonconflict situations. In nonconflict situations, people seem to define themselves broadly, as shown in Diagram 1. People may also come to see themselves through the lens of conflict (Diagram 2). Therefore, people engaged in gender conflicts may perceive being "male" or "female" as their primary or sole identity. In conflicts involving race, people may see themselves as primarily "white" or "black."

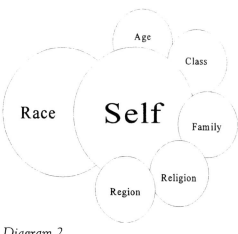

Diagram 2

8. The way an individual or group defines others also differs in conflict and nonconflict contexts. In nonconflict situations, people are less likely to stereotype others or categorize them according to only one social group. However, the process of assigning a stripped-down identity to another person or group seems to increase during conflicts. For example, in the United States white people do not usually judge the personal characteristics of other white people based on skin color alone. However, many Americans who have been socialized in a racist setting will make immediate judgements of the character of people of color based solely on the color of their skin.

9. Because of the connection between conflict and identity, perceptions of self and other may need to be transformed in peacebuilding efforts. Rehumanizing oneself and one's enemy requires transforming the perceptions of the ways people are identified. This occurs by increasing the flexibility or relative importance of the ways people identify themselves. As people become aware of their interdependence with many other social groups, including with their enemy, they gain a fuller sense of their own and their enemy's identities. For example, Palestinian and Israeli women who have met and discussed the many shared aspects of their lives as mothers, sisters, wives, widows and victims of conflict have gone through a process of rehumanizing their sense of self and other. Together they are in a stronger position to build peace in the region.

10. Perceptions of identity change according to physical and relational contexts. At the workplace, a person may relate to others through her professional identity. When at home, a person will interact with others according to her family role as mother, wife or daughter. The typical negotiation room is sterile and encourages people to identify each other as "negotiators" or members of a single identity group related to the conflict. Peacebuilders can intentionally create contexts where adversaries are encouraged to see themselves and others through lenses that allow a fuller definition of both self and other.

–Lisa Schirch
© MCS 2000, from *Conciliation Quarterly*, Vol. 19 No. 1

Know Thyself

Effective conflict management begins with self-management and self-management begins with self-awareness, with knowing and understanding oneself. The value of such understanding is magnified in conflict. As individuals become aware of the way they tend to react in the stress of conflict, they can make choices to modify their behavior—behavior that might be hurtful to self or others.

The next step is understanding and respecting the styles of others, which may be very different from one's own. One might discover, for example, that the style of a colleague is not really dysfunctional or obnoxious, but appears that way because the combination of some styles is prone to mutual frustration and misunderstanding. An understanding of and appreciation for style differences is crucial to the person who wishes to positively manage conflict.

Many instruments exist to assist individuals in assessing their "style" in conflict.

Thomas-Kilmann Conflict Mode Instrument

One of the best known instruments is the Thomas-Kilmann (T-K) Conflict Mode Instrument, developed by Kenneth W. Thomas and Ralph H. Kilmann. The T-K posits five distinct styles in responding to conflict: Accommodation, Avoidance, Compromise, Competition, Collaboration. It is useful for working with groups, as it demonstrates a range of responses to conflict among individuals. The T-K can be administered and interpreted relatively quickly.

One limitation of the T-K is its narrow focus on responses to conflict. The five T-K "styles" are actually better described as "approaches," and not styles, as the term is used by other instruments which describe a broader range of personality aspects. Researchers who have worked with a variety of style instruments suggest using more than one to provide more information. One can consider one's T-K conflict "style," for example, alongside one's Myers-Briggs or Gilmore-Fraleigh profiles, which provide a broader picture of one's orientation to life.

Myers-Briggs Type Indicator

The Myers-Briggs Type Indicator (MBTI) is a preference sorter using four continua to indicate extroversion/introversion, sensing/intuition, thinking/feeling, and judging/perceiving. The 16 possible types are determined according to where one fits on each of these scales. In conflict situations it is helpful to understand if an individual characteristically values openness or privacy, method or intuition, fairness or mercy, and early closure or information gathering with spontaneous action.

The Gilmore-Fraleigh Style Profile

Many conflict practitioners use the Gilmore-Fraleigh (G-F) Style Profile, developed by Susan K. Gilmore and Patrick W. Fraleigh. The G-F is similar to the MBTI in that it focuses on broad personality function. But it is less sophisticated—therefore easier to interpret—and more directly focused on how individuals *interact* with one another. This makes it a good tool for learning about interpersonal conflict.

The G-F instrument posits just four styles, reminiscent of the four humors of medieval wisdom (sanguine, phlegmatic, choleric and melancholic). These are Accommodating/Harmonizing, Analyzing/Preserving, Achieving/Directing and Affiliating/Perfecting.

A particularly helpful characteristic of the G-F instrument is that it provides two sets of scores, one for "calm conditions" and one for "storm conditions." The assumption is that many individuals respond differently in the stress of conflict (storm) than in normal interaction. Understanding this "stress shift" allows one to anticipate and better manage oneself under "storm conditions," and understand and relate better to others whose behavior changes under stress.

Another helpful characteristic is that the G-F highlights both the *strengths and the weaknesses* of each of the four styles. It is difficult to use the Thomas-Kilmann material without communicating a strong bias toward the use of "collaboration" in most conditions. Therefore, most users will likely find the G-F more affirming and empowering than the T-K.

The G-F provides considerable information regarding how the styles interact. This knowledge enables users to strategically plan how to bring the best out of others and to communicate clearly their own needs in working out differences. The G-F is available in three versions, intended for work colleagues, students and "intimate partners." Other materials, including a manual for trainers, are available.

Enneagram

The Enneagram is an ancient typology that identifies nine separate and distinct personality types. See the article by Larry Hoover on page 62.

The MCS Style Inventory

On page 64 is a style inventory developed by Ron Kraybill. While this instrument has not been used as widely nor tested for validity as have the T-K, the G-F and other instruments, it is a simple instrument that can serve as a starting point for reflection about one's preferred approach to conflict. Like the T-K, Kraybill's instrument focuses more narrowly on conflict behavior and not broadly on a variety of personality factors. Like the G-F, the instrument provides a "calm" and a "storm" score so users can consider their responses under varying conditions.

Like the T-K, the Kraybill inventory tends to place more value on one approach, collaborating. It is important to note that each of the approaches can be appropriate given the situation, and that each has its drawbacks or "costs" if overused or if used in *every* situation. A key benefit of the awareness of our predominant style and the other approaches is realizing we can make *choices* in response to most conflict situations.

After completing and scoring the inventory, consider (and discuss with others) these questions:
1. Do you agree that the approaches which received the highest scores are your predominant approaches to conflict?

2. What conflict approaches in other people do you find difficult to understand or work with?
3. What approaches would you like to strengthen, aside from those which received the highest scores? How might you work at that?

Styles and Culture

There are many factors which influence our tendencies in conflict. Many personality researchers note that many of our preferences and ways of interacting are "set" at a very young age. While biology plays a role in influencing our behavior, we are also strongly shaped by the many "cultures" of which we are a part—culture defined much more broadly than "race" or "ethnicity." Some of these other cultural influences include our gender group, socioeconomic class, geographical location, education, institutions we are a part of, etc.

In their training manual *Conflict Analysis and Resolution as Education* (UVic Institute for Dispute Resolution, 1994), Michelle LeBaron and Victor C. Robinson propose these questions for reflection and discussion:
1. What did I learn about conflict from my family/ different cultural groups with which I affiliate?
2. What does this information about my conflict handling style mean for me when I am involved in a conflict?
3. What does this information about my style mean for me as an intervenor?

Conclusion

Key to helping others in conflict is knowing and understanding one's own tendencies in conflict. Self-reflection is an ongoing task for peacemakers, and not a "once and done" thing. Each person does have a predominant style of doing things in life, including "doing conflict." We can combine self-awareness, knowledge of the variety of responses to conflict that are available, and continual skill-building to work at responding more constructively to the conflicts—the "differences heated up"—that are a part of our lives.

–David Brubaker and Jim Stutzman
© MCS 1995, 2000. Portions of this article first appeared in *Conciliation Quarterly*, Vol. 6 No. 3.

Ordering Information

Thomas-Kilmann Conflict Mode Instrument and *Myers Briggs Type Indicator:* Consulting Psychologists Press, PO Box 10096, Palo Alto, CA 94303; 800-624-1765; www.cpp-db.com
Gilmore-Fraleigh Style Profile: Friendly Press, 5120 Franklin Blvd #3, Eugene, OR 97403; 888-541-0336

Self-awareness and Conflict: The Enneagram as Catalyst

Mediation and conflict transformation training typically includes some instruction in self-awareness, the ongoing attention to one's internal state. It emerges in the use and discussion of conflict styles that help us understand our differences in dealing with conflict. It is a part of the discussion and learning around listening exercises as trainees are encouraged to reflect on and articulate their insights when they experience empathic listening. It is central to the understanding of mediator bias. It is fundamental to the critiquing process following role plays or simulations. And it is seen as the key to understanding and improving emotional intelligence.

While we intuitively know what it is, it might be useful to examine it more closely and not just in the context of other elements of conflict transformation. In so doing we may get some helpful insights into ways that we can understand and, in turn, share with others the connection between self-awareness and taking responsibility for our own thoughts and actions. Moreover, we may get an enhanced vision for ways that we can transcend the limitations of our ego and personality structure and search for new ways of knowing and being.

Self-Awareness Defined

Buddhist practitioners call it mindfulness. It has been personified as the inner observer, a second self who is able to watch with dispassionate curiosity as the primary self struggles. It is a phenomenon unavailable to animals and perhaps the central component of human consciousness. At its best it is the nonreactive, nonjudgmental attention to inner states. Jon Kabat-Zinn is a well known proponent and teacher of mindfulness. He describes it as paying attention in a particular way: on purpose, in the present moment, and nonjudgmentally.

Of course it is not as easy as it sounds. While we may have received some instruction or experience in meditative or mindfulness practices, we are painfully aware of the omnipresent self-talk, chatter or distraction that we live with which interferes with our purpose, our being in the present moment and our acceptance of self and others. We are less aware of the deep-seated and more painful habit patterns of thought, emotional reactions and assessment.

Enneagram Defined

The Enneagram is an important tool for developing self-awareness. Based on a 1500-year-old system for gaining self knowledge attributed to the Sufi mystics, the Enneagram has been adapted into psychological terms and used as a personality typology. The system identifies nine separate and distinct personality types, each of which has identifiable characteristics for patterns of thinking, feeling and acting. Each of the patterns is based on an explicit perceptual filter, which determines what you pay attention to and how you direct your energy.

When we were infants we were surrounded by those who cared for our every need; life was delicious and uncomplicated. Then came the pain of separation and exposure to an uncertain and often unloving environment. So we developed a system of coping with the world, a system of thinking, feeling and acting that became our personality or ego.

Each of us has developed one of the nine patterns to protect a specific aspect of our self that felt threatened as our personality was developing. As we discover our personality type, we discover more about our original whole self. We will also understand more about the unconscious motivation from which we operate. Discovering our "enneatype" can also help us understand how to focus effectively on becoming more productive, proactive and responsible. It allows our true and best self to emerge and can change the way we relate to others.

Enneagram in Teaching and Practice

I have used the Enneagram for the past five years as a component of mediation and conflict transformation training and teaching, as an initial exercise in interventions where working relationships have broken down and as a self discovery tool with friends and family. Thanks to the excellent literature and competent training available, the Enneagram system is accessible and user-friendly. Helen Palmer has made a major contribution to this work, especially through the use of the "oral tradition." This consists of the principle of self-discovery and panel interviewing.

The inventory method allows us to "type" ourselves by determining with which of the nine descriptions we most identify with. A coach or self administered guide and feedback from friends and family then help us confirm the choice. Panel interviewing places persons who identify with the same type in a group or "panel" so they can share the commonalities of their type and world view. Through this approach we can experience how similarities related to type and world view can cut across ethnic and cultural differences. We can also move beyond the psychological typology of personality and learn more about our identity and how we order and create meaning in our lives.

Teaching about personality styles in conflict is based on the premise that knowledge of our own style in conflict and understanding and respecting the styles of others are essential to personal conflict management. While we have always considered managing our own behavior in conflict as an important component, I believe it is becoming increasingly clear that it is the most important component. This helps explain the interest in and support for the articulation of the transformative approach to mediation and the focus on personal empowerment and understanding and respect for the point of view of others. For me, the Enneagram has been an increasingly important component of my training, teaching, intervention and personal growth.

On the Enneagram, I am a "nine," the description of which is "mediator" or "peacemaker." This is a term chosen to represent one of the strengths of this type, i.e., being able to see all points of view easily and therefore good at helping people resolve their differences. The downside is my tendency to be more aware of other people's positions, agendas and personal priorities than my own. Indecisiveness and distractions are problems and my attention is easily diverted to trivia. I also like life to be harmonious and am a conflict avoider. These are my "automatics," my habits of mind. Understanding this has been helpful. Now when my heart pounds during a heated exchange, I am willing to see it as cue to speak up, rather than clam up.

–Larry Hoover
© MCS 2000

Intervention

I have used the Enneagram in interventions with a conflicted family business and with several groups of professional practitioners who were approaching dysfunction in their practices. In all cases the insights gained by the participants about their own and the other participants' personality types opened the door for successful relationship rebuilding. Understanding that behaviors which precipitated a breakdown in relationships could be attributed to habit of mind rather than motive was transformative.

With friends and family, the Enneagram allows issues that have been off limits because of painful history to be put on the table and discussed in a different way. It's as if the "edge" is removed from difficult issues with old baggage. Conversation about problematic patterns and habits is particularly difficult because old wounds are reactivated and we easily move into our automatic defenses. Discussing personality patterns and habits of mind is different, like a "reframing." Communicating in this way opens doors and lets us see old issues in a new manner.

Conclusion

In the major spiritual traditions, habits of mind have been viewed as passions or vices. Spiritual growth depends on our ability to move beyond these fixations. Jesuit priest Anthony deMello said spirituality is "waking up." An awareness and understanding of our habits of mind from a psychological perspective is a good place to start. The Enneagram is an excellent tool not only for awareness but for personal and spiritual growth. It gives us a vision for who we are meant to be once we experience freedom from the limitations of our habits of mind. It also encourages us to think nondualistically by recognizing our personality or ego as a friend and not an enemy—a friend that has helped us cope with the problems of an imperfect world and an ally and fellow traveler on our spiritual journey.

Personal Conflict Style Inventory

Please Note: The reflection this inventory can create is more important—and more reliable—than the numbers the tally sheet yields. There are no "right" or "wrong" answers, nor have we "standardized" this instrument. Some takers agree with the results; others disagree. Whether you like the results or not, you should rely on them for an accurate picture of yourself only after further self-scrutiny and discussion with others. The inventory is merely a tool to enable these larger tasks.

Instructions: Consider your response in situations where your wishes differ from those of another person. Note that statements A-J deal with your **initial** response to disagreement; statements K-T deal with your response **after the disagreement has gotten stronger**. If you find it easier, you may choose one particular conflict setting and use it as background for all the questions. Circle one number on the line below each statement.

When I first discover that differences exist. . .

A. . . . I make sure that all views are out in the open and treated with equal consideration, even if there seems to be substantial disagreement.

Not at all characteristic ← 1 — 2 — 3 — 4 — 5 — 6 → Very characteristic

B. . . . I devote more attention to making sure others understand the logic and benefits of my position than I do to pleasing them.

Not at all characteristic ← 1 — 2 — 3 — 4 — 5 — 6 → Very characteristic

C. . . . I make my needs known, but I tone them down a bit and look for solutions somewhere in the middle.

Not at all characteristic ← 1 — 2 — 3 — 4 — 5 — 6 → Very characteristic

D. . . . I pull back from discussion for a time to avoid tension.

Not at all characteristic ← 1 — 2 — 3 — 4 — 5 — 6 → Very characteristic

E. . . . I devote more attention to feelings of others than to my personal goals.

Not at all characteristic ← 1 — 2 — 3 — 4 — 5 — 6 → Very characteristic

F. . . . I make sure my agenda doesn't get in the way of our relationship.

Not at all characteristic ← 1 — 2 — 3 — 4 — 5 — 6 → Very characteristic

G. . . . I actively explain my ideas and just as actively take steps to understand others.

Not at all characteristic ← 1 — 2 — 3 — 4 — 5 — 6 → Very characteristic

H. . . . I am more concerned with goals I believe to be important than with how others feel about things.

Not at all characteristic ← 1 — 2 — 3 — 4 — 5 — 6 → Very characteristic

I. . . . I decide the differences aren't worth worrying about.

Not at all characteristic ← 1 — 2 — 3 — 4 — 5 — 6 → Very characteristic

J. . . . I give up some points in exchange for others.

Not at all characteristic ← 1 — 2 — 3 — 4 — 5 — 6 → Very characteristic

If differences persist and feelings escalate. . .

K. . . . I enter more actively into discussion and hold out for ways to meet the needs of others as well as my own.

Not at all characteristic ← 1 — 2 — 3 — 4 — 5 — 6 → Very characteristic

L. . . . I put forth greater effort to make sure that the truth as I see it is recognized and less on pleasing others.

Not at all characteristic ← 1 — 2 — 3 — 4 — 5 — 6 → Very characteristic

M. . . . I try to be reasonable by not asking for my full preferences, but I make sure I get some of what I want.

Not at all characteristic ← 1 — 2 — 3 — 4 — 5 — 6 → Very characteristic

N. . . . I don't push for things to be done my way, and I pull back somewhat from the demands of others.

Not at all characteristic ← 1 — 2 — 3 — 4 — 5 — 6 → Very characteristic

O. . . . I set aside my own preferences and become more concerned with keeping the relationship comfortable.

Not at all characteristic ← 1 — 2 — 3 — 4 — 5 — 6 → Very characteristic

P. . . . I interact less with others and look for ways to find a safe distance.

Not at all characteristic ← 1 — 2 — 3 — 4 — 5 — 6 → Very characteristic

Q. . . . I do what needs to be done and hope we can mend feelings later.

Not at all characteristic ← 1 — 2 — 3 — 4 — 5 — 6 → Very characteristic

R. . . . I do what is necessary to soothe the other's feelings.

Not at all characteristic ← 1 — 2 — 3 — 4 — 5 — 6 → Very characteristic

S. . . . I pay close attention to the desires of others but remain firm that they need to pay equal attention to my desires.

Not at all characteristic ← 1 — 2 — 3 — 4 — 5 — 6 → Very characteristic

T. . . . I press for moderation and compromise so we can make a decision and move on with things.

Not at all characteristic ← 1 — 2 — 3 — 4 — 5 — 6 → Very characteristic

Style Inventory Tally Sheet

When you are finished, write the number from each item to the tally sheet. For example, on item B, if you selected number 1, write "1" on the line designated for B on the tally sheet. Then add the numbers. B 1 + H 4 = 5 Calm Write the number you circled for each situation beside the corresponding letter. Add each of the 10 columns of the tally chart, writing the total of each in the empty box just below the double line.

A ___	K ___	B ___	L ___	C ___	M ___	D ___	N ___	E ___	O ___
G ___	S ___	H ___	Q ___	J ___	T ___	I ___	P ___	F ___	R ___
Calm	Storm	Calm	Storm	Calm	Storm	Calm	Storm	Calm	Storm
Collaborating		Forcing		Compromising		Avoiding		Accommodating	

Now list your scores and the style names in order from highest score to lowest in both the calm and storm columns below.

Calm

Response when issues/conflicts first arise.

_____ _____
score   style

_____ _____

_____ _____

_____ _____

_____ _____

Storm

Response after the issues/conflicts have been unresolved and have grown in intensity.

_____ _____
score   style

_____ _____

_____ _____

_____ _____

_____ _____

Interpreting the Scores

This exercise gives you two sets of scores for each of the five approaches to conflict. **Calm** scores apply to your response when disagreement first arises. **Storm** scores apply to your response if things are not easily resolved and emotions get stronger. The higher your score in a given style, the more likely you are to use this style in responding to conflict. The highest score in each of the columns indicates a "preferred" or primary style. If two or more styles have the same score, they are equally "preferred." The second highest score indicates one's "backup" style if the number is relatively close to the highest score. A fairly even score across all of the styles indicates a "flat profile." Persons with a flat profile tend to be able to choose easily among the various responses to conflict.

–Ron Kraybill
© MCS 1987

Approaches to Conflict

Forcing ("my way")

Overview: Control the outcome; discourage disagreement; insist on my view prevailing.

Perspective on Conflict: Conflict is obvious; some people are right and some people are wrong. The central issue is who is right. Pressure and coercion are necessary

Often appropriate when . . .
- an emergency looms.
- you're sure you're right, and being right matters more than preserving relationships.
- the issue is trivial, and others don't really care what happens.

Often inappropriate when . . .
- collaboration has not yet been attempted.
- cooperation from others is important.
- used routinely for most issues.
- self-respect of others is diminished needlessly.

Collaborating ("our way")

Overview: Assert your views while also inviting other views. Welcome differences; identify all main concerns; generate options; search for solution which meets as many concerns as possible; search for mutual agreement.

Perspective on Conflict: Conflict is natural, neutral, so affirm differences, prize each person's uniqueness. Recognize tensions in relationships and contrasts in viewpoint. Work through conflicts of closeness.

Often appropriate when . . .
- issues and relationship are both significant.
- cooperation is important.
- a creative outcome is important.
- reasonable hope exists to meet all concerns.

Often inappropriate when
- time is short.
- the issues are unimportant.
- you're overloaded with "processing."
- the goals of the other person are wrong beyond doubt.

High Concern for Issues
9

8

7

6

Compromising ("half way")

Overview: Urge moderation; bargain; split the difference; find a little something for everyone; meet them halfway.

Perspective on Conflict: Conflict is mutual difference best resolved by cooperation and compromise. If each comes halfway, progress can be made by the democratic process.

Often appropriate when . . .
- cooperation is important, but time or resources are limited.
- finding **some** solution, even less than the best, is better than a complete stalemate.
- efforts to collaborate will be misunderstood as forcing.

Often inappropriate when . . .
- it's essential to find the most creative solutions.
- when you can't live with the consequences.

Low Concern for Relationship

1   2   3   4

High Concern for Relationship

6   7   8   9

Avoiding ("no way")

Overview: Delay or avoid response; withdraw; be inaccessible; divert attention.

Perspective on Conflict: Conflict is hopeless; avoid it. Ignore differences; accept disagreement or get out.

Often appropriate when . . .
- the issue is trivial.
- the relationship is insignificant.
- time is short, and a decision is not necessary.
- you have little power, but still wish to block the other person.

Often inappropriate when . . .
- you care about the issues *and* the relationship.
- used habitually for most issues.
- a residue of negative feelings is likely to linger.
- others would benefit from caring confrontation.

4

3

2

1
Low Concern for Issues

Accommodating ("your way")

Overview: Accept the other's view; let the other's view prevail; give in; support; acknowledge error; decide it's no big deal or it doesn't matter.

Perspective on Conflict: Conflict is usually disastrous, so yield. Sacrifice your own interests; ignore the issues; put relationships first; keep peace at any cost.

Often appropriate when . . .
- you really don't care about the issue.
- you're powerless, but don't wish to block the other.

Often inappropriate when . . .
- you are likely to harbor resentment.
- used habitually in order to gain acceptance (Outcome: depression and lack of self-respect).
- when others wish to collaborate and will feel like forcers if you accommodate.

–Ron Kraybill

© MCS 1986, 2000, titles adapted from the Thomas-Kilmann Conflict Mode Instrument and from David Augsburger

Commitment to be Constructive

In any conflict there are three main considerations: people, problems, and process.

Sometimes someone in a conflict says "Let's just deal with the issues here. Let's leave out all relationship and personality stuff." I don't think that it is possible. I think that every time you work on issues, the relationships of those involved will be impacted. Vice versa, working on the relationship will impact work on the issues. What I have observed is an interrelationship that cannot, or should not, be ignored.

Frequently, the idea of trying to find a cooperative resolution, whether between two people or within a group, is viewed as a very time consuming process which often ends in frustration. We can be much more efficient and effective when utilizing a cooperative resolution process if we keep reminding ourselves of our "commitment to be constructive." I have chosen this aspect of the relationship between individuals in conflict because I believe it is more critical than simply "whether the relationship is important."

The vertical continuum in the diagram represents the issues in the conflict. High means that the issue is important to me. Low means the issue is not important to me. On any issue we discuss, we are all somewhere on the continuum between high and low. The horizontal continuum represents my commitment to be constructive in this relationship as it relates to the issue being discussed. High means that I am willing to act in way that demonstrates my willingness to search for some way of handling this problem which will be constructive for all parties. Low means that I am not willing to act in ways that demonstrate my willingness to look for a constructive resolution for both. This means that my actions might be destructive for at least one of the parties.

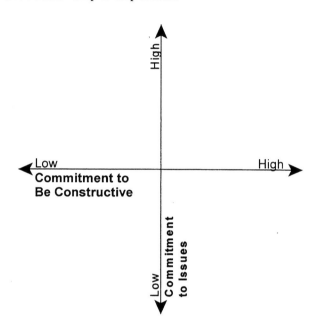

There is a cartoon that says: "Sure, that's right, just walk out of the room. You know what your trouble is? You can't take destructive criticism." It is an accurate and concise illustration of one of the options—walking out—when one party perceives another as being destructive.

Constructive Style

I use this diagram in training events to help individuals consider how their personal style of handling conflicts will likely impact those with whom they relate.

I ask participants to work in groups of two or three and place all of the styles (avoiding, compromising, collaborating, forcing, accommodating) on the grid, assuming all you know about the person is the style you see being acted out. In other words, "Based on the style, what is your sense of their commitment to the issues (high or low)? Of their commitment to being constructive in the relationship (high or low)?"

I think that it is possible to use all of the styles in all of the quadrants, but using some on the right-hand side would require much more conversation and convincing to persuade the other party that you are on the constructive side of the continuum. The purpose of this is to increase awareness of the *impact* of the style on others. Whatever our style, we need to ask ourselves "In which quadrant do I think someone would put me if all they knew about me was the style I use?" And, "Is that the quadrant in which I want to be perceived?"

Constructive Negotiation

I also use this diagram to help individuals determine their readiness for using mediation to resolve a conflict and, when a mediation gets "stuck," whether they should continue trying.

In my first meeting with parties, individually or together, I draw the diagram and explain to them what it is intended to illustrate. At the end of the description I suggest that it would be possible in their case for each of them to stay high on both the issues and high on the commitment to be constructive. I point this out to illustrate that they have a number of options in terms of how to relate in this dispute.

I ask them if they are willing to work on the right-hand side. I say that I realize from time to time they may forget and move toward the left-hand side, but I wonder if they would be willing to allow me to ask them throughout the mediation if they are still on the right-hand side.

I tell them that as I understand my role as a mediator, it is important only to bring those people together in a mediation who have agreed to work on the right-hand side. That's what mediation is all about—people agreeing to try to work together constructively. Often in an individual meeting, the first response to me is that they probably could be on the right-hand side but their opponent, they are sure, is not. I then remind them that it is my responsibility to only bring them together if they *both* say that they are willing to work on the right-hand side.

Then I ask again if they would be willing to commit themselves to work on that right-hand side. If they both say yes, then I bring them together in a mediation and start that meeting by again drawing the diagram and saying, "I have met with both of you and you have each assured me that your intention is to work on the upper right-hand side, isn't that right?" If they don't both say yes, we are not ready to start the mediation.

A problem I have observed and experienced is that if we don't get agreement on the issues (in a reasonably short time or sometimes even after a long time) we often feel like we have to make a choice between being constructive or staying high on the issues (standing up for my convictions).

Another problem I have observed is the difficulty in sorting out my feelings and how I am going to choose to act. Sometimes, when I don't have very constructive feelings, choosing to act in constructive ways seems to feel like just that, "an act," as "fake" or "phony" or at least incongruent. I suggest that this is normal and that as (or if) things are worked out, feelings will catch up with the decision to be constructive. Sometimes if things aren't worked out soon the need to live with the incongruence is very difficult.

This is what I think that Jesus was saying in his teaching to "love your enemies." He was suggesting that it is possible, and it is God's preference, for one to stay on the constructive side of the continuum even with someone who has very different goals or objectives or has very different positions on issues, even when those issues are very important to you.

Constructive Peacemaking

I think that all peacemaking starts with a decision on the part of at least one of the parties to be constructive. The easiest situation in which to make peace is when the other party also decides to be constructive. But, I can still decide what I am going to do about being constructive regardless of whether the other is on the constructive side.

Shalom-peace is defined as peace which results from right relations. The Bible does not suggest that peace exists when we have no differences or conflicts. Rather, shalom-peace is the kind of peace that results from knowing that when conflicts emerge, there will be a constructive way of dealing with the conflicts. It is important here to recognize that I am not suggesting "giving in" on the issues of concern. What I am suggesting is that we need to remember that the issues are on the other continuum. That means that it is possible to remain high on the commitment to be constructive while also being highly committed to the issues.

There are no guarantees that things will come out the way I want or in my favor in the short view, but maintaining an unconditional commitment to being constructive is, as I understand it, what it means to know God. In the words of I John 4, "God is love (agape—unconditional love). Those who love (agape—are unconditionally committed to being constructive) know God. Those who do not love (non-agape—are not committed to being constructive) do not know God."

–Ron Claassen
© 1995. Used by permission.

Part 2

The Relational Dimension

To actively listen we must create space in the cluttered corridors of our minds for communication to happen. When our cups are full—minds overflowing with our own affairs—we have no room for the concerns of another. The meaning of the words cannot enter; we cannot listen. When we choose actively to listen, to make space for another, we exercise a power that can have startling, life-giving effects.

–Kori Leaman-Miller

Understanding Conflict: Experience, Structure and Dynamics

Conflict is the gadfly of thought.
It stirs us to observation and memory.
It instigates us to invention.
It shocks us out of sheep-like passivity,
and sets us noting and contriving.
Conflict is a sine qua non
of reflection and ingenuity.

–John Dewey, 1930

Conflict Images and Metaphors

Most discussions of conflict start by defining what "conflict" is. We prefer to start by asking what conflict is like. Think for a minute. How would you complete these sentences:

> *Conflict is like. . . ?*
> *My family does conflict like a. . . ?*
> *I do conflict like a. . . ?*

What images come to your mind? What symbols or metaphors? Consider, for example, the broad differences that exist between Western and Eastern conceptions. In the Western world, "conflict" is rooted in the Latin word *confligere*. Literally this means "to strike together." It leaves us with an image of flint and stone, sparks, heat and fire. "Heat" is one of the most common metaphors for conflict. How many times have you heard or used one of these phrases: a "heated" discussion; "boiling" mad; an issue too "hot" to handle; or problems "simmering" below the surface? The Chinese, on the other hand, form the symbol for "crisis," which we associate with conflict, by combining two terms: danger and opportunity. Such a view does not perceive conflict in terms of collision, force and heat, but rather as a challenge.

When people talk about their conflicts they often describe them metaphorically. Metaphors are a tremendous source for perceiving how people understand and experience a particular event or relationship. For some time we have been "collecting" conflict metaphors, and using them both as analytical and intervention tools. For example, in one seminar a woman described her family conflicts as an earthquake:

> *There are not many warning signals, the pressure building up from the bottom is not visible. It just hits. The ground shakes and splits. The noise of crumbling emotions is great. And then, a deep silence settles over the destruction. Now nobody can trust the ground, and the clean-up appears impossible.*

The power of metaphors is their innate ability to tap into our experience and feelings about a situation. They evoke emotions, images and insights that we often are unable to provide in literal descriptions or analysis. In the above metaphor we can feel the uncertainty, vulnerability and hurt this person has experienced in her family conflicts. "In a nutshell" we have a view of the situation, a description of problems that are otherwise hard to name, and the beginnings of what interventions may be useful. These descriptions that naturally emerge in people's efforts to talk about their problems provide a resource for the aware conflict manager.

The Structure of Conflict

Conflict often appears overwhelming, confused and unmanageable to those involved and to potential intervenors. We have found that a simple, yet useful approach is to view conflict as composed of three elements: people, process and problems. Any of these, or combinations of them, can be the cause of conflict, and will always be present in the development and outcome of a dispute. Let's consider each of these in more detail.

People refers to the relational and psychological elements of the conflict. Included here are peoples' feelings, emotions, self-esteem, and individual perceptions and conceptualization of the problems and others. In terms of outcome, this aspect of conflict represents the possibility of reaching psychological closure and interpersonal reconciliation. As intervenors we need to be aware and analyze how the "people" part of the conflict affects their interaction. Our efforts are aimed at:

- understanding and eliciting the expression of emotions and feelings;
- recognizing human need to explain, justify, and vent those feelings;
- taking time to listen and show respect for the basic dignity of people as human beings;
- supporting, not threatening, their self-esteem;
- probing deeper into their perception and conceptualization of the situation and of others;
- identifying how others' behavior and the situation in general has affected them and their lives.

Process refers primarily to the *way* decisions get made and how people feel about it. We often overlook the process of decision-making as a key cause of conflict, but it is here that resentment, feelings of being treated unfairly, and a sense of powerlessness are rooted. People who feel excluded or sense they cannot influence decisions affecting their lives will rarely cooperate with and support those decisions. They may not overtly reject the decision, but their behavior will disrupt the relationship in subtle and covert ways. The goal of conflict management is to empower people to function as equals, structure a process of decision-making that involves those affected by the decisions and that feels fair to them. Our efforts are aimed at:

- uncovering the patterns of communication as it relates to decision-making;
- discovering how people feel about how decisions have been made;
- understanding the power balance or imbalance in the relationship;
- developing a process that feels fair and includes the people affected by the decisions.

Problems refers to the specific issues and differences people have between them. These usually involve things like different values, opposing views about how to make a decision, incompatible needs or interests, and concrete differences regarding use, distribution or access to scarce resources (land, money, time). These are often referred to as the "real" root causes of conflict and people tend to "lock into" a position over these issues, creating an impasse. Ideally creative conflict management helps identify the needs and interests underlying peoples' perspectives, rather than arguing over "positional" solutions. Our efforts are aimed at:

- clarifying areas of concern and specific issues separating people;
- uncovering the basic needs and interests underlying those issues;
- establishing mutually acceptable criteria/process for decision-making;
- identifying principles and values held in common.

The Dynamics of Conflict

Researchers suggest that conflict, at almost all levels, also has certain predictable dynamics. Consider how several of these are related to our structure of people, process and problems.

1. Often what starts out as a disagreement is transformed into personal antagonism. Differences over specific problems get translated into charges against the other person and inferences about their character, intentions and motives. Instead of focusing on the problem they share, the people view the other person as the problem.

   - People share and are responsible for the problem.

   A

   Problem

   B

• The other person is viewed as the problem.

B ⟵ ⟵ ⟶ ⟶ A

2. In most conflicts there is a pattern of change in issues as the conflict intensifies. Initially, a conflict emerges around a single issue; however, over time new and different problems "crop up." Peoples' "talk" about the issues is increasingly less specific and more general. The pattern is one of issue expansion and proliferation, leaving a sense of confusion and unmanageability.

3. Communication is increasingly less direct and accurate. People have less contact and dialogue with their opponent, and more with those who agree with them. Increased intensity and emotional involvement corresponds with decreased ability to listen and communicate. Consider the figure below.

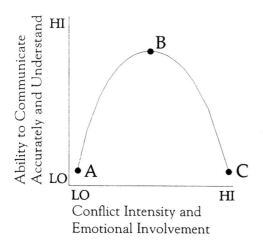

Conflict Intensity and
Emotional Involvement

Here conflict intensity and communication accuracy are compared. Point A on the graph suggests that little interaction and conflict result in little communication or mutual understanding. In other words, increased conflict serves to "get us thinking," and helps us understand what the other person believes. Point B represents the ideal. Here we have the maximum level of conflict intensity and emotional involvement that can be handled productively. Our communication and understanding is at its highest. However, increased intensity from here produces less and less understanding. Point C symbolizes high intensity and emotional involvement and a complete inability to listen, communicate or understand.

4. The dynamics of an "eye for an eye" set in. This is what some scientists call "reciprocal causation." People respond, not to the original issue or concern, but rather to the most recent response received from the other side. Escalation, both of hostility and personal antagonism, leads to a spiral of ever increasing intensity, mistrust and miscommunication.

5. In groups like congregations and neighborhoods conflict often brings a change of social organization. As problems intensify, polarization sets in and people feel obligated to move into "one camp or the other." It is difficult to stay on, or even find, neutral ground. Moderate stabilizing people have less influence, while more extremist influences emerge and become key players.

In sum, these dynamics together produce outcomes that are destructive to the relationship and rarely resolve the key issues in a satisfactory manner. Left unmanaged and unrestrained the most harmful components of conflict drive out those that hold potential for regulating the interaction: extremism replaces moderation; antagonism replaces disagreement; assumptions and attributing motives replaces dialogue and listening; original concerns are lost in the preoccupation of responding to the latest insult; and people are seen as the problem.

–John Paul Lederach
© MCS 1992, adapted from *Conciliation Quarterly*, Vol. 6 No. 3

Social Transformation of Conflict

7. Polarization

    Change in Social Organization

6. Antagonism → Hostility

5. Eye for an eye

    Reaction and Escalation

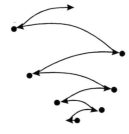

4. Triangle

    Talk *about* not with

3. Issue proliferation

    From specific to general

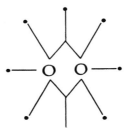

2. Shift from disagreement to
    personal antagonism

    Person seen as problem

1. Problem-solving

    Disagree, but share problem

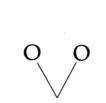

Destructive

MORE VIOLENCE

LESS TRUST

LESS ACCURATE COMMUNICATIONS

LESS DIRECT CONTACT

Constructive

–John Paul Lederach
© MCS 1989

Centered Communication — Listening

I want to write about the great and powerful thing that listening is. . . . Listening is a magnetic and strange thing, a creative force. . . . When we are listened to, it creates us, makes us unfold and expand. Ideas actually begin to grow within us and come to life. . . . There is this little creative fountain in us all. It is the spirit, or the intelligence, or the imagination - whatever you want to call it. . . . It is when people really listen to us, with quiet fascinated attention, that the little fountain begins to work. . . to accelerate in the most surprising way.
–Brenda Ueland, Strength to Your Sword Arm: Selected Writings

We all know about prophetic speaking, but prophetic listening means listening to others in such a way that we draw out of them the seeds of their own highest understanding, of their own obedience, of their own vision, that they themselves may not have known were there. Listening can draw forth out of people things that speaking to them cannot.
–Elise Boulding, New Call to Peacemaking Conference, Dartmouth College, 1980

What Is It?

Centered listening means tuning my energy into the heart of the other, into the center of their being. It seeks to both hear the words and hear beyond them in order to understand deeply the essence of their message. It means setting aside, for the moment, my agenda, my opinions, my feelings and focusing, with all my capability, on the other and what is important to them.

Centered listening emerges from, and communicates, a profound respect for the other. It says,"You are a person of great worth and, whether or not I agree with you, I want to hear what's in your heart." Centered listening is not an easy task, especially in conflict and especially with those closest to me. It is a spiritual act, akin to prayer, and it demands commitment, discipline and vulnerability. It reaches out open hands to receive rather than fists to hurt or folded arms to protect.

Centered listening is rare because few people really know how. Few of us know how to momentarily shelve our own agenda. Few of us can refrain from advising, judging, interrogating or interrupting with our own stories and opinions. An enterprising entrepreneur in Kansas is charging $80 an hour just to listen. No advice, no therapy, just listening. And he's booked full. Ueland says, "Who are the people to whom you go for advice? Not to the hard, practical ones who can tell you exactly what to do, but to the listeners; that is, the kindest, least censorious, least bossy people that you know. It is because by pouring out your problem to them, you then know what to do about it yourself."

Why It's Transformative

Centered listening is transformative precisely because it enables people to solve their own problems. It invites them, without judgment, condescension or hint of disdain, to bring out their woundedness, their doubts and their fears. Bringing these shadows into the light lessens their binding power and enables people to deal with the shadows directly and openly.

Centered listening gets people in touch with the best of who they are. If I think someone is smart and I listen to them expecting them to be smart, they *will be*. And if that keeps happening, they'll believe it more and more and keep getting smarter. Or funnier. Or kinder. My listening helps create them.

Centered listening is especially transformative in the midst of escalated conflict. It is a concrete and powerful manifestation of a change in the conflict's direction, a loosening of clenched fists, new life breaking in. In my opinion, this kind of listening in a conflict is often 75% of its transformation.

Ueland says, "And so try listening. Listen to your wife, your husband, your father, your mother, your children, your friends; to those who love you and those who don't, to those who bore you, to your enemies. It will work a small miracle. And perhaps a great one."

–Carolyn Schrock-Shenk
© MCS 1995

Does Listening Really Work?

Active listening really works! Try it outside of conflict interventions. Try it with coworkers, family members, friends. It will slow down the rate of conversations and actually improve your understanding. It necessarily means that you are not spending time mentally composing your response while "listening" to the other person. It means you are truly attending to what is being said verbally and nonverbally. This skill is used not only in conflict resolution. It is used by counselors, health care practitioners, business people and many others. Here are some of the things people first using active listening say.

"It feels artificial."

New skills often feel artificial until they can be fully integrated into our repertoire. You may become so concerned with practicing active listening correctly (the mechanics) that you lose sight of your desire to communicate with warmth and immediacy. Sometimes people also worry that reflecting feelings and content with which they disagree will be taken as agreement. It is important to frame comments clearly, and to be clear yourself that active listening means an understanding of feeling and substance, but not necessarily agreement with what is being said.

"It is irritating."

Use of active listening can put people off. My young son is likely to respond with comments like "Don't psychologize me, Mom." At the same time, if done well, active listening is very affirming and becomes part of the normal cadence of conversation. Practice definitely helps in moving toward a sense of genuineness in its use. If you find that it is not working in a particular situation, and even escalating the conflict, try another approach.

"It can escalate the conflict."

If you are personally involved in the conflict, then using active listening can do just that. While I have several personal experiences that confirm its usefulness in conflicts where anger is targeted at me, I know to use it with caution. Depending on the history between you and the other, the intensity of the conflict and the point in the anger cycle where you and other party are at the moment, it may be most adaptive to do something other than "try to find out more."

"I am not a good guesser. I do not know what the feelings are behind the substance. I do not want to alienate the person by making wrong assumptions or guesses. Especially not repeatedly."

This is a good point. Active listening should not turn into a game of cat and mouse (I wonder if you are feeling sad? No, then maybe disappointed? No, then. . .) If you are stuck, ask an open question: "You spoke of missing the boat and the inconvenience it caused; I am wondering how that felt?"

"Cross-cultural communication is complex; active listening may be harder in such settings. I am also concerned that my use of active listening may be misinterpreted in cross-cultural situations."

Cross-cultural situations indeed are more difficult. It becomes even more important to be sure that accurate communication is taking place. This is a reason to use active listening. At the same time, it would be inappropriate or disrespectful to use active listening in a situation where the speaker may take offense. In some cultural contexts, it is disrespectful to engage in a back and forth clarifying, questioning pattern of conversation. Rather, it is important to let all parties speak without any interruption or response. Or, it may be appropriate to defer to an elder speaker without responding with questions or requests for clarification. You will have to make decisions about the use of active listening based on your knowledge of the cultural contexts of the parties, cues you receive from the parties directly, observations you make of parties' nonverbal communication and, where appropriate, from cultural informants external to the process.

–Michelle LeBaron

© UVic Institute for Dispute Resolution 1994, from *Conflict Analysis & Resolution as Education: Culturally Sensitive Processes for Conflict Resolution*. Used by permission.

Centered Communication — Speaking

Definition: Centered speaking comes from the heart, the center of ourselves. By providing information about what is happening at the center of ourselves we invite others to also share from their "center." Christianity has taught for centuries that to know God, we must open our hearts to God. Talking about God does not bring us into meaningful relationship. Only opening ourselves and allowing God to know what is in our hearts enables us to establish that relationship. "Centered speaking" applies this Christian concept to human relations as well. If we wish to "love one another," we must approach others and open the center of ourselves to them.

How to recognize uncentered speaking: *Un*centered speaking is easily recognized because the word "you" appears continually. My attention blurs away from my personal center and fastens on you in negative ways, usually by *blaming, mind-reading* (claiming to know your intentions), or *demanding*. This is also called "you messages." Examples of uncentered speaking:

- "When are you going to start showing a little respect for me? You think you're the only one with a busy schedule!" (demanding, blaming, mind-reading, conveys little information about me)
- "You're just trying to make things difficult for the rest of us!" (blaming, mind-reading)

How to make speaking centered: The focus of centered speaking is on giving information about myself: my emotions, my needs, the impact of a situation on me, my preferences. This is also called "I-messages." Examples of centered speaking:

- "I feel all torn up inside about the things you said last night." (information about my feelings)
- "It's very frustrating for me when you show up half an hour late." (information about my feelings) "It puts me behind schedule for the whole evening." (information about impact on me)
- A useful way to formulate centered speaking is to say: "I feel. . . when you. . . because. . . ." or "The effect of this situation on me is. . . ."

How can I talk only about myself if the situation involves another person? Of course there will be reference to the other person. But centered speaking returns quickly to providing information about self: describing my emotions and vulnerabilities, the impact of others' actions on me, my regrets and preferences for the situation.

Talking about myself is difficult! Centered speaking *is* hard, especially with people closest to us. It requires self-awareness (what exactly do I feel?), vulnerability (am I willing to reveal what is in my heart?), careful thought and self-discipline. Only those motivated by mature love are willing to invest the effort in this emotional and spiritual discipline that gets easier with practice. The rewards are substantial: greater understanding with others, greater personal clarity before God.

Other characteristics of centered speaking:

- Speaks only for self, does not pretend to speak for others.
- Most powerful when rooted in here-and-now, the feelings I have at this moment as I am talking.
- Talks about events at specific times and places, not "general problems."
- Takes responsibility for self first of all. My first job is to stay centered and change me, not to change you. Even if another person is not centered, I can grow from a painful conflict if I can stay centered.
- Does not seek to excuse own behavior by pointing to the behavior of others; doesn't wait for others to act first in reconciliation. Centered communication keeps the focus on my responsibility.
- Helps others get centered by listening deeply.

–Ron Kraybill
© MCS 1988

Why Don't I Speak? Why Do I Speak?

Why Don't I Speak More Often and More Forcefully?

- **I don't know how I feel.** People sometimes remain silent, especially in a conflict, because they can't identify the emotions that are frothing inside of them. Rather than risk saying something they'll regret or don't mean, they say little or nothing. This silence can be interpreted as apathy, anger or strategic disengagement by other parties. Such perceptions can lead to misunderstandings and further conflict.

- **I want you to know what I'm thinking.** Sometimes people remain silent in a conflict, especially with a significant other, because they think the other should be able to guess what they're thinking and feeling. Many of us have been hoodwinked by the myth of magic intimacy—if you really love me, you should know what I'm feeling without my having to *say* it. Such mind reading is not only impossible but also undesirable. If I want you to know what is going on inside of me, I must tell you. It is by the very act of telling—and your listening—that this elusive and holy thing called intimacy is brought into being.

- **I have not been allowed to speak in the past.** A history of not being heard, whether as a person or member of a group, is hardly the best encouragement to try speaking now. Sometimes people don't speak because layers of oppression and a history of violence prevent speech. Such power imbalances not only disable people from speaking their minds and hearts; they cheat the whole group out of those persons' ideas and perspectives. It's important to attend to reasons one woman in a roomful of men isn't speaking or the lone African American among whites remains silent.

Why Do I Speak Too Often and Too Forcefully?

- **I don't know how I feel.** If I am unaware of my emotions and unable to name them, I may become forceful and even oppressive instead of remaining silent. Distance from my emotional center may make me insensitive to others' emotions as well. This in turn may make me railroad my ideas past others without listening to theirs. Insecurity is commonly and often rightly considered a reason to remain silent—but it can also lead to forceful expressions of opinions and domineering conversational techniques. Often when someone is oppressive or even lashing out, that aggression is emerging, consciously or unconsciously, from deeper pain, woundedness or self-doubt.

- **I want you to know what I am thinking.** Much of the speech in the media and public arena these days is contentious and divisive. Growing up in this society, children learn that the goal in any argument is to win. By extension, the goal in any conversation is to convince. If I speak too often and too forcefully, chances are that I am operating in this paradigm that honors the debater and belittles (or at least ignores) the collaborator. In our increasingly litigious culture, we are taught to present evidence, to prove something happened or didn't happen, and to "make a case." In other words, we learn to document, defend and declare. All of this makes it easier for many of us to let others know what we are thinking than to listen to what they have to say.

- **I have always been allowed to speak.** If I am a member of a group with a history of dominance or that currently wields much power, I may be accustomed to speaking freely and to having the upper hand in conversations. I may come across as overbearing without knowing it. Recognizing my own power and learning to give others time and space to speak rather than filling every second with my own words is crucial.

–Valerie Weaver-Zercher

Part 3

The Structural Dimension

All polishing is done by friction.   –Mary Parker Follet

Power and Conflict

I. Definitions of Power

The ability to get things done or to influence outcomes. The ability to affect and be affected by the feelings, attitudes, beliefs, opinions and behavior of others.
                                          –Don Freeman, Lancaster Theological Seminary

The ability to take one's place in whatever discourse is essential to action and the right to have one's part matter.
                                          –Carolyn Heilbrun, *Writing a Woman's Life*

II. Key Principles/Assumptions About Power

1. No one is completely powerless; to be alive is to embody and exercise power.

2. Power exists between people. It does not lie in the individual, but in the social relationship.

3. Power is not a finite resource nor is it a distributable commodity; it is relational, fluid and difficult to measure.

4. Power itself is neither positive nor negative but it can be used constructively or destructively.

5. The denial of one's power is a small step away from the abuse of it. It is critical to be aware of, and acknowledge, one's power.

6. Significant power inequities become occasions for the abuse of power. Over time, these inequities are destructive to people and relationships.

7. Individuals internalize societal patterns of domination and oppression and are shaped by their membership in a particular identity group. But individuals are not completely defined by this identity since each also has the power to act in his/her own interests.

8. Constructive conflict transformation will work from or towards a relative balance of power.

9. God's desired order is a domination-free order.
                                  with thanks to John Paul Lederach; Juliana Birkhoff; and Hocker and Wilmot, *Interpersonal Conflict*

III. Kinds of Power

* **Exploitative power**—*power upon*; literal use of physical force or threat to use such force with apparent intent to do so if necessary.

* **Manipulative power**—*power over*; use of promises or threats involving the interests, desires, needs or other wants of the other person(s) or group, but short of the use of force as such; often indirect or implied.

* **Competitive power**—*power against*: contesting to win against another of relatively equal power by superior application of one's own power or deflection or diminution of the other's power.

* **Nutritive or nutrient power**—*power for*: use of one's own power for the empowerment of another or development of the other's power.

* **Collaborative or coalescent or coalitional power**—*power with*: pooling power together to increase the likelihood of mutually desired ends.
                                  drawn from Rollo May, *Power and Innocence*, and Don Freeman, Lancaster Theological Seminary

IV. Sources of Power

1. **Formal authority.** The power that derives from a formal position within a structure that confers certain decision-making prerogatives. This is the power of a judge, an elected official, a CEO, a parent or a school principal.

2. **Expert/information power.** The power that is derived from having expertise in a particular area or information about a particular matter.

3. **Associational power** (or referent power). The power that is derived from association with other people with power.

4. **Resource power.** The control over valued resources (money, materials, labor, or other goods or services). The negative version of this is the ability to deny needed resources or to force others to expend them.

5. **Procedural power.** The control over the procedures by which decisions are made, separate from the control over those decisions themselves (for instance, the power of a judge in a jury trial).

6. **Sanction power.** The ability (or perceived ability) to inflict harm or to interfere with a party's ability to realize his or her interests.

7. **Nuisance power.** The ability to cause discomfort to a party, falling short of the ability to apply direct sanctions.

8. **Habitual power.** The power of the status quo that rests on the premise that it is normally easier to maintain a particular arrangement or course of action than to change it.

9. **Moral power.** The power that comes from an appeal to widely held values. Related to this is the power that results from the conviction that one is right.

10. **Personal power.** The power that derives from a variety of personal attributes that magnify other sources of power, including self-assurance, the ability to articulate one's thoughts and understand one's situation, one's determination and endurance, and so forth.

from Bernard Mayer, "The Dynamics of Power in Mediation and Negotiation," in C.W. Moore, editor, *Practical Strategies for the Phases of Mediation, Mediation Quarterly*, vol. 16. (Jossey-Bass Inc., 1987).

V. Power and Conflict Transformation

Power is integral to all conflict. Conflict transformation practitioners must become aware of their own power, their assumptions about power and the values and goals they bring to conflict situations. They must also explicitly assess how power is operating in the conflictive relationships, evaluate their own role, and seek the appropriate process in conflicts of significant power imbalance.

In each conflict situation, it is important to ask questions such as: What are the sources of power for those in conflict? Is there a significant power imbalance? Is power being misused or abused? How can the less powerful become more empowered? What intervention is most appropriate?

The criteria for evaluating any conflict transformation process should be whether it moves the situation toward more justice and the people involved toward right and equal relationships.

–Carolyn Schrock-Shenk
© MCS 2000

Perspectives for Assessing and Working With Power

Mutual Dependence

Emerson has suggested that power is directly linked to dependence in any relationship. He provides the following equation:

$$P_{ab} = D_{ba}$$ The power (P) of A over B equals the dependence (D) of B on A.

This is best understood in terms of goals and needs. If I need you to reach my goals, then you have power over me for that situation. This is further refined by noting the *importance* of the goal and whether there are *alternative avenues* for reaching it. This perspective provides several direct questions for balancing power.
- Who is dependent on whom for meeting what goals?
- Can the person who feels in low power change their goals, or make them less important?
- Can the lower power person discover alternative ways of reaching the goals that do not depend on the other?
- In what subtle and implicit ways does the "high" power person depend on the low power person? What are ways of raising awareness about that dependence?

Consider several examples of how this works. Oddly, the strategy of "caring less" is a form of balancing power. For example a teenager abuses his curfew privileges and the parent decides to punish by removing his access to the car (resource control). The teenager responds, "Big deal. I'll just go with Joey." ("Who cares" translates into "I am changing my goals and am not dependent on the car or you to meet them" = increased sense of power, further enhanced by the parent's sense of anger at not being taken seriously and feeling powerless to alter the teen's behavior.)

Or consider how the dynamics of labor/management conflicts illustrate these power dynamics and the fluid nature of seeking a balance. Labor feels they deserve a raise. Management refuses. At first assessment labor is dependent on management for the raise, thus management has power over labor and refuses to negotiate. Labor then opts to demonstrate how management is dependent on them. They go on strike, slowing production and work. Management responds by hiring scabs as a way to reach the goal of continuing production and thereby demonstrate their independence of labor. Labor then begins a broader appeal calling for a boycott of the product by the general public, thus highlighting a different way that management is dependent, this time on the buyer who is sympathizing with laid-off workers. The battle for power and dependence now turns to the media: whoever controls the media and the way the problem is framed and understood by the public may determine in whose favor the power balance will shift.

Currencies

Hocker and Wilmot (*Interpersonal Conflict*) talk about currencies as a way to understand power. Power, they suggest, depends on controlling currencies that other people need and value, and can be used for, against or with others. They list these in several general categories.
- *Expertise*: Knowledge, skill or talent in a specific subject or matter provides expertise others need and gives you power.
- *Resource control*: Controlling the rewards or punishments, often accompanying your position in an organization or system, provides power. Often these are related to economic resources, although a key to many conflicts is who controls information.
- *Interpersonal linkages*: Here power emerges through coalition formation, the bringing together of people who share a common goal. Coalitions, shifting alliances, polarization are all related to the ebb and flow of relational power and efforts to balance or maintain an imbalance of power.
- *Intimacy*: This relates to the ability of forming intimate bonds with others through love, sex, caring, nurturing, inclusion. Often conflict is expressed through the offering or removal of intimacy currencies. The "silent treatment" for example is a common form of intimacy currency withdrawal.

We also can add several ways that power is used and created in many social settings.

- *Authority*: Here power is located in the position, rank or status which one person occupies and that others view as legitimate. Where viewed as illegitimate, authority still carries the threat and use of sanctions that go with the position.
- *Presence*: Self-confidence, charisma, clear values and articulation, assuredness all translate into power in social interaction.

Mediator power, for example, is based on *expertise* about the process, *authority* (legitimacy to exercise process control), and *presence* by connecting with disputing parties, maintaining a non-anxious demeanor and pursuing just and fair solutions.

Tips for Balancing

When power imbalances become apparent and need addressing mediators can look to short and long term solutions. Short term assumes we are already "at the table," long term means there is an unwillingness for the higher power party to even enter into mediation or negotiations.

Short Term
- Provide special education or training to prepare lower power party to put forth their perspective and interests.
- Use support person or advocate to be with the lower power party in the process.
- Use resource expanders outside the mediation, like counselors, accountants, lawyers.
- Use caucus to check that people understand the implications of certain solutions that appear to favor higher power person.
- Explore the unidentified currencies and resources lower power party has and the links of mutual dependence.
- Enforce ground rules.
- Move conversation to a new venue; find new storytelling methods.
- Bring more stakeholders to the table.
- Do joint fact-finding.

Long Term
- Educate and raise public awareness concerning issue and legitimacy of concerns
- Develop strategies to demonstrate mutual dependence, e.g., non-cooperation, boycotts, strikes
- Develop strategies to demonstrate illegitimacy of abuse of power, e.g., civil disobedience
- Use mediation to articulate the legitimacy of low power position and interests

As a bottom line, mediators must recognize that mediation is not always the most appropriate conflict resolution strategy. In situations of power imbalance, injustice and abuse, other strategies should be pursued, particularly when the situation has long-range ramifications for many people who are not likely to be represented in a face-to-face mediation.

One key is to develop the right forum for appropriately handling the conflict. For example, in a case of racial discrimination at work, the individuals involved can meet face-to-face and work on that particular situation. That forum, however, does not address the broader issue of institutional or systemic discrimination which must be addressed in another forum.

–John Paul Lederach
© MCS 1989, 2000

Three Domains of Power

In practice, I believe power is a dynamic between and among people, a multilayered and ever-shifting set of relationships. We therefore need tools to describe and understand patterns of behaviors, overt and implicit, that are taking place in any given moment. When I analyze power as I practice conflict resolution, I think of it as operating dynamically in three domains. Like all theoretical constructs, this one is less than exhaustive. But I offer it as a start to evolving working tools for understanding how power works in conflict resolution and how we as interveners need relate to it. In each of these arenas, power is exercised differently, with particular consequences for collaborative work and particular challenges to the practitioner. To illustrate this way of thinking about power, I present snips of a conversation with Eleanor Smith of Atlanta, who founded Concrete Change, a group seeking to improve accessibility of new houses for people with disabilities. Eleanor Smith is herself a wheelchair user and eloquently describes a little-recognized reality she often encounters:

> I don't think it's obvious to everyone that the way homes are built severely excludes a pretty big portion of people. [Take] one little architectural feature, . . . the bathroom door. Typically a new home . . . will have a narrow bathroom door that the wheelchair won't go through. . . . The fallout on people's lives is tremendous, just from that one detail. . . . People stop and think, "If I knew I couldn't go to the bathroom if I went to dinner, would I go?" . . . And then if we do go, we really take a very major risk. We learn to really be ashamed of what we need. . . . It's very shame-inducing; it's very health-threatening to try to develop a bladder that will hold it that long. . . . Those few inches [on a bathroom door] really are humongously important in terms of being able to be at anyone's house, including your own.

Transactional: Everyday behaviors that occur between and among us—choice of words, body posture, eye contact, and so on—communicate and negotiate power.

> . . . We went to [a charity housing organization, and talked] to the chairman of the board. He came over to the house, and there were eight of us talking with him. He leaned back, his arms folded over his chest, taking a very rational, seemingly pseudo-rational approach: "Who else is doing this in the country?" "Well, nobody we know of right now." "Well, we don't want to slow down the learning curve."

The body-posture and style of speaking of the chairman conveyed an exercise of power. His gestures—leaning back, crossing his arms—expressed confidence in his position, a certain unwillingness to budge, a sense of command over the situation in which he found himself. His mode of speaking—asking in a reasonable tone of voice for a precedent, speaking in terms of learning curves—communicated a disinclination to solve the problem at hand.

Who speaks first, how long a person speaks, tone and volume of voice, vocabulary, command of language, style of reasoning: these are only a few of the many ways we exercise power. Some of these behaviors can intimidate (yelling, for instance), while others negotiate power by casting doubt on another person's credibility. Becoming attuned to transactional power moves reveals their wide array.

Contractual: Sets of agreements, tacit or explicit, create environments in which power is distributed in particular ways.

> He meant they didn't want to even think about doing one thing different because then they couldn't build houses quite as fast. As women, we really felt disempowered, too, I might say. He was one man and we were eight women, talking about house construction.

The chairman took charge of the shape of the dialogue, and the committee members tacitly consented. Agreements often take the form of unchallenged assumptions. The chairman assumed that his highest value, to build houses quickly, was universally accepted; that it was technically inevitable that building accessible houses would slow that process down; and that his goal and the committee's were therefore fundamentally in conflict. The women were thus presented with the task of articulating and countering his assumptions. Gender entered into the process. The chairman's invocation of technical expertise suggested that he, a man, would of course know more about such matters. The women, themselves schooled in a social world of gender inequality, quietly succumbed to a sense of inferiority—although only temporarily.

Structural: Both face-to-face transactions and group situations exist in the context of greater social structures, which define an underlying set of power relations.

> Then one very stubborn woman in our group wrote to every board member, and somehow that changed it. There were some board members that wanted to try it. So then [the organization] began doing it, finding out that it hadn't been that hard.

> We wanted to then parlay that into state legislation. Four years ago we started trying to get a state law through that every new house would have basic access. The Home Builders' Association, which is one of the strongest national lobbies, has so much clout that they have full-time lobbyists in every state. . . . They were putting out outlandish cost figures of what it would cost to have a wider bathroom door in new construction. . . . They could afford to fax everywhere in the state, and they could afford to pay their full-time lobbyist. And, they are one of the biggest donors, even on a state level, to the legislative campaigns.

The construction industry is better funded than are disability-issues activists. That is a structural fact of life in modern-day America which is the context for any dialogue or negotiation between the two groups. Matters of money, political access, educational and technological resources, group status based on culture, age, gender, physical ability, ethnicity, and so on, influence every interpersonal transaction, more or less decisively depending on its content and context, and on the degree of inequality of the participants. Very often, structural components of power dynamics seem indirect and are therefore not visible to those living them.

These three domains in which power operates are not distinct from each other. Each shades into the others and helps to form it. Cultures of gender, for instance, deeply inform Eleanor Smith's experience of intimidation on a transactional level, as she experienced the chairman from the charity housing organization leaning back in her living room and crossing his arms over his chest. Gender is a construct that is negotiated through ongoing interpersonal transactions (in personal relationships between men and women) and imbued with power because of characteristics of social structure: the greater earning power of men, for instance, which in turn derives from the higher value placed on traditionally male occupations—CEOs as compared with secretaries, for example. The tacit agreements that allowed the chairman to define the question—as a technical matter of what would be needed to make the changes the activists sought and how that would affect the "learning curve"—were credible because he held structural power as the representative of an organization with enough resources to build houses. The power accruing to the manner in which he considered that question—rational, weighing one set of possibilities against another—grew from a deeply imbedded set of structural characteristics of the gendered economic and social system in America.

–Beth Roy
© MCS 2000

Conceptions of Peace

For some people "peace" has been understood as the absence of violence. By this, people normally mean the absence of overt physical harm to persons and property which emanates from wars, riots, murders, vandalism, etc.

This conception of peace holds that the maintenance of "law and order," the pursuit of stability and a relatively safe social and political order are primary objectives of peace. In this understanding of peace, the presence of a relatively small amount of visible (overt) violence in society provides an indicator of successful peace and peacemaking. Police forces, courts, and prison systems are usually the instruments used to bring about and enforce this type of peace in the domestic arena. Internationally, the equivalent concepts include balance of power, nuclear deterrence, and hierarchical power structures in which the bigger and more powerful states become the arbiters or policemen of global affairs. This approach to peace has been characterized as negative peace since its focus is on the absence of violent conflict and war.

One major shortcoming of this conception of peace is that in its preoccupation with controlling overt violence[1] it may condone or perpetrate another kind of more covert violence which has come to be called structural violence. Structural violence has been defined as social and personal violence arising from unjust, repressive, and oppressive national or international political and social structures. According to this view, a system that generates repression, abject poverty, malnutrition, and starvation for some members of a society while other members enjoy opulence and unbridled power inflicts covert violence with the ability to destroy life as much as overt violence, except that it does it in more subtle ways. In other words, it is not only the gun that kills. Lack of access to basic means of life and dignity does the same thing.[2]

For others, peace is viewed as a condition of tranquility where there is no disagreement or dispute, where conflicts are banished, and people, individually and collectively, live in calm and serenity. A major shortcoming of this conception of peace is its failure to recognize conflict as a fact of life. Instead of acknowledging its existence and learning to use appropriate mechanisms to deal with it, this notion of peace can lead people into the misguided percep-

tion that if you avoid conflict, it will go away.

For still others, peace goes beyond a preoccupation with the absence of conflict or violence. It is seen as the transformation of conflictual and destructive interactions into more cooperative and constructive relationships. This understanding equates peace with "conflict transformation and resolution." In this view, peace is not simply a state of general tranquility or an imposed order that suppresses discord, but is rather a network of relationships full of energy and differences. However, in this conception of peace, structures are available through which personal and social differences can be identified and worked out in ways satisfactory to all involved parties as well as to the society at large. Sometimes in this process, the status quo may be disturbed or long-standing structures may be shaken; but this definition maintains that peace is achieved only when the root causes of the differences or conflictual relationships are explored and resolved.

From this perspective, peace and peacemaking are not just techniques deployed to patch up differences when conflicts erupt, but are larger concepts having application even in situations that are not visibly conflictual. Peace is a philosophy, and in fact a paradigm, with its own values and precepts, which provides a framework to discern, understand, analyze, and regulate all human relationships in order to create an integrated, holistic, and humane social order. What, then, are the values and principles underlying this definition of peace?

Values and Principles

The following is a brief summation of some of the most important values and principles:

1. **One cannot resolve conflicts and thus make peace unless the root causes of the conflicts are identified and dealt with.** The implication of this is that for conflicts to be resolved, one must look beyond surface issues and address the substantive and emotional issues as well as the parties' needs and interests that are at the root of the conflicts. In other words, lasting peace between conflicting parties is possible only when deeper needs are accommodated and satisfied.

2. **It is not possible to resolve conflicts and attain peace unless attention is given to the justice and fairness of the process as well as the outcome of the settlement.** In other words, peace without justice is a rather meaningless concept, although this is not to suggest that the pursuit of justice and the pursuit of peace are one and the same thing.

In this context, the search for justice requires concern for the impact which the settlement of the dispute might have on parties not represented in the peacemaking process. In other words, this definition of peace disavows dispute settlement which favors the interests of the parties in conflict at the expense of the interests and well-being of non-represented parties and society in general.

3. **People's deeper needs are not totally incompatible.** Parties in conflict can discover commonality of interests and objectives which can lead to mutually acceptable solutions to their problems. Often the help of third parties, whose perceptions have not been distorted by the conflict, may be necessary in such explorations. If parties operate on the level of human needs, it is possible to arrive at creative solutions satisfactory to all the contestants.

4. **Conflict resolution and therefore peacemaking involves a restructuring of relationships,** a transition from an order based on coercion to one based on voluntarism; from a relationship characterized by hierarchy to one marked by equality, participation, respect, mutual enrichment, and growth.[3]

Holistic Peacemaking

Peacemaking that embodies these values and is guided by these principles is about individual and social transformation. It is about change from immature to mature relationships, from dependence or independence to interdependence, from destructive competition to energizing cooperation, from hierarchy and coercion to equality and voluntarism, from pursuit of selfish interest to mutuality, and from an economic model that focuses simply on material prosperity to a model that integrates material development with social cohesion, psychological and spiritual growth. In other words, this peacemaking paradigm is not simply about controlling or solving conflict; it is about fostering harmony by promoting a change process aimed at building a just and humane social order. It is about constructing national and continental visions which could point ways out of the crises besieging our societies.

The paradigm indicates not only end objectives but also identifies approaches to be utilized in bringing about the desired changes. These processes entail dialogue instead of coercion, accepting responsibility instead of assigning it to others, receiving by giving instead of by taking, negotiation instead of win/lose decisions, focusing on needs instead of wants and positions, cooperation instead of competition, etc. Consistent with these processes, the paradigm also suggests roles for actors leading the kinds of change and transformation processes indicated here. Some of these roles are those of bridge-builders, consensus-seekers, mediators, reconcilers, healers, catalysts for the creation of humane relationships and a compassionate social order, and most important of all, leadership by example.

[1] See Johan Galtung, "Violence, Peace and Research," *Journal of Peace Research*, No. 3, 1969.
[2] See Paul Wehr, *Conflict Regulation* (Boulder, CO: Westview Press, 1979), p. 14.
[3] See John W. Burton, "Generic Theory: The Basis of Conflict Resolution," *Negotiation Journal* Vol. 2, October 1986, pp. 333-44.

–Hizkias Assefa
© Nairobi Peace Initiative 1993, from "Peace and Reconciliation as a Paradigm," NPI Monograph Series, No. 1. Used by permission.

"Revolutionaries" & "Resolutionaries": In Pursuit of Dialogue

In a recent and rather animated discussion on the polarity between mediation and nonviolent advocacy approaches, a colleague with longstanding advocacy leanings spoke rather poetically. *"Mediation,"* he said lifting his head and breathing slowly and deeply through his nose, *"it's the aroma."* Indeed, mediation seems to lend itself to olfactive processes. To some it smells sweet as the dew on the beard of Aaron. To others the perfume is so sweet it stinks, used to cover up less desirable winds swirling under the surface. But the tension between these sister circles of peacemaking exists and occasionally catches us off guard.

Activists in nonviolent and rights advocacy circles critique mediation as glossing over and taking a middle road, often toward solutions of mediocrity. They believe mediation is based on superficial understanding of structural problems, best depicted as the reduction of injustices to "problems of communication." They question whether the benign and naive face of mediator's good intentions covers an unspoken, but powerfully manipulative, ideology of harmony that ultimately benefits the rich, powerful and conservative. They are at times frustrated with the popularity and all too "palatableness" of conflict resolution for the mainstream of peace church constituency and society at large. In the end the question is posed: Is there integrity in *not* taking a stance, in *not* standing by the oppressed and downtrodden?

Practitioners in conflict resolution and mediation critique the activist orientation for a superficial understanding of what mediation is about and how it works. They question whether activists are interested in learning the processes, skills and discipline of listening, engaging seriously with all viewpoints and reconciling deeply fractured relationships. They are at times frustrated with the sense of self-righteousness implicit in the activist spirit, which suggests for itself a deeper, more integral adherence to the call of faith.

Perhaps my descriptions of views shock you. On several occasions recently, the lack of contact between these views has struck me as showing signs of nonconstructive conflict that I have in part reflected here. Generalizations and stereotypes tend to dominate. An either/or mode of thinking is usually prevalent. Activists talk with activists about mediators. Mediators talk with mediators about activists. Rarely do the two communities engage in direct dialogue. The times when I have had the opportunity to do the latter, I have found it most enlightening and productive. As a contribution toward dialogue I would like to offer three ways for framing the issues I have found useful.

1. Different But Not Incompatible

As a starting point for discussion, I suggest a return to one of the earliest conceptual pieces developed in conflict resolution by Quaker conciliator Adam Curle. He suggests that the movement from unpeaceful to peaceful relationships can be charted in a matrix comparing levels of power with levels of awareness of conflicting interests. The matrix is

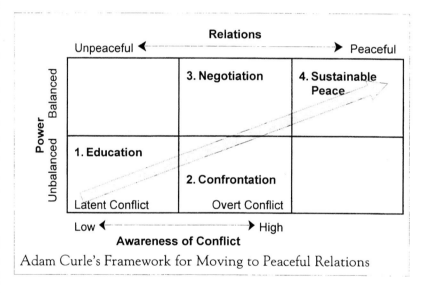

Adam Curle's Framework for Moving to Peaceful Relations

useful for plotting where we are in a given conflict, but also for suggesting the potential roles we choose to take at a given time. The three major roles which emerge are education, active confrontation or advocacy, and negotiation.

The roles emerge as we follow a typical path of conflict. Education, or *conscientization*, is needed when the conflict is hidden and people are unaware of power imbalances and injustices. It is the superficial circumstance of false prophets crying, *"Peace, Peace,"* when there is no peace.

Increased awareness of issues and interests leads toward demands for change, which rarely are immediately attained and more likely are not even heard, given the imbalance of power. Change and the balance of power is then pursued through some form of confrontation. If successful, the confrontation will increase awareness of interdependence and balance power, legitimizing in the process the demands the lower power party has put forth. Negotiation now becomes possible and can lead to agreement for restructuring the relationship and increased justice. At any point the path can jump back. Conflict does not always lead to restructured relationships.

We notice several important, but often overlooked, aspects in the typical process of conflict. First, mediation and advocacy share the goal of change and restructuring unpeaceful relationships, the common pursuit of justice. When justice ceases to be the goal of *either* intervention, the strategy must be questioned. Where any approach is used as a ploy to co-opt or manipulate the less powerful and disadvantaged, it should not be pursued.

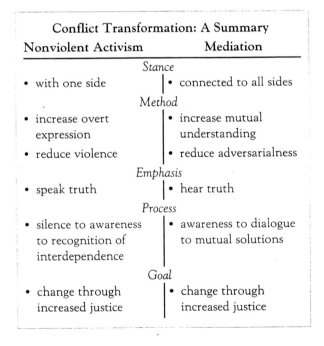

Conflict Transformation: A Summary	
Nonviolent Activism	Mediation
Stance	
• with one side	• connected to all sides
Method	
• increase overt expression	• increase mutual understanding
• reduce violence	• reduce adversarialness
Emphasis	
• speak truth	• hear truth
Process	
• silence to awareness to recognition of interdependence	• awareness to dialogue to mutual solutions
Goal	
• change through increased justice	• change through increased justice

Second, nonviolent advocacy and mediator roles overlap, complement and, more importantly, are mutually dependent. Negotiation becomes possible when the needs and interests are articulated and legitimated. This happens most often through confrontation and advocacy, which translate into a recognition of mutual dependence. On the other hand, restructuring the relationship toward increased equality and justice does not emanate auto-matically from confrontation, unless we assume the total elimination of one side. Mediation can and should facilitate the articulation of legitimate needs and interests of all sides into fair, practical and mutually acceptable solutions.

Where the two differ is in connection to the people and perspectives involved and the immediate goals pursued. Nonviolent advocacy chooses to stand by one side for justice's sake. Mediation chooses to stand in connection to all sides for justice's sake. Nonviolent advocacy moves to *produce and increase* overt expression of conflict, while reducing violence. Through conflict it seeks to move from silence and complacency to awareness and change. Mediation, building on acute awareness of conflict, moves to *produce and increase* mutual understanding, while reducing adversarialness. Through conflict it seeks to move from awareness to understanding to change. The former is experienced as "increasing" conflict; the latter as "reducing" conflict. More correctly stated, both are conflict transformations.

2. Conflict Transformation

Terminology that dominates a field or discipline often evolves with the changing conceptual processes of its practitioners. Such is the case in mediation. "Conflict resolution" was the early and currently dominant concept. The concept indicated the need to understand how conflict evolves and ends. It encouraged the development of strategies and skills for dealing with the volatile and too often destructive outcomes of conflict. At times, however, "resolution" conceptually promotes the notion that conflict is bad and should be eliminated. Legitimate questions are raised about whether that is the goal, or whether we ever really "resolve" a conflict. Certainly, specific decisions are made and expressions of conflict end. But if there is an ongoing relationship conflict remains. "Resolution" does not capture that ongoing nature nor the need for a relational ebb and flow, and sometimes may inappropriately push for the premature reduction of confrontation.

Some years ago conflict "management" entered practitioner parlance. Heavily western in conception, management pointed toward the idea that conflict follows certain predictable patterns and dynamics that could be understood and regulated. Like building a bridge over a raging river, or damming it up to produce electricity, we likewise can channel conflict energy toward productive outcomes. But experience tells us we do not really control human action and interaction, nor is the object of our work to simply reduce volatility. Thus "management" only partially depicts the goal and work of mediators.

Recently I have moved toward the characterization of conflict "transformation." Transformation suggests we do not eliminate or control, but we do impact the path of conflict. This is true in at least two ways. First, we can transform *perceptions*. Conflict is always based on how issues, actions and others are perceived. At times those perceptions are clear and accurate, often they are not. Second, we can transform *expressions*. Conflict will always be expressed by some means, be that overt and direct or covert and subtle. The chosen expression conflict takes is amenable to change.

With this concept we again find an inclusive, rather than mutually exclusive, way of looking at nonviolent advocacy and mediation. Both view conflict as legitimate, necessary and potentially healthy. Both are working at transforming conflict in pursuit of justice. Nonviolent activism often works at "raising awareness" on an issue, the transformation from not perceiving or not caring to "seeing" and "doing" something about it. This is the movement from silence to awareness, and from awareness to balancing power. It pays close attention to the *expression* of conflict, choosing to *escalate and confront* in ways that respect the human integrity of those with opposing goals and positions.

Mediation works at the perception people have of each other, their goals and the conflict itself. It *transforms* the expression modes toward dialogue and interdependence. Nonviolent advocacy, while concerned about process, places primary energy in achieving substantive change. Mediation, while concerned that people address their substantive concerns, places primary energy in process change. This is the movement from awareness of

–John Paul Lederach
© MCS 1989, from *Conciliation Quarterly*, Vol. 8 No. 3

interdependence to dialogue and mutually acceptable solutions.

3. Empowering the Community of Voices

A professor of mine, Elaine Yarbrough, wrote an insightful article titled, "Making peace with yourself." (*Working for Peace*, Neil Wollman, ed.) She proposed that each individual is made up of a community of internal voices, each having a perspective and needs. These voices are at times in conflict and are too often viewed as being incompatible opposites. Our tendency is to pay more attention to one set of voices and subconsciously deny a voice to others. *"When we deny certain parts of ourselves they often gain influence rather than disappear,"* Yarbrough writes. They leak into our communication and relationships, often empowering themselves at inappropriate times. Speaking for my intrapersonal community, I find this true for my mediator and activist voices. When I deny or disenfranchise one of the voices, I lose part of who I am and the resources at my disposal.

This perspective sets up a challenging paradox. We must simultaneously be about the task of empowering the voices-as-community and the community-as-voices. In practical terms, activist and mediator voices need each other. When and where we deny our different voices, we clip the wings of growth and lose crucial resources in the difficult climb toward justice.

Moreover, I believe that these voices, when empowered as community, enhance the individual roles each must play. The best nonviolent activists know and use the skills of an adept mediator. The best mediators have the passion and vision of activists. Yarbrough suggests that a good way to accept those internal voices which you find negative and perhaps overwhelming is to "hang around others" who represent and promote those voices. Their acceptance of you may help you accept your hidden voices. Therein lies the challenge of the justice dialogue.

When Mediation Is Not Enough

With the increasing popularity of mediation over the last number of years, many involved in the struggle for peace have embraced mediation as a positive practical approach to working at the world's problems. We must ask whether we have shortchanged ourselves and the vision we once held. The time has come to once again examine where we are going.

Like many others, I came into the mediation field out of concern and desire for reconciliation between conflicting peoples. But we soon realized that "reconciliation" sounded a bit presumptuous, so we opted for "conflict resolution." Then as we gained experience, we realized that "resolution" was not always possible, so we shifted to what we now call "conflict management."

While these changes accurately reflect realistic terminology for what we are doing, they indicate a shift we have rather unconsciously made away from a belief that reconciliation, embodying both peace and justice, is our goal. Our desire to be neutral and gain rapport with all parties involved has caused us to shy away even more from earlier commitments. We have concentrated on technique over values.

Has the mediation movement helped us work at putting these values into practice? If not, where have these values gone? Has conflict mediation become the "opiate of the peacemaker," as someone has coined it?

Current Model

The mediation model held by many today views most disputes as neither good nor bad, but as situations of competing interests and needs among parties that are generally neither right nor wrong. Perceived differences can be settled by improving communication and understanding and then negotiating a settlement, preferably through one or several face-to-face sessions. While this model serves us well in many disputes, it falls short when there are significant differences of power between the parties involved, when violence is institutionalized into relationships, and when larger socioeconomic problems prevent a realistic negotiated resolution of the conflict.

As mediators, we automatically face a dilemma in these types of disputes. We want to maintain our credibility with both sides. Yet we are uncomfortable with certain injustices that may or may not be open for discussion by those involved. With our orientation toward neutrality, we hope that the parties themselves will confront the larger problems of violence and injustice. Unfortunately, the reality is that sometimes they do not—or cannot—and we are left with our conscience. In the end, a negotiated settlement might serve to reinforce an unjust system.

Admittedly, there have been alterations in the mediation model to make a better fit with certain types of disputes. Many mediators now work at power differences, redress for injustices, and agreements addressing long-term solutions for change. But to a large extent, many conflicts do not easily adapt to this model. To compensate, many argue that some types of conflict, such as domestic violence, are never suitable for mediation.

Another alteration has been to limit the agenda according to the limitations of the mediation format itself. Since broader issues of racism or classism reach far beyond those present at the table, mediators tend to limit discussion to specific disputes facing a neighborhood, school, or company. When individual disputes are merely symptoms of a larger unhealthy system, however, a transformation must take place at the system level for the specific conflicts to subside. The third party must decide whether to stick to the specific disputes or address the larger systemic problems. Even if the broader agenda comes forward, it becomes unwieldy to work through in a few mediation sessions.

And let us not forget what remains the number one limitation to mediation—getting people to the table. If one party is unwilling to negotiate, even after a number of skillful maneuvers by the mediators, the fact is that mediation has failed. Somehow we have let this limitation take a back seat, leaving many people disgruntled with mediation as a viable alternative. In my work in Central America and in this country, I have encountered many disputes where it is simply not in the perceived best interest of one party to sit down to negotiate. This is especially true when society reinforces a party's position through machismo, racism, classism, etc.

Finally, at yet another level, we must recognize that with all of the emphasis on mediation throughout the past decade, our world is not a safer or kinder place. Both in this country and worldwide, we have seen a massive proliferation of violence and the use of force to solve problems. The disparity between the rich and poor is unparalleled. The "richest country in the world" is also one of the most violent societies, where homelessness abounds and one in nine children suffer from malnutrition. In response, we lock up more people per capita than any other country in the world. The choice to kill over 160,000 Iraqis when sanctions and negotiation still held promising possibilities—and then express practically no remorse for the dead—is a chilling reminder of where we are today in our quest for peace.

That is not to say that mediation has failed. It is rather a statement of how little trust we place in peaceful means and just solutions. Should we be working more directly at promoting alternative values and speaking out for the victims in our violent world?

An Alternative: Conflict Transformation by Active Nonviolence

To address the serious problems facing our world, we first need to be clear with ourselves regarding our goals and values. To assume that we are a disinterested third party in the case is to imply that we do not care. It is not enough to say we will let the parties determine the agenda. The conflict may be larger than the parties involved, who are often caught up in addressing the symptoms of a more basic conflict. Paradoxically, we must state up front our commitment to confront violence, injustice, and oppressive systems, while seeking a process that empowers ALL those involved to determine their own futures. We must seek to bring about just and lasting solutions to the larger social problems, as well as to a specific disputes—in short, a transformation of the individuals, relationships and systems.

Then, with this clear value commitment, we can focus on conflict as the appropriate arena for our work as peacemakers. Conflict provides the energy, motivation and heightened awareness necessary to bring about change. But we must not assume that

mediation is the prescribed methodology to reach just solutions. It might, in fact, serve to decrease confrontation, to reinforce an unjust status quo. Instead, we need to sit down with one or more of the parties to discern desirable outcomes and the best methodology to help us get there. Those involved must have a greater voice in what processes will be chosen, based on their own assessment of the situation and the willingness of each party to participate. Mediation may be an appropriate option. But advocacy or a boycott may be just as or more appropriate.

Mediation remains an important effective alternative, but not the overriding paradigm from which we operate. We have experienced first-hand the power of getting people together to work at their differences and we must continue to pursue this as an essential component of a larger, more comprehensive model. But mediation is probably best seen as a powerful tool, rather than a moral framework for peace.

The following principles represent an attempt to clarify where transformation based on active nonviolence differs from traditional mediation:

1. Our overall position is not a neutral or disinterested one or even an impartial one. We are for solutions that are just and which empower all those caught up in conflict. There are points where mediating without siding with any one party is essential, but that is not our overall position.

2. The goal is not to get the parties to the negotiation table or even to reach a mutually agreed upon settlement. It is to establish more just, equitable and peaceful relations. Transformation of social structures and systems that create conflict must also be included in our goals.

3. Socioeconomic problems are as important in the process as the issue at hand. Lack of education and employment opportunities, easy access to weapons, lack of positive community interaction, and excessive violence on television, etc., must be taken into consideration if we are to achieve a lasting peace.

4. Conflict does not happen in a vacuum, but in the context of community relationships. This

fact influences who is involved, where work should take place, and the relationship of a "third party" to those directly involved in the conflict. It might be beneficial for those who intervene to be known and respected by all parties, instead of someone unknown from the outside.

5. Working for a lasting peace includes the transformation of persons, as well as the dispute. All too often we separate the inner self from the issues at hand, only to regret that someone did not have good faith after leaving the negotiating table. Adam Curle states that "external change never begins at all unless changes in the internal goals and perceptions have to some extent already occurred." We should cultivate an atmosphere where internal change can take place.

6. We cannot assume people have the knowledge and skills to work toward just and peaceful solutions. An orientation to the peacemaking process is essential—to the needs, risks, available alternatives and importance of reaching peace. Before moving ahead with mediation or any other alternative, the parties must also have some basic preparation in communication and nonviolence skills. This is not paternalism, just the opposite; for it empowers all involved with the knowledge and skills usually privy to mediators and outsiders.

7. Peacemaking is first of all an educational process. From the point of intervention on, we are engaged in education—modeling and promoting living alternatives for people who want to know a better way.

–Mark Chupp
© MCS 1991, excerpted from *Conciliation Quarterly*, Vol. 10 No. 3

The Transformation Process

A holistic approach to conflict and social problems is not new. But it has lost some of its luster over the years. With the disillusionment of the 60s and 70s, many have steered clear of approaches that lead toward community-oriented solutions. Yet the problems we face are very complex. The promotion of violence, war and oppression is based on sophisticated models, reinforced with popular language and high technology.

In North America, those of us in the mediation movement are convinced that ends do not justify means, that process is as important as outcome. But have we gone too far the other way? Does good process always assure good outcomes? Have we lost sight of the prize? What are the goals of our work, beyond a mutually agreed upon agreement?

Recognizing the immeasurable contributions that have come in the last decade from the exploding field of mediation, we now must ask where we are headed in the next decade. Ultimately, we will need to clarify the overall goals of our work. As we come clear, stating a desire for peace with justice, these goals will reshape our views toward mediation.

We have a rich history from which to draw. Many creative alternatives already exist. When we are able to unite these alternatives under one conceptual framework, we will be better prepared to unite many groups already working at related goals. We will also be better prepared to respond to the wide range of conflictual situations many now live in here and abroad.

Restorative Justice

"A revolution is occurring in criminal justice. A quiet, grassroots, seemingly unobtrusive, but truly revolutionary movement is changing the nature, the very fabric of our work." These are the opening words in a 1996 publication of the National Institute of Corrections. Characterizing the combined community and restorative justice movements, author Eduardo Barajas, Jr., a program specialist for the NIC, goes on to observe that the changes extend beyond most reforms in the history of criminal justice: "What is occurring now is more than innovative, it is truly inventive, . . . a 'paradigm shift.'"

The restorative justice movement has come a long way since 1974, when we began our version of victim/offender mediation (entitled the Victim Offender Reconciliation Program, or VORP) in Elkhart, Ind. Who could have imagined that we were at the vanguard of a movement with the potential to revolutionize justice?

Today's interest at the national level follows several decades of innovation and experimentation on community and state levels. As Barajas' observation above implies, restorative justice is not a matter of adding some new programs or tinkering with old ones. Instead, restorative justice involves a reorientation of how we think about crime and justice. The problem with past reform efforts—which have so often gone astray—is that they have not challenged us to look at our problems and our solutions through a new "lens."

While the restorative justice concept can be framed in a variety of ways, two ideas are fundamental: restorative justice is *harm-focused* and promotes the *engagement* of an enlarged set of stakeholders.

Restorative justice views crime first of all as harm done to people and communities. Our legal system, with its focus on rules and laws, often loses sight of the reality that crime is essentially harm. Consequently, it makes victims at best a secondary concern of justice. A harm focus, however, implies a central concern for victims' needs and roles. Restorative justice, then, begins with a concern for victims and how to meet their needs, for repairing the harm as much as possible, both concretely and symbolically.

A focus on harm also implies an emphasis on offender accountability and responsibility—in concrete, not abstract, terms. Too often we have thought of accountability as punishment, pain administered to offenders for pain they have caused. Unfortunately, this is often irrelevant or even counterproductive to real accountability. Little in the justice process encourages offenders to understand the consequences of their actions or to empathize with victims. On the contrary, the adversarial game requires offenders to look out for themselves. Offenders are discouraged from acknowledging their responsibility and are given little opportunity to act on this responsibility in concrete ways. The "neutralizing strategies"—the stereotypes and rationalizations that offenders use to distance themselves from the people they hurt—are never challenged. So the sense of alienation from society experienced by many offenders, the feeling that they themselves are victims, is only heightened by the legal process and the prison experience.

If crime is essentially about harm, accountability means being encouraged to understand that harm and to begin to comprehend the consequences of one's behavior. Moreover, it means taking responsibility to make things right in so far as possible, both concretely and symbolically. Wrong creates obligations; taking responsibility for those obligations is the beginning of genuine accountability.

The principle of engagement suggests that the primary parties affected by crime—victims, offenders, members of the community—are given significant roles in the justice process. They need to be given information about each other and to be involved in deciding what justice requires in this situation. In some cases, this may mean actual dialogue between these parties, as happens in victim/offender mediation or family group conferences, to come to a consensus about what should be done. In others it may involve indirect exchange or the use of surrogates. In any event, the principle of engagement implies involvement of an enlarged circle of parties as compared to the traditional justice process.

At the risk of oversimplifying, the restorative justice and the usual traditional justice approach (or retributive justice) might be summarized like this:

Retributive Justice	Restorative Justice
Crime is a violation of the law, and the state is the victim.	*Crime* is a violation or harm to people and relationships.
The *aim of justice* is to establish blame (guilt) and administer pain (punishment).	The *aim of justice* is to identify obligations, meet needs and promote healing.
The *process of justice* is a conflict between adversaries in which offender is pitted against state rules and intentions outweigh outcomes and one side wins while the other loses.	The *process of justice* involves victims, offenders and community in an effort to identify obligations and solutions, maximizing the exchange of information (dialogue, mutual agreement) between them.

To put restorative justice in its simplest form: Crime violates people. Violations always create obligations. Justice should involve victims, offenders and community members in a search to identify needs and obligations so that things can be made right so far as possible.

"Restorative justice" is a term which quickly connects for many people and therein lies both its strength and weakness. Many professionals as well as lay people are frustrated with justice as it is commonly practiced and are immediately attracted to the idea of restoration. "Restorative justice" intuitively suggests a reparative, person-centered, common sense approach. For many of us, it reflects values with which we were raised. As a result, the term has been widely embraced and used in many contexts.

But will the term be used simply as a new way to name and justify the same old programs and goals? There are many programs—such as community service—which can be compatible with restorative justice *if* they are reshaped to fully account for restorative principles. If they are not reshaped as part of a larger restorative "lens," however, at best they will be more of the same. At worst, they may become new ways to control and punish.

Already we are seeing programs which are not truly grounded in restorative justice but operating with that name. When they are unsuccessful, they tend to discredit the movement. Restorative justice will be simply one more in a long line of fads if we do not think carefully about its principles and their interrelationship. This means attention to values. The "restorative justice signposts" on the following page are intended to serve as a checklist.

All this is not to say that there is such a thing as "pure" restorative or retributive justice. Rather, justice may been seen as a continuum between two "ideal types." On the one end is our western legal system. Its strengths—such as the encouragement of human rights—are substantial. Yet it has important weaknesses. Criminal justice tends to be punitive, conflictual, impersonal and state-centered. It encourages the denial of responsibility and empathy on the part of offenders. It leaves victims out, ignoring their needs. Instead of discouraging wrongdoing, it often encourages it. It exacerbates rather than heals wounds.

At the other end is the restorative alternative. Victims' needs and rights are central, not peripheral. Offenders are encouraged to understand the harm they have caused and to take responsibility for it. Dialogue—direct or indirect—is encouraged and communities play important roles. Restorative justice assumes that justice can and should promote healing, both individual and societal.

Criminal justice is usually not purely retributive. On the other hand, we will rarely achieve justice that is fully restorative. A realistic goal is to move as far as we can (and it will vary with each program and case) toward a process that puts victims, offenders, members of the affected community—their needs, their roles—at the center of our search for a justice that heals.

–Howard Zehr
© Howard Zehr, 1997, originally published in *Corrections Today*, December 1997. Used by permission.

Restorative Justice Signposts

We are working toward restorative justice when we . . .

I.   . . . focus on the harms of wrongdoing more than the rules that have been broken,

II.   . . . show equal concern and commitment to victims and offenders, involving both in the process of justice,

III.   . . . work toward the restoration of victims, empowering them and responding to their needs as they see them,

IV.   . . . support offenders while encouraging them to understand, accept and carry out their obligations,

V.   . . . recognize that while obligations may be difficult for offenders, they should not be intended as harms and they must be achievable,

VI.   . . . provide opportunities for dialogue, direct or indirect, between victims and offenders as appropriate,

VII.   . . . involve and empower the affected community through the justice process, and increase its capacity to recognize and respond to community bases of crime,

VIII.   . . . encourage collaboration and reintegration rather than coercion and isolation,

IX.   . . . give attention to the unintended consequences of our actions and programs,

X.   . . . show respect to all parties including victims, offenders, justice colleagues.

–Harry Mika and Howard Zehr
© Mennonite Central Committee U.S. Office on Crime and Justice 1999. Used by permission.

For free "Restorative Justice Signposts" bookmarks, contact the MCC U.S. Office on Crime and Justice at ocj@mccus.org.

Toward a Transformative Practice of Restorative Justice

One of the most persistent critiques of the field of restorative justice (RJ) is that it still fundamentally fails to address the structural dimensions of criminal conflict. Current mediation and conferencing strategies focus too much energy on the interpersonal dimensions of crime and ignore the deeper roots of the trouble as found in class, race/ethnicity, and gender-based, systemic conflict. Practitioners have largely *not* been trained to think of their work within systemic frames of reference and so, by default, tend to carry out their role as if peace and conflict in one's life were a purely personal responsibility and prerogative. While few, if any, critics claim that RJ practitioners intend these grave effects, the net result, they conclude, is the same: participants in informal justice models are persuaded, through affective strategies, to focus on interpersonal accommodations and are effectively anesthetized to larger questions of consciousness and action.

Harry Mika draws on a real-life case study to illustrate the problem. His case study involves a matter in which criminal charges were laid and the principal combatants were ordered to participate in a RJ mediation program. The precipitating incident concerned a protracted conflict over street parking. It revolved, on the surface of things, around who "was 'allowed' to park in front of whose house." Although a wide range of neighborhood residents had been affected by this dispute, one person, whom Mika refers to as "Rio," appeared to be especially central. Rio's refusal to allow a certain African-American man to park in front of his home meant that he and a few other players were gathered, albeit somewhat reluctantly, for facilitated deliberations. Lengthy sessions were conducted which allowed participants to express their feelings. Detailed agreements were pursued which stipulated specific behavioral expectations for the various individuals at the meeting with the emphasis on "technical issues, such as who would park where, how late and how loud parties would be, and the like."

By mapping out this conflict's deep-seated connections to a far more complicated web of community forces and societal patterns of racism, sexism, classism, addiction, homophobia, violence, repression/control, and dependence, however, Mika powerfully demonstrates the shortcomings of the mediators' interpersonal and issue-focused approach. As the author puts it so well, Rio may be sexist, racist, homophobic and violent, but "he draws his definitions of masculinity and his license for the macho prerogatives he holds dear from a shared culture that tolerates intolerance and invidious distinctions between human beings." Mika concludes that although the mediators' efforts in the parking dispute were undoubtedly "better than nothing," their emphasis on affective, interpersonal accommodations has very limited potential to truly address the underlying sources of the trouble.

"Reaching Toward" a Structural Analysis

While I am not sure that we can hope to develop a practice which *clearly, demonstrably, and consistently* addresses the shortcomings Mika has articulated, I am convinced that it is possible to develop an approach which *reaches toward* change at the structural level in the sense that it makes such change more likely. As a minimum starting point, it seems particularly crucial to more consciously and consistently train mediators/facilitators to *think* in systemic/structural terms (rather than maintaining an almost exclusive focus on skill building).

Dugan's "Nested" Conflict Foci

One critical conceptual dimension of a more structurally attuned practice can be found in the work of Maire Dugan. This conflict theorist identifies four different levels of conflict as issues-specific, relational, structural/subsystemic and structural/ systemic (Dugan, 1996). She argues that those seeking to address conflict on one level need to be cognizant of the way that same conflict may be manifested or rooted in the other levels (Ibid.).

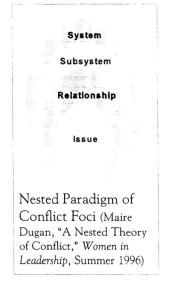

System

Subsystem

Relationship

Issue

Nested Paradigm of Conflict Foci (Maire Dugan, "A Nested Theory of Conflict," *Women in Leadership*, Summer 1996)

This suggests that if we truly wish to work at the roots of a problem, RJ practitioners must be engaged on multiple levels in a multiplicity of roles drawing on multiple forms of intervention/action. We must move beyond the traditional focus of mediation—meeting with Rio and the man who wants to park in front of his house—or even that of group conferencing—meeting with these two plus a handful of others from their neighboring homes—"because the problem and its possible solutions go well beyond" these individuals (Ibid., p.17). Instead, informal justice programs must be prepared to respond to this problem as it:

1. emerges from our dysfunctional paradigms of race relations, power, and socioeconomics (structural systemic);

2. is reinforced in the specific policies, traditions and procedures of our various institutions which are, or are perceived to be, inequitable or ineffectual, such as the police, the courts, and other civic structures (structural subsystemic);

3. surfaces in the ongoing patterns of interaction and feelings between the principal combatants and their associates/social circles (relational); and

4. is exhibited in the specific issues which emerged at the surface level of the conflict, such as who should park where (issues-specific).

Lederach's "Nested" Time Dimension

John Paul Lederach supplies another key dimension for a structurally transformative approach to RJ. His diagram illustrates the vital importance of "nesting" one's response to a problem in one time frame with a clear understanding of the implications of that response for other phases of one's work. In other words, we must not respond to a moment of crisis (e.g., a crime) in such a way as to undermine our long-term vision of our desired future together. Rather, our activities in the *immediate* (2-6 months), *short-range* (1-2 years), *decade time frame* (5-10 years), and *long-term, generational vision* (20+ years) must be integrated and comprehensive.

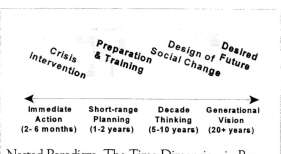

Nested Paradigm, The Time Dimension in Peace and Justice Building (John Paul Lederach, *Building Peace: Sustainable Reconciliation in Divided Societies*)

Focusing *all* or *most* of one's attention as a RJ facilitator on working out a detailed agreement on the most immediate issue of who will park where in Rio's neighborhood is a classic example of the crisis-driven, "quick fix" reactions which Lederach advises against. While addressing the immediate issue of parking, this approach arguably increases the threat of a more destructive outbreak of violence in the long term when the deeper structural roots of the parking problem give rise to new "weeds" (i.e., disputes). These, in turn, are experienced as all the more distressing and provoke a higher level of reactivity because participants were "led on" to believe these tensions were behind them. When we initiate processes whose time frames and numbers of participants only permit a focus on one or two immediate concerns, it is only a matter of time before other issues, such as someone's barking dog, loud children, or dilapidated fence, "sprout" yet again.

Another way of saying this simply is that you resolve issues, but you don't resolve relationships or communities, hence the need for a comprehensive strategy of transformation, not just restoration. At the level of time frames, this suggests that facilitators and participants alike must be encouraged to think in humble, realistic ways about what can be accomplished in one or two meetings. RJ practitioners should seek to respond to the immediate crisis of the neighborhood parking dispute, wherever possible and appropriate, with models of intervention which reflect a belief in the need for an ongoing process. In the same way, we must strive to include a representation of people which reflects the belief that relationships and networks are the soil in which long-term, structural change takes root.

Dugan and Lederach in Combination

Lederach brings Dugan's concept together with his own in *Building Peace: Sustainable Reconciliation in Divided Societies*. In so doing, he creates a model that is useful in assisting RJ mediators/facilitators to cultivate a longer and deeper view of their tasks.

Lederach articulates five questions that emerge from this new model which move us toward a more long-term response to conflict. The questions prompt strategic thinking as it relates to crisis management, crisis prevention, transformation, root causes and vision. These questions can be usefully adapted and applied to the realm of RJ practice and training along the following lines:

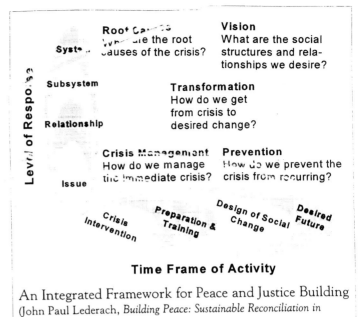

An Integrated Framework for Peace and Justice Building
(John Paul Lederach, *Building Peace: Sustainable Reconciliation in Divided Societies*)

1. How do we respond to the immediate crisis/issues/wounds created by the violation of one community member (i.e., the victim) by another community member (the offender)? How do we respond to the immediate crisis the violation causes for the community as a whole? (**Crisis Management**)

2. How do we prevent the crisis of violation and injury from recurring? (**Prevention**)

3. How do we get from the immediate crisis of this offense to desired change in the offender and in our society? How do we get from the immediate aftermath of violation to desired healing in the victim and our community? (**Transformation**)

4. What are the root causes of the violating behavior in the offender, the community, and society at large? (**Root Causes**)

5. What are the social structures and relationships we desire? (**Vision**)

A Broader Framework of Peacebuilding and Social Change

A final critical conceptual framework is found in the work of Adam Curle. Curle's model affirms the need for consciousness raising education, advocacy, and negotiation/conciliation/mediation (i.e., dialogue). All of these are framed within an overarching goal of long-term peacebuilding for socioeconomic and relational-spiritual transformation (the wide arrow in the chart at right represents the progression of conflict and change). Furthermore, the model assumes an unembarrassed value orientation in favor of less powerful groups gaining voice as a precondition of true

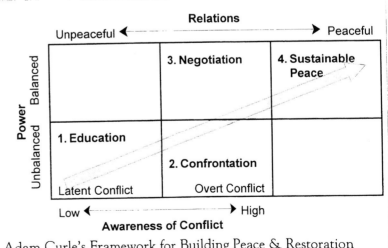

Adam Curle's Framework for Building Peace & Restoration
(John Paul Lederach, *Preparing for Peace: Conflict Transformation Across Cultures*)

transformation. In many ways, then, his work is an earlier articulation of the themes explored by the writers I have already reviewed.

Like Dugan, Curle affirms the need for a multiplicity of roles to be utilized at different times throughout the peacebuilding process. Like Mika, he also recognizes the dangers of "cooling out" or pacifying a conflict by prematurely facilitating dialogue in a situation which should be helped to progress from the covert to overt stages. His model suggests that unless both the disempowered and more powerful parties begin to recognize the structural nature of their problems, facilitated dialogue is actually counterproductive to building peace.

Curle's work has clear and dramatic implications for our understanding of RJ. It adds the critical dimensions of power analysis, awareness, and latent and overt conflict. As such, it reflects the additional insight that crime often grows out of frustration. This frustration stems from the fact that some individuals and groups in society have more power than others and that this situation of injustice remains largely unrecognized and unacknowledged. This argument is supported by the simple fact that the vast majority of persons who are arrested, prosecuted, and imprisoned for committing crimes belong to the lower socioeconomic strata of our society.

RJ practitioners, then, can be helped enormously to understand these realities by learning about Curle's model. More specifically, they can be assisted to reflect critically on the implication that *facilitated dialogue (e.g., Victim-Offender mediation or conferencing etc.) may well serve to reinforce power imbalance and structural conflict because of its premature use at the first level of unbalanced and unaware relations.*

In the final analysis, however, while the sources of crime may be largely structural, the effects are primarily personal. Curle's model, therefore, does not suggest the inappropriateness of Victim-Offender dialogue as "the opiate of the peacemaker," by definition, so much as it makes clear the need for RJ practitioners to: A) be wary of the ways their work may reinforce structural injustice; B) work cooperatively and respectfully with social activists, advocates, and other community partners who are pursuing the avenues of *education* and *confrontation* more directly; and C) design models of RJ intervention that are more able to serve the ends of interpersonal healing *while also* promoting the goals of education and confrontation with respect to the structural sources.

–David Dyck

© Contemporary Justice Review 2000. A longer version of this article appeared in *Contemporary Justice Review*, Vol. 3, Issue 3. Used by permission.

Part 4
The Cultural Dimension

Our first task in approaching another people, another culture, another religion, is to take off our shoes, for the place we are approaching is holy. Else we may find ourselves treading on someone's dreams; more serious still, we may forget that God was there before our arrival.

–Max Warren

Introduction to Culture

Culture refers to the patterns of behaviors, values and communication styles which best describe the unique characteristics of an organization or a particular ethnic or culture group.

Because cultural conflict is deep-seated and structural, we are all, by definition, already participants in the conflict. The question is "How can we construct a learning environment that will allow members of diverse cultural groups to conflict creatively?" For all practical purposes, conflict is a natural part of a process that is committed to bridging cultures.

It is critical to recognize that some degree of conflict is inherent in almost any multicultural setting where relations between cultures have been socially institutionalized according to a dominant-subordinate dynamic. Conflicts are particularly acute around issues related to land, economics and racism. Generally, conflict increases as cultural diversity increases.

–Roberto Chené

There are few things in the conflict transformation field as challenging and complex as the cultural dimension. Were there simply a multiplicity of cultures whose unique characteristics were valued equally by all, there would be challenge enough. The expression of anger or the meaning of silence or the nuances of a body movement can vary greatly depending upon who you are and where you come from. The very reality of these cultural differences can cause conflict. Or exacerbate it.

When one adds to this very colorful mix of cultural variations the reality of unequal power and of domination and oppression, the path to navigate becomes something of a mine field. Every conflict is about power in some way. When one is dealing with conflict in which a party is in power over another, especially when that power is abusive, the path to conflict transformation becomes considerably different.

In these pages we have tried to look at culture through the eyes of multiculturalism as well as through the eyes of domination and oppression. (See also the previous pages on power.) We know that we have a long way to go to do both well. We continue to be aware that the major players in the conflict field, the majority of the models used and the bulk of the writing continue to be from a white, dominant-culture perspective. So we keep adding people and processes and ideas that emerge from the rich color in our midst. Our goal, however, is shifting from an "adding on" modus operandi to a manual—and a practice—that is truly multicultural, truly primary and integral to who we are. We hope this edition of the manual is another step in that direction.

–Carolyn Schrock-Shenk
© MCS 2000

Culture and Values: Some Givens

A definition of culture: What everybody within a group knows that everybody else in the group knows.

1. Cultural assumptions are beliefs which are so completely accepted within the group that they do not need to be stated, questioned, or defended.

2. Everyone is ethnocentric. We see the world through culture-colored eyes.

3. We compare people and events based on our own systems and perspectives.

4. Each culture thinks its own ways are superior.

5. Our culture determines many of our values.

6. We all have biases and prejudices.

7. Our values/biases show up in our interactions with people.

8. Discussing biases and prejudices is risky, because it is easy to be misunderstood.

9. There are no cultural absolutes, in terms of responses, only "right" or "wrong" responses within a given culture. Groups are not "better" or "worse"—but different.

10. Not every conflict involving people who are different is caused by a cultural problem.

11. We cannot know all things about all cultures.

12. We can increase our effectiveness as intercultural communicators and problem-solvers.

13. We can be more aware of what there is to be aware of regarding cultural differences.

14. Cultural conflict does not disappear because we decide to ignore it.

15. There is ambiguity in diversity. Tolerance for diversity, an open mind, hope, patience, and faith are important for improving our relations with others.

16. Intercultural relationship development comes through commitment, not accident.

–adapted from the **Community Board Program**
© The Community Board Program, 1540 Market Street, #490, San Francisco, CA 94102. Used with permission.

The Mediator's Cultural Assumptions

Introduction

In January, 1985, I conducted a series of "pilot" workshops on mediation and conflict management skills in three Central American countries. The materials and presentations were given in Spanish. However, during reflection times, the participants reported a feeling of "uneasiness" with aspects of the mediation procedure I presented. One person noted, "it seemed very North American." Referring to his Guatemalan compatriots who had role-played a conflict, he continued, "they acted more like gringos than like us."

In the workshops I shared a model of conflict management which I had found useful, but one that brought with it the assumptions and premises that emerged from and are relevant to a North American setting. I was a "change agent," exporting a prescriptive model of conflict management from one context to another, and I was encountering the limits of my own cultural assumptions about conflict when applied to another culture. If I was to have anything useful to contribute in this setting, it would be essential for me to first accomplish two important tasks:

1. Learn more about myself, to become conscious of the cultural assumptions I bring to conflict.
2. Learn more about others, that is, become conscious of and learn from the cultural assumptions present in the culture of others and draw from the resources of that culture in exploring effective ways of responding to conflict there.

This is a study of the "subculture" of professional mediation. I wish to clarify how North American definitions of mediation may produce crucial points of tension when directly exported to other cultures. I also wish to suggest factors I believe deserve careful attention when mediators move from one cultural setting to another, in or outside of the United States. As a point of reference, I will compare North American assumptions about the use of a third party with Latin American conceptions.

Mediator Monologue as Mirror on Cultural Assumptions

Consider the purpose and genre of the talk used by the North American mediator in the monologue. The monologue is a short uninterrupted introductory speech given by mediators to disputants at the beginning of mediation. The monologue explains the rules, similar perhaps to the referee's explanation of the rules of the game to the boxers. It is a practiced performance, permitting disputants to "take an emotional time-out from their initial anxiety while the mediator is busy explaining the structure" (Folberg and Taylor, 1984).

The language of the monologue as used by North American mediators I have studied reflects cultural values about conflict, and these values are reinforced by the physical setting in which mediation normally takes place. One value is formality, that is, explicitly stated rules and explanations, consciously defined and organized limits on what is acceptable behavior and what is not.

Formality is reinforced by setting. In the North American model, mediation formally "takes place" in a bounded, indoor setting. The scene invokes the formalized language in the monologue, and the language formalizes the scene.

The formality established by language and setting is further reflected in the mediator's conception of time. Urban, Anglo North Americans generally have a "bureaucratic" conceptualization of time. It is a commodity to be rationally and efficiently used. This conceptualization of time underlies the structure of mediation. Mediators "schedule" mediation "sessions," they "block out" time in their schedules, mediation is "terminated" until the next session.

All this suggests several continua that affect how people make decisions, manage conflict and use third parties. Consider the implications for conflict management and mediation of five characteristics sociology has identified:

Characteristics of Modern and Traditional Societies Affecting Mediation

Modern	Traditional
Autonomous/ Individualistic	Familial/Group Dependent
Impersonal/Professional	Personal/Relational
Rational/Formal	Affective/Assumed
Technical/Specialized	Informal/Holistic
Achievement/ Accomplishment	Ascriptive/Personal Network

Over time, mediation as a speciality in the United States has progressively become a more formalized, rationally technical and professional process. It is not just a folk art, it is a business. Practically, formal structure provides a sense of security for persons living in modern bureaucratic society. We are familiar with professionals and adapt easily to "business-type" relationships.

However, the view that formal structure helps control and "facilitate" interaction is not universal as indicated by both sociological and cross-cultural literature. Levine and Padilla note Hispanics generally have a preference for "interpersonal relations based on trust for people mingled with a distaste for formal, impersonal institutions or organizations." This parallels the positive emphasis placed on *personalismo* or "affectivity" in Latin cultures.

Personalismo has practical implications for mediation. Relationships and responsibility to the primary group are considered more important than schedules and immediate task accomplishment. People in a more traditional setting may not experience a formalized structure as "providing security" and "facilitating" discussion of problems. Anglo North Americans tend to treat human relationships as fast, easy-come, easy-go. Friends are made quickly, but rarely are friends permanent. For the Latin American, friendships are not lightly developed nor ended. Priority is given to people over tasks and schedules.

Assumptions About the Role of the Mediator

For North American mediators, reaching agreement is the outcome goal of mediation. The solution must be "acceptable" to both parties; a solution that both can live with. Here, "outcome" means that an interpersonal conflict is resolved if the parties directly involved reach agreement. Notice again the "individualistic" orientation to conflict, fitting neatly a modern, bureaucratic context. It does not necessarily take into account the wider social networks of the disputants.

In traditional contexts familiarity with the use of a third party is more prevalent than in middle class Anglo settings. However, it is not formalized, viewed as a technical-specialist role, nor called mediation. Rather an informal structure pervades: a structure not explicitly stated in terms of rules and official expectations, but emerging from expectations inherent in generally accepted ways of thinking and acting in a group. A good example is the use of godparents in Latin America as go-betweens between the children and parents. Godparents serve as non-technical mediators who help smooth and stabilize conflictive relations in the family structure.

In the North American model, ignorance and distance, that is anonymity, provide legitimate "rational-legal" authority. Other cultures may expect that the mediator is known, and in fact is an integral element maintaining the stability of group life. It is the human bond that establishes both trust and continuity through the process. Relationship to and knowledge of disputants and their social context provide legitimate "traditional" authority. Differences in the norms of interpretation of this role can produce important misunderstandings between disputants coming with one expectation and the mediator another.

We naturally assume that conflict can be "managed." In mediation this means parties themselves—alone—can resolve, control and direct the solution. By concentrating on reaching agreement among parties "at the table," a conflict situation is conceptualized as something that can be acted on and changed in isolation from any larger surrounding context. The structure "facilitated" by a third party provides a control.

Not everyone shares this assumption. Persons in traditional societies may look to third parties for counsel, education and advice precisely because they feel the solution is outside their control. The initiative for change is not perceived to be in the hands of the person with the problem, but rather it lies with the third party.

Assumptions About Norms of Interaction

The basic assumption underlying North American norms of interaction is a cultural preference for "direct" communication between antagonists. The explicit rules establishing this structure assume that face-to-face negotiation between disputants is desirable. However, Hispanics may prefer to use intermediaries as "surrogates," as a buffer to limit the face-to-face confrontation of antagonists.

Further, the Anglo preference to directly deal with problems is usually accompanied by a fast pace of self-disclosure and working immediately on the issues. Anglos tend to give "I-topics" an early slot in the course of dialogue. Mediation demands it. However, Hispanics place them later. This can lead to considerable confusion. Anglos may feel Hispanics "beat around the bush" and "don't get to the point." Hispanics may feel Anglos are too forward and socially impolite, not showing proper deference and respect.

Our temporal organization of interaction provides another comparison. Hall suggests two models of organizing time, "events scheduled as separate items—one thing at a time, as in Northern Europe, or following the Mediterranean model of involvement in several things at once." He terms the "one thing at a time" as *monochronic*, and the "involvement of people and completion of transactions rather than adherence to preset schedules" as *polychronic*. The strength of the polychronic model is its orientation to people, or *personalismo* as Latinos call it. Its weakness is "inefficiency" from a rational viewpoint.

To the monochronic culture it is only logical that to manage a discussion, one thing must be processed at a time. Anything else is confusing. Not all cultures share this notion of process or confusion. Take for example a typical open marketplace in Latin America, where vendors attend to many people at once. People are engaged in multiple conversations and tasks at one time. Latinos have developed more sensitive polychronic listening and interaction skills. We have not. What appears as confusion to us, may not be at all confusing to others.

A Proposed Ideal Type of Mediation

The above discussion identified several important factors affecting the usefulness of mediation as it moves from one context to another. It is now possible to suggest, in preliminary fashion, what considerations would assist a mediator in deciding on a culturally appropriate model. In this paper I focused on Latin America as a more "traditional" setting. The suggestions here will relate to that context, although some of the ideas may well apply to other "cultures" in the broadest definition (e.g., the culture of ethnic groups, of social workers, of an inner city neighborhood, etc.).

Designing specific intervention strategies for a Latin context should involve several important procedures and considerations. First, the process followed for entering disputes should incorporate *personalismo*. Here the mediator emphasizes the relational over the structural elements of the process. Direct personal contact is pursued in the setting familiar to those involved as opposed to a "professional" anonymous approach. The Spanish word *la platica* best describes the nature of this approach.

Literally, *platicar* means to "talk" or "converse," but it carries with it a connotation of informal, open conversation. The mediator has less control of the process and the issues discussed, but the approach should feel more personable and less threatening to the parties. The mediator must also expect this will take more time and that the pace of self-disclosure and direct discussion of the important issues will occur only after other obligatory topics have been handled. S/he should encourage broad discussion of many aspects of the disputants' lives that may seem unrelated to the central problem. They are not. People who positively value group affiliation tend to think in terms of their social network. That is, they look at the whole, not the parts as the point of reference.

Second, the mediator must situate the conflict in the disputants' frame of reference, what I call "contextualization." The mediator must know how a person interprets the boundaries and context of the conflict. Contextualization is the exercise of "ethno-conflictology", the study of how people make sense of conflictive situations and appropriate "common-sense" methods of resolving them. As such, contextualization helps the mediator decide on an appropriate style and format of intervention. S/he must be sensitive to the parties' potentially varying preferences for formality, temporal organization, pace and sequencing in the different phases of the interaction, and to the context of their wider social networks. In other words, *la platica* and contextualization are preliminary steps that help the mediator assess what "range of options" of the various components are appropriate in the particular context s/he is working.

Conclusion

In summary, the most important assumptions affecting mediation include the following:

1. The North American model evolved in a modern, urban bureaucratic context. Mediation was increasingly identified as a *"formal"*

process with specialist roles. The North American model assumes that a "formalized structure" for discussing volatile issues provides both a sense of security and purpose for disputants. "Formalization" takes place through the interaction of language and setting, in other words, the social definition of time and space.

2. The North American model assumes that *direct communication* between conflicting parties is desirable for an acceptable outcome and is the mode of interaction preferred by the disputants. As such, much of the mediator monologue is used to establish the "rules of speaking" that will govern the session. Sociologically, this "facilitation" is the social control of direct communication. Formalizing the roles and process explicitly establishes this control.

3. The *temporal organization of the model is monochronic.* Mediation assumes that a task-oriented, linear, "one-thing-at-a-time" approach is the most ideal manner of resolving problems. As such, it tends to be more "analytical" than "relational," and assumes a directed, fast-paced style of communication and self-disclosure from the disputants.

4. As a structured, task-oriented process, the primary goal of mediation is "reaching agreement" on the issues. Disputants are expected to take responsibility for making decisions to resolve the issues. This assumes a criteria of *autonomy and individualism in decision-making,* rather than one of responsibility to a wider social network. Further, it tends to be pragmatic, concen-

trating more on resolving the issues than on reconciling the disputants or reestablishing wider community relations.

5. The mediator is presented as a *technical specialist. As* such his/her relationship to the disputants is defined as professional, and therefore somewhat anonymous and impersonal. A professional role relationship with the disputants is assumed preferable in resolving their dispute. A written agreement is preferred and the mediator is essentially "in and out" of their lives.

In conclusion, this paper should serve as a word of caution. We need to become more aware and sensitive to the fact that mediation in North America evolved in and adapted to a modern, mostly professional and bureaucratic society. Techniques and processes developed in this context are based on premises which may not be shared, nor appropriate in others. Our mistake is to assume that what is "logical" and works in one setting can be directly transferred to another.

I have endeavored to show the existence of a wide variety of possible options for accomplishing the basic tasks that mediation proposes. I have further suggested that it is incumbent on mediators to make the design of a particular intervention in other cultures problematic and to proceed with a spirit of "discovering" what feels comfortable and appropriate to the parties involved. This is a corrective step for avoiding cultural imperialism, even with something as well-intentioned as the management of conflict.

–John Paul Lederach

© MCS 1986, from *Conciliation Quarterly*, Vol. 5 No. 1 (excerpted from "Mediation in North America: An Examination of the Profession's Cultural Premises")

See chart on following page.

Continuum of Cultural Expectations

Stages of Mediation	Components	"Pure Formal"	"Pure Informal"
Entry	Setting	*1. Public/ Bureaucratic	Private/Interpersonal
	Expectations of Participants	*2. Professional/Anonymous Contact	Known/Friend/In Person
		*3. Restricted Access	Unrestricted Access
	Third Party & Disputants	#4. Facilitate Direct Communication	Surrogate for Direct Communication
		*5. Relationship to Issues	All Aspects of Life Involved
		*6. Autonomous Decision Maker	Groups Dependent Decision Maker
Introduction	Process/Structure	*7. Directive/Formalized	Nondirective/Assumed
	Rules of Talk	*8. Spoken/Overt	Assumed
	Priorities	*9. Tasks First	Relationship First
	Roles	*10. Formalized	Assumed
Story-Telling	Interaction	#11. Face-to-Face	Via Third Party
	Topic Sequencing	#12. I-Topics Early	I-Topics Later
	Speaker Sequencing	#13. Restricted/One-at-a-time	Unrestricted
	Purpose	*14. Analytical	Relational
Problem-Solving	Temporal Organization	#15. Monochronic	Polychronic
	Purpose	*16. Focus on Issues	Reconcile Relationship
	View of Conflict	*17. Issue Focus/Isolated from Social Network	Focus on Issues as Embedded in Social Network
Agreement	Form	*18. Written/Signed	Personal Word/ Relational
	Relationship to Third Party Following	*19. No Relationship	Responsible to Parties and for Agreement

* = Item fits Modern/Traditional Dichotomy
\# = Item suggested by cross-cultural literature.

–John Paul Lederach
© MCS 1986, from *Conciliation Quarterly*, Vol. 5 No. 3 (excerpted from "Mediation in North America: An Examination of the Profession's Cultural Premises")

Assessment in Intercultural Conflict Resolution

Before deciding on a process, or even deciding whether to engage in a conflict resolution exercise, it is important to conduct a thorough assessment. The assessment will give you information about the appropriateness of intervention, timing, identity of intervenors, appropriate parties, history of interaction between or among the parties, and many other factors that will be critical to:

- The decision to intervene or to decline to intervene
- Process design
- Timing and setting of intervention
- Make-up of an intervention team
- Who needs to be included as a party or a participant
- How it might be best to proceed, e.g., do you need to provide some training first in order to assist participants to have a productive negotiation?

Here are some elements to consider when making an assessment. These items should not be explored in a linear way as in a questionnaire, but woven into a discussion with potential parties and interested others about their needs and perceptions of the issues.

Issues

What is the nature in the issues of the conflict? Are there hidden issues that relate to the history between the parties or the history between the groups from which the parties come? Are the issues such that they suggest long, complex discussions, or are they fairly distinct? How divergent are the parties' opinions of the issues? What are the real conditions affecting the issues and how amenable are these conditions to change? What is the "cultural common sense" of the parties regarding what to do when such issues emerge?

Process

What kind of process fits with the "cultural common sense of the parties?"

Here you will want to assess the degree to which back-and-forth dialogue directly between parties is comfortable to the parties. Will the parties be comfortable meeting together? Is this a case where you simply need to gather some information, present options to the person requesting assistance, and connect them with resources? (Not all requests for service will merit a face-to-face meeting between one person in conflict with another). What do the parties want from the process—a decision, an apology, a chance to tell the other how they experienced the conflict, healing, an agreement, a chance to prove they were right, or something else? Given the parties' expressed desires and your information about the nature of the conflict, what kind of process makes sense?

Process Options Include
- arbitration by referral to a person trained in this process
- CARE (face to face Conflict Analysis and Resolution as Education)
- ombuds intervention (a one-step removed voice with some standing or authority who can try to effect an action that so far has not succeeded)
- referral to small claims court (where a legal remedy is clearly indicated by virtue of the nature of the case)
- conciliation (shuttle conflict resolution where the parties do not necessarily meet)
- involvement of elders and respected others in assisting with processing the conflict (either advising on process, convening process or engaging in the process)
- a local or traditional process that is acceptable to both parties
- referral to another agency whose resources are more suited to the kind of conflict described
- assessment and analysis (where a matter is complex and multiple parties are involved, it may be important to gather much more in-depth information before a process can be initiated)
- no process (it may be determined that the timing is wrong, that a key player will not play, or that in some other way the conditions for intervention are not ripe; it is better to take no action than to intervene without a clear sense of how intervention may meet the needs and objectives of the parties)

What setting would feel most comfortable for all of the parties?

If the setting that fits one party would feel awkward to the other, is there a way of including some elements of both in order to model collaborative problem solving? What is the level of formality each desires? What is most convenient for all concerned? How can you choose a setting and also be mindful of the power issues in the relationship? (You may not want to arrange a meeting between an individual and a representative of an institution at the institution's board room. If the individual is already feeling intimidated, this setting choice could only intensify the experience.)

What timing framework would feel comfortable to the parties?

In this discussion, be mindful of the parties' cultural common sense of what to do when faced with conflict. Some traditions involve long, open-ended discussions. Others are more structured and require considerable advance planning. Check on the urgency of dealing with the issues from all parties' perspectives. Watch that time is not used as a "power move," e.g., to pressure the other into something with which that person may feel uncomfortable.

Parties

- Who are the parties to the immediate conflict?
- What are the power dynamics between the parties?
- Who else may have input into a decision over the issues?
- Who should we avoid surprising?
- Who will be affected by any decision that is made?
- Who do the parties see as individuals or groups whose interests should be represented?
- How will representation be structured?
- What kind of communication currently exists among parties, and how will communication be maintained throughout the intervention?
- What would feel comfortable to the parties concerning inclusion of others not immediately involved?
- What languages do the parties speak?
- Is there a communication barrier?
- If a conflict resolution process is convened, how will effective communication be assured?
- What are the pressures or stresses on parties that may play a role in their behavior in conflict resolution sessions and also outside?
- Is there any history of physical altercation between the parties? If so, this is a red flag, and intervention should be done by those with extensive training and experience, if at all.
- What are their individual BATNAs (Best Alternative To a Negotiated Agreement) and WATNAs (Worst Alternative To a Negotiated Agreement)?
- Are all parties willing to come to the table?
- What do the parties' cultures tell them about . . .   . . . the nature of the conflict?
  . . . appropriate behavior when in conflict?
  . . . what is private and what is public?

Intervenors

- Who would be a "natural" as an intervenor?
- Who has already intervened and what has been their experience?
- What qualities are most needed in an intervenor in this situation?
- How important is confidentiality and does this indicate that an intervenor from outside the communities of the parties might be best received?
- Is there an intervenor with whom the parties would feel a high level of trust either for linguistic, cultural, professional, or other reasons?
- How would the value systems of potential parties fit with the value systems of the proposed intervenor?
- What personal qualities in an intervenor are most important?
- What affiliations of intervenors could be counterproductive or productive in the process?
- What professional or job affiliations might be helpful in the situation?
- What is the role of gender in this conflict and what does this mean for intervenor selection?
- What are the power dynamics in this conflict and what does that mean for intervenor selection?
- What is the likely duration of this conflict, and is the potential intervenor available for ongoing follow-up?
- How can a team of intervenors be structured so that it will be balanced and effective in taking all factors into account?

All of these questions will not be relevant in every conflict. Some of the questions you will need to ask will emerge from the context of specific situations. It would be helpful if you keep a list of those questions you find useful in assessment in addition to those listed here.

–Michelle LeBaron

© UVic Institute for Dispute Resolution 1994, from *Conflict Resolution and Analysis as Education*. Used by permission.

Beyond Prejudice Reduction

"What will the U.S. be like when whites are no longer the majority?" So *Time Magazine* postulated in its cover story of April 9, 1990. The writers point to the rapid demographic changes in this country and the imminent reality that, by the year 2056, the majority of this nation's population will be Asian, African American, Hispanic, Native American, and Pacific Islander.

The tone of the article strives to be objective, but underneath is a clear indication of anxiety, if not fear, of what this change will mean to the current majority culture of this nation. The authors frame their primary concern well: "History suggests that sustaining a truly multiracial society is difficult, or at least unusual."

I believe that how the conflict resolution field defines itself and its models, in preparing to respond to the realities of a multicultural society, is the most critical developmental task our field will encounter. The topic of working at conflict resolution in multicultural and multiracial contexts is being considered more frequently at conferences and other settings. It is my observation, however, that some serious reexamination of our objectives and methodological directions is in order. I'm particularly concerned with the current emphasis on techniques geared only to "prejudice reduction."

I acknowledge that, as a black woman, my perspective on this may be different. The popularity of the film "Driving Miss Daisy" provides a handy illustration of some of my concerns. "Driving Miss Daisy" is the story of an aging Jewish woman, no longer able to drive herself safely. Her son insists on hiring a black man, only a few years her junior, to be her chauffeur.

Miss Daisy is quite hostile to the idea and to her new driver at first. Over time, he is able to break down the walls of hostility enough to do the job which he was hired to do—that is, driving Miss Daisy.

At the end of the film is a rather touching scene in which Miss Daisy, now confined to a nursing home, is fed by her former employee. There is a sense in which she has discovered something of his humanity. Indeed, the film depicts a very real level of "prejudice reduction," but also underscores my fear. As much as the film leaves one with a sense of the warmth that has come to be present between them over the years, it is still Hoke (not *Mr.* Anybody) who serves *Miss* Daisy. While the friendliness is apparent, their social and economic roles are still very much intact.

The aims of "prejudice reduction," "bias awareness," "cultural sensitivity," and other such processes are helpful. But these are incomplete approaches—or perhaps simply entry points—to the task of resolving conflict between persons of different races and cultures in this society. The flaw that is inherent in these methods is that they are limited to the adjustment of individual attitudes, and do not give consideration to the fundamental realities of *power*. Their danger lies in the possibility of enabling people to "feel good" about one another, while leaving undisturbed the attendant social realities that may underlie the conflict.

My fear is that the field of "multicultural conflict resolution" could unwittingly be seduced into becoming one more means of social control that attempts to neutralize the need to strive for justice. As I look at who is working in this area, I find that Roberto Chené makes a helpful contribution to this discussion. Chené, who directs the Southwest Center for Cross-Cultural Relationships, in Albuquerque, conducts workshops which consider the role of dominant/subordinate relationships in conflict in an explicit way.

In this society, there is a "dominant culture" that by implication relegates all other cultures to a "subordinate" status. Whether intentional or not, the dominant culture has the power to set the standards, determine norms, and, in effect, define reality. Using this analysis, one can easily see the linkages between a culture that is able, through domination, to define parameters, and the concomitant realities of racism, sexism, classism, ageism, heterosexism, etc.

The prevalence of racism and other "isms" cannot be routed by the adjustment of individual attitudes alone. They are present in the very fabric of the society and become systemized in institutions, dominant mythology, and law. I would press us, therefore, to examine more closely one of the fundamental tenets of conflict resolution through mediation. I remember a statement I read about a decade ago: "If one is only to be non-discriminatory, one ends up being racist and sexist." I would amend that statement to read, "If one is only neutral, one ends up enforcing dominant reality (and being racist, etc.)."

In other words, I would suggest that there is a "myth of neutrality." Just as modern biblical scholarship has come to understand that it is not possible to read the Bible from a neutral posture, neither is it possible to enter the realm of conflict and ignore the way in which race, gender, class, cultural background and history give both subtle and explicit definition to the exercise of power.

At the recent Southwest Conference on Peacemaking and Dispute Resolution, the theme was "Multicultural Perspectives/Critical Issues in the Field." In that context, John Paul Lederach urged North American mediators critically to assess "What are we up to?" I would reply that the appropriate role of mediator is perhaps not that of "neutral third party," but rather that of "advocate for equality." It is "impartiality"—which Webster's defines as treating or affecting all equally—that will give integrity to the process, and not indifference towards issues of power or justice.

I believe four things are required, if we are to be advocates of equality and seek just methods of effective multicultural conflict resolution.

1. **Critical self-understanding:** Effective trainers or mediators in multicultural and multiracial conflict settings must understand the dynamics at work in their own assumptions and attitudes. They have to be willing to understand their own cultural perspectives and social situations, and the strengths or limitations of their openness to others.

2. **Willingness to allow persons to define their own realities:** The primary ingredient here is the ability to truly "listen." Listening, in this respect, is not simply a "tool" to enable another person to "feel heard;" it must include opening ourselves to the possibility of learning and being changed, as well.

One of the negative effects of the dominant/subordinate relationship is that it minimizes the ability of the one in the dominant position to hear and take seriously the perceptions and differing experience of the one in the subordinate position. The dominant party has the ability to "define reality" from his or her perspective, and to use that as the standard by which to measure and judge the claims of the subordinate party. While it is nearly impossible to avoid taking information and organizing it according to our own categories, at least a different consciousness might first ask the questions: "How can I be present in a way that most gives honor or respect to the values that this person or culture holds?" Rather than, "What can I do to be successful?" or "How can I get *my* ideas across?"

3. **Social analysis and historical perspective:** How do people's personal and social history give shape to their access to and perceptions of power? Can this information help me to understand another's distrust or wariness of a given situation? For instance, it may be nearly impossible for a census taker to get information on the number of people living illegally in one dwelling by simply asserting that the government-solicited information is confidential.

4. **Development of appropriate methods:** We must analyze the cultural premises inherent in the professional conflict resolution models developed in the U.S. While such methods may be perceived as "objective" by members of the dominant culture, they are inherently biased against people who function according to other cultural realities.

The usual expectation of the dominant culture is that the "other" person must change in order to "fit" or "blend in." Instead, the mediator must make every effort to equalize the footing, by learning the processes and requirements necessary to make the person from the non-dominant culture feel comfortable and confident enough to work toward appropriate resolution of conflict. This should be deliberate, and both parties should be made aware of it. A vital part of acknowledging the humanity of both parties is to integrate their culture and heritage, as well.

These elements suggest the development of a process or approach which I call "transformational." It assumes some degree of conflict between cultures, and invites people to examine the dynamics of a conflict not only on an individual level but also within the social dimensions that are implicit: power, class, race, sex, history, as well as culture and tradition. The goal is to be as self-conscious in seeking to understand the total contexts of people, as we now are in seeking to understand the "issues."

I don't deny that we need the kinds of work now going on under names such as "prejudice reduction" and conventional mediation models. I personally want to keep the dialogue open with those practitioners. But we must also be open to the ongoing need to critique these and other models currently promoted in the field. While it is possible for trainers and mediators to critique their own preferred models, the field itself should also expand to include new trainers and mediators who reflect more fully the multicultural and multiracial dimensions of society.

In saying this, I want to caution against an urge to "colorize" the field and our models. This is not what I mean. As Roberto Chené stresses, simply having a mix of people is not enough. What is needed is people who are willing, from their own diverse cultural, social, and historical perspectives, to engage the field in the tough questions which lie ahead.

–Dale Susan Edmonds
© MCS 1990, from *Conciliation Quarterly*, Vol. 9 No. 2

Reflections on the Basics of Intercultural Leadership

As a teacher and trainer in the practice of intercultural leadership, I have come to understand over the years that leadership initiatives or models that are not explicitly intercultural are seriously limited. They do not fully embrace the challenge of living in a society that is culturally diverse and has only recently begun to seriously acknowledge that fact. To lead social change in the new millennium, we are in desperate need of leadership models that are inherently intercultural in their understanding and boldly creative in their implementation. Intercultural leadership is rooted in the profound awareness that human reality is culturally diverse. We are in it and affected by it whether we choose to be or not. Racial, ethnic, gender, religious, sexual preference, and other likely unlimited diverse characteristics constitute the world and universe in which we live.

A tremendous amount of work has been and is being done in the area of diversity. I think, however, that there is much that is yet to be attempted. I consider this a new field of study and practice.

New Curriculum for Society

To deepen our understanding and focus on leadership, we have to acknowledge that our society has institutionalized chronic conflict among people who are different. The conflict is so pervasive and the need to address it so urgent, that I think leadership must be intercultural. To keep society focused on the urgent need to deepen our problem-solving skills, we do not have time for leadership that is not intercultural. To live in diversity we have to move up the learning curve as quickly as possible—or we may be outstripped by the interracial, interethnic, inter-difference conflicts that have been institutionalized in social policy as well as at the personal level.

I find that organizational leaders and their staffs are often poorly prepared to address these institutionalized, intercultural conflicts, and lack the knowledge, ability, and skills to approach the problem with understanding and leadership. We continue to treat the issue of intercultural differences, by and large, as an "add on" or an afterthought, often spurred by some federal or legal constraint, or by a conflict that reminds us, "Oh yes, diversity."

We need a model of problem solving that begins with the premise that reconciling differences is the problem to be solved and we "add on" the rest as energy and resources allow. The extent, depth, and the violent outcome of the problem require a shift in our approach as quickly as possible. We need to reframe our problem-solving paradigm so that it is exactly the opposite of the current approach—the curriculum for our society, not an addition to it.

I believe each of us is immersed in the relationship dynamics of difference and that when we act as if we are not, the result is some degree of conflict. If the conflict is creative and we are open, we learn from the difference. If the conflict is raw and hurtful, we retreat to avoidance of difference. The resultant polarization fuels the hopelessness that so many people feel today about ever bridging our differences, whatever they may be. We attempt to overcome the hopelessness by intensifying the rhetoric of change, reasserting our commitment to a new order, or placing our hopes once again in our youth. All this while we fail to acknowledge the reality that youth are excluded from the center of our adult communities. The hopelessness needs to be overcome by accessing hope in the context of viable and trusting recreated intercultural relationships. This includes the recreation of adult-youth relationships.

Beyond Celebration of Differences

So how do we define this problem, and where do we need to start to begin to solve it in the new millennium? Do we have the leadership capacity to take it on?

To restate, we have only one problem: Our society and the world have historically used dominance and the exercise of power and privilege as the primary strategy for reconciling differences. We are all aware of slavery, the multiple colonizations of the U.S. Southwest, the chronic conflicts in Ireland and the Middle East, the effect of the Americanization process on people of color, to name a few. The exercise of power and privilege is a totally flawed methodology, does not of course really reconcile anything, and sets in motion conditions for endless conflict. This approach to reconciling differences between human beings is dysfunctional, and, in my view, antithetical to the mutually trusting nature of healthy human relationships. Its inherently violent nature has not prevented it from continuing to be the primary strategy for working out differences—however benign it appears at times, however creative the rhetoric used to design new forms of dominance. As one immersed in the field of intercultural leadership, diversity, and multiculturalism, I have learned that there are unlimited levels of co-optation, including the use of words like diversity, multiculturalism, and intercultural leadership, which can create the illusion that we are actually addressing the issue of dominance. A common form of denial is to equate diversity with celebration or the model that asserts that we all have a culture, as if cultural assimilation is not, in practice, a cover for cultural dominance. No, when we have institutionalized racism and sexism, celebration will not make a dent. We have a conflict that needs to be unraveled and healed.

The perspective I am articulating can feel big and, to some people, quite hopeless. I have no illusions that the world is going to come around on this issue anytime soon. But for the sake of realistic problem-solving and analysis, let us at least acknowledge that dominance is at the heart of the problems we are trying to solve.

Simply put, we are not in conflict because of our racial, ethnic, gender, religious, linguistic, and other differences. Conflicts related to those differences are real but minor. We are in conflict because these differences are structured into relationships based on dominance. Dominance is the root of the conflict, not the differences. The differences between us could be worked out rather easily without the dominance-subordination structure and conditioning in which they are imbedded.

Dominant and Subordinate Relationships

I have learned from my experience that there are some very predictable behaviors related to dominant/subordinate patterns. If, for example, one understands the legacy of dominance in any relationship and the dynamics of white privilege, in particular, one knows that conflict is inherent in any diverse situation. In interracial situations, for example, because of the nature of exclusion, people of color come to a situation expecting some conflict and discomfort in the process of building trust. White people come to the situation expecting harmony and are shocked or offended if conflict

and discomfort arises. Conflict seems to be avoided if people of color simply remain polite and do not speak from their reality or identity. In other words, diversity is often popular until the moment the actual differences become explicit. As people of color, we have learned to choose how much conflict or discomfort we want to elicit or have the energy to manage. When the subordinated side pushes for inclusion, the included side, in knee-jerk fashion, quickly falls into defensive patterns that cause dominants to feel that whites are the real victims.

In such interracial situations, as a rule, rather than admit to discomfort, whites fall into silence or pretense. People of color pick this up, and either their anger or their frustration arises. In any case, it does not take much for the mutual discomfort level to escalate; at that moment, we are already in conflict. People of color have learned to assess if whites are sophisticated enough to handle the tension without reverting to silence or victim behavior. Beyond the harmony expectation, whites also are wondering if they are going to be attacked, or if anger from people of color will overtake the agenda. The common outcome of these dynamics is mutual flight. To some degree, people of color stay and whites leave, or whites stay and people of color do not return to the next meeting, leaving whites to wonder why their recruitment efforts are not working.

Another scenario is to get a mediator or intercultural facilitator and work it out. The best outcome occurs when the conflict becomes transformed into knowledge and everyone's capacity to relate interracially is enhanced. Too often, however, the encounter feels too hurtful to participants, and they desperately hang in until the project or whatever brought them together is over, then swear never to come back. What is needed at this point, of course, is healing and perspective as well as understanding. We meant so well and tried so hard. What happened?

Time Oppression

In a speeded-up, over-stressed society, healing and understanding take time that most people feel they do not have. What I personally think of as "time oppression," in combination with lack of inter-difference relationship capacity and leadership, has us locked into waves of incredible efforts to change accompanied by backsliding into various degrees of polarization. When you add time pressure and the conditioned reaction to it, the scenario I describe remains unresolved.

The dominance implications are that white participants will leave wondering why their world should be subject to be shaken and lamenting how the current emphasis on diversity is the real cause of the conflict. (This mindset did not exist prior to the civil rights movement.) In the southwestern United States, where I am from, people of color will leave convinced that it is impossible ever to bridge the generations of violence and exclusion that started with Columbus. For variations on these dynamics I could have just as easily drawn on youth-adult, women-men, gay-straight, or any other configuration. The point I want to make is that these dynamics are related to any dominant-subordinate structure. It's a "set up" for conflict.

Intercultural leaders understand intimately the institutional and personal dynamics of exclusion and oppression, understand intimately their socially assigned role as victim or as one who perpet-uates exclusionary behavior, and have chosen to liberate themselves from that imposed assignment. They also choose to help lead the way out of the mess we are in and have the capacity to articulate a vision that clarifies the problem we are trying to solve. To foster healing, it is imperative that we help people separate the institutionalized oppression from the variety that operates interpersonally. Intercultural leaders describe a path that we might take while, with cultivated self-awareness, acknowledging how they are taking responsibility for their own growth. Denial or pretense is out of place in intercultural leadership.

Our challenge as intercultural leaders is to get clear on how we are all affected by the umbrella of dominance so that, in the next millennium, we can facilitate the creation of mutually trusting relationships and institutions. If we hope to move to the height of what celebrating diversity should really be about, the journey is going to have to be intentionally and specifically led by people who wish to let the journey transform them.

–Roberto Chené
© Roberto Chené 2000, from *Cutting Edge Leadership 2000* (College Park, MD: James MacGregor Burns Academy of Leadership)

Theories of Gender, Conflict and Peacebuilding

There are several theories related to the development of differences between the sexes. One theory asserts that there are major biological and psychological differences between men and women. Another asserts that differences between men and women result from cultural socialization. The extremes of these two theories are outlined below, particularly as they relate to conflict, violence and peacebuilding.

While researchers have examined these theories, there is little that can be said to be "true" for all women and men. Beliefs about the roles and characteristics of men and women vary across cultures. The following survey is designed to raise the issues and beliefs often shared in cross-cultural conversations on these topics, not to provide answers or facts.

Theory: Differences Between Men and Women Are Biological

Basic Beliefs

Biological and psychological differences exist between males and females that affect their approaches to conflict and peacebuilding.

Biological Fact	Conclusion
Females can bear children.	Females care more about children, relationships and life than do men.
Males cannot bear children.	Males are less concerned about children and life-giving.
Females experience the patterns of the menstrual cycle.	Females are closer to the rhythms of nature and more in touch with the environment.
Males tend to be physically larger and stronger.	Males are better able to assert their power through physical force than women are.

Some Implications

- Because of their physical strength, men are more likely to depend on the use of force to solve problems.
- Many women have needed to develop alternatives to violence (nonviolent action, negotiation and peace-building) because of their relative lack of physical strength compared to men.
- Women are naturally more inclined to peacebuilding than men.
- Since men are more prone to violent conflict and war, women are often seen as more neutral than men in conflicts. Women's neutrality may increase their ability to build peace.
- As primary caretakers of children, women may be seen as more legitimate conflict activists, since a mother's concern for her children is seen to be natural. As a result, mothers may not be targeted with as much violent repression as other activists for raising conflict issues that concern their children.
- Women's identities as mothers, sisters and daughters of men who fight and/or die in war may contribute to their ability to find common ground with women from different sides of conflict.

Theory: Differences Between Men and Women Are Sociological

Basic Beliefs

- "Gender" does not necessarily refer to biological sex, but to culturally learned characteristics. A person's gender may or may not be the same as their biological sex.
- Boys are socialized to have "masculine" gender characteristics; girls are socialized to have "feminine" characteristics.
- Boys who have "feminine" characteristics and girls who have "masculine" characteristics are often punished or sanctioned by their community.
- Gender roles are constantly produced and reinforced by society.
- Men and women may learn and practice different ways of communicating, thinking and relating to other people if they are socialized in distinct genders cultures.

- Examples of stereotypical gender characteristics in North American society:

Masculine	Feminine
Aggressive	Passive
Competitive	Cooperative
Rational	Irrational/Emotional
Express power through violence	Express power through nonviolent communication and relationships
Independent	Dependent/Interdependent
Strong/Steady	Weak/Compassionate
Leaders	Submissive followers
Income earners/Family providers	Child rearers/Housekeepers

Some Implications

- Men and women may come into conflict with each other because of the different ways they communicate, learn and relate to others that develop from their distinct gender cultures.
- Men and women may have different approaches to dealing with conflict based on their "gender cultures."
- In many cultures, masculinity is defined in part by the use of violence; males are encouraged to use violence because it makes them "men."
- Women are discouraged from using violence because it decreases their femininity.
- Because they have grown up learning feminine skills and characteristics, such as empathy, compassion and communication, women may more easily develop related peacebuilding skills.
- Since women are socialized to find power through relationships *with* others rather than through power *over* others, they may be less threatening to others and less likely to use violence to solve problems.

Superiority and Power

No matter what theory one chooses to explain the origins of differences between the sexes, North American culture places greater value on men and "male" characteristics (assertiveness, independence, competitiveness, rationality, etc.). This acceptance of male superiority leads to the construction of social structures that benefit men and discriminate against women. Men and women may come into conflict with each other because of the unequal access they have to power structures. Men are the leaders in most organizations, companies and nations; men own most of the world's wealth and are paid more on average for their work than women. These basic power imbalances may lead to conflict between men and women in all areas of life.

This belief in the superiority of men and masculine characteristics leads to the prevalence of violence against women. In many cultures, 40 to 60 percent of women are victims of rape, domestic abuse and/or incest at least once in their lives. Public violence, such as crime and war, appears to be connected with incidents of domestic violence against women. The rape of women is now a frequent military strategy to humiliate and colonize the enemy. Militaries cultivate and war validates masculinity. Military language is "gendered." It connects killing and winning to masculinity, and losing and/or nonviolence/negotiation to a loss of masculinity or to being feminine.

Questions for Discussion

1. Which approach, biological or sociological, makes most sense to you? Why?
2. If gender differences are culturally constructed, are gender roles "sacred" or open to challenge from those who see the roles as oppressive?
3. If gender differences are based on biology, is violence to be expected as the normative response men have towards conflict?
4. Does concentrating on women's strengths in peacebuilding perpetuate traditional sex role stereotypes?
5. What can peacebuilders do about the connection between masculinity and violence?
6. What can they do about the widespread plague of violence against women?
7. What role can peacebuilders play in breaking down the acceptance of male superiority and the resulting social structures?

–Lisa Schirch
© MCS 2000

Gender, Race and Power

When I am asked to give a talk or workshop, after finding out the details of time, place and subject matter, I always ask, Who are the women who will be involved? I do this not because I am concerned about their credentials, but because I am concerned that there be women represented fully in whatever I do. Similarly I ask who are the people of color participating on the panel, presenting at the conference, etc. In a sense it is a polite way to inquire if people of color and white women will be included, and not just at token levels. When I was asked to write this article I asked the same question about this periodical. The response I received was that, "Yes we are concerned about that too, and we are working on it." Since I have heard this response before, I asked about how they are working on it and to what results are they holding themselves accountable.

After these questions my next question is often, What kind of follow-up are you doing? Is this a limited focus on gender issues or racism (or any other issue) that will then be discontinued or is gender or race going to be included as part of the core content of this organization from now on? How? And how are women and people of color going to participate and take leadership in that process?

With these questions, even before I speak or write anything for this particular project, I have raised issues of power and participation, gender and race, tokenism and change. It is never inappropriate to ask these questions and to expect serious and considered responses.

We live in a society where people are divided into groups with more power and groups with less power as listed below.

Powerful	Less Powerful
adult	youth
men	women
white	people of color
rich	poor
boss	worker
adult	elder
heterosexual	lesbian, gay and bisexual
people without disabilities	people with disabilities
Gentile	Jew
Christian	Moslem, Buddhist, Jew, atheist
"normal"	"fat"
teacher	student
born in U.S.	recent immigrant
formally educated	not formally educated

Groups with less power are vulnerable to violence from people in groups with more power. Children are vulnerable to physical, sexual and emotional abuse from adults. Women are vulnerable to all of that as well as economic discrimination, sexual harassment, inadequate childcare and health care. People of color are vulnerable to physical, sexual and emotional abuse as well as job and housing discrimination, police brutality, etc. People with more power are always working to make white, male, well off, heterosexual, physically abled, Christian, etc. the norm, the center, and to push everyone else to the margins.

Locate yourself in the chart above. You will probably notice that you are on both sides of the chart, in more powerful groups and less powerful groups, vulnerable to violence at times and privileged at times. That means that we know what it's like to be less powerful and can build alliances with other people in less powerful groups to challenge the status quo. We also know what it's like to have the privilege of being in a powerful group and can use our resources to be allies to people in less powerful groups. For example, as a white male worker I can be working for economic justice for all workers, while at the same time be an ally to women and youth and people of color. We are not responsible for or guilty for where we are in the chart. We are responsible for what we do about it.

To keep my priorities clear and to challenge this system of power, inequality and violence I need to be constantly asking the questions, *Who has the power? Who makes the decisions? Who has the resources? Who is vulnerable to violence?*

And then I must ask the more specific questions, *Where are the women? Where are the people of color? Where are the poor and working class? Where are the lesbians, gays and bisexuals?*

This system of power and violence is gender based. It is based on a male model of power as power over others—control. We teach boys to be tough, aggressive, in control, not to show feelings, not to cry and never to ask for help. What are boys and men supposed to do with their feelings, with the pain, hurt, sadness, excitement, and frustrations of life? We train them to funnel the feelings into anger and turn the anger into violence. We teach them to find someone with less power, more vulnerable than they are and pass on the abuse. The target could be anyone—another man, a woman, a younger person, a member of a group with less power. This is how the control and exploitation of people based on gender, race, class, etc., operates, by training men to enforce the system through the use of violence.

And women's role provides the model for being exploited. Take it, be passive, be dependent, don't challenge men, look good, be available, take care of things, don't complain. This role is enforced by rape, incest, domestic violence and street harassment. If women fight back or protest, men blame women for "provoking" them.

You and I can challenge this system of structural inequality and injustice by fighting back, building alliances and using those important questions to keep us clear about our goals—safety, the redistribution of power, and the full and equal participation by everyone, at all levels, at all times.

You may have noticed that I have not talked about tolerance, or prejudice, or white people unlearning racism, or men sharing the chores. Those things are important, but the issue is injustice, and the question is about power, not prejudice. We need to be less concerned about personal attitudes and more concerned about social change.

Gender and race are not just "interesting" issues. They are the core of our lives together; part of the everyday reality that binds and separates us, that produces injustice and violence. How are you going to take these issues into your family, school, workplace and community relationships? Are you going to keep asking those questions even when it is awkward, or embarrassing, or scary or dangerous? These are simple questions and I want to ask them of you.

Where is the power? Where are the people of color? Where are the women? What are we going to do about it?

–Paul Kivel
© Paul Kivel 1994, from *Conciliation Quarterly*, Vol. 13 No. 1/2. Used by permission.

Anger and *The Color of Fear*

Several years ago now, I saw a video that was unforgettable. In his own words, filmmaker Lee Mun Wah's *The Color of Fear* offers a fascinating exploration of the transformative forces that can be unleashed when "people of all cultures come together to speak about their fears and prejudices in a peaceful, confrontive and intimate way." The film powerfully explores themes related to power, culture, racism and the place of anger in conflict transformation and change-making.

This film features unscripted dialogue between eight men of African, Asian, European, Latin American and Native American origins who come together for three days of intense interaction. Through many hours of honest encounters, they eventually come, one by one, to reveal the ways in which racism has scarred each of their lives. They also appear to develop the type of deep bond and trust for one another that can only come through honest dialogue.

This does not happen easily or painlessly. Crying, pleading and shouting are at least as much a part of the dialogue as is the relatively calm exchange of perspectives more commonly associated with attempts to make peace. Throughout much of the video, David, a white man, consistently minimizes the racism the men of color in the room had experienced. Despite others' polite attempts to name this tendency, David appears completely impenetrable. He frequently proffers advice about how other cultural groups can "improve themselves" and "make their own way."

After yet another condescending remark along these lines from David, Victor finally reaches a breaking point. An African American man, Victor describes his intense anger and frustration at continually being told that he can "come over" and be like the "white man." He shouts with rage at the injustices he and his people have experienced. During this gripping segment, the physiological symptoms associated with anger become clearly visible and audible with Victor. The veins stand out on his temple, his voice becomes high pitched and very loud, his words become coarse, though never abusive, and his breathing very heavy.

In the silence thick with tension which follows, David is for the first time left speechless. While it is impossible to know exactly what David is thinking or feeling, it seems safe to assume that he is feeling at least a little shocked and overwhelmed. Nevertheless, while Victor's outburst does not lead to a miraculous conversion on the part of David, it later becomes apparent that it marks something of a positive turning point for him. Eventually, he comes not only to acknowledge that racism exists but confesses that he himself has been deeply wounded by it.

So what do we, as conflict transformation practitioners, have to learn about anger from the experience of the brave men who volunteered to participate in Mun Wah's project? From his demeanor and facilitation of the sessions, it seems apparent that Mun Wah strongly believes in the role of confrontation in addressing deeply rooted conflict. Far from quickly intervening to "defuse" Victor's anger, he let him go on to a point I believe many in the field of conflict resolution would consider inappropriate. Mun Wah chose to remain silent during the height of Victor's rage and to allow all, perhaps especially David, to sit in the discomfort of that anger. In turn, it was only in this discomfort that David's wall of denial seemed to finally be penetrated, allowing the first light of understanding to begin to creep in.

Frequently criticized by social activists for being too quick to try to neatly package the pain associated with systemic conflict, practitioners in the field of conflict transformation might do well to likewise move cautiously in our response to anger. Had Mun Wah intervened too quickly, the power of the exchange would have been neutralized and ultimately the transformational opportunity between Victor and David would have been suppressed, if not lost. A critical dimension of the exchange's positive function seemed to reside in the fact that the person in the socially low-power position (Victor) was expressing anger toward the person in the socially high-power position (David). Had David been shouting at Victor it is much more likely that the exchange would have been merely abusive, with the inequitable power structures simply reinforced.

In the final analysis, however, the film demonstrates clearly that when people gather in a safe setting to address deep-seated conflict, the expression of anger can sometimes act as a catalyst for breaking down barriers. It can move people to value and share their experiences of pain while motivating others to finally begin listening and recognizing the need for personal and corporate change.

–David Dyck
® The Network: Interaction for Conflict Resolution 1996, from *Interaction*. Used by permission.

Conflict and Cultural Identities

I remember one of the first conflict resolution workshops I attended when I began this work 15 years ago. The facilitator drew a pyramid divided into sections by a series of horizontal lines. Each section identified different types of conflict issues—things people fight about—with "facts" at the top followed by "methods" and "goals." With the issues arranged top-to-bottom from the simplest to the most difficult types to resolve, the section at the base of the triangle identified as non-negotiable such issues as "values," "security" and "identity."

At the time, that made a lot of sense and helped me as a new mediator. I learned to listen carefully for the way people in conflict often frame matters as worse than they really are, and to reframe many of those same issues (when at all possible) as more manageable.

It also helped me to understand that core principles and values, slowly developed over the course of a lifetime and even more slowly changed, were to be downplayed when at odds with one another and emphasized when held in common. However, my experience over the last couple of years has left me wondering if *any* issue can be said to be entirely non-negotiable as the diagram (and conflict resolution theory) suggests.

Why Identity?

Recent international, regional, community—even denominational—conflicts have shown the increasing importance of identity in a world where individuals and groups struggle for recognition. Cultural, racial, religious or gender differences are often a key factor in fueling hatred and, at times, violence. Prejudice and racism often ignite conflict where other factors (such as economic disparity) may already exist in an unjust but otherwise "tolerated" situation.

Identity conflict, says conflict resolution theorist and practitioner Jay Rothman, arises from the heart and is therefore "about who we really are and what we care about most deeply."[1] For this reason, asserts Miroslav Volf—a theologian concerned with identity, conflict and reconciliation—"it might not be too much to claim that the future of our world will depend on how we deal with cultural identity and difference."[2] The most difficult and challenging conflicts testify to its importance. Identity matters.

Changing Views of Culture & Identity

In the mid-1980s, culture (an important part of human identity) gained a lot of attention in the field of conflict resolution. As in other fields, our understanding of culture has changed over time (see chart). Early on, culture was largely viewed as a catalog of rules and practices which determined interaction among diplomats and business negotiators (Column 1). We learned, for instance, appropriate cultural greeting rituals and the importance of attitudes toward time and disagreeing openly (or not). And, we were told in stereotypical fashion, *all* Japanese or *all* Mexicans follow the same customs in *all* situations, including conflict and negotiations.

As the field of conflict resolution began to take culture more seriously, it was increasingly recognized as a complex variable rich in symbolic meaning, capable of affecting both conflict processes and outcomes (Column 2). As something which shaped human behavior from one setting to the next, both theorists and practitioners focused on overcoming culture-based *differences* between disputants.

When I first began my research in Labrador in 1995, I was interested in learning how cultural differences between Aboriginal groups and non-Aboriginal groups there made conflicts and their transformation more

Culture, Identity and Conflict Resolution Theory

← Descriptive	Symbolic	Constructed →
Culture as a static catalog of rules and practices (focuses on the "content" of culture).	Culture as structure (focuses on how culture shapes behavior).	Culture as socially produced and transformed (focuses on how culture emerges and is put to use).
Culture expressed in forms of human behavior.	Culture provides a blueprint for human thought and action.	
Homogeneous.	Culture → Human action	Human → Culture action

Implications for Conflict Resolution

Follow etiquette, customs. May or may not impact process below the surface.	Treated as a variable capable of affecting conflict processes and substantive outcomes.	Conflict (and conflict behavior) shapes and reshapes culture (and cultural identities).
Knowledge of culture determines diplomatic, negotiation protocol.	Overcoming cultural *differences* as obstacles to settlement.	Focus on processes capable of transforming conflict behavior (and sense of self).

complex. Two years later, as a potential mediator, I sought to learn as much as possible about the cultural groups and their differences so I could become a more effective third party.

However, once I began talking to people, I soon saw a different "directionality" in the culture-conflict relationship that I had not considered before. Culture was not only affecting conflict; conflicts also seemed to be having an impact on the cultures and cultural identities of people in Labrador (Column 3).

Negotiating Identities?

In Labrador, persons taking the "wrong" position on an issue could be accused of not being a "real" Indian or a "real" Labradorian. Others either minimized or promoted certain cultural characteristics (e.g., ancestry) and practices (e.g., language) in order to gain advantage over others. For example, a person making a racist comment about Inuit one day to gain leverage in a dispute might be seen obtaining a benefit as a member of the Inuit Association the next.

People talked to me about the ways their sense of self had changed over the years, often as the result of conflict. They spoke of how their lives might be changed as a result of present conflicts or future decisions about them. I saw how the outcome of one conflict clearly influenced the ways in which individuals and groups chose to deal with the next conflict. And, over a longer period of time, I could see how this changing conflict behavior was beginning to transform cultural practices, understandings and even the groups themselves.

I began to wonder: If cultures and identities changed as the result of past processes (such as colonization), could they also be changed through present conflict transformation processes (protest, negotiation)? At the root of this question was another I had learned not to ask before: Are cultures and identities negotiable? What I observed and experienced suggests they could be.

Identity and Land

At the heart of my observations is the issue of land, a key aspect of cultural identity and an important issue in identity-based conflicts around the world, from the Mideast to Europe to the Americas. For Palestinians and Israelis, Native Americans and other indigenous peoples, cultural identity is not merely shaped by a person's relationship to the land but equated with the land. Contrary to what conflict resolution theory tells us, land does not simply *satisfy* individual and group identity needs: land *is* identity. People for whom this is true are profoundly aware of the ways that land issues impact their sense of self.

For example, the Labrador Innu are trying to negotiate a deal over a proposed nickel mine on their land. Dependent on the caribou and other wildlife freely roaming the snow-covered land eight months of the year, the Innu are concerned about the potential impacts of such a huge development project on their traditional hunting and fishing activities, which have been a central part of their culture and identity for thousands of years. As they experience conflict and negotiate over these issues, the main question they are asking is not "What will we get?" but "Who will we become?" Underneath that lies a more ominous question emerging from an awareness of genocide elsewhere: "*Will* we be?"

To complicate matters, as part of ongoing treaty negotiations, the Innu are attempting to settle the amount of land which they will ultimately control. Many Innu believe that accepting anything less than their full land claim is a recipe for cultural extinction. Inseparable from the land being discussed, Innu cultural identity is literally "brought to the table" for negotiation. What makes resolving this conflict even more difficult is the fact that in Labrador the land is also a major part of Inuit, Métis and Settler identity.

Practice Meets (and Challenges) Theory

It is widely accepted in the field of conflict resolution that identity-based conflicts are prone to escalation, resistant to resolution and altogether non-negotiable. As we have seen in Kosovo, Northern Ireland and elsewhere, the first two characteristics are no doubt true. But what about the third claim of non-negotiability?

Take a typical dispute between neighbors. If one insists on building a fence to keep the other's dog out of her yard, our knowledge of classic positions and interests tells us that perhaps a leash will work just as well for meeting everyone's needs. The need for security can be met without any impact on her identity as a resident of the neighborhood. However, if an imposed or negotiated agreement includes building a fence, the resulting change in communication patterns, borrowing habits and other aspects of her relationship with her neighbors would almost certainly and immediately impact her image and actions as a "neighbor."

"Yes," conventional conflict resolution theorists might concede, "as land is negotiated, individual and group identities are affected, albeit indirectly. But land merely *satisifies* the basic human need for identity. It is a means for providing identity, not identity itself. And while land may be negotiable, identity is not."

In some instances it may be true that one thing will "satisfy" an identity need just as much as something else, especially when both contribute equally to our overall sense of self. But identities are not the same as interests. Certain characteristics (such as gender) and practices are central to who we are. We might ask, for example, what exactly is required for a farmer to maintain his or her identity as a farmer. Is a farmer still a farmer without a tractor? Crops? Land? Conversely, merely having such things does not make one a "farmer."

Since the boundaries of our self are constantly shifting (this process is especially intense for some rapidly changing cultural groups, immigrants, refugees and people experiencing war), identifying what is at the core of our identities can be difficult. And since the make-up of our identities is a complex mixture of many different factors, it can be difficult to know how a change in one will affect the whole of our self. Whether something makes an impact on our identity "directly" or "indirectly" can be beside the point.

Perhaps it would help to think of so-called "non-negotiable" issues as being more like positions than interests. This is especially true when an identity need is met primarily (or, in some cases, only) with one "satisfier" (that is, "only *this* land will allow us to be who we are"). As with classic positions, interveners can attempt the difficult task of searching for alternatives to meet an identity need, while remembering that such needs are resistant to resolution, prone to escalation when threatened, and potentially transformed by conflict *and our remedies to it*, including negotiation.

Returning again to Labrador, I participated in one First Nation's negotiations with federal and provincial governments. I observed and interacted with Aboriginal leaders who were directly negotiating aspects of their cultural identity—issues related to land, language and cultural practices. For those groups, the theoretical distinction between a "need" such as identity and a "satisfier" would simply not make sense. How useful then is such a distinction in practice?

Implications for Transformation

This complex foray into the world of conflict resolution theory must now be brought back a bit closer to the ground. I will suggest some of the practical implications for all of this in a more general way.

As I noted above, how we view culture and identity influences the consideration we give them as factors in conflict situations. If we think of cultures and identities as unchanging, then we will almost certainly not think of them as negotiable. Neither will we view them as a fruitful or even necessary part of conflict transformation. Understandably, some still feel that delving into the complex morass of cultural and identity aspects of a conflict is a dead-end venture down a one-way street. However, I suggest that in spite of any intent to avoid going down that road, much of what the best practitioners already do enables disputants to understand the complex personhood of their adversary and gain insight into how their own identity is inextricably intertwined with the other, if only through the conflict they share.

Identity needs must be acknowledged and addressed if we are to make a difference in conflicts involving such issues as race, gender, sexual orientation, culture and religion. The important difference between identity needs and classic interests supports the idea that identity-based conflicts are a distinct form of conflict and require a special approach to transforming them. That understanding is perhaps why some keep searching for the Holy Grail of interventions in identity-based conflicts. I'm not yet convinced such an approach exists apart from the best practices used in other complex conflicts which seek to address the full range of needs of those involved while empowering them to pursue personal and systemic transformation and change.

As interveners in identity-based conflicts, we need to be intentional about creating opportunities for people to actively participate in negotiating the emergence of a new, shared identity which recognizes our increasing interdependence. The risks involved in doing so are great, especially for those whose identities are threatened or are in danger of being "negotiated away." But the risks of not doing so are even greater as the conflicts of this millennium become those of the next.

[1] Jay Rothman, *Resolving Identity-Based Conflict*, (Jossey-Bass Publishers, 1997), p. xiii.
[2] Miroslav Volf, "Cultural Identity and Recognition," in Brennpunkt Diakonie (Neukirchener, 1997), p. 216.

–Larry Dunn
© MCS 2000, from *Conciliation Quarterly*, Vol. 19 No. 1

Refugees and Conflict

In 1996, I began working on a project for the Office of Refugee Resettlement to develop a model for use by refugee resettlement workers in orienting refugees and their receiving communities to conflict management and resolution in the United States. My assumption then was that refugees and immigrants were the same in terms of conflict issues. That idea was quickly dispelled.

There are some useful similarities. One of the larger issues for all new Americans is the basic difference between the Euro-American understanding of how to deal with conflict and the view held by most of the world's people.

Residents of the United States whose cultural background emanates from Western Europe generally believe that conflict is best handled directly: If I have a problem with you, the best plan is to talk to you about it. If I don't talk to you directly, there is something wrong with my morals. This view may be influenced by Jesus' instructions in Matthew 18, but world Christians do not universally embrace the Euro-American understanding of it.

Generally speaking, people outside North America and Western Europe don't think this way. The difference has to do with cultural assumptions and values concerning "face" and "space."

David Augsburger describes the phenomenon well in *Conflict Mediation Across Cultures.*[1] Western cultures are most concerned about space, the ability to act independently. Eastern cultures are more concerned about face, the recognition that I am not an independent actor, but part of a larger whole which is affected by my actions. In "high-context" or "face" cultures it is unacceptable to make another lose face and unthinkable to put oneself in the position where face can be lost. The entire family or clan loses face when one of its members does. "Low-context" or "space" cultures, such as that of Euro-Americans, care about face, but it is much less important than the ability to be an independent actor.

The high-context culture develops methods for conflict resolution which minimize opportunities for loss of face. High-context cultures develop elaborate indirect methods for working with

conflict. The usual pattern is for a person in conflict to go to the designated (not officially designated, but commonly accepted) wise person to describe the problem. In each cultural setting the requirements for this person are different. It could be a village elder, or it could be your mother-in-law. One common thread is that the wise person must have status at least as high as the highest status person in the conflict.

The wise person then visits with the other party and separately advises both parties how to get through the conflict. There can be no loss of face in following the advice of the wise person. The closer the parties are to a village setting, the more force the wise person's recommendations carry. To ignore the recommendations would be to cause the wise person to lose face, which is unacceptable.

Persons from low-context cultures are willing to risk loss of face if independence is maintained. Meeting directly with the other person in the conflict carries the risk of loss of face, but since only you are affected, the risk is acceptable.

Bringing people from these two types of cultures together for conflict resolution is commonly done by North Americans who have no idea just how damaging the process is for the high-context person. Both immigrants and refugees are regularly violated by well-meaning people. The very fact that people are asked to deal directly with differences is a grave affront to the high-context person. Language and status issues make it very difficult for the high-context person to complain, since to complain would make the higher status American mediator lose face, which is disallowable. The degree of acculturation which has taken place for the parties in conflict makes a difference, but should not be assumed.

While this dynamic is similar for both refugees and immigrants, there are challenges unique to both as specific groups. For example, immigrants decide to move, sometimes for reasons very similar to those causing refugees to flee. Immigrants most often come to a new country with others of their group, or come after a community has been established by pioneers. Some immigrants have the critical mass of people necessary to maintain cultural practices, such as indirect conflict resolution. Refugees flee for their lives, usually winding up in camps where they stay for long periods before being resettled to a country they know nothing about, into a hostile community which resents them. They feel at the mercy of resettlement workers and face systems they do not understand.

Refugees often have no cultural base in the new country. Many or all of their "wise people" are gone. Their culture is fractured or destroyed. Even if others from their country are resettled in the same area, they may be from different clans, even from the very group that made the refugees flee. Refugees from the Balkan States find themselves resettled in small groups which include both Serbs and Croats. Somalis from warring clans share apartment complexes. Deadly enemies are thrown together by a well-meaning resettlement community into poor neighborhoods which are already divided into gang turf. The results are predictable.

One of our most basic suggestions arising from this project is for conflict resolution systems to be established in neighborhoods receiving refugees. The refugees cannot use their traditional methods of conflict resolution, since the people around them don't recognize wise persons both groups can turn to for indirect conflict resolution. Directly addressing conflict is unthinkable for most refugees. By establishing recognized mixed groups of refugees and long-term residents it is possible to reestablish the indirect communication vital to conflict resolution involving persons from high-context cultures. Our project teaches resettlement agencies to create these groups. The key is creation of a mixed group of refugees, resettlement workers and community representatives.

We have learned that mediation styles exist on a continuum, which can be described in at least two ways. The description best understood by low-context people is the continuum between evaluative and facilitative behaviors by the mediator. The more the mediator expresses opinions about the efficacy of the emerging agreement, the more evaluative the process is. The less active the mediator is, and the more the mediator focuses on guiding the parties only in good communication, the more facilitative the process is. It is common to compare the evaluative style to how lawyers operate and the facilitative style to how counselors operate.

–**Duane Ruth-Heffelbower**
© MCS 1999, from *Conciliation Quarterly*, Vol. 18 No. 2

Less well understood is what I call the continuum between conciliation and mediation. There is similarity, but the conciliator is a chosen wise person whose opinion is respected as embodying the mores of the group, while the mediator is seen as a helping person with skill, but without as much moral authority. Low-context cultures relate to the evaluative-facilitative continuum, and high-context cultures relate to the conciliation-mediation continuum.

One of our usual training roleplays is aimed at helping the group understand the role of the Western mediator. We have a step-by-step script for a facilitative Western mediator to use, and give the group a scenario. A group of Kurdish refugees used this script in a roleplay, which they did in Arabic. I asked them afterwards to describe the process. The "mediator" described it this way: "He told me how he saw it, and then the other man told me how he saw it, and I told them what to do." I asked whether they had carefully followed the script, and the mediator replied, "Oh, yes. Every detail."

High-context persons cannot readily comprehend the idea of Western facilitative mediation. Even trying faithfully to follow a script which requires face-to-face discussion, they instead do conciliation by an indirect method. This experience is faithfully repeated by high-context persons in all of our trainings. In consequence, we do not recommend trying to force high-context persons into low-context dispute resolution models; in our experience, low-context persons take more readily to the high-context conciliation form, turning to the agreed-upon wise person for advice.

Refugees in conflict are violated daily by well-meaning people. They have no way to respond; familiar and trusted ways of doing so often fail them. Our hope is that through this project, resettlement workers and dispute resolution practitioners will be better prepared to manage such cross-cultural disputes.

[1] Augsburger, David W. *Conflict Mediation Across Cultures: Pathways and Patterns.* Louisville, KY: Westminster/John Knox Press, 1992. Especially helpful sections on face, space and high- and low-context cultures include pp. 28-35, 84-96 and 264-266.

Contemporary Values and Practices of Original Americans

The romantic images some people have of Original Americans as being very peaceful among themselves and warlike with others needs to be replaced with a contemporary realistic view. The 545 federally acknowledged tribes of approximately two million Original Americans have various types and combinations of tribal courts and traditional peacemaking forums and vary in the degree to which they walk a traditional path or a mainstream American path. Nevertheless, there are some general tendencies among Original Americans when it comes to defining the type of justice and, therefore, the peacemaking procedure which feels, and is, Indian.

The tribal court, which was imposed upon tribes by the U.S. government, does not reflect traditional ways. The courts keep the focus on the intellectual level, rather than on the spiritual, the heart, relationship building. They concentrate on distributive justice (the equitable distribution of resources) and wild and rough justice (revenge, punishment, control, determining who is right). The court process for handling conflicts separates people; it increases distances.

Sacred Justice

Among themselves, Original Americans are generally not as concerned with distributive justice or rough and wild justice, as they are with what I term sacred justice. Sacred justice is Indian justice. Sacred justice is concerned with mending broken relationships: relationships among people, with other animate and inanimate beings, and with the higher spirits. It means that the underlying causes of a disagreement have been addressed. It delivers healing solutions, ones that cleanse and fortify those on all sides of the problem. Sacred justice helps people reconnect with the higher spirits; seeing the conflict in perspective to the higher purposes.

What is Traditional Peacemaking?

We know that there is no "Native American way" to make peace. Each tribe has its own methods, but there are some common features among Native Americans. At its core, "traditional peacemaking" (TPM) is inherently spiritual: it speaks to the connectedness of all things; unity; harmony; the balance between the spiritual, intellectual, emotional and physical dimensions of a community of people.

TPM is viewed and used as a "guiding process" to assist people in their journey back into harmony with one another and all aspects of the universe. Peacemaking is directed at healing hurts and wounds. It includes the widest circle of people concerned, each having a voice.

Unlike mediation, TPM is relationship-centered, not agreement-centered. It is giving advice, reminding people of their responsibilities to one another. A traditional peacemaker, peace chief, law mender or council of elders has the respect and trust of tribal members based on an exemplary life. The peacemaker is not someone with school-based or workshop-based training in conflict resolution skills. Peacemakers have learned by observation and listening in natural settings throughout their lives. Traditional forums are more a guiding court than a punishment court. The peacemakers often give advice to each concerned person about living up to their responsibilities to family and community; facilitate circle talk; ask for apologies; or request that restitution be made, relatively small fines be paid, and community service be performed, often to help the elderly. They want everyone to leave with their tails up, not as in courts where one person leaves with a tail up, one with a tail down. They tell stories which impart the expected behaviors and beliefs by which people should live. Spiritual leaders and healers may be consulted. The "third party" is actually considered to be the whole community.

The Exemplary and the Actual

While some tribes have kept their peacemaking ways vital, there are other tribes where the more traditional ways of helping people are, although still alive, not always well and not used by many tribal members. It is frequently acknowledged by tribal members that traditional ways of handling conflicts are preferable to the courts, resulting in solutions considered fair to all concerned. Systematic nourishment of traditional methods, however, is not common.

A few Native communities have made modifications in their traditional peacemaking procedures by blending them with non-Indian procedures. For example, they now have some restrictions on the amount of time taken to handle the conflict.

Each TPM program has a different structure and different relationships to the institutions in its immediate and larger community. None are costly for anyone, and they tend to be relatively uncomplicated, simple procedures with a slow pace. Deep listening, thoughtful and respectful telling of stories, looking for and accepting guidance are parts of each process as it seeks sacred justice.

A Revitalization Movement

Government-imposed adversarial courts have been recognized as contributing to the weakening of Indian communities. A thoughtful move towards developing comprehensive tribal justice systems (a system with courts, traditional peacemaking modified for the contemporary context, and violence-prevention programs) is occurring across Indian Country. It's been said that "we are learning again how to disagree without being disagreeable." There is evidence of a TPM revitalization movement.

As traditional peacemaking is being kept alive and/or revitalized today, the need for the use of courts is not gone. Today's Original Americans live in multiple worlds. They need to have an appropriate mixture of conflict resolution methods available to them, woven into a strong beautiful braid of the new and the old.

Original Americans are concerned about the spiritual, social, health, economic and cultural disintegration of their tribes. Tribal customs and beliefs must be protected and enhanced. Indian values and practices which are an integral part of peacemaking strengthen communities. Peacemakers perform a vital role in keeping tribes healthy; it is very important that tribal peacemaking be nurtured.

Justice: A Comparison

Generic Native American	Mainstream American
Relationship-centered	Agreement-centered
Follow the old ways	New, change is best
Cooperation	Competition
Communal "ownership"	Private property
Harmony with nature	Mastery over nature
Humility, anonymity	Win a prize, announce it
Submissive, accommodate	Aggressive, assertive
Look at present needs	Look at future needs
Share resources	Save resources for self
Time is always with us	Time is limited
Win once; let others win, too	Win as often as possible
Extended family, clan	Current nuclear family
Everything is interrelated	Categorize things
Success measured through giving, relationships	Success measured by material accumulation
Progress maintains traditions	Progress is change
Thinking based on wisdom	Logic based on strategy
Reasoning based on experience	Scientific explanations
Less formal, less structured	More formal, structured
Oral communication, teaching	Written forms
Verbal agreements	Written transactions
Acceptance based on age, experience, reputation	Acceptance based on education, social status
Group consensus	Individual, boss decides
Decision based on effects on future generations and on everyone	Decision based on immediate personal gain, and on offender
Trust honesty of statements, expressions of feelings	Use of facts, evidence, witnesses important
Nurture, support given to all, restore dignity	Degrees of punishment, Restore goods
Peacemaking is healing, spiritual	Conflict resolution is problem-solving

Summary

There is concern that traditional ways of handling serious disagreements are being replaced by the courts and that peacemaking is being lost with the passing of elders. There is also evidence that this concern is being dealt with by the creation of programs to institutionalize and legitimize sacred justice. Many tribes today are actively working at revitalizing their customary laws and traditional peacemaking forums. Tribal members recognize that in the 1990s they cannot walk a path that is strictly traditional, nor can they walk a path that totally ignores who they have been and who they are.

–Diane LeResche
© MCS 1999, from *Conciliation Quarterly*, Vol. 18 No. 4

Ritual: The New (Old) Tool in the Conflict Transformer's Toolbox

Dancing under the stars. Sharing a cup of tea. Waving smoke over one's head. What do these have to do with conflict transformation?

Many in the field of conflict studies would utter: "Nothing!" There is almost no mention of the word "ritual" or of any symbolic actions in the field of conflict studies. The Western-based field of conflict studies has sought to bring some order into a world filled with chaotic violence. In seeking order, the field has neglected to see the power in the oldest form of dealing with conflict. Ritual taps into the core of our perceptions and beliefs about the world and molds these beliefs into symbols. Ritual uses these symbols to communicate. Ritual acts to recreate and transform the world.

Since the beginning of time, conflict and ritual regulated relationships in communities, serving as ways of defining identity and means of relating to and separating from others. Western conflict theory has only begun to explore the perceptual dimension of conflict; that is how humans symbolically create the world through world view lenses that shape how they see, value, interpret and act. Reaching back into history toward one of the oldest habits of humanity, perhaps we can find a new key to the future of working with conflict.

Types of Ritual

There are many kinds of ritual, such as: formal ritual vs. informal ritual, traditional vs. improvised, and rituals that deal specifically with cosmological notions of the universe vs. those that deal more generally with one's world view.

Formal: For many, the term ritual connotes formality. Taking communion, participating in Catholic Mass, creating a special holiday and attending a wedding or a funeral are all examples of formal rituals.

Informal: We participate in informal rituals every day. We may not feel like we are engaging in a ritual when we eat a meal, brush our teeth, walk the dog, or write in our journals, yet these patterned, everyday actions have special meaning in our lives. If we interrupt or break these informal rituals, we are likely to be more conscious of what they mean to us.

Traditional: Many rituals are patterned traditions of the past. Traditional rituals are based on cultural beliefs that are passed from generation to generation through ritual action. The Native sweat lodge, the British changing of the guards, and the exchange of rings at a wedding are all examples of traditions that are passed on through ritual action. While the meaning may change from generation to generation, the basic form of ritual stays the same.

Improvised: Not all rituals are based on traditions. In North America today there is an active movement to create new rituals through improvisation. Feminist theologians and women's spirituality groups have been reviving the use of ritual in recent decades. Using the symbols both of their own and of borrowed ritual traditions, women's spirituality groups design and improvise meaningful rituals with the intent and belief that ritual has a power to transform and re-create. For example, one woman planned a ceremony to bury a childhood dress in a formal funeral as a way of putting the "abused child" part of her identity to rest and transforming herself into a "survivor."

Cosmology: Rituals may reflect cosmology or religious beliefs. Cosmological rituals focus on the connection between humans and the larger powers in the universe. Catholic Mass or Indigenous purification ceremonies are both examples of rituals with religious meaning.

World view: Other rituals are not explicitly religious. For example, high school graduation ceremony marks an important life event and reflects the cultural traditions of a group of people, but does not include religious meaning.

Definitions and Functions of Ritual

Definitions of ritual differ widely in the literature. The working definition of ritual I have found helpful is: A contextual *frame* which links people together in symbolic actions which *communicate* a transforming message.

Frames: Ritual frames the interaction in a context. Rituals seek to create a "liminal" or "in-between" space that is separate from normal time and space. This "special space" is often called a "safe space" in the field of conflict studies to indicate the need for conflict intervenors to help *create an atmosphere conducive to transforming relationships* and world views. Many intervenors are already highly skilled in making sure chairs are arranged in a circle or that round tables are used, as these indicate equality and cooperation. Many successful international efforts at mediation have had major breakthroughs when the people in conflict were eating dinner, smoking, dancing, or interacting in some location other than a negotiating room. Rituals help frame interactions between people in a way that may be more conducive to transformation.

Links: Ritual expresses relationships between people, their world view and the environment. Ritual's liminal frame allows for changes in how we see ourselves and others. In conflicts we fixate on one particular identity, e.g., ethnicity, race, gender, religion, profession. In being with each other in a ritual frame, a liminal space, we can see each other as mothers, fathers, community leaders, tennis players, or sacred beings with many different identities. This shift in identity helps ritual participants begin relating to each other differently. Trust can be built from the common ground found in identifying common frames and common identities. As our perceptions of our identities and relationships change and/or expand in our minds, a space is made for creating a new structure of relationships.

Communicates: Ritual is a form of communication which transmits *both verbal and nonverbal* messages. Anthropologist Edmond Leach claims, "We engage in rituals in order to transmit collective messages to ourselves." Humans create the world through their intent and action in the world. Ritual communicates in a unique way, using symbolic rather than rational, verbal forms of communication and using the entire body of senses rather than just verbal.

Symbolic: Ritual communicates through symbols, metaphors and stories which allow for multiple, even contradictory meanings. In ritual, we observe the world from a different perspective than we

normally do. Complex problems or paradoxes can be solved in ritual by actually allowing our brain to think differently. Neurobiologists write about how one's world view is actually a biological pattern in the neural networks of the brain. Our brains become trained to work in certain ways. In rituals, such as meditation, the shiver up our back or the actual change of consciousness actually change the neural pathways in our brain and the way we perceive the world.

Actions: Ritual involves physical postures and actions. The use of the full body in ritual allows for the full range of ways people know and understand the world. Some cognitive theorists understand the process of learning as involving the whole body rather than just mind. In addition to the bodily expression of emotions such as crying, shouting or laughing rituals often employ all of the body's senses by finding meaning in what is seen, heard, smelled and tasted. The Indigenous smudging ceremony is an example of how ritual's power comes through the body as each individual bathes in the sweet-smelling smoke, invoking presence and awareness in the gathering.

Transforming: Ritual is a process for undergoing change. In ritual we are able to change our perceptions of the world, and in particular, of conflict. Nonviolent action is a type of ritual as it engages in symbolic, transforming, communicative action. African American people sitting at the lunch counters, boycotting city buses, marching through the streets and gathering in Washington, D.C., were ritual actions that changed perceptions and beliefs of both White and Black Americans.

As the field of conflict studies rediscovers the power of ritual to communicate, frame and transform conflict through symbolic actions, we link with the history of humanity. Let us walk through the doorway that ritual opens, allowing ourselves to move from our heads to our bodies, from our rational thinking to our emotions—to engage our full beings in the pursuit of peace.

–Lisa Schirch
© MCS 1998, from *Conciliation Quarterly*, Vol. 17 No. 3

Resources for Further Study on Conflict Transformation Theory

Augsburger, David W. *Conflict Mediation Across Cultures: Pathways and Patterns.* Louisville, KY: Westminster/John Knox Press, 1992.
> Blends theory and stories from many cultures, inviting readers to "unlearn" their common sense about conflict and learn new perspectives from other cultures.

Auruch, Kevin. *Culture and Conflict Resolution.* Washington, DC: U.S. Institute of Peace Press, 1998.
> Offers a challenge to scholars and practitioners not only to develop a clearer understanding of what culture is, but also to apply that understanding to more effective conflict resolution processes.

Burton, John. *Conflict: Resolution and Prevention.* New York: St. Martin's Press, 1990.
> Calls for problem-solving processes derived from human needs theory that can revolutionize legal, political, diplomatic and military approaches to deep-rooted conflict.

Bush, Robert A. Baruch, and Joseph P. Folger. *The Promise of Mediation: Responding to Conflict Through Empowerment and Recognition.* San Francisco: Jossey-Bass, 1994.
> Explores and promotes the transformative potential of mediation as it critiques the field of mediation today. Very worth reading.

Curle, Adam. *Tools for Transformation: A Personal Study.* Stroud, UK: Hawthorn Press, 1990.
> A book about transforming ourselves and the world we live in by looking at psychology, physics, Buddhism and Quaker practice.

Dugan, Maire A. "A Nested Theory of Conflict," *A Leadership Journal: Women in Leadership—Sharing the Vision.* Vol 1. July 1996.
> A highly accessible article which presents both a new theoretical perspective on conflict and the story of how the author developed this theory.

Fisher, Roger, and William Ury. *Getting to Yes: Negotiating Agreement Without Giving In* (2d ed). New York: Penguin Books, 1991.
> The most popular small book on basic principles of win-win negotiation, using interest-based collaboration.

Herman, Judith. *Trauma and Recovery: The Aftermath of Violence—from Domestic Abuse to Political Terror.* New York: Basic Books, 1992.
> A classic in the field of psychology, offers an analysis of trauma and the process of healing.

Hocker, Joyce L., and William W. Wilmot. *Interpersonal Conflict* (3d ed.). Dubuque, IA: William Brown, 1991.
> An excellent introduction to conflict dynamics and expressions of conflict in interpersonal and group situations.

Lederach, John Paul. *Building Peace: Sustainable Reconciliation in Divided Societies.* Harrisonburg, VA: Eastern Mennonite University Press, 1994.
> An essay examining what it takes to build peace in today's conflicts.

Lederach, John Paul. *Preparing for Peace: Conflict Transformation Across Cultures.* Syracuse, NY: Syracuse University Press, 1995.
> Explores conflict resolution training and its relation to culture.

Mayer, Bernard. *The Dynamics of Conflict Resolution: A Practitioner's Guide.* San Francisco: Jossey-Bass, 2000.
> An essential guide that shows how successful mediators, facilitators and negotiators draw on their creative internal process to resolve conflict.

Ross, Rupert. *Returning to the Teachings: Exploring Aboriginal Justice*. Toronto: Penguin Books, 1996.
   Excellent illustration of the conflict between the Native American philosophy of justice and the Western judicial system.

Rothman, Jay. *Resolving Identity-Based Conflict in Nations, Organizations and Communities*. San Francisco: Jossey-Bass, 1997.
   A look at identity conflicts for both theorists and practitioners.

Singer, Linda R. *Settling Disputes: Conflict Resolution in Business, Families, and the Legal System*. Boulder, CO: Westview Press, 1990.
   A survey of dispute resolution models throughout the field, especially in relation to conventional legal structures.

Wehr, Paul. *Conflict Regulation*. Boulder, CO: Westview Press, 1979.
   A classic in the field. Looks at conflict dynamics through the exploration of several varied case studies. Excellent appendices of training exercises.

Wehr, Paul, Heidi Burgess and Guy Burgess. *Justice Without Violence*. Boulder, CO: Lynne Reinner Publishers, 1994.

Zehr, Howard. *Changing Lenses: A New Focus for Crime and Justice*. Scottdale, PA: Herald Press, 1990.
   A classic on restorative justice.

Periodical

Conciliation Quarterly Newsletter. Mennonite Conciliation Service, PO Box 500, Akron PA 17501; 717-859-3889; mcs@mccus.org; www.mcc.org/mcs.html
   Often has articles related to the interplay of dispute resolution, peacemaking and justice.

Chapter 3

Interpersonal Communication and Problem-Solving

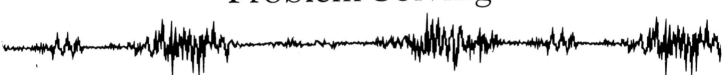

I believe that our world is on the verge of self-destruction and death because society as a whole has so deeply neglected that which is most human and most valuable and the most basic of all the work of love—the work of human communication, of caring and nurturance, of tending the personal bonds of community.
—Beverly Wildung Harrison

Introduction

The Role of Communication

Communication is the simple exchange of meaning—the giving and receiving of feelings, opinions, ideas or beliefs. Communication lies at the heart of all interactions. It is central to all conflict because it *causes conflict* through miscommunication and misunderstanding, it *expresses conflict*, verbally and nonverbally, and it *is a vehicle for conflict transformation*, positive or negative.

In reality, there is nothing "simple" about communication. The meanings of words and actions vary widely among people of different cultures, as well as between people in unequal power relationships. The approach of a police officer, for instance, on a dark city street may communicate protection and be a cause of relief to an affluent white tourist who has lost his way. For a young African-American man in dreadlocks who lives on that same street, however, the policeman's approach may communicate danger and cause fear. A woman who was once beaten by a lover many years before may hear something very threatening in her current partner's tone of voice, something a mediator, unaware of her history, wholly fails to hear. Issues of culture and power are thus intrinsic to communication. Understanding the "politics of meaning," that is, how power is transacted through nuances and styles of communication, is an important part of the mediator's role.

Attitude and Skills

The ability to positively transform conflict is largely dependent on two key elements of communication: attitude and skill level. Of these two, attitude is the most critical. This means "being" before doing—being truly "present" with the other, being sincere, respectful and caring, being aware of my own feelings and agenda, possessing a commitment to being constructive and a desire to understand as well as to be understood. Without this kind of being, our proficiency with specific skills are merely "noisy gongs and clanging symbols."

It is very important, however, to understand that good skills and helpful processes are critical as well. Built on a solid attitudinal foundation and combined with an awareness of our own personal style and the styles of others, these skills and processes open the door to healthier interactions, more collaborative work and play and, ultimately, a more peaceful world.

Assumptions We Bring to Communication in Conflict

1. All people with their diverse styles, gifts and opinions are created in God's image, and deserve respect.
2. Attitude and skills are both critical for conflict transformation.
3. Most people genuinely want to be constructive in conflict and can learn skills that will increase their ability to do so.
4. Obstinacy and vindictiveness usually emerge out of woundedness and insecurity rather than out of strength.
5. Most people will negotiate reasonably if they feel heard and respected.
6. Only occasionally is constructive communication not possible due to significant emotional problems or bad-faith intentions of one party.

A Note of Caution

Communication skills training is not an easy task. Many training participants bring resistance at a variety of levels. "Oh no, not again!" "It feels so fake." "I don't like being psychologized." "It doesn't work anyway." These are important feelings that, first and foremost, need to be elicited and heard non-defensively. That process itself is cathartic. Additionally, I find it helpful to constantly ground these skills in a discussion of a constructive attitude, noting often that being truly present with someone is much more critical than flawless skills. I also find it helpful to acknowledge the different levels of exposure to and experience with these skills and to acknowledge that, given how absolutely critical they are in conflict transformation and given my own struggles as a trainer to "walk my talk," I return to them once again, unapologetically.

–Carolyn Schrock-Shenk, with thanks to Ron Kraybill, Alice Price and Beth Roy
© MCS 2000

Blocks to Empowering Others

Nonverbal blockers: These are disempowering body language that say I am not interested or willing or able to really listen. They take many forms: fidgeting, distracting gestures, yawning, flat or judgmental facial expressions, fixed eye contact or wandering eyes, tense or overly relaxed body posture, and so on. Studies show that only about 15% of communication is the words or content while 25% is tone of voice and 60% *is nonverbal*.

Verbal blockers: These are verbal responses that *may* be useful at certain places and times. Most of the time, however, they block listening and *disempower* others. They imply: "You are not good enough, smart enough, strong enough; *I* am the one who knows." Here are some examples:

> **Advising:** Telling the speaker how to solve their problem.
> - "Why don't you just. . . ."
> - "Maybe you should. . . ."
> - "I'd just try to relax and not take it so seriously."
>
> **Judging:** Negatively evaluating the speaker and/or their problem.
> - "Don't get so uptight about it."
> - "That's not a very constructive attitude."
> - "I think you're the one that's got to face up to problems."
>
> **Analyzing/Diagnosing:** Telling the speaker about their motives, root causes, etc.
> - "What's *really* bothering you is. . . ."
> - "Your insecurities are coming through. That's why you're so sensitive."
> - "Maybe she reminds you of your mother who. . . ."
>
> **Questioning:** Probing for information about the speaker's problem, often implying judgement.
> - "Why did you do that?"
> - "Are you being as kind and considerate as you can?"
> - "Have you considered just forgiving him?"
>
> **Reassuring/Minimizing:** Trying to make the speaker feel better by minimizing their experience.
> - "Don't worry about it. Just trust yourself. You'll do fine."
> - "You did the best you could, so stop fretting about it."
> - "Cheer up. A month from now things will look different."

Key Concepts

1. **Empowerment comes through presence.** Most people get connected to their own good ideas and inner resources if others can truly be present. Learning to empower others is not a matter of learning the "right" answers but rather learning to be truly present to them. Being present means devoting full attention to the other person and their perceptions, setting aside my ideas, reactions, and experiences. Presence is a discipline of healthy self-denial that takes time, energy and commitment.

2. **Presence precedes problem-solving.** Our ideas and advice are often short-cuts to problem-solving. "I'll skip getting into your shoes since I'm the one with right answers to solve this." Efforts to skip presence and move quickly to problem-solving result in *resistance* (people start arguing with your advice) or *dependency* (people perceive you as the one with power to resolve things, not themselves).

Small Group Exercise

1. In a group of three, take turns talking for five minutes about "something that really bugs me." Others select "blocks" from the list above and slip them into the conversation.

2. After five minutes, stop using the above responses. Continue the conversation for another five minutes, focusing on *hearing* without advising, evaluating, or analyzing.

3. Discuss the experience. What was easy/difficult? What was helpful or unhelpful to the speaker?

–MCS Staff
© MCS 1988, 1992, 1995

Exercises/Discussion Starters on Listening

For personal reflection or journaling

1. Think about yourself as a listener. List five people with whom you interact regularly. On a scale of 1-10 (1=poor, 10=excellent), rate how you think each of these people would perceive your listening skills and your ability to be present with them.

    - What factors affect the different ratings?
    - Which scores do you consider worth improving?
    - What personal changes do you need to make to improve them?
    - How will you go about making those personal changes?

2. Think about the last conflict in which you were a participant. Describe the kind of listening you did in the midst of the conflict.

    - Were you able to be non-defensive and momentarily shelve your agenda in order to really hear the other person?
    - Did you communicate respect and caring for the other person? If so, how? If not, what blocked you from it?
    - What kind of changes do you want/need to make to be a centered listener in conflict?
    - How will you go about making those changes?

For discussion in pairs or small groups

3. Think of the person who is your best listener. What characteristics make that person stand out as a listener?

4. When you are experiencing intense conflict with another person, what are some of the things that you often need or want to talk about?

5. What, if anything, might cause someone with whom you are in conflict to be hesitant about sharing her/his concerns or perspective with you?

6. Think about a person with whom you have a hard time sharing concerns and feelings. What specific behaviors make it difficult for you to be open with this person? What comments or questions from you might have a similar effect of "shutting down" others?

7. Think about a person with whom you have an easy time talking about your concerns and feelings. What approaches or questions have made it easier for you to talk about difficult circumstances? In conflict situations, what sorts of questions create an atmosphere in which people feel they can share?

–Carolyn Schrock-Shenk and David Dyck
© MCS 2000

Cooperation Skills

Cooperation involves two seemingly contradictory movements: *asserting self* and *supporting another*. One asserts one's own needs and interests, and at the same time supports the needs and interests of others. The challenge is to do them simultaneously, since they operate like a *push* and *pull*. Many people are skillful at one of these; few are skillful at both. The combination is remarkably effective. With practice anyone can learn it!

Supportiveness Skills (listening)	Assertiveness Skills (speaking)
1. Paraphrasing	1. I-Messages
2. Openness	2. Preference Stating
3. Agreement Stating	3. Purpose Stating

Supportiveness Skills: The "Pull" of Listening

Paraphrasing

Reflecting in one's own words the essence of what the speaker has said. This is the most useful listening skill in that it demonstrates one's commitment to understanding.

How to paraphrase
- Keep the focus on the speaker. "So you felt. . .," "You're saying. . .," "You believe. . . ."
- Restate briefly in your own words, rather than simply parroting the speaker.
- Reflect both *content and feeling* whenever possible and appropriate.
- Match, to some extent, the emotional intensity of the speaker in your paraphrase.

Why Paraphrase?
- Demonstrates understanding and/or the attempt to understand.
- Clarifies the communication. (If you misunderstand, they'll correct you.)
- Affirms worth of speaker and encourages them to say more.
- Reduces defensiveness of both you and the speaker.
- Slows down a fast or angry conversation, helping to reduce the intensity of the conflict.

Examples
- "So you were really frightened when. . . ."
- "You felt I was being unfair to you when. . . ."
- "Let me make sure I'm understanding you. You're saying you don't want that responsibility. . . ."

Openness

Communicating openness to receive more information about others' perceptions and needs, even if those may be critical or competitive. This is often important in order to clarify the situation before attempting to respond.

Examples
- "Say more about. . . ."
- "Tell me what you have in mind."
- "Give me a specific example."

Agreement Stating

Acknowledging where one agrees with others in the midst of a disagreement.

Examples
- "I agree with you that. . . ."
- "I can see what you're saying about. . . ."
- "I share your concerns about. . . ."

Assertiveness Skills: The "Push" of Speaking

I-Messages

A clear, nonthreatening way to confront that focuses on oneself rather than on the other person. It communicates the impact of the situation on one's *emotions* or *performance*.

How to Use I-Messages
- Focus on yourself and own the problem: "I. . . ."
- Name the feeling: "I felt used. . . ."
- Name the problem behavior: "I felt used when you put your name on the work I did. . . ."
- Describe the impact on you: ". . .because I put a lot of time and energy into that project."

Why use I-Messages?
- I take responsibility for my feelings
- Avoids blaming or accusing the other
- Reduces defensiveness and de-escalates conflict
- Expresses strong feelings in a way that preserves the relationship

Examples
- "I felt angry when you told me to meet you at noon and then you didn't come or call, because I had changed my plans so we could meet."
- "It's very upsetting for me when you get your projects in late. I get behind with my deadlines and then others get on *my* case."

Preference Statements

Communicating clearly one's preferences or desires rather than stating them as demands or forcing others to guess. Defining oneself clearly also invites others to do the same.

Examples
- "My preference is. . . ."
- "What I'd like is. . . ."
- "It would be helpful to me if. . . ."

Purpose Stating

Making known one's intentions so others do not unknowingly operate at cross-purposes. By supplying information about your aims, a purpose statement enables others to understand what you are about and if possible, help achieve your purpose without needless misunderstanding.

Examples
- "What I'm trying to accomplish is. . . ."
- "I'm hoping to. . . ."
- "My intention was to. . . ."

I-Message Exercise

1. Ask participants to stand back-to-back in pairs. Read a brief scenario after which the partners turn around and the designated partner blasts the other with a blaming you-message. The partner is encouraged to respond as s/he might in "real life." When the voices and tension escalate, intervene and stop the exercise.

2. Then ask the partners to replay the scenario using an I-message instead. (Here, encourage them not to get "hung up" on exact wording but to focus instead on the purpose or spirit of an I-message.

3. After several such exchanges with both partners getting a chance to deliver and receive both you- and I-messages, debrief with a focus on how people felt when delivering and receiving the two kinds of messages (i.e. focus less on the mechanics of creating I-messages and more on feelings).

–MCS Staff
© MCS 1988, 1992, 2000

Practice Cooperation Skills

1. A friend says: "Life really seems miserable right now. At work they keep pressuring me to get more done. Our oldest child is going through some kind of a rebellious stage in the last month. On top of that are the problems we've been having with the pastoral search committee at church!" YOU RESPOND:

2. A neighbor says: "Look at the junk in that guy's yard! It's so typical of poor people—to have trash over the whole place!" (The yard *is* a mess but you don't want to ignore a classist statement.) YOU SAY:

3. You are leading the sermon discussion group. You have just written a focusing question on the board. Bob ignores the question and asks what people think about a recent political development. YOU RESPOND:

4. A group of five people are trying to choose a restaurant. Two have spoken in favor of Mexican food, and now it's your turn to speak. You dislike spicy food. YOU RESPOND:

5. You're in the middle of an important planning session with your family. A friend calls up and says she wants to discuss a problem at work. YOU RESPOND:

6. In a committee Susan keeps her eyes on the floor most of the evening and resists your efforts as chair to draw her into discussion. Near the end you ask her to contact others about a special meeting Friday morning. She says, "Since you run the whole show anyway, why don't you just do it yourself!" The room falls silent. YOU RESPOND:

7. There's a work project you have to finish before you can leave on vacation, scheduled to begin two days from now. Your 10-year-old nags you to play with her, complains that you're *always* working and don't care about her anymore. YOU PARAPHRASE, THEN CONTINUE:

8. Your neighbor frequently parks his car so close to your driveway you have to drive on the grass to get out. YOU CONFRONT HIM:

   After you confront him, he says defensively: "Come on, don't get so uptight about things. What's the big deal about having to run on the lawn every once in a while?" YOU RESPOND:

   Later still in the conversation, he says, "Since we're airing our beefs today, I might as well tell you, you haven't been such a great neighbor yourself." YOU SAY:

–MCS Staff
© MCS 1989

The Open Question

Open questions are questions that cannot be answered with a "yes" or a "no." They have the effect of opening up discussion, of expanding issues, of broadening perspectives and of encouraging inductive thinking. The use of any type of question must be evaluated carefully in cross-cultural settings. At times and in certain settings, questions could be considered intrusive, disrespectful and inappropriate. Be aware of the cultural context and move forward with care.

Open questions may:
- Open up the options when parties seem stuck;
- Help parties to move away from a fixed position on something;
- Help parties to see things from the perspective of the other;
- Help explain the broad context in which a behavioral choice was made, making it easier to understand the behavior and enhancing trust among the parties;
- Function as an agent of reality by asking the party to look at the practical effect of his or her expressed view;
- Slow down the process where parties are engaged in a heated back and forth exchange.

Kinds of open questions:
- *Probing Questions* ask for more information.
- *Clarifying Questions* seek to sharpen the listener's understanding of what has been said.
- *Justifying Questions* ask the speaker to give some evidence for the view expressed.
- *Consequential Questions* are used for reality testing; to ask about potential solutions or look at possible consequences.

Probing questions

These questions ask for more information. They seek to identify what it is about something that makes it important to a party. For example: "You mentioned a moment ago that when his aunt left the room, you felt you had lost an opportunity. Can you tell me more about what you hoped would happen while his aunt was there?"

Ways to phrase probing questions
- What is it about this that concerns you the most?
- When was it that you realized how much the entire service was going to cost?
- How did you come to decide to choose another place for the next course?
- Please tell me more about how you came to feel/think that?

Clarifying questions

These questions seek to sharpen the listener's understanding of what has been said. For example: "So, it was not so much the loss of the contract that concerned you as it was the loss of the relationship?"

Ways to phrase clarifying questions:
- When you say "the meeting," which time are you referring to?
- You said a few minutes ago that you thought it was possible to recover part of what had been lost. Can you tell me what you meant by the word "recover"?
- You spoke of immigrants. Did you mean people who are recent arrivals, or some other group?

Justifying questions

These questions ask the speaker to give some evidence for the view expressed. They are useful when there is some incongruence between what the speaker has said and his or her body language. Use these questions with caution when dealing with parties from a hierarchical culture or organization: They may incite defensiveness or alienation. For example: "Mariel, you said a few minutes ago that you had written Agit off. Now you are talking about a continuing business relationship. Can you tell me how those might fit together?"

Ways to phrase justifying questions:

- Earlier you said. . . , and just now I thought I heard you say that. . . . Can you tell me how you plan to move forward?
- When you said you were going out of town, I thought I heard a note of finality in your voice. Just now you used the word "maybe" when I asked about your plans to travel out of town. Could you help me with my confusion?

Consequential Questions

These are questions to "reality test"; to ask about potential solutions, to look at the possible consequences of a position taken or a solution. For example: "If you go on as planned, who do you think will be most affected?"

Phrasing for consequential questions:

- How do you think the sequence will change the plan you had earlier?
- Have you thought about the down side for you if the market turns before the units are built?
- What do you think your response might have been if this suggestion were made by Surjeet two months ago?

–Michelle LeBaron
© UVic Institute for Dispute Resolution 1994, from *Conflict Resolution & Analysis as Education*. Used with permission.

Probing and Paraphrasing Exercise

Objective: The following exercise is to assist you to become more proficient and comfortable with the vital skills of probing and paraphrasing as they are used in effective communication. The particular challenge in this exercise is to be curious rather than judgmental, to listen well in the context of emotionally charged topics, especially when you disagree with what the speaker is saying.

Roles and Instructions

Divide into groups of three. Each person in a group should have an opportunity to play each role once.

Listener: As the listener, your goal is to use open-ended questions and paraphrasing to help you uncover the interests (needs, wants, fears, concerns, hopes) of the other party.

Speaker: As the speaker, your role is to initiate the exercise by reading one of the positional statements from the list below. It is important to pick a statement you actually agree with and have interests in. If the listener responds by using open-ended questions and listening well, please reveal your interests. However, if the listener asks close-ended, leading or adversarial questions, please react as you might, when feeling defensive.

Observer: Your role is to record the questions and paraphrases of the listener, noting body language and tone. Stop the conversation after 3-5 minutes. Assist the group in analyzing the exercise by reviewing the "transcript" together. Finally, be especially sure to "make space" for the speaker to describe how s/he was reacting/responding to the listener and why.

List of Controversial Statements

- The Bible is clear in its message that homosexuality is outside the will of God. Therefore, while we love the sinner, we cannot condone the practice of homosexuality in our churches.
- It's hard enough in this world to find someone you love. If you're lucky enough to find a match for your soul, why should it matter whether they are of the same or opposite sex?
- Although men and women are equal, they have different roles. There are many ways other than preaching that a woman can minister.
- God created men and women to be equal. Why is the pulpit excluded from that equality?
- The Bible says, "Thou shall not kill," period. Abortion is killing, and even though we recognize the unfortunate circumstances surrounding some pregnancies, ending the pregnancy is never the right option.
- Issues are not always cut and dried. Although abortion is not a perfect option, rape and incest victims must be allowed to make their own choices.
- The Constitution gives every person the right to bear arms. It's a fundamental right that can't be taken away.
- There is no legitimate reason for anyone to possess a device capable of murder. All guns should be banned.
- There are just some people who can never be rehabilitated. It's foolish to keep a mass murderer in jail while we work to pay for his room and board. He should receive the same fate as his victims.
- Regardless of how evil a person may seem, it's not our place to play God by executing criminals. The Bible says, "Thou shalt not kill."
- Now we're supposed to say "African American." What was wrong with "Black"? There's no way to keep up with this political correctness.
- It's time for white people to recognize the privilege and power that our skin color gives us. We need to be sensitive to what our brothers and sisters of color are telling us.

–**David Dyck, with Michelle Armster and Kristin Reimer**
© MCS 2000

Recognizing Feelings

Any conflict, indeed any interaction, is wrapped in feelings. What feelings are present, how they are expressed, how much they need to be "unpacked" in a situation varies greatly depending upon many factors. But feelings are valid, important and a very necessary part of conflict transformation.

Eliciting Feelings

1. Create a safe space.

   - Work at ways to build trust and community.
   - Elicit and use ground rules appropriate to the situation.
   - Emphasize the importance of feelings as part of the transformation process.
   - Acknowledge the existence and validity of many different—and even conflicting—feelings.
   - Acknowledge and accept feelings as they are expressed.

2. Observe body language and tone of voice.

   - Listen "beneath" the words.
   - Be sensitive to timing, to people's readiness to be vulnerable.

3. Create opportunities to name and describe feelings.

   - Ask open questions:
     "How do you feel about that?"
     "Gail, how did that incident in the hallway affect you?"
     "Tyler, you got really agitated while Mrs. Arnold was talking. What was happening to you then?"
     "What was it like for you to grow up without a mother?"
   - Allow for and be comfortable with times of silence.

Responding to Feelings

- Develop a vocabulary for a variety of emotions. (See list on the following page.)

- Validate the expressed feelings by listening without judgment and reflecting them back to the speaker.

- Be tentative in naming a feeling, but don't fear guessing the wrong one. Correcting the guess will help clarify the feelings.

- Help the speaker distinguish between feelings/emotions and behavior/action.

- Invite the speaker to elaborate, to be specific about what they feel and why. Encourage them to vent until they are ready and able to make positive behavior choices.

- If someone wants to change a feeling, ask what s/he needs in order for that to happen.

–Carolyn Schrock-Shenk
© MCS 1995

See also "Healing Strategies: Addressing Feelings" on page 179.

Identifying Feelings

Abandoned
Affectionate
Afraid
Ambivalent
Angry
Annoyed
Anxious
Appreciative
Ashamed
Attacked
Betrayed
Bewildered
Bitter
Blamed
Bored
Brave
Burdened
Calm
Cared for
Cheerful
Comfortable
Comforted
Competent
Concerned
Condemned
Confident
Confused
Contented
Created
Crushed
Cut off
Defensive
Delighted
Desperate
Determined
Disappointed
Disappointing
Discontented
Discounted
Discouraged
Dissatisfied
Distracted
Disturbed
Doubtful
Drained
Dread
Eager
Embarrassed
Empty

Energetic
Enthusiastic
Envious
Exasperated
Excited
Exhausted
Fearful
Foolish
Free
Frightened
Frustrated
Furious
Glad
Good
Great
Guilty
Happy
Helpless
Hopeful
Hopeless
Horrified
Hurt
Ignored
Important
Imposed upon
Impressed
Incompetent
Indifferent
Infuriated
Intimidated
Irritated
Isolated
Jealous
Judged
Left out
Lonely
Lost
Loved
Mad
Miserable
Misunderstood
Needed
Optimistic
Overwhelmed
Paranoid
Patronized
Pleased
Pressured
Proud

Put-down
Puzzled
Reassured
Rejected
Relieved
Remorseful
Resentful
Resigned
Ripped-off
Sad
Satisfied
Scared
Self-sufficient
Selfish
Settled
Shamed
Shocked
Shy
Silly
Skeptical
Spiteful
Squeezed
Stuck
Surprised
Sympathetic
Tentative
Terrible
Thoughtful
Threatened
Tired
Trapped
Troubled
Trusted
Trusting
Uncertain
Uncomfortable
Undecided
Understood
Uneasy
Unimportant
Upset
Used
Useful
Useless
Vulnerable
Wonderful
Worried
Worthwhile
Wounded

–MCS Staff
© MCS 1995

Anger and Conflict

Anger is a critical emotion—there are many things in this world that should make us angry. Anger informs us and motivates us to change or make changes. Like fire, anger is a transformative force. When directed appropriately, it is powerfully productive. Undirected and uncontrolled, it is powerfully destructive.

The power and intensity of anger often makes us feel uncomfortable and out of control. Staying centered and nondefensive when encountering an angry person is extremely difficult but important because defensiveness and agitation tend to negatively escalate the conflict. Staying centered and nonattacking when one is angry at another is equally important. This does not mean staying quiet and nonconfrontive. In fact, implosion or the denial of one's anger can be as destructive as explosion. The challenge is to stay in control of my anger and to direct it appropriately so I do not injure myself or another.

It is important to remember that anger is a secondary emotion. Under it usually lie fear or powerlessness or victimization. Understanding and addressing the root causes of the anger is key in directing and managing it. It is also important to remember that how one expresses one's anger is determined by many factors, such as ethnicity, gender, social status, family patterns, health (mental, physical, emotional and spiritual) and immediate context.

Responding To an Angry Person

- Allow the person to vent—that alone helps diffuse the anger. Listen carefully. Ask clarifying questions to understand the concerns. Try to hear the primary feelings causing the anger.
- Remain nondefensive and stay emotionally connected. (This is hard!) Be calm but not nonchalant—you are taking this seriously as well.
- Paraphrase the concerns as you understand them, including the feelings.
- Explore what needs to be changed in the situation causing the anger.

Responding As an Angry Person

- Listen to yourself. Be aware of your feelings, the level of intensity, the effect on your body. Breath deeply. Take the time you need to focus.
- Look deeper. Examine what is below the anger, the root causes (this is not easy when you're very angry).
- Confront assertively. Do so after you're sure your anger will not rage out of control and injure the other. Use nonblaming I-messages and name your deeper concerns.
- Listen back. When you are able, listen to the other's feelings and perceptions.
- Explore next steps together.

Responding to Anger Exercise

In pairs, roleplay the following situations, taking turns being the listener/responder.

1. Your daughter has just broken your neighbor's window while playing. Your neighbor has frequently complained about being disturbed by your children—now this. He comes storming over to your back yard and begins to yell at you.

2. While facilitating a meeting, you asked Chris, who had spoken more than anyone, to "sit tight" for a bit and give Miguel a chance to respond to the issue on the table. You thought you had asked in a good spirit but Chris got extremely angry and begins accusing you of controlling and manipulating.

3. You have repeatedly been the brunt of subtle negative comments about your heritage. Finally you can no longer stay silent.

–Carolyn Schrock-Shenk
© MCS 1995, 2000

Where Technique Ends and Real Life Begins
(or "This Stuff Won't Work Where I Come From")

"You don't understand—this stuff won't work where I come from," one of the young men says during a seminar I am leading on I-messages and other communication skills. Voices around the room chime in in agreement. "Maybe if I were from some nice neighborhood where everyone talked like that, it'd work. But if I started talking that way in my neighborhood, I'm telling you, it wouldn't do any good. The only language people understand there is fists."

I stutter around for awhile, trying to defend these techniques while letting them know that I know that as an upper-middle-class white woman, I don't have any idea how tough it is to grow up in their streets. Inside I am kicking myself for even presuming to be able to teach them anything; these ideas are culturally foreign and probably inappropriate. I shouldn't have even agreed to lead this workshop, I think. Why should they listen to me?

Then a young man in the front row speaks up, turning slightly to his peers. "You don't have to use her words, like 'I feel this' and 'when' and 'because' and all that," he says. "But you can still let people know what effect they're having on you—especially people you really care about—by

being honest about stuff and not acting all tough all the time." He then proceeds to offer an honest, "un-tough," and self-possessed I-message—completely devoid of formula—for an example we had just been discussing.

A couple others nod their heads, and we all sit in silence for a moment. I smile gratefully and a little meekly at the man in the front row. He and I and everyone else know that his words have moved mountains that mine never could.

Our speech is laden with all that we have accumulated from our histories, families, churches, and neighborhoods. Recognizing that the very same words carry different and even opposite meanings for people of different cultures and backgrounds can move us toward an understanding of both the fragility and power of speech. Ultimately, the impact of our words will depend more on our sincere desire to communicate than on the speaking techniques we employ. Indeed, a deep and abiding hunger for holy, compassionate, and inspired communication is the first and last step toward speaking for ourselves, listening to others, and ultimately speaking and listening to the Word that formed us.

–Valerie Weaver-Zercher

Some Cultural Differences that Affect Conflict Expression

Conflict expression can vary widely and can have opposite meanings as in the contrasting statements below. Dominant culture assumptions about expression can be misleading.

Expressing strong emotions	Strong feelings must be gotten out of the way first so negotiation can progress through calm, rational communication. Being objective and reasonable is associated with legitimacy.	Progress must be made in negotiation *before* participants can let go of intense expressions of emotion. Strong feelings are associated with legitimacy of a concern.
Trustworthiness of a third party	Impartiality is important, therefore someone who is a stranger to all parties is most likely to be trusted.	Caring and involvement are important, therefore someone familiar who is known and respected by all parties is most likely to be trusted.
Site of problem-solving	The conflict should be separated from outside influences, therefore a neutral location is best.	Problem-solving should take place in the context where the conflict occurred.
Getting to the point	It is important not to beat around the bush; identify and discuss the key issues in a conflict quickly.	It is rude to name problems too quickly; better to spend some time in casual interaction first.
Issue organization	Talk about one thing at a time.	Deal with several topics at once, or move back and forth between issues.
Saving face	Admitting that you have been wrong, or backing down, is unpleasant, but appropriate in some circumstances.	Losing face is completely unacceptable.
Structure of problem-solving	Conflict resolution works best when organization is formal. There should be clear roles, rules and demarcation of beginning, ending and the stages in between.	Conflict is best resolved in a climate of informality that resembles casual, social interaction.
Attribution of fault	When someone defends him/herself against an accusation, it is a sign of innocence; silence signifies guilt.	When someone defends him/herself against an accusation, it shows they are guilty; to ignore an accusation is a sign of innocence.
Threats	Threats represent a real intention to do harm. They are meant when they are said.	Threats represent a safe way to let off steam without doing real damage. They should not be taken literally.
Function of argument	Heated argument escalates conflict and interferes with finding solutions.	Heated argument is part of the truth-seeking process and helps resolve conflict.
Active listening	Nodding, saying "mm hmm," etc., means, "I am paying attention to you."	Nodding, saying "mm hmm," etc., means, "I agree with what you are saying."
Being silent while others discuss	Silence is neutral; it simply means someone is not ready to speak.	Silence represents agreement with what is being said. Or, not speaking when others exchange views is a refusal to help resolve the conflict and is obstructive.
Eye contact	It is natural and respectful to look directly at the person you are talking with. Looking away can signify evasion or deception.	It is natural and respectful to look away while talking with someone. Direct gaze can signify challenge or attack.
Questions	Questions indicate interest and genuine concern.	Questions are a form of attack; it is intrusive to require someone to explain themselves.

–Michel Avery
© Friends Conflict Resolution Programs (Philadelphia). Used by permission.

Triangles and Indirect Communication

Triangling

The concept of *triangles* is central to understanding communication from a systems perspective (see general systems articles in chapter six). It is a normal phenomenon. When anxiety grows in a two-person relationship, one individual will typically find a third person with whom to ally—often for the purpose of talking about the other individual or otherwise relieving the tension or imbalance in the first relationship. In families, for example, children frequently *get triangled by* or *triangle* parents. Triangling patterns in families and other organizational groups become predictable over time. Unchallenged, triangles become ingrained patterns of indirect communication.

Everyone has experienced patterns of indirect or *triangled* communication in the groups to which we belong.

- Mary always calls her mother when things are not going well between Mary and her husband, Joe.
- Fred is silent in congregational business meetings when the youth pastor asks for input, but never fails to talk to Sara afterwards in the parking lot.
- In the Smith family, all communication of dissatisfaction with others goes through brother-in-law Larry.

De-triangling

In order for systems to change—to move from indirect communication to open dialogue and self-definition—one can resist getting "triangled in" by giving the problem back to "A" and helping them to look at it constructively. Below are some helpful steps when person "A" is attempting to triangle you (C) into their relationship with person "B":

1. Listen carefully to understand A's story.
2. Acknowledge A's feelings without agreeing, disagreeing or adding any of your own opinions or stories.
3. Paraphrase A's underlying concerns about B's actions. Why were the B's actions hurtful and what would A like to see happen in this situation?
4. After hearing A's concerns, problem-solve together. Encourage A to confront B. You may offer to accompany A, serve as a mediator, or help find other ways to make the confrontation safe.
5. If A refuses to deal directly with B, set clear limits with A regarding ongoing discussions about the problem.
6. Do not pass on A's story to B or anyone else. Continue to support emotionally, encouraging A to be direct with B. Stick to your set limits.

Roleplay Exercise

With a partner, roleplay a situation where someone (A) attempted to triangle you (C) into their relationship with B. You play the role of A and your partner plays you (C), attempting to follow the steps above. Debrief. Discuss how your partner's response was similar or different from your response in the actual situation. Which response would most encourage direct communication? Switch roles and repeat the exercise.

For Discussion

What relevance does this view of triangling have in cultures that routinely use trusted third parties as go-betweens to address and resolve conflict? What might direct confrontation mean in these cultures?

–Alice M. Price and Carolyn Schrock-Shenk
© MCS 1989, 1995

Negotiation

Everyone negotiates. Whenever two or more people need to agree on something, they use negotiation. Many tend to think of negotiation only as a formal process, with a clear beginning and ending, that involves representatives working toward an agreement on behalf of a group. Examples include contract negotiations between a labor union and management or negotiating a treaty between two countries.

The most common images in society emphasize a winner-take-all view of negotiation, referred to as *competitive or distributive negotiation*. One party's gain necessarily means the other party's loss. This view of negotiation is based on a *win-lose* approach that stresses aggressive maneuvers, managing impressions and manipulating information to gain advantage over an opponent. The drawbacks are obvious, as one party stands to lose everything and relationships suffer regardless who wins.

Dissatisfied with competitive negotiation, many people assume the only alternative is to see *compromise* as the essence of negotiation. Each party must make a series of trade-offs to reach agreement in order to arrive at some middle ground. You give a little, you get a little. While less destructive, this approach ignores many creative options and not all problems can be resolved through compromise. When two people engaged to marry want to live in two different cities, deciding to live halfway between the two may not be a viable solution.

A more creative approach is *collaborative or integrative negotiation*. Instead of trying to outsmart an opponent or meet them halfway, this approach searches for solutions that meet goals and objectives of both sides. Unlike competition, parties emphasize their commonalties and jointly work at resolving their differences. It implies an interdependence where both parties work together to preserve the relationship. Collaboration is based on trust and a free flow of information. Solutions emerge by dealing constructively with differences. There is joint ownership in any decisions and collective responsibility for future direction. Mediation generally utilizes this approach, also known as "principled negotiation," which comes from the classic work, *Getting to Yes*, by Fisher, Ury and Patton.

Refer to the "Comparison of Negotiation Approaches" on the following page to further distinguish distributive/competitive negotiation from integrative/collaborative negotiation. The arrow points to a continuum of negotiation approaches, because in reality most negotiation is not strictly one approach but a combination of the two.

Collaborative Negotiation

Stages (Principles) of Process (from *Getting to Yes*)
1. Identify and define the problem (separate people from the problem)
2. Identify and discuss each party's interests and needs (focus on interests, not positions)
3. Generate options/alternative solutions (generate possibilities before deciding)
4. Evaluate and select alternatives (decide on objective criteria or standards)

In *distributive* negotiation, parties are encouraged to approach any negotiation with a *bottom line* or preconceived notion of the worst acceptable outcome. Without disclosing their bottom lines, parties are encouraged to reject any proposal below that line. While considered a way to protect a party's vital interests and needs, bottom-line thinking is rigid and may be based on inaccurate or arbitrary information.

Fisher and Ury invented a more powerful alternative to the bottom line, coined the *BATNA* (Best Alternative To a Negotiated Agreement). Used in integrative or collaborative negotiation, parties should consider their BATNA prior to entering into negotiation. The negotiation must then produce something better than your best alternative in order to be acceptable. Power comes from the ability to walk away from a negotiation. The way to increase your power is to further develop any opportunities for an alternative settlement. Fisher, Ury, and Patton (p. 106) state that "developing your BATNA thus not only enables you to determine what is a minimally acceptable agreement, it will probably raise that minimum." For example, knowing the salary and benefits of an alternative job offer increases your ability to negotiate for the salary and benefits you want at the job you want.

Finally, Fisher, Ury and Patton suggest seven strategies for dealing with perception problems that often arise in the midst of negotiation.

1. Try to see from the other's perspective.
2. Don't deduce the other's intentions from your own fears.
3. Avoid blaming the other for the problem.
4. Discuss each other's perceptions.
5. Seek opportunities to act inconsistently with the other's misperceptions of you.
6. Give the other a stake in the outcome by making sure they participate in negotiation.
7. Make your proposals consistent with the principles and self-image of the other.

These stages and strategies of principled bargaining work ideally when both parties come to negotiation with a collaborative approach. They also work, however, if you use them unilaterally, and can become contagious. The other party might start out with the low-trust competitive approach and be persuaded by your openness and focus on interests instead of positions. Asking questions to find out why they hold their position will lead to an exploration of their interests and needs, and soon to a joint brainstorming of options to meet both parties' interests.

Comparison of Negotiation Approaches

Distributive or Competitive Negotiation		Integrative or Collaborative Negotiation
Zero sum game (win-lose)	**Content**	Joint gain (win-win)
Each party focuses exclusively on their own self-interests	**Parties' focus**	Enlightened self-interests (your interests in light of the other's interests)
Hard (unfriendly)	**Relationship**	Soft (friendly)
Maximize your own gain, minimize loss Emphasize differences in goals and interests Quantitative versus relational goals	**Goals**	Both parties gain in light of diverse and common interests, separate and interdependent needs Emphasize common goals and interests Include both quantitative and relationship goals
Rigid (confrontational)	**Identity/ face-saving**	Flexible (supportive)
Withhold data and conceal information, use it selectively and strategically	**Flow of information**	Create free and open flow, full disclosure of relevant information
Start extreme, concede slowly; manipulate intentions, resources and goals; resist persuasion; convince other you can give no more Perceived as logical, step-wise progression	**Process**	Build trust; identify each other's interests; creatively maximize joint benefits; expand perceived limited resources; generate and evaluate options; make a joint decision
Military maneuvers (the best defense is a good offense)	**Metaphor**	Group lost in the wilderness (group survival)
Biased toward confrontation (threatens relationship) Against responsiveness and openness Encourages brinkmanship (to the point of danger) Difficult to predict other's responses Overestimation of payoffs of competitive (e.g., legal) action	**Disadvantages**	Biased toward cooperation (compromise) Avoids confrontational strategies Over-sensitive to others (easily manipulated) Requires skills and process knowledge Requires confidence in one's own ability to assess situation and perceive others

–Mark Chupp
© MCS 2000

Stances for Collaboration

Giving and receiving feedback responsibly is a key to healthy and respectful relationships. The following tips are provided to help you prepare for dialogue.

Listening Stance

Pay attention. Be ready to summarize what you hear.

- Body language which says, "I'm listening."
- Silence is okay, as long as you are truly paying attention.
- Brief summaries: "You're saying. . . ." "The way you see it. . . ." "So you feel. . . ."

"Inform Me" Stance

Be open to and ask for more information.

- Avoid questions which "cross-examine" or carry a prejudgment: "How can you think that?" "Why would anyone do that?" "Who told you that?"
- Ask for specifics or examples, if the information is too general: "Help me understand that better with an example."
- Seek depth: "Say more about that." "Could you explain why you're feeling that way?" "Tell me what you have in mind."

"Inform Others" Stance

Be open to express your ideas and feelings.

- Speak for yourself, not others.
- Own your ideas and feelings with I-messages: "I feel. . . ." "I'm confused about. . . ." "I think. . . ."
- State an opinion not an ultimatum; remain open to others' ideas/needs: "My preference is. . . ." "What would meet my needs best is. . . ." "If it were just me. . . ." "What I'd like to see happen is. . . ." "What I'd find helpful is. . . . What about you?"
- Let people know how you've personally been impacted by things: "The reason I've felt upset is. . . ." "I felt really hurt when. . . ." "This has affected me by. . . ."
- Let others know your purpose for sharing information, especially if it is sensitive: "What I'm trying to accomplish. . . ." "My intent in sharing is. . . ." "I'm hoping. . . ."

Areas of Agreement and Affirmation

- Positive feedback helps build trust and lets others know what you need and like.
- Say "thank you" when someone has given you helpful information or new insights: "It helps to understand your perspective on that."
- Be willing to honor areas of agreement, even if you disagree on other things: "I agree that. . . ." "I see what you're saying and want to add. . . ." "I share your concern, but. . . ."

–Ron Kraybill, as adapted by Alice M. Price
© MCS 2000

A Process for Working at Interpersonal Conflict

1. Break the cycle of destructive conflict: Name the conflict

Often just asking, "What's happening between us?" can break the cycle so that each person can begin to reflect on the situation and her/his role in the conflict. Take some time alone if needed and then plan a time when both of you are able to work on the conflict.

2. Listen to yourself

Take time to listen to your feelings and reflect on where they are coming from. Think how you want to treat yourself and the other person in this conflict, reminding yourself of the importance of the other person and of your relationship.

3. Tell your stories (uninterrupted time)

Create the space to listen to each other, allowing each person to tell her/his story. This includes past unresolved hurts, each person's perspective on what has happened, and what concerns remain. Ideally, it is a process of moving from blame to discovery, of uncovering what happened and what is important.

4. Identify the issues creating tension

Once each person has told her/his story, make a list of all the issues that are creating tensions in the relationship. Try to make one joint list and include tangible disagreements as well as past hurts.

5. Identify commonalities and move toward healing

Take time to acknowledge and validate the other person. This is also a time for identifying what you hold in common about a particular issue. If there are hurts, name the feelings and discover the roots to them. It might be helpful to allow each person time to write if the issue provokes a lot of emotions.

6. Work together on one issue at a time

Clarify what the issue is, why it is important, and what each person's interests are concerning the issue. This is another stage of discovery where different perspectives are expected and welcome.

7. Generate options for reconciliation and resolution

Brainstorm options for meeting each person's concerns. Avoid critiquing a suggestion or jumping to agreement at this step. Do not be afraid to make a request, but also consider what you can offer the other person.

8. Build a plan that satisfies both

Choose from the options in the previous step, discussing the pros and cons of the most promising ideas. Several ideas are often combined together to satisfy both parties on a particular issue. It is a good idea to write down your plan, specifying *who* will do *what*, *when* and *where*.

9. Focus on relationship and agree to check back

After you have crafted an agreement take time to reflect on your relationship now that you have worked through this process. Discuss how you can learn from the conflict, let go of the power it has over you and release the other person. Be generous and gracious with each other, acknowledging the hard work you have done and the positive contributions each made to the process.

10. Agree to check in

Make a commitment about how and when you will support each other and check back on the progress you are making.

–Mark Chupp

© MCS 2000. Many of these concepts are drawn from *Making Peace with Conflict: Practical Skills for Conflict Transformation*, Carolyn Schrock-Shenk and Lawrence Ressler, editors (Herald Press, 1999).

How to Confront

Suggestions for More Effective Interpersonal Confrontation

Very few people enjoy confronting someone else. Even fewer relish being confronted. A primary reason is that our experiences in confrontations have often been very painful. For that reason, most people tend to avoid confrontation at all costs. The result is that unresolved issues fester because no one is willing to deal with them. These "suggestions" are intended to offer guidance in knowing when and how to confront.

When to Confront

Not every issue on which you disagree with someone else merits confrontation, but some do. Not every relationship matters enough to you to justify the emotional energy of confrontation, but some do. A good rule of thumb: When you care a lot about both the *issue* and the *person* it may merit confrontation.

Plan the Confrontation

Effective confrontation requires planning. Think through how you will approach the person, what you will say, how the person might respond. The goal is to prepare yourself mentally and emotionally for the confrontation, not to become obsessed with all the possible nuances.

Seek a Safe Environment

The confrontation will more likely result in a positive outcome if the environment feels "safe" to the person you are confronting. Examples of "unsafe" environments: in front of a large group of people, or across from your desk if you are the person's superior. Try to find more informal, neutral or "home" turf for the person you are confronting.

Ask Permission

Most people will respond better to confrontation if you allow them the opportunity to help schedule it. Some personality styles insist on this, and will respond negatively with a demand to "talk about this issue now." A better approach: Inform the person that there is an important issue that you would like to discuss with him or her. Ask when would be a good time to get together and talk about it. The person may respond, "Let's do it right now," but will nonetheless appreciate the opportunity to have declined.

Be "Hard on the Issues, Soft on the Person"

When confronting, it is important to be open about the issues which concern you. "Beating around the bush" is often perceived as manipulative and confusing. But dealing clearly with the issues does *not* mean you also have to be hard on the person. It is often helpful to (honestly) affirm things you appreciate about the person even while you are identifying issues that concern you. If you are in a long-term relationship with that person, affirm your ongoing commitment to that relationship.

Own Your Feelings and Beliefs

During the confrontation, speak for yourself, not for others who aren't there. It is particularly unhelpful to say things like, "Everybody else feels this way about you but doesn't have the courage to tell you." Instead, own your own concerns through the use of "I-Statements." An example: "I felt angry and confused last Thursday evening when you said that no one in our group cared about you. I care a lot about you and it hurt me to hear you say that I don't."

Be Honest About Your Own Preferences

The general reason for confronting is that we are hoping for a change of behavior in the person we are confronting. Thus, it is generally helpful to be honest about your own preferences, rather than to leave the person guessing as to what you are hoping to see. An example of a preference statement:

> "I would prefer that in the future you come to me personally when I do something that concerns you. I've found that I respond best when I'm confronted one-on-one, rather than in front of a group."

Be Prepared to Listen

Any time we confront someone we are asking them to take seriously our concerns. Often these concerns are issues of a personal nature about which the person may feel very strongly. Thus, it is essential that we be prepared to *listen* to the person after we have shared our concerns. A possible way of helping this to happen: "Thanks for listening so carefully when I shared my concerns with you. I don't expect you to instantly agree with everything I said, and really want to hear your perspective. How do you think and feel about the things I've said?"

Accept Confrontation as a Normal Part of Life

While few relationships need daily confrontation, it is inevitable that in most caring relationships confrontation will occasionally need to occur. Once it has, accept it as part of life. It would be unhelpful to try to pretend that it never occurred, or refuse to talk about it later. In fact, the person confronted may need ongoing opportunities to talk about the issues that were identified in the initial confrontation. At a later meeting, you may wish to offer this opportunity. "Thanks again for the way you listened to me the other day when we talked about X. Have you had any further thoughts since then that you'd want to share with me?"

Be Confrontable

When someone else confronts you, concentrate first on understanding their concerns. This is best done with paraphrasing, or "active listening." Before responding to the person's concerns, state something like: "Before I respond to that I want to make sure I understand what your concerns are. If I understood correctly, you're concerned about X, Y and Z. Is that right?"

Of course, these considerations will not guarantee a "painless" confrontation. When we identify issues of personal concern we are risking our own vulnerabilities by asking another person to be vulnerable with us. Such a process is not without risk, and there is no assurance that we will maintain control of it.

But people who have confronted with these considerations in mind report that the experience was generally more positive than they expected. When we deal clearly with issues which divide us, rather than attacking the person who disagrees with us, we often develop new insights and even a deeper relationship with the person with whom we disagreed.

For Discussion

1. What relevance do these principles of confrontation have in cultures that value indirectness?

2. What other principles might be more appropriate?

–David Brubaker
© MCS 1988

Resources for Further Study on Communication

Augsburger, David. *Caring Enough to Hear and Be Heard*. Scottdale, PA: Herald Press, 1982.
    Provides useful insight into listening and speaking; uses personal illustrations, diagrams, exercises, psychological principles and case histories.

Bartel, Barry. *Let's Talk: Communication Skills and Conflict Transformation*. Newton, KS: Faith and Life Press, 2000.
    A workbook for group study, written for high school youth and adults. Includes a personal inventory on conflict management styles, discussion guides, personal reflection exercises, and roleplays for active listening and appropriate speaking. A leader's guide is included at the back.

Bolton, Robert. *People Skills: How to Assert Yourself, Listen to Others, and Resolve Conflicts*. New York: Simon & Schuster, 1986.
    A helpful book focusing on communication skills.

Duryea, Michelle LeBaron. *Conflict Analysis and Resolution as Education: Culturally Sensitive Processes for Conflict Resolution (Training Materials)*, Victoria, BC: UVic Institute for Dispute Resolution, 1994. Also: Michelle LeBaron Duryea and Victor C. Robinson. *Conflict Analysis and Resolution as Education: Culturally Sensitive Processes for Conflict Resolution (Trainer Reference)*. Victoria, BC: UVic Institute for Dispute Resolution, 1994.
    Designed to assist mediation trainers and mediators to address culture in a comprehensive way. Highly recommended.

Fisher, Roger, and Scott Brown. *Getting Together: Building Relationships As We Negotiate*. Boston: Houghton Mifflin, 1988.
    Builds on Fisher's previous book, as the subtitle suggests.

Gilmore, Susan K., and Patrick W. Fraleigh. *Communication at Work*. Eugene, OR: Friendly Press, 1993.
    Suggests ways to accept and celebrate style differences between yourself and others. Teaches interpersonal skills and self-management strategies and gives practical, sensible suggestions for improving communication in working relationships.

Hocker, Joyce L., and William W. Wilmot. *Interpersonal Conflict*, 3rd ed. Dubuque, IA: William Brown, 1991.
    Basic text on the components of conflict and conflict intervention. Includes excellent material on communication patterns such as triangling.

Kochman, Thomas. *Black and White Styles in Conflict*. Chicago, IL: University of Chicago Press, 1981.
    A classic in understanding cultural differences, including the impact of culture on communication patterns.

Lawyer, John W., and Neil H. Katz. *Communication and Conflict Resolution Skills*. Dubuque, IA: Kendall/Hunt Publishing, 1985.
    Manual to be used for courses and workshops as well as self-study. Includes theory presentation, skill development examples, self-testing exercises.

Lawyer, John W., and Neil H. Katz. *Communication Skills for Ministry*. Dubuque, IA: Kendall/Hunt Publishing, 1983.
    Workbook designed to teach interpersonal skills to individuals and teams dedicated to helping others. Includes theory presentations, skills practice, evaluation of progress and results.

Lerner, Harriet G. *The Dance of Anger: A Woman's Guide to Changing the Patterns of Intimate Relationships*. New York: Harper and Row, 1997.
    Reissued, this book shows women how to turn anger into a constructive force for reshaping their lives.

Miller, Sherod, Daniel Wackman, Elam Nunnally and Phyllis Miller. *Connecting With Self and Others*. Littleton, CO: Interpersonal Communication Programs, 1988.
> A good book on understanding communication. There is an exercise book available to make the content more practical. Certain sections are more helpful than others.

Nh'ât Hanh, Thích. *Being Peace*. Berkeley, CA: Parallax Press, 1987.
> The Vietnamese Zen master and peace activist provides, among other thoughts, a look at the Buddhist system of seven practices of reconciliation.

Schrock-Shenk, Carolyn, and Lawrence Ressler (eds). *Making Peace with Conflict: Practical Skills for Conflict Transformation*. Scottdale, PA: Herald Press, 1999.
> A practical guide to understanding and transforming conflict based on biblical and Anabaptist principles.

Ury, William. *Getting Past No: Negotiating With Difficult People*. New York: Bantam Books, 1991.
> A book on communication and negotiation.

Chapter 4

Interpersonal Mediation:
One Model

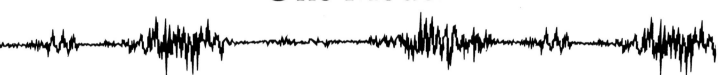

Throughout the world, there are literally thousands of different and legitimate ways for two parties to reach an agreement. Just because <u>we</u> feel comfortable with one set of rules and etiquette does not mean that it is necessarily the most logical, efficient or desirable method for everyone.

–Jan Jung-Min Sunoo

Mediation: An Overview

While various forms and arenas of mediation have existed for many years and in many settings, the popularization of mediation in North America has been on a tremendous rise since the early 1970s. Its influence can be seen from high-level international negotiations to the "barking dog" cases brought to local neighborhood centers. And its proponents likewise run from Supreme Court justices and university professors to grassroots community organizers and ten-year-old volunteers on school playgrounds.

What is Mediation?

In simple terms, mediation is a process, facilitated by a third party, by which disputants discuss their concerns and issues and explore possible options for mutually satisfactory solutions to differences. Typically, the process is a voluntary one and the parties have selected the third party. Without taking sides or imposing solutions, the mediator's role is to assist the parties in identifying their needs and interests, generating options, and documenting agreements. On a continuum of conventional problem-solving models, mediation (along with its even less formal counterpart of conciliation) is a facilitated negotiation process, set up by and for the parties themselves. It stands in contrast to arbitration, litigation, and other fact-finding or evaluative processes, where the format is adversarial and decisions are made and imposed by a third party.

What is the Attraction of Mediation?

For some, it is its practicality. Disputes which would otherwise take extensive time and money to be processed through traditional legal channels—or simply languish in growing court backlogs—can often be managed more quickly and affordably through Alternative Dispute Resolution programs sponsored by courts, industry groups, private agencies or volunteer-based community centers. Settlement rates run high (80% and greater) in many of these established mediation programs.

For others, however, the attraction of mediation is more than a utilitarian one. Settlement is not the sole objective. Rather, mediation is a vehicle for empowering individuals or groups to identify and articulate their needs and interests, and to fashion their own solutions from a range of options. Because mediation is a discipline of careful listening and dialogue, the potential for transforming people

and problems goes far beyond the "quick fix" of some mediation proponents. Conflict resolution becomes an opportunity to strengthen the individuals and relationships directly involved by fostering both mutual recognition and gain and, ultimately, to bring about genuine change in communities.

Why this Particular Model?

The mediation process outlined at the beginning of this chapter is fairly typical of the mediation processes which have evolved in North America over the past three decades. Similar outlines will be found in training and program manuals in public, private, and community-based settings across the U.S. and Canada. (And now, with the growing exportation of mediation, in training and program manuals around the globe.) As you can gather from the foundational chapters in this manual, the understandings of Mennonite Conciliation Service (MCS) about conflict's transformation grow out of underlying faith understandings about ourselves, others, and the broader world. As these understandings of our practice mature, we have struggled with carrying one "prescriptive" model of mediation into diverse racial and ethnic communities here and abroad. We also struggle against the use of mediation as a "quick fix" in complex disputes or situations of significant injustice and power imbalance.

Our desire is that the mediation outline offered below will be viewed and used thoughtfully within the broader context and caveats of this manual and MCS's work. While the mediation outline itself may be rather conventional, we attempt throughout this chapter and in our training events to convey and emphasize our own distinctive assumptions and values about mediation and the mediator role. We invite you to draw upon, alter and even reject this model in ways which: 1) are appropriate to specific settings and cultures; 2) maximize your own peacemaking gifts; and 3) best realize your own and others' understandings of mediation's potential.

–Alice M. Price
© MCS 1995

Refer to "Mediator's Cultural Assumptions" (page 101) and other articles in the Cultural Dimension section of Chapter Two.

Transformative Mediation

The authors of a recent book, *The Promise of Mediation*, popularized the notion of "transformative mediation" which is based on the premise that when we are in conflict with each other we are generally two things to varying degrees:

1) We are *weak*
   - confused and unsure
   - fearful and anxious

2) We are *self-absorbed*
   - only able to see our own needs and wants
   - which usually makes us defensive and suspicious

The authors believe that popular mediation has been based largely on the "Satisfaction Story" which has reaching agreement and improving relationships as its primary goals. Mediation, they believe, has the potential to do much more; it can transform people's lives. Specifically, they believe that mediation can move people:

1) From weakness to *empowerment*
   - an increased sense of personal value and strength
   - increased self-respect, self-reliance and self-confidence
   - an increased capacity to handle life's problems

2) From self-absorbed to *recognition*
   - an acknowledgment and concern for the situation and problems of the other
   - an increased ability to be empathetic, compassionate and considerate

	The Satisfaction Story	The Transformation Story
Dispute	a problem to solve	opportunities for moral growth and transformation
Success	agreement over issues identified by the mediator	parties experience moral growth through empowerment and recognition with or without reaching agreement
Process	5-7 steps directed by the mediator	guided by mediator but parties have ownership of process

The mediation we promote in this manual does not fit cleanly into either of the "stories" but carries many elements of both. We do promote searching for agreements to specific conflictive issues if that is what the parties are seeking, and we present a variety of ways to work toward agreement. We are committed to improving the relationship of the parties both by addressing the tangible issues as well as the hurts and misunderstandings between them. We also believe that mediation can transform individuals and that what happens at the intrapersonal level affects the interpersonal level deeply, as well as the structural and cultural levels. So we also promote ways to address the deep feelings disputants bring, their needs for clarity and acknowledgment and healing and reconciliation. Perhaps the real art of mediation is the ability to move between these "stories" depending on the needs of the disputants with whom we are working.

–**Carolyn Schrock-Shenk**
© MCS 2000, drawn from Robert A. Baruch Bush and Joseph P. Folger, *The Promise of Mediation*

A Dispute Resolution Continuum

More
Control

Informal Discussion and Problem-Solving: Majority of disagreements are handled this way, some satisfactorily, others simply get "dropped."

Negotiation: A bargaining process around differences entered voluntarily by parties who try to educate each other about their needs and interests, to exchange resources, or to address intangible issues such as future relations.

Conciliation: A process in which a third party attempts to help parties to collaborate, but less structured or formal than mediation. (Conciliation is also used as a broad term for many conflict management/resolution processes.)

Facilitation: An impartial third party leads a collaborative process in which individuals and groups with divergent views meet to reach consensus on a goal or to solve a problem. Similar to mediation, but generally does not involve an impasse.

Mediation: A facilitated negotiation; a process by which a mediator assists disputing parties to collaboratively discuss their concerns and problem-solve their issues. Mediators assist in documenting any mutually acceptable points of agreement the parties may reach. The mediator does not have authoritative decision-making or enforcing power and participation by the parties is voluntary, private and face-to-face.

Arbitration: A private process conducted by one or more third parties who decide how the dispute will be resolved. The outcome may be "binding" or "nonbinding"/"advisory."

Judicial Approaches (Including Litigation): Intervention by socially recognized authority to decide the issues and enforce the decision. It is generally a public process where parties lose control of outcome, but may gain from forceful advocacy of their point of view.

Legislative Approaches: Another public and legal means of problem solving where win/lose decisions are determined by voting. Individuals have only as much control/influence as they can mobilize.

Less
Control

–Jim Stutzman
©MCS 1994, 2000

A Negotiation Paradigm

Most mediation models draw on a paradigm known popularly as "principled negotiation" or "reconciling interests." This model focuses the parties on "interests" rather than "positions" as the foundation for negotiation. Below, the key attributes of "principled negotiation" are contrasted with more adversarial and accommodating styles of bargaining.

–MCS Staff

Problem		Solution
Positional Bargaining: Which game should you play?		Change the Game— Negotiate on the Merits
Soft	Hard	Principled
Participants are friends.	Participants are adversaries.	Participants are problem-solvers.
The goal is agreement.	The goal is victory.	The goal is a wise outcome reached efficiently and amicably.
Make concessions to cultivate the relationship.	Demand concessions as a condition of the relationship.	**Separate the people from the problem.**
Be soft on the people and the problem.	Be hard on the problem and the people.	Be soft on the people, and hard on the problem.
Trust others.	Distrust others.	Proceed independent of trust.
Change your position easily.	Dig in to your position.	**Focus on interests, not positions.**
Make offers.	Make threats.	Explore interests.
Disclose your bottom line.	Mislead as to your bottom line.	Avoid having a bottom line.
Accept one-sided losses to reach agreement.	Demand one-sided gains as the price of agreement.	**Invent options for mutual gain.**
Search for the single answer: the one *they* will accept.	Search for the single answer: the one *you* will accept.	Develop multiple options to choose from; decide later.
Insist on agreement.	Insist on your position.	**Insist on using objective criteria.**
Try to avoid a contest of will.	Try to win a contest of will.	Try to reach a result based on standards independent of will.
Yield to pressure.	Apply pressure.	Reason and be open to reason; yield to principle, not pressure.

–Roger Fisher, William Ury and Bruce Patton
From *Getting to Yes*, 2nd edition. Copyright © 1981, 1991 by Roger Fisher and William Ury. Reprinted by permission of Houghton Mifflin Company. All rights reserved.

A Matter of Attitude

Why does mediation work? Skills and technique are important, but the mediator's attitude is an essential ingredient.

Attitude Toward the Parties

Respect is the key. Mediators need to respect the dignity and competence of each party. Mediators must also respect the responsibility of the parties for resolving their own conflict.

Attitude Toward Oneself

Humility helps. Jim Laue has aptly described the importance of an "ego container" for a mediator—an imaginary box to constrain one's self importance.

Attitude Toward the Process

Keep it simple. Mediation is an uncomplicated, flexible process that makes sense. Mediators need to resist the urge to make it more complex.

Attitude Toward Conflict

Conflict is a normal, natural part of life. Mediators who interact collaboratively with people who are in conflict are modeling positive problem-solving behavior.

Attitude Toward Interplay of Emotions and Rational Thought

Legitimize feelings. Mediation allows for the safe and productive expression of feelings. Parties need to do this before they can negotiate rationally and productively.

Attitude Toward Reconciliation

True reconciliation brings healing. It may seem impossible or at least unlikely, but mediators need to be willing for the parties to have it—they deserve it.

–Community Mediation Center
© Community Mediation Center (Harrisonburg, Va.). Used by permission.

Listening Skills for Mediators

Listening skills are critical during the entire mediation process, from intake and assessment through follow-up. In addition to the following review, see Chapter Three as well pages 184-186 on reframing for a more in-depth look at a range of important communication skills.

1. **Use your body** to say "I'm listening." But always remember to take cues from the speaker about what is comfortable and culturally appropriate for them in terms of eye contact, body orientation, touch, etc.

2. **Use *echo* responses**, repeating a word or phrase spoken by the speaker. This unobtrusively focuses the attention of the speaker on things which may be unclear to you. Echo responses allow you to direct the flow of conversation without major interruptions.

3. **Paraphrase** or restate the speaker's views in your own words, focusing on the speaker, including both facts and feelings, and being non-judgmental. Reminder: Paraphrasing is a powerful tool for building rapport with many, but not all people.

4. **Summarize** the basic viewpoints of the speaker as you've heard them. A summary is an extended restatement of the key points offered by the speaker. Use summaries to focus on the issues and solvable problems, not on personalities. In the final summary, obtain the agreement of the speaker that you have summarized both accurately and completely.

5. **Launder** unhelpful language parties use; ask questions that elicit more useful information and move the discussion to meaningful levels.
    - *Generalizing*: "He's always late." (Mediator responds: *"When does he come in late? What is he late to?"*)
    - *Unspecified noun or verb*: "I don't like that sort of thing." (*"What is it that you dislike?"*) "She just bugs me. . . ." (*"In what way does she bug you? When does she bug you?"*)
    - *Speaking for others*: "I happen to know that no one else here can get along with him either." (*"Speaking from your own experience with Mr. Brown, could you tell us more about what you're upset about?"*)
    - *Attacks*: "She's a liar." (*"You see things differently."*)

6. **Watch for and highlight** hidden offers, commonalities and conciliatory intentions: "I can't wait for this to be over." (*"So you are really looking for a way to put this behind you. Tell me more about what that would look like for you."*).

7. **Be careful** with questions, since they impose your agenda on the speaker (leading) rather than allowing the speaker's experience to structure the interaction (pacing). When possible, hold questions until the speaker has finished, then use "open" (*"Could you say a little more about Mrs. Jones?"*) rather than "closed" (*"Who is Mrs. Jones?"*) questions.

    Aim for inviting, imperative questions (*"Explain. . . .," "Say more. . . .," "Help us understand. . . ."*) rather than interrogatives (who, why, when). As rapport builds, interrogatives become more acceptable. (See page 181 for more on drawing out interests.)

8. **Maintain** a listening atmosphere. Be firm about the "no interruptions" ground rule. Respond to the first few interruptions and ignore later ones (instead of the reverse). If people feel they must respond to "lies," give them pen and paper to take notes. Stay in the "I" mode and avoid you-statements. (*"I'd like to remind you . . . ,"* rather than *"You're breaking the ground rule"*) Respond to their interests. (*"John, I know you have a different perspective on this. I want to hear your view as well in a few minutes."*)

–MCS Staff
© MCS 1987, 1992, 1995

Intake and Assessment

Intake begins with the initial contact with each party. It has been said that 80% of the work of mediation is done before the parties even get to the table. The terms pre-mediation, or intake, refer to the initial conversations with potential mediation parties and can really be considered the first stage in the mediation process. When adequate time is taken to prepare both mediator and parties for the work of mediating, the fruitfulness of the session(s) together is heightened.

Listen. Listening begins immediately. Whether it is by phone or in person, the mediator or program staff member listens to and seeks to understand how each person sees the situation and why they are considering mediation. Nonjudgmental attentiveness and the ability to ask open, inviting questions are critical for assessment and for trust-building with each party. How much of each person's experience you need to hear at this stage and how long it takes varies greatly depending on the needs of the parties.

Assess the appropriateness of mediation. It is important to determine if there are any elements or dynamics which may make the situation inappropriate for mediation (i.e., if problem has no identifiable other party, if one party is not available or willing, if violence or intimidation exists between the parties, or if there are issues that are not negotiable). Referring people at this stage to other resources and services as appropriate can be your best and most successful mediation strategy.

Reduce surprises. You want to try to eliminate some surprises in the mediation session and save everyone time and frustration during the sessions. Be aware of dynamics such as the need for language interpretation, existence of very strong emotions, or desire for the presence of support persons or party advocates. Making sure that all involved parties are identified and contacted is critical as well. This avoids the surprise—and delay—of discovering in the mediation session that someone with a critical role in the conflict situation is not present.

Educate the parties about the process. This is the time to begin educating the parties about the process. Describe mediation, including the role of the mediators and the way decisions are made; clear up any misperceptions; build commitment; and generally prepare participants for the process.

Reduce resistance. Anger, hopelessness, suspicion and fear are all common emotions from parties at this stage. There are times when getting a party to see beyond any of these enough to take the step of mediation takes a long time and lots of listening and paraphrasing. Arguing and pressure tactics generally increase resistance. Focusing on understanding and naming underlying concerns decreases it. If it is clear that no amount of attentive listening will prepare a party, you may want to help them look at their options. You can ask, "If you don't try mediation, what do you think will happen?" Then, "If that does happen, is that okay with you?" If the answer is "yes," thank them for their time, wish them wisdom and courage, and say good-bye. They clearly are not ready for mediation or mediation may not be a good choice in their situation.

–Sandi Adams and Carolyn Schrock-Shenk
© MCS 2000

When to Mediate?

Guidelines for Deciding When Mediation is Appropriate

The growing acceptance of mediation as an "alternative" means of resolving disputes has propelled the process into nearly all areas of North American society. Mediation is used in business disputes, community and family problems, congregational conflicts, victim-offender reconciliation, schools, environmental disputes, farmer-lender negotiations, international and cross-cultural conflicts and labor-management relations. Yet mediation is not a cure-all. Though mediation deserves even greater use than it is now enjoying, not all conflicts can or should be resolved by mediation. Knowing what process to use in a given dispute and when to implement it are initially the most crucial issues in successful dispute resolution.

Following are guidelines for determining if and when to choose mediation:

Mediation is not an appropriate substitute for therapy or counseling.

When one or several parties to the conflict are emotionally ill, or under so much stress that rational discussion would be impossible, mediation should be avoided or delayed. Be careful though; parties in conflict are often quick to assume mental illness or evil intent on the part of their adversaries. In the cases in which psychological help is needed, Christopher Moore suggests referring the party to an appropriate resource. Moore's "Code of Professional Conduct for Mediators" states: "Mediation shall not be conducted with parties who are either intoxicated or who have major psychological disorders which seriously impair their judgment."

This does not preclude mediation as *an addition to* professional counseling or therapy. The process of resolving differences with an adversary can contribute to personal healing and emotional well-being. As Josie Medina has stated, "Although mediators are not therapists, mediation is therapeutic." One factor to weigh: Are the problems at hand unique to this relationship, or do they appear as a pattern in many other relationships for the individual? Mediation addresses specific problems well, but handles general patterns poorly.

Mediation should not be used as a coercive means to an end.

Mediation is a voluntary process (except in criminal cases). Individuals should generally not be ordered or required to participate in mediation. Reconciliation happens only by invitation. However, be clear about the alternatives if a person does not wish to participate in a mediation session. Threats and coercion, though, are incompatible with the nature of mediation.

Mediation should not be used as a substitute for the proper exercise of authority.

When laws have been broken and/or individuals victimized, the church and/or society must act to stop the victimization. Action at this stage inevitably produces conflict, as the perpetrator is censured for his or her behavior. A rush to mediate would be inadvisable at this stage, although it may become appropriate at later stages. For example, Victim Offender Reconciliation Programs (VORPs) have successfully mediated restitution between offender and victim. However, this is only done *after* the offender has admitted to the wrongdoing.

Mediation is not appropriate when trained mediators are not available.

Mediation is a specific process which requires training and practice to learn. A person unskilled in the mediation process may be extremely useful in the roles of supporter, advocate, researcher or even discussion facilitator. However, such roles should not be confused with that of mediator. Every person can and should serve as a "peacemaker" at times, to assist two friends or family members who are in conflict. Mislabeling the experience, however, is unfair to the process, the parties and the would-be "mediator."

Mediation should be avoided when power should *not* be balanced.

Mediation is effective in part because it works to balance power differentials at the table, placing the company president, for example, on the same bargaining level as the union organizer. For the vast majority of disputes, especially in a culture which values "democracy," this is appropriate and helpful in the resolution process. In some situations or cultures it may be highly inappropriate to attempt to balance power.

Consider for example a traditional culture in which a village resident has violated a strongly-held precept of the village. According to custom, the village elders will meet to determine how to resolve the problems which have been created. Instead, a visiting North American mediator urges the parties to consider mediating the dispute. The village elders are torn between their desire to please the visitor and their knowledge that they dare not compromise their authority. To sit down as "equals" with the offender would demean the elders in the eyes of the village. It would also wrongly imply that future violations of this nature would be negotiable.

"Mediation is inappropriate if the goal is repression or revolution."

"Mediation is an appropriate process for resolving a community conflict if both parties are seeking a middle range of goals, such as redistribution of resources, grievance machinery or tension reduction. In some instances, mediation simply may

–Dave Brubaker and Ron Kraybill
© MCS 1988

assist an establishment group in coopting the challengers." (Jim Laue)

Given the effectiveness of mediation in resolving disputes, the process may be contraindicated if used too early with surface issues that do not resolve the root causes of conflict. Minority or subordinate groups would be especially prone to misapplied mediation. John Paul Lederach has suggested that a "mediator's nightmare" would be someone mediating the dispute between Rosa Parks and the Montgomery bus company which tried to force her to give up her seat in the 1960s. Without the opportunity to gain recognition through a conflict-producing act of resistance, subordinate groups can be further hampered even by well-meaning mediators.

These six instances are not intended to be a complete list. Nor do we suggest that such cautions will serve as complete guidelines in any situation. Our primary purpose is instead to caution that mediation, like any other process, is not appropriate to *all* disputes.

Additional information on screening cases for mediation and special areas for concern is included in Chapter Six.

Mediating Intercultural Relationships

When bias reduction and conflict resolution intersect well, the focus of the conflict resolution process is primarily on the human relationship and secondarily on the conflict resolution process. Someone who is too biased or too scared has to rely on the mechanics of the agenda or the formula of the conflict resolution process. In a worst-case scenario, particularly in intercultural work, the mediators' bias or fear can negate their effectiveness and they can actually become part of the conflict.

In intercultural settings, people of color are looking for the behavioral and verbal clues which communicate that the mediator is willing to be in relationship. Between people of color and white people, bias which is not overtly expressed may come across as aloof or cold behavior which can communicate, "I do not want to get involved with you." The bias and aloofness, of course, can run both ways. The reconciliation, though, for everyone is found in a willingness and ability to be in mutual relationship.

Coercive Assimilation

From my point of view, the mediator, to be most effective, needs to understand the legacy of coercive assimilation, what that means in practice, and what that means to various populations in the United States. By coercive assimilation (I emphasize "coercive" because our system teaches the myth that the process has been benign) I mean dynamics that have locked us into totally unworkable one-sided relationships where some of us have been historically oppressed into being like others.

A mediator can help bridge some of the conditioned polarization in the room by their ability to help the participants balance task and process. In intercultural problem solving and conflict resolution, getting to task is often a number one priority, what I call a "dominant culture" agenda—very tight, very task-oriented. It says by its structure that the task is more important than the community. If biases crop up or a participant gets enraged about something, the mediator says, "We don't have time to deal with that now; we'll look at that later." But the participant is already feeling it and thinking it. The mediator has asserted his or her own power and silenced the participant's voice by not going in the participant's direction. Eventually, the participants are ready to hang the mediator (who may be a person of color who is assimilationist; we all live in a dominant culture and take on its character).

Making Relationship Top Priority

Getting to process or relationship should also be a number one priority because of the need to bridge these patterns of dominance and subordination (in the form of assumptions about what is important and how things will happen) in which the parties in the room are already locked and which will play out in the room in a free flow manner unless the intercultural relationship is facilitated. If relationships are not made the focus of the work, then completing the task at hand will be number one because deadlines, meeting real needs, and so on—what I consider time oppression—dictate that it be number one.

The common tendency is to treat getting to task as the number one priority and the process or relationship piece as number two. The mediators' biases or fears can cause them to focus on tasks because that feels easier than relationship. Aligning task and process this way, as one and two, is a dominant cultural approach. What I see happen repeatedly when I'm called in to mediate (sometimes too late) is that the de-emphasis of relationship building starts to alienate the people of color from the reconciliation process because a critical part of who they are gets squeezed out of the agenda in the urgency of getting to work.

More Than Good Intentions

In general, people of color have great awareness and skill in understanding people of the dominant culture who generally don't have a similar ability to understand the other side—to understand people of color. There is an "understanding deficit." So often we encounter defensiveness from mediators of the dominant culture; they don't know that they don't know. They tend to think that good intentions are enough, but there is a profound lack of knowledge. If we all apply some good conflict resolution skills and some ventilation and healing, we can all manage our discomfort and reveal what we need to know about each other.

Fear of conflict is a major problem. As soon as people of color sound too angry and white people get too scared, polarization takes over the room. Dialogue becomes an exercise in academic futility, with everyone pretending to work it out. Our biggest problem, as people who do conflict resolution, is that conflict scares us. We pretend to be in charge. It would be a breath of fresh air to admit our fears to each other.

From the perspective of people of color, conflict is institutionalized—it's just a question of when it flares up. If you're surprised when it flares, you don't understand the nature of conflict. Often, a white mediator with good intentions will be surprised when his or her attempt to do good "on behalf of" people of color results in conflict. Such mediators don't understand the dominance and oppression with which people of color live.

The fear of conflict can cause people to put together interventions that protect them, framing agenda topics to steer away from the real conflict, using a dominant culture agenda so it looks like something's happening when it's actually an avoidance of conflict. We can train people in conflict resolution and they can still avoid the rage of people of color because that's the scariest issue. When that rage is expressed, the mediator can say it is outside the scope of the work. If an intervention is avoiding issues of difference and rage around difference, it's inauthentic conflict resolution. It's a sham. The mark of good conflict resolution is its capacity to elicit rage in the room and to teach people how to direct it.

–Roberto Chené
© MCS 2000

Working Assumptions for Intercultural Mediation

- Some degree of conflict is inherent in almost any intercultural setting where relations between cultures have been socially institutionalized according to a dominant-subordinate dynamic.

- When working with members of diverse groups, conflict is a given when the goal is to create an intercultural community.

- Because cultural conflict is deep-seated and structural, we are all, by definition, already participants in the conflict.

- Without education, training and participation in a forum designed to bridge cultural differences, it is difficult for many people from the dominant culture to perceive the need for or develop the skills to help create a multicultural community based on equality.

- Members of minority cultures—without an opportunity for communication with members of the dominant culture in which they feel that their point of view has been heard and taken seriously—are unlikely to give up their anger or have any desire to create a multicultural community.

Relationship Requirements for Conflict Partners

- Commitment

- Flexibility

- Persistence

- Ability to tolerate discomfort

- Ability to give positive instruction

- Ability to take instruction

- Ability to listen to anger

- Ability to curb anger

- Ability to nourish support for self (eliminate isolation)

–Roberto Chené
© Roberto Chené. Used by permission.

Common Barriers to Intercultural Mediation

- Fear of retaliation

- Reluctance to hurt other's feelings

- Fear of one's own anger

- Fear of intercultural conflict

- Fear of starting a conflict that can't be controlled

- Actual reluctance to share power

- Mediator discomfort and anxiety

Beginning Guidelines for Intercultural Mediations

To maximize effectiveness a responsible mediator or dispute resolution practitioner will make every effort to learn about the cultural and social expectations of the people he or she will be dealing with. . . .

I offer the following short list of observations and suggestions that have arisen from my studies and experiences in the field. Many of these guidelines will be recognized as universally applicable principles and may already be familiar to some mediators. Much of what follows is simply good common sense. But primarily, these suggestions focus on rules of conduct that are especially applicable to situations involving cross-cultural mediation.

Expect different expectations. Differing expectations are brought to the bargaining table when individuals from different cultures confront each other. Responses are often misinterpreted, and otherwise assumed "rules of the game" cannot be taken for granted.

Do not assume that what you say is being understood. The same words spoken in English often have different meaning and emphasis to people from different cultures.

Listen carefully. Determine what concerns and interests each party is trying to communicate with their proposal.

Seek ways of getting both parties to validate the concerns of the other. For example, you might say, "Mr. Manager, just to make sure we are all communicating with each other clearly, can I ask you to restate the union's concerns about the vacation schedule?" Ask the union to do the same thing regarding a company issue.

Be patient, be humble, and be willing to learn. Americans often expect instant gratification, instant results, instant responses. Many people from other cultures work on a different, often more slowly paced timetable. Impatience is viewed in many cultures as a sign of immaturity rather than enthusiasm; loud displays of confidence may be interpreted as arrogance; and insistence on the rules of the game may be seen as disrespect for how others have learned to interact. In separate caucus, take time to point out potential differences as cultural difference and encourage each party to accept and learn something from the other.

Apply "win-win" negotiating principles to the negotiation rather than traditional adversarial bargaining techniques. Define issues rather than taking hard initial positions. Discuss the interests and concerns of both sides. Try to come up with multiple options for solving the problems of both parties. Apply fair standards to select the options, and work through a consensus process to arrive at solutions rather than using power plays.

Dare to do things differently. Throughout the world, there are literally thousands of different and legitimate ways for two parties to reach an agreement. Just because **we** feel comfortable with one set of rules and etiquette does not mean that it is necessarily the most logical, efficient, or desirable method for everyone.

–Jan Jung-Min Sunoo
© Plenum Publishing 1990, excerpted from "Some Guidelines for Mediators of Intercultural Disputes," *Negotiation Journal*, October 1990. Used by permission.

Intercultural issues and the design of appropriate processes can be complicated. Please refer to the articles on culture in Chapter Two and the resources suggested on page 127.

The Use of Co-Mediators

We encourage using two mediators working together as a team whenever practical. There are many advantages to this, both for the mediators and for the disputants. This is especially true in cases involving cross-cutting issues of race, ethnicity, gender, class, age, etc. Some of these advantages are:

Advantages

For the Disputants

- The mediation team can represent disputants' diverse characteristics (e.g., male/female, Anglo/Hispanic, old/young, etc.)
- A disputant has a better chance of feeling a sense of trust with at least one of the two mediators.
- The disputants have the advantage of the combined skills of two mediators, whose skills usually enhance and complement each other.
- Co-mediators can model cooperative problem-solving and direct dialogue for disputants.
- There is a better "check" on mediator bias or other shortcomings.

For the Mediators

- Having a partner eases the load and tension of mediation, especially in difficult cases and multi-party situations.
- Tasks can be comfortably divided when mediators are intentionally paired (e.g., a person skilled at handling emotions paired with a person skilled at practical problem-solving).
- A team is less likely to be accused of being "co-opted" by a party.
- Co-mediators can learn new techniques from each other in the process.
- Sessions can be debriefed and strategies planned with a partner.
- A co-mediator can "intervene" if a partner "loses it" in some way.
- A less-experienced mediator can work with a more-experienced colleague.

Possible Disadvantages

Although we feel the advantages of co-mediation far outweigh the possible disadvantages, some of these are listed below for your consideration:

For the Disputants

- They must discuss painful, embarrassing, and/or complicated matters with yet more people.
- Co-mediation usually raises the cost of mediation sessions, if the disputants are paying a mediation fee.
- Working with a team can sometimes complicate scheduling of sessions.
- Disputants can experience what seems to be a "divided mind" between the mediators about what should be happening in the process.

For the Mediators

- Co-mediating with someone you haven't worked with regularly can feel awkward and frustrating.
- Coordinating a case with another person can sometimes feel like more work than it is worth.
- The co-mediation format can lead to mediator "laziness" or inattention.
- A co-mediation team which isn't well-matched can feel out-of-balance and uncomfortable to one or both mediators, depending on differences in mediation style, personal style, experience, etc.
- It can be costly to mediation programs to field mediation teams for all or even most cases.

–Alice M. Price
© MCS 1989, with thanks to Jennifer E. Beer, *Peacemaking in Your Neighborhood* (New Society Publishers, 1986)

A Mediation Process: An Overview

Mediation is a process designed to meet the needs of the disputing parties. The intake process and getting people "to the mediation table" are critical, often challenging, and precede the process below.

The steps below are fairly standard but include our bias toward the need to include personal and relational issues. While it is presented here as a linear process, it rarely is. Most mediations will cycle through the various stages a number of times, and sometimes not in a particularly logical order. It is also presented as a very formal process. Much interpersonal problem-solving and informal third-party assistance follows similar kinds of steps. This is a "map," from which all of us can, and should, deviate as the situation requires.

I. Introduction (by the mediators) (page 172)

    A. Greeting/affirmation/seating/logistics
    B. Describe the process and the role of the mediators
    C. Establish ground rules

II. Storytelling (page 173)

    A. Each party describes the situation from their viewpoint
    B. Mediator summarizes each one's perspective after they speak
    C. Listen for key issues/concerns, feelings, commonalities

III. Identifying Issues (page 175)

    A. Mediator lists joint issues
    B. Check with all parties to make sure list is inclusive
    C. List can include less tangible relationship issues as well as tangible, concrete ones

IV. Problem-solving/Healing (page 177)

    A. Choose one issue and ask each participant to describe the related problem in more depth
        1. Help participants discover the interests under their positions; what matters most to them
        2. Encourage parties to generate options jointly
        3. Note commonalities whenever possible
        4. Encourage parties to examine and be open about their feelings
        5. Encourage constructive communication (I-messages, active listening, empathy, etc.)
        6. Help parties focus on the future ("How can we relate peacefully?") rather than getting stuck on the past ("Who was right/wrong yesterday?")
    B. Most conflicts include both tangible issues and relationship issues. Which need to be addressed first will vary.
    C. Encourage and acknowledge moments of individual empowerment and/or recognition of the other

V. Agreement/Resolution (page 189)

    A. Be specific about concrete agreements—who does what, when, where
    B. Be balanced and nonjudgmental
    C. Address approach for future problems
    D. Intangible, relationship actions can be noted/summarized in addition to the tangible agreements or in place of them (apologies, acknowledgment of responsibility, affirmation, etc.)

–MCS Staff
© MCS 1989, 1992, 1995, 2000

Introduction Stage

The opening minutes are critical. People generally come with a history of poor communication and a breakdown of trust. They are often anxious, fearful, suspicious of each other and uncertain about what the next few hours will hold. Thus, mediators have the opportunity to set the atmosphere for a different way of being and relating which is much more important than getting all the suggested components exactly right.

Specifically, mediators can set an atmosphere of
- respect (of each other, of the disputants, of their conflicts, etc.),
- calmness (a non-anxious presence) and
- confidence (a sense of purpose and order, not arrogance).

Before Parties Arrive

1. Have newsprint, markers, paper and pencils available.
2. Check signals with your co-mediator.
   a. Who, if anyone, will take "lead" role.
   b. How will you divide tasks: various stages; note-taking; process vs. task focus, etc.
   c. Anticipate any special difficulties in this mediation session.
   d. Personal mediation styles, including ways to increase collaboration.
3. Check the environment (Is it neutral territory?).
   a. As comfortable and informal as possible.
   b. Seating arrangements; table or no table.
   c. Place for private meetings.
   d. Personal needs: tissues, bathroom, beverages, waiting & smoking areas.

Opening Statement

1. Welcome and introductions—set appropriate tone. Consider spiritual and/or cultural rituals, prayer, silence, readings, humor, etc. for centering and release of anxiety.
2. State the purpose and affirm parties for their willingness to use mediation.
3. Process:
   a. Each person will describe situation from their perspective.
   b. Mediators will summarize and help parties create a list of issues to address.
   c. Discuss the issues one at a time.
   d. Work to reach agreement or other closure; or identify next steps.
4. Mediators' role
   a. To help parties talk to each other and find their own solution.
   b. Not to decide right and wrong, or tell them what to do.
5. Mediator confidentiality, including any exceptions.
6. Taking a break:
   a. Parties may ask to take a break at any time.
   b. Mediators sometimes take a break.
   c. Mediators sometimes meet separately with each party (caucus).
7. Ground rules/guidelines:
   a. Mediators ask both parties to agree to listen when other person speaks.
   b. Add additional ground rules as needed and appropriate.

–Ron Kraybill and MCS Staff
© MCS 1984, 2000

Storytelling Stage

Goals

- To build rapport and trust with both parties by modeling empathy and respect regardless of beliefs, words or conduct.
- To summarize concisely the essence of each party's perspective.
- To listen for key issues, feelings and commonalities.

Process

- Each party describes the situation from their perspective while the other party and the mediators listen.
- Mediators briefly summarize as each party finishes. Include:
  - general story
  - main concerns
  - feelings

Who Goes First?

Mediators use a variety of ways to determine which party tells their story first. One is to begin with the party which initiated the complaint or made the request for mediation. Another is to begin with the party who seems the most talkative and volatile, so they can let off some steam and listen when it is the other party's turn to speak. Still another is simply to flip a coin.

A Sense of Being Understood as the Primary Goal

Earning the trust of the parties is more important for the mediator at this stage than mastering all the facts of the situation. Grasping facts and the sequence of what happened is useful, of course, but if you make this your primary goal, you are likely to end up interrupting the parties with constant questions and creating an atmosphere of interrogation. Allow a speaker to finish his or her account and then raise questions or hold your questions until the Problem-Solving Stage which follows, when you will have opportunity to deal with each issue in depth. Often, however, there are more effective ways of getting the information you need than by asking questions, as we shall see in the next section.

Questions vs. Statements

Questions are one of the most frequently abused forms of communication. In fact, many conflicts are conducted in the form of questions.

Questions are especially problematic where trust is low. They control the person being questioned, limiting the way in which he or she can respond. For this reason, they are frequently used by lawyers in courtroom or by police in interrogating suspects. For example, "Did you or did you not. . . ?" Or, "What were you doing on the evening of March 19?" Behind the question in such settings lies a hidden agenda, to trap the speaker. Questions can of course be used sincerely, without intending to trap or interrogate others but where trust is low, their use tends to arouse defensiveness and resentment. Even where trust is high, communication is likely to become more effective and clear if people use questions only when a question is truly needed.

The alternative is to use a statement which invites people to share information which you seek. Instead of asking questions like, "Who is Mrs. South?"; "What did you do then?"; "What did you do that for?"; "Who, why, what, when, etc.?" mediators can make statements that will do the job as well and create a greater sense of openness at the same time. For example, "Say more about Mrs. South." "I don't understand what you were doing when this happened." "Tell us about what happened that day." "Describe, clarify, expand, etc." "I don't understand the connection between these two events." "Please say more about. . . ."

Dealing with Interruptions

A major challenge, particularly in the early stages of mediation, is how to deal with interruptions from the parties. Both sides are so eager to be listened to and so fearful that they will not be heard, that they may repeatedly interrupt the other party. It is important that mediators develop good skills in addressing this challenge, for failure to do so can rapidly lead to a loss of control over the discussion, and loss of faith by the parties in the entire process. After the parties have had a chance to see how mediation works, they realize that everyone will be heard and interruptions usually become much less of a problem.

Be firm about the ground rule of "no interruptions." Respond immediately to the first few interruptions and ignore those that come later, not the other way around. Have extra pen and paper handy and give them to the interrupter to make notes. For example: "Excuse me, Mr. North, I'd like to remind you of our ground rule about not interrupting. Here's a pen and paper, maybe you could make notes of your concerns so you don't forget them. We'll give you a chance to respond later. Thank you. Continue now, please, Mrs. South."

Taking Notes

Vast amounts of information pour from the lips of parties in conflict. Keeping track of who thinks what is a difficult challenge! It is sometimes tempting for mediators to take detailed notes, but this can be a great block to building trust. A mediator with his or her nose stuck in a writing pad does not convey deep personal interest in the parties! The parties need support and human contact if they are to open themselves to new and unfamiliar ways of communicating. Learn to listen for key words so you can keep writing to a minimum. If there are two mediators, another option is to agree that only one mediator will take notes at a time. This ensures that there is always at least one person giving full attention to the parties.

Dealing with Provocative Statements

Often in the Storytelling Stage, people say things that are highly provocative. "Our housing forum was going fine until these bandits sitting across the table today decided we were easy prey. . . ." Mediators need skills to cope with such provocative statements.

- If you sense that someone is getting provoked by the account of an opponent you can say: "John, I know you have a different perspective and I want to hear your view as well in a few minutes." Offered as an occasional aside to listening parties, such a comment by mediators can help them keep their anger under control.
- Soften provocative comments with a neutral paraphrase. For example, paraphrase "she's lying" into "you see things differently from the way she does."
- Often it helps to ask for specific examples. If Party East says Party West is "inconsiderate and totally irresponsible," the mediator could respond by saying: "Please give us a specific example of what you have in mind." Specific examples move the discussion out of the category of character assassination into the arena of specific events where there is often more room for negotiation or "agreeing to disagree."
- If name-calling or swearing is becoming a prominent feature of the discussion, the mediator can propose a ground rule that they be avoided, and get the commitment of both parties to observing this ground rule.
- If an emotional explosion takes place and the mediators feel they have no other means of regaining control, they can ask to meet separately with each of the parties in caucus.

–Ron Kraybill and Carolyn Schrock-Shenk
© MCS 1984, 2000

Because listening skills are especially important during this stage, please see "Listening Skills for Mediators" on page 162.

Issue Identification Stage

Issue identification is the critical bridge between storytelling and problem-solving and serves as an agenda or framework for the remainder of the mediation. The list of issues, created by the mediators from their listening during storytelling, can help move the parties from opponents to collaborators working on a common agenda.

Considerations

1. Identify the issues *early* in the process

It is usually done after both have spoken once since much of what they say on the second round is either a deepening of their story or a rebuttal to the other's story. ("You will get a chance to talk more about that as we problem-solve together.")

2. The *mediators* do the listing, preferably on newsprint or chalkboard

As mediator listening objectively to all parties, you should be the one to list the issues. It is helpful to jot down concerns in your notepad as you hear them during storytelling so that you can summarize the list from your notepad onto the newsprint. You may feel the need to check in with your co-mediator first.

3. Create a *joint* list

The list should combine the major concerns of both parties into one list.

4. *Frame* the issues to make them *acceptable* to both

Launder the language to avoid reflecting anyone's viewpoint. For example, "responsibility for the accident" is more neutral than "Joe wrecked Ann's car." Relationship issues and attitudes are the most difficult to name in a neutral way. "Respect for each other" is more neutral than "Rob's obnoxious attitude."

5. State the issues in a *simple* and *general* way

This will help keep the list short (three to five is good) and make the task more manageable. For example, "financial concerns" may be more helpful than "car payments," "mortgage" and "medical bills." (The latter three can be listed as sub-points.)

6. Check the list *verbally* with both participants

Ask them, "If we successfully worked through all of these issues, would that take care of the problem for you?" You may need to add to or modify the list based on their responses. After agreement, move to problem-solving! It is not uncommon, however, to add an issue that emerges later in the process.

–Carolyn Schrock-Shenk
© MCS 1993, 2000

See the following page for more on mediatable issues.

Does This Issue Belong in Mediation?

Types of Negotiable Issues

Behaviors

- How people treat each other
- Sharing space
- Respecting boundaries
- Communicating about problems
- Noise
- Following through on promises and responsibilities
- The ways people do their work

Things, money

- Property
- Reimbursement
- Arranging payments
- Repairs
- Loans
- Maintenance

Structure and Systems

- How decisions are made
- Rules and regulations
- Procedures
- Schedules
- Job responsibilities
- Access

Concerns That Can Be Discussed, But Not Negotiated

- Beliefs
- Principles, Values
- Child-raising
- Attitudes
- Anger

- Personal Style
- What happened
- Hurt Feelings
- Perceptions
- Management style

- Interpretations
- Prejudices
- Trust
- Blame, Fault
- Rights

Issues That Usually Cannot Be Mediated

- Determining the truth of what happened.
- Determining fault and punishment.
- Addictive behaviors.
- Pathological or abusive behaviors.
- Wide gap in power between the parties.
- Issues where the real decision-maker is not present.

- Issues where people who may be affected by a decision or whose cooperation is necessary are not represented.
- Issues requiring investigation and disclosure before fair negotiation can take place.
- Situations where the parties do not understand the complexities of the issues or their legal options.

Dealing with Unmediatable Issues

- Feelings, attitudes and other non-negotiable concerns often point towards negotiable issues. Reframe those pieces that can be translated into specific behaviors.

- Support expression and discussion of key concerns without trying to get agreement. When they are ready, encourage them to address the things they can negotiate.

- State that certain topics cannot be resolved, then suggest aspects or related topics you think can be negotiated. Some caution is needed here. Negotiating side issues or aspects of behavior may be pointless when the main issue remains a source of active conflict. And when the main problem is an abusive relationship or large power difference, fair and safe negotiation of side points is probably impossible.

- Ask the parties to agree on another place or method to deal with their unmediatable issues.

- Postpone the session until all necessary parties agree to attend.

- If there's nothing left to mediate, end the session. Consider drawing up a session summary.

–Jennifer E. Beer and Eileen Stief

© Friends Conflict Resolution Programs 1997, from *The Mediator's Handbook*, 3rd ed. (British Columbia: New Society Publishers). Used by permission.

Problem-Solving/Healing Stage

I. Mediator's choice whether to:

- initiate problem-solving (negotiating practical issues), or
- focus on healing.

This stage consists of alternating back and forth between these two tasks. No formula works—the key is adeptness in both and good timing in switching from one task to the other. Many mediators are more comfortable in one area than the other—push yourself to grow in the hardest area!

II. Problem-Solving Steps

A. Note common goals and concerns. (Mediators can point out commonalities whenever they emerge.) See "Summarizing Points of Agreement" on page 188.

B. Choose one issue to begin.
1. **Easiest First.** This is useful when things are tense and trust is low. Often success on small items creates momentum for larger ones. Just the opposite of #2 below.
2. **Most Important First.** This is difficult when tension is high but if one issue keeps cropping up, take it on rather than try to ignore it.
3. **Alternating Choice.** Parties take turns picking issues for discussion.
4. **Party Agreement.** See if parties can agree on a common issue with which to start.

C. Issue-focused storytelling. Each describes in turn what's happening around that issue. "Let's begin with the exchange during the coffee break. Paul, can you describe in more detail your impression of what happened?"

D. Identify interests. Each says what they need, what is important to them, regarding this issue; mediators can list these on board or newsprint.

E. Generate ideas for resolution:
- as many as possible
- encourage creativity
- no judgment or commentary
- help parties state what they want, not what they are against.

F. Evaluate ideas. Consider pros and cons of each option; does it meet interests?

G. Agree on solution. Choose solution acceptable to both; often a combination of several ideas. "If Alex would drop the charges, would you be willing to pay for the window?"

If you get stuck in any of these steps, move to another issue, or caucus.

III. Healing Strategies

A. Be ready to take plenty of time; don't be afraid of periods of silence.

B. Highlight commonalities between parties, including pain and hurt.

C. Acknowledge feelings, especially with paraphrasing. Invite parties to elaborate.

D. Coach paraphrasing and direct dialogue as appropriate.

E. Highlight good intentions, offers of accepting responsibility, apologies, requests for forgiveness, etc.

F. Affirm small steps in the healing process.

G. Recognize the deeply spiritual nature of the interaction.

See the following pages for more on healing strategies.

IV. Reminders in this Stage

A. It's their problem, not yours. Disputants sense quickly if you take emotional ownership for resolving things—they'll be happy to sit back and watch you sweat.

B. You're in charge of the agenda. Be flexible, open to suggestions, but never passive about choosing or switching issues for discussion. Be prepared to say: "The issue you raise is important, but for the moment I'd like to set it aside and come back to that later."

C. Stay in "I" mode. "I would like to ask you to. . . ." "It's difficult for me to keep things going when you ignore the ground rules, so I'd like it if. . . ."

D. Direct discussion between the two parties is always preferable so long as it's constructive. Look for ways to encourage it.

E. Be comfortable with silence.

–MCS Staff
© MCS 2000

Healing Strategies: Addressing Feelings

No one can heal others. Trying to do so—a genuine temptation—hinders them from finding their own true healing. The challenge and calling for mediators is to create a space, an environment, in which healing can occur and then to walk with the participants as they find elements of their own healing.

Mediators are not therapists and should not try to unravel deep-rooted personal wounds. But mediation is therapeutic and does address feelings which surround every conflict, even those that seem practical or institutional. The critical questions are whether the parties will acknowledge their feelings directly, whether that acknowledgment is needed for transformation of the conflict and when and how a mediator addresses the feelings effectively.

It is important to remember that stubbornness, rigidity, fierceness, etc., appear to come from strength but in reality come from deep vulnerability. People who intimidate are deeply wounded. Many of them know it and are actually frightened and scared behind their facade. The wounds are either: a) fears and insecurities about the current situation (appropriate to address as a mediator), or b) distant, often unconscious memories of past injuries from others, frequently childhood experiences.

Various cultures express feelings and emotions quite differently. For example, public expression of strong feelings may not be appropriate in one cultural setting. In another, high emotional expressiveness even with strangers may be the norm.

Goals of the Mediator

1. To enable people to get in touch with their feelings in ways that do not create resistance.

2. To acknowledge the feelings of both sides without implying who is right or wrong.

3. To enable parties to state their feelings directly to each other, which often provides opportunity for healing.

4. To assist parties in clarifying what they need in order to experience healing, particularly when it involves someone else at the mediation table. If the wounds lie with others, enable parties to get the help they need, including personal counseling if necessary.

5. To do all this so that if one or both parties are not ready to acknowledge their feelings and experience healing, the mediator can still remain an effective, credible assistant in resolving the more tangible issues.

Strategies

1. Paraphrase feelings.

2. Push for specifics; don't be content with generalizations. Attempting to work constructively with feelings is fruitless except in the context of specific events. E.g., "You've felt like a helpless victim in your relationships with Henry. Give us some specific examples that would help us understand what has been happening."

3. Ask people to "describe the impact of an event on you personally."

4. Interview each party about an emotional event, encouraging I-statements, and asking the listening party not to interrupt. E.g., "I'd like to take a little time to hear from each of you about what has been going on inside of you while this has been happening. I'd like to start with William. Paul, I'd like to ask you to lean

back and listen for a couple minutes without interrupting. William, tell me the things you see/hear/feel when you put yourself back in that situation."

5. Coach paraphrasing. E.g., "Paul, I'd like to ask you to say in your own words to William what you understand him to be saying just now." Then, "William, tell Paul what he's understanding correctly and what he's missing."

6. Coach direct communication. E.g., "William, could you turn to Paul and tell him directly what you just told me." (This is effective only when one party makes positive statements, or uses I-messages to state his or her feelings.)

7. Use caucus to explore difficult emotions, especially if people seem stuck in a very high or very low expressive mode. Check for possible cultural dimensions to their expression level, as well as for any concerns still unspoken in the joint session. Test whether and how key feelings and concerns can be shared appropriately with the other party.

8. Ask people to rate themselves on a scale of 1 to 10 about readiness to let go of feelings about a given experience. (1 = definitely not ready; 10 = definitely ready)

9. Ask people to give you some idea of what they need in order to let go of their feelings.

10. After progress has been made in talking through feelings, invite people to say something to each other that they believe may help the other to let go of their emotions. Sometimes it helps to give ideas, e.g., "You may want to say any one of several things. You may wish to apologize for something, or you may simply wish to say 'I would do it differently if I could.' Or you may wish to express appreciation for something. Finally, you may wish to make a statement of commitment about the future."

11. When people really seem stuck on feelings, tell them it's important not to let go of them too quickly. People should hang on to deep feelings until they are tired of them and want to let go of them. Paradoxically, the mediator's spoken observation that a person may not be ready to let go of a strong emotion, such as a need to hold a grudge, sometimes unsticks that feeling. Then the person feels genuinely free to move on to new options.

12. Give parties opportunity to withdraw and possibly write a summary of their feelings.

13. Encourage private counseling. Be cautious here, though. Do it only in caucus.

–Ron Kraybill, as adapted by Alice M. Price
© MCS 1989, 1992, 2000

Positions vs. Interests

Helping parties to focus on interests—not positions—is a critical underlying strategy throughout all stages of the mediation process. However, it gets particular emphasis during the problem-solving stage. See also "A Negotiation Paradigm" on page 160.

Understanding Positions vs. Interests

Positions

Positions are statements or demands framed as solutions. Parties in conflict naturally think and talk in "positions," which often contain incomplete information, hidden agendas, and "bottom line" posturing. Positional bargaining leads to impasse or compromise, but rarely to creative, win/win solutions.

Interests

Interests are broader than positions and are essentially what each party needs for satisfaction or resolution. Interests are the reasons behind the positions and they encompass such things as needs, concerns, and hopes. Interests can arise from substantive, procedural or emotional factors.

Exploring interests helps parties in a variety of ways:

- Understanding one's own interests increases self-awareness and personal empowerment.

- Understanding one's own interests more clearly unlocks new ideas.

- Understanding the interests of another leads to recognition of another's basic needs.

- Parties discover that they share many basic interests (e.g., financial security, ending of hostilities, neighborhood safety).

- Parties can often find resolution that addresses interests on both sides.

Strategies for Exploring Interests

- Make a list of each side's interests, as they surface, including basic human needs.

- Reframe locked-in positions as interests: "The dogs have to go!" becomes "You're really concerned about the noisy barking when you are sleeping."

- Ask why a particular demand is being made, to draw out underlying interests.
  "Tell me more about why that's so important to you."
  "Say more about your basic concerns with this."
  "What matters most here for you?"

- Ask why a particular proposal is not satisfactory, to understand their concerns better.
    "Help me understand why you feel that's not a workable solution."
    "Say more about what seems unfair here."
    "Tell me how that affects you."

- Point out similar interests.
    "You both seem very concerned that . . . ."
    "Better communication is really important to both of you."

- Test for new solutions which meet apparent interests and look ahead.
    "Tell me what would help you feel better about that."
    "How would you want to have that handled, if it happens again?"

Examples of Positions and Interests

Examples of Positions	Possible Interests
Shut the window!	Eliminate a draft; too much noise coming in, need to concentrate
Pay me $500 right now, or I'll evict you!	Reliable rental income; pay own bills; needs money
Either I pick or we don't go to the movies!	Assure don't see violent film; to have a good time
I want $1.50/hour raise!	To earn the same as others doing same work; fairness

–MCS Staff
© MCS 1988, 1989, 2000

Positions and Interests Exercise

As stated earlier, positions are statements or demands made by a party as their solution. They believe this is what is needed to resolve some concern, problem, or need they may have. These are the interests that mediation focuses on: what needs to be satisfied, what the party needs resolved. There may be a single interest or multiple interests driving someone's position. There can be any number of possible solutions to interests.

In mediation it is not necessary to guess parties' interests. We are able to hear and clarify them by questioning and paraphrasing. In this exercise, however, try to imagine what the interests may be.

Example: Position: "I must have a dishwasher in the new house."

Interests (possible):
- Wants to be sure that dishes are very clean and sanitary
- Doesn't want to see dishes piled up in or near new sink
- Wants to use time to do things other than chores

1. "There will be no pets in this house."

2. "You can't use the car Saturday night."

3. "We won't negotiate until the protests stop."

4. "We won't stop the protests until you negotiate the working policies."

5. "My son must be in that other class."

6. "I want $250 for the damaged wall."

How did you do? Here are some possible interests for each of the positions.

1.
   - to have a clean house
   - to keep cleaning chores to a minimum
   - to save money for other needs
   - to have few obligations so family can travel when able.

2.
   - needs to get to own event that night
   - concerned about safety of driving home that late
   - needs full tank of gas to get to long-distance meeting early in the morning.

3.
   - needs to get business going again, as soon as possible
   - wants to minimize likelihood that protests will be seen as a method to force change or negotiations
   - wants to maintain their legitimate authority.

4.
   - want to assure that negotiations and changes will occur
   - don't want to be taken advantage of
   - want continued focus on concerns and visibility gets it
   - want other to see strength of shared concern and effort.

5.
   - believes son will do better in a smaller class, which the other class is
   - doesn't understand teaching methods of current teacher
   - other classes' schedule allows son to be in a special program that is held the same time as current class.

6.
   - needs that much money to repair wall
   - wants compensation for time and trouble to repair damage
   - wants person to take responsibility for their behavior.

–Sandi Adams
© MCS 2000

Reframing a Conflict

A U.S. Flag in the Sanctuary

Joe's concern stated as a position:

"The flag stays!"

Positions

are

incompatible

John's concern stated as a position:

"The flag goes!"

Joe's underlying concerns:

"The state should be respected and we should be thankful for freedom to worship."

Ignore positions

Explore their interests

John's underlying concerns:

"The Church is an international body and Christian allegiance should be to Christ."

Reframe the conflict
Translate incompatibilities into *differences that are not incompatible*

1. Joe wants to communicate:
   - gratitude for freedom to worship;
   - respect for the state as an institution ordained of God.
2. John wants to affirm that:
   - all peoples are welcome here;
   - final allegiance belongs to God, not sovereign states.

Help parties generate multiple solutions that hold potential for meeting all concerns. For example:

- Special worships dedicated to expressing gratitude for freedom of religion;

- Banners inviting all nations to worship here;

- Placing flags of all U.N. nations in the sanctuary.

–John Paul Lederach
© MCS 1989

Reframing Opportunities

Reframing simply means responding to the speaker in a way that both validates the speaker's experience and allows her/him to move from a particular perspective and response to a potentially more constructive one.

From General to Specific

To help the speaker focus more clearly on specific actions or events underlying feelings and opinions.

- "He's the most uncooperative employee I've ever had." *Tell us about some of the ways you see him as being uncooperative.*

- "I just don't like that sort of thing." *What specific kinds of things bother you the most?*

Identifying Underlying Feelings

To identify and acknowledge the feelings that underlie the words of the speaker.

- "I can't believe they would fire me without ever talking to me or warning me." *Sounds like you're really feeling betrayed.*

- "I'm trying to do my best but I have five people telling me what to do." *That must be really frustrating. Can you say more about how it affects you?*

Laundering/Neutralizing Attacks

To validate the intensity of feelings by understanding and focusing on underlying concerns.

- "The lazy slob is always late." *Being on time is very important to you, isn't it?*

- "He's a lying traitor. There isn't an ounce of truth in what he said." *Wow. You see things completely differently.*

Identifying Hidden Offers/Points of Agreement/Commonalities

To hear, respond to, and build on hints of progress and positive movement.

- "They expect me to do all this work, but they've never offered to train me for it." *So if you had adequate training, you believe you could handle the work.*

- "If he would act responsibly, I could get my work done." *What specific things from him would help you get your work done?*

Responding to Triangling Attempts (With Mediator)

To validate the speaker but avoid being triangled.

- "Don't you believe what he did was totally irresponsible?" *Clearly you believe it was irresponsible.*

- "Wouldn't you be angry if she did that to you?" *I'm interested in hearing more about your anger.*

Responding to Speaking for Others

To encourage ownership of the problem by the parties present and discourage indirect communication.

- "Nobody in this church likes that family." *Could you tell me more about your interaction with them?*

- "John and Mary have had the same problem believing his stories." *Say more about the stories you have struggled with.*

Responding to Contradictory Stories

To bring clarity to a situation or to reach agreement on how to proceed from here.

- "I wasn't even there." *I'm confused; you say you weren't there, but a bit ago you talked about seeing Nakita.*

- "She keeps saying I knew about the money but I didn't." *Say more about the things you did know.*

Responding to Blaming Statements (Toward Mediator)

To avoid defensiveness or counterattack. To respond to underlying fears, concerns, pain.

"Well, it's clear you're taking her side in this." *Sounds like you feel I'm being unfair. Say more about that.*

"You must get off on throwing your power around here, huh?" *So you feel like I'm taking too much control here. How could we do things differently?*

–Carolyn Schrock-Shenk
© MCS 1995, 2000

Practice Exercises for Reframing

Write quick responses to the statements below. Try to validate the speaker, while moving towards a more productive focus. Share some of your examples with a partner and/or the larger group.

1. They're jealous, that's the problem. _____

   _____

2. That whole bunch is an irresponsible lot. _____

   _____

3. She's the most uncooperative employee I've ever had. _____

   _____

4. People around here are cold and unfriendly. _____

   _____

5. Everyone on the block has trouble with him. _____

   _____

6. That's just the way men are. _____

   _____

7. If he'd just start acting responsibly, I could take care of his old fence. _____

   _____

8. It is absolutely untrue that we're trying to create a fuss and make trouble for you! _____

   _____

9. I'm trying to do my best! But how can I get all this work done when three different people are telling me

   what to do? _____

   _____

10. This whole situation has been a royal pain from start to finish! _____

    _____

11. I hate this kind of bickering. If you'd just act reasonably we could solve this mess. _____

    _____

12. If you had done what I asked you to six months ago, this never would have happened! _____

    _____

Generating and Evaluating Options

Once underlying interests are more clearly identified, parties can be encouraged to explore multiple options for meeting their needs. Once a good range of options are on the table, various tools can be used to evaluate them in light of the underlying interests.

Generating Options

Brainstorm

Purpose: To stimulate creativity by generating as many ideas as possible in a short period of time, unhindered by critical evaluation.

Procedure: 1. Explain the purpose, stressing that evaluation will occur later and that all ideas are welcome, both serious and nonserious.
2. Frame the problem in a how-to format: "How can money be located to pay the partnership debts without requiring a further cash investment by either party?"
3. Welcome each idea and list it on newsprint, discouraging any evaluative responses.
4. Encourage participants to "piggyback," taking previous ideas and modifying them.
5. Keep it short—five minutes should suffice.

Card Sort

Purpose: Similar to brainstorming but less threatening for some people. Also usually less creativity-inducing.

Procedure: 1. Invite parties to jot down ideas on 3 by 5 cards or other paper, one idea per card/sheet. Generate as many ideas as possible.
2. Place cards in the middle of the table or tape sheets on the wall for review.

Variations to Broaden Input

Brainstorming or card sort by parties who are not principal disputants. When people are present who are not key actors, they can be invited to generate ideas along with or for the benefit of disputants. Designated experts (e.g., lawyers, accountants, consultants) can also be invited to fill this role. If parties are returning for another session, "homework" can be assigned to stimulate further generation and research of options.

Evaluating Options

Plus/Minus Chart

For any given option, create a chart divided down the middle. One side is for the pluses (advantages) of this option, the other is for the minuses (disadvantages). This is a simple tool for organizing discussion.

Anticipated Impact Chart

For a given course of action, list possible impact on each person involved. This helps to objectify emotions about why a course of action is or isn't acceptable. Possible impacts: feelings about self/others, time, money.

List Criteria for Solution

Before evaluating possible solutions, create a list of objective criteria for evaluating them. These criteria normally parallel the parties' deepest underlying interests. Good for complex cases.

–Ron Kraybill and Alice M. Price
© MCS 1989, 2000

Summarize Points of Agreement

People in conflict get so caught up in the heat of disagreement that they often lose perspective of the total picture. This makes the damage of conflict much higher than it needs to be, for even where people may not care for each other personally, in many situations they agree on important things, share certain values or goals, or need each other in inescapable ways. Mediators can be a powerful moderating force by helping the parties make decisions based on more than the anger and resentment they may be feeling at the moment, repeatedly reminding the parties of the things they agree upon or have in common.

Pointing Out Commonalities in Early Problem-Solving

One particularly effective time to summarize points of agreement is after the parties have agreed on the list of issues needing discussion, but before they have actually begun an in-depth discussion. After Storytelling, the mediator can summarize the issues, get the parties' agreement that these were the things they wished to discuss, then summarize their commonalities:

- They may have both stated a desire to be reasonable or to get the conflict resolved.
- They are both likely to benefit a great deal from the resolution of the conflict.
- The fact that they have both been willing to attend the mediation session probably indicates a desire to resolve things.
- They may have both said that this conflict has been painful, frustrating, costly, burdensome, etc.
- They may have both talked about their commitment to the community, institution, church, party, etc., which indicates that they have common commitments.
- They may have both talked about the steps they took in the past to resolve things. Even if these failed, these efforts indicate a willingness to work things out.
- They may both be victims of the same larger social forces, such as unemployment, racial discrimination, violence, low wages, etc.
- They may have both indicated that they have made mistakes or over-reacted in the past.

It is almost always possible to identify several areas that the parties agree upon or share in common, even in the most polarized conflict. Pointing these out repeatedly throughout the discussion process is an important contribution to the emotional atmosphere of discussion. But be cautious! Pointing out commonalities is not:
- . . . making up nice things that aren't true. Be sure that any commonalities you talk about reflect things the parties have already said or have agreed upon or that are obviously true.
- . . . telling the parties that they don't have any real disagreements or that the disagreements aren't significant. At all times the mediator accepts that there are real conflicts. In pointing out commonalities you are merely pointing out that in addition to the areas of conflict, there are also some things the parties agree about.
- . . . suggesting that resolution is going to be easy. On the contrary, the point is that there is hard work ahead, and that as they enter into this work, it would be helpful for the parties to remember those things that they share in common.

Your credibility as a mediator is probably your most important asset with the parties. Never lie and never exaggerate the prospects for peace. Whatever commonalities you point out have to be real and believable.

Summarizing Negotiated Agreements

As the parties begin to discuss and negotiate, small concessions are often made. The larger issues may still be unresolved and the tone of discussion may still be hostile but it is important that mediators be alert for agreements or concessions no matter how small, and summarize these as a way of improving the atmosphere.

If there is progress in the negotiations, the list of agreements gets longer and longer. By regularly reminding the parties of what they have accomplished, the mediator reduces the chances that they will fall back into attacks and recriminations. The list of agreements already reached helps establish an atmosphere of progress and cooperation that can help in addressing what may be the most emotional issue on the agenda.

–Ron Kraybill
© MCS 2000

Agreement Stage

While resolution can happen without reaching specific agreements, many successful mediations do result in a form of contract that addresses future actions. Any agreements reached should state clearly WHO is agreeing to WHAT, WHERE, WHEN and HOW. The disputants' wording can be used whenever possible. An effective mediation agreement should:

1. **Be specific and be clear about deadlines.**

   Avoid ambiguous words (e.g., "soon," "reasonable," "cooperative," "neighborly," "frequent," "quiet"). Use specific words, dates and times that will more likely have the same meaning to both parties. For example, "Mrs. Wrangle and the McBickers agree to build a 5-foot high board fence along the property line between their houses. Mrs. Wrangle agrees to buy the building materials by May 8, and the McBickers agree to construct the fence by May 30."

2. **Be balanced.**

   Ideally, both parties gain something and both give something. Sometimes naming the "intangibles" can help balance things (Kate has apologized for. . . . Gerald agrees to accept Omar's payment plan).

3. **Be positive.**

   When possible, encourage disputants to name what they *will do* in the future, rather than what they won't do or will stop doing.

4. **Be realistic.**

   Can the disputants live up to their agreement? It is best if the agreement speaks only for the disputants themselves, i.e., actions that they personally have control over. Check wording of each item with each of the parties to make sure you are writing what they agree to.

5. **Be clear and simple.**

   Avoid legalese. When possible, use the disputants' language. Be sensitive to the needs of parties who don't read very well or don't have a good command of the English language.

6. **Name the "intangibles."**

   As appropriate, name acknowledgment of responsibility, statements of apology, forgiveness, affirmation, etc. For example, "Erika acknowledged that she was responsible for spreading the rumor about Monique and apologized. Monique accepted Erika's apology."

7. **Address the future.**

   Help disputants decide how they will address problems that arise in the future. You may want to schedule a progress check-in method.

8. **Be signed by everyone present.**

   Upon completion, read to the parties and get their responses. Does it cover all issues? Do they pledge to live up to it? Should we agree on some way to review progress in the near future? Then sign and date the agreement, and give copies to both parties.

–MCS Staff
2000, adapted with permission from Friends Conflict Resolution Program

Some Sample Agreements

Mediation agreements can range from the very simple to the very complex in format, content and length. An agreement should be written in a style and in language appropriate to the parties. It should be drafted in a way that will be clear to them and will maximize their ownership. All agreements should be signed by the parties and the mediators. Several sample agreements are included on this page and the next.

Sample Partnership Dissolution

The parties, Raymond Herman, Hugh Herman and Frank Herman, have met four times with a mediator to seek a mutually acceptable solution for dividing a family farm partnership. At present, Raymond has a 50% interest and Hugh and Frank each have a 25% interest. The goal was to allow Raymond and his wife to continue farming, while allowing Frank and Hugh to receive a fair market value for their shares.

After discussing several different approaches and options, the parties are in agreement that the partnership should be dissolved, ideally before the end of the calendar year. The only asset of the partnership, approximately 103 acres of agricultural land and buildings, will be distributed as follows:

1. Approximately 25 acres at the west end of the ground will be transferred from the partnership to Hugh and Frank. It is understood that this land is the most readily available for development.
2. The remaining agricultural acreage and buildings will be transferred from the partnership to Raymond.
3. In addition, Raymond and his wife will transfer to Hugh and Frank an adjacent portion of personal real estate, of approximately five acres.

Raymond agrees to make arrangements to have appropriate surveying done to effectuate these transfers. He will also consult with the family attorney to have the necessary documents prepared for the land transfers, as well as for the dissolution of the partnership itself. Each party will let the attorney know exactly how they wish to receive title, whether jointly, in common, or otherwise. Raymond agrees to be the primary contact for the family attorney in completing these transactions, but will stay in touch with Frank and Hugh as appropriate. Frank and Hugh agree to make themselves available for meetings, as needed.

If, in consulting with the family attorney, Raymond should learn of significant matters which need to be decided by the partners—especially if there is a significant benefit to arranging for transfer of the 30 acres directly to one or more developers or other third-party buyers—he will discuss this with Frank and Hugh. In this event, the parties will weigh these benefits against the time delays and other factors to determine whether their agreement should be adjusted accordingly.

In terms of the sale of the 30 acres to third parties, it is agreed that preference should be given to selling some of the acreage to the retirement home adjacent to the farm, in line with the overall market value of the land.

All costs associated with the execution of this agreement and the dissolution of the partnership shall be paid from the partnership account. It is acknowledged that this account will probably not be adequate for all the related costs, and each party agrees to pay any balance of expenses in proportion to his or her interest in the partnership.

–**Alice M. Price**
© MCS 1995

Sample Agreements Between Family Members or Neighbors

1. *A nineteen-year-old living with her mother.* (A balanced agreement is often a problem in family mediations involving teenagers, even in this fairly even-handed contract.)
   - May Ellen agrees to be flexible about the Saturday curfew time if Ginnie calls before midnight.
   - Ginnie and May Ellen agree that Ginnie will contribute $30 per week towards rent and groceries.
   - May Ellen agrees to clean up after every dinner.
   - Ginnie agrees to tell her mother where she is going at night, and with whom.
   - May Ellen agrees not to ask questions about Ginnie's social life.
   - May Ellen and Ginnie agree to talk over any problems during lunch on Sunday.

2. *An older neighbor and a young family next door.* (Note that the parents do not make agreements for their children: "Jeanne and Marc agree to talk. . ." not "Jeanne agrees that Joe will. . . .")
   - Arthur agrees to return the frisbees, baseballs, and the football tomorrow morning.
   - Marc agrees to pay for and repair the fence before April 7.
   - Marc and Jeanne agree to talk with their children about the mediation and about talking back to Arthur.
   - Arthur agrees to stop cursing and scaring the children.
   - Arthur and Jeanne agree to phone if more problems come up.

3. *Common driveways*
   - The Jamisons and the Tomlins agree that cars will only be left in the driveway while loading and unloading.
   - Bill and Toni Jamison agree to talk to their daughters about parking their bicycles on the porch.
   - The Tomlins agree to call before 9:00 p.m. if the driveway is blocked.
   - Paul Tomlin agrees to mow the driveway strip.

–Friends Suburban Project
© Friends Conflict Resolution Programs 1990, from *Mediator's Handbook*. Used by permission.

Tools for Breaking Impasse

Avoid the Trap of Over-Responsibility

As a mediator, you will function more effectively and with greater confidence and calmness if you recognize that the mediators cannot make peace, only the parties can. The mediators can of course assist in the discussion process, but in the end it is the parties' conflict and they are responsible for the outcome.

Mediators who feel over-responsible for the outcome of a conflict function poorly in their role. If things go well, over-responsible mediators often seek personal credit for success and thereby arouse resentment in the parties. If things go poorly, over-responsible mediators often become frantic and begin pushing the parties to accept their own suggestions for resolution. The parties usually resist this pressure and before long the mediators find their energy consumed by arguments between themselves and the parties.

To the extent that mediators act in ways that suggest they feel *over-responsible* for resolving a conflict, the parties often become *under-responsible*. If the parties see that the mediators feel responsible to come up with solutions and push hard for their acceptance, they tend to become passive and take a mostly negative role.

If the mediators recognize what is happening and know how to change their behavior so that the responsibility passes back to the parties, the dynamics often change. By refusing to become over-responsible for the lives and problems of others, mediators can often increase the likelihood that others will take responsibility for their own problems. If the parties do not object to the possibility of the mediator withdrawing, then this is a sign that indeed there may be little further that the mediator can do, and that it is time to end mediation efforts.

Trust the Process

Rather than feeling personally responsible for providing solutions, experience teaches many mediators to trust the discussion process to bring solutions. They know that any mediation process will have ups and downs; they also know that the only way to get to the ups is by going through the downs. If they can just keep the right kind of discussion process going resolution will often eventually emerge.

Focus on Understanding Each Side

The "right" kind of process is a process in which the parties feel increasingly confident that the mediators understand their needs and interests. Ideally each side understands the other side but if the mediator does her job well of understanding the parties *in the presence of both sides*, this often takes care of itself over the course of the discussion. Often the parties gradually begin to understand each other as they overhear the mediator trying to understand their opponents.

If mediators know and believe this, their task is easier than it seems. Rather than seeking to persuade or pressure parties, sometimes it is more effective to simply seek to understand them. If mediators focus on asking good questions, it is surprising how often solutions begin to emerge.

> *Help us understand the concerns you have about this particular proposal.*
> *Are there particular points, concerns, feelings that you especially want the other party to understand (or that you feel they have not yet understood)?*
> *What do you hope to get out of this discussion?*
> *On the long term, what do you see as most important for you/your people in this situation?*
> *How would you like to proceed if we are unable to come to agreement today? What do you see as the benefits and the costs associated with that path?*

Draw the Parties into Joint Information-Gathering

A strategy often used in group facilitation is to draw the parties into a joint effort to gather information relevant to the conflict. Negotiations are set aside for a time to allow for this. The parties might together make a trip to the site of a disputed property. They might agree to jointly hear input from a respected community leader or professional person with expertise related to the conflict. They might agree that one side will gather information regarding relevant legal issues and the other side regarding financial issues. If the matter is a community conflict involving numbers of people, they might agree to jointly go and hear the perceptions of others involved.

Often such information-gathering is employed as a first step in complex talks, for it offers a way to ease into the issues, build relationships, and set the stage for negotiation later. But it can also be used at the time of impasse as well. It gives a new focus and changes the dynamics, offers the parties something immediate and practical to cooperate on, and sometimes uncovers new grounds for resolution.

Switch from Problem-Oriented Tasks to People-Oriented Tasks

Mediation involves not only problem-solving skills for negotiating difficult issues, it also requires relationship-building skills for working with people who are hurt, angry, and suspicious. Success in mediation requires a good sense of when to switch from one set of tasks to the other. When things get difficult it may be time to make such a switch. For example, if the parties are stuck on how to resolve an issue it might be useful to spend some time pointing out areas of commonality and areas of agreement, or giving each side an opportunity to express their feelings and experience the empowerment that often comes from being listened to by an attentive listener.

Use Caucus

A caucus is a private meeting between the mediator and only one party. Caucus should be used sparingly. If the goal is the empowerment of others to solve their own conflicts, mediators need to mediate in ways that reduce the dependency of the parties on them. Caucus often has the opposite effect. The parties have little contact with each other. They wait to be called by the mediators who engage in the hard work of finding solutions. This leaves little room for the parties to build trust or develop new patterns and skills for resolving future conflicts.

Yet despite its shortcomings, caucus is a powerful tool that is sometimes essential in maintaining control and making breakthroughs in times of impasse. Mediators should know how to use it effectively for those moments. (See the following page for information on caucusing.)

Deadlock-Breaking Mechanisms

In some situations the parties might be willing to employ a deadlock-breaking mechanism. One such mechanism is arbitration, that is, the parties agree to submit a particularly difficult issue to arbitration. In standard arbitration, a person or panel of persons are agreed upon by both parties and requested to come up with a solution to the conflict which both parties bind themselves in advance to accept. Once the decision is rendered, the parties have no option but to accept it, and are legally bound to do so.

–Ron Kraybill
© MCS 2000

Calling a Caucus

What Is a Caucus?

A caucus is a closed meeting between the mediator(s) and one party at a time. To keep things balanced, mediators almost always caucus with both parties, first with one and then with the other. While direct dialogue between the parties in joint sessions is always the preferred objective of mediation, a private caucus may be needed, at times, to move the parties toward direct exchange. In extremely volatile or sensitive disputes, the use of caucus can even eclipse joint discussion as the primary means of communication, but this is, and should be, rare.

Call a Caucus . . .

- When storytelling has been rocky and you detect no willingness to make concessions as you move into the problem-solving stage.
- To explore concessions or get information that parties seem unwilling to discuss in joint sessions.
- When you reach an impasse at any time.
- If one or both parties show signs of high stress by repeatedly breaking ground rules or engaging in disruptive behavior.
- If one or both parties seem to distrust you.
- If you aren't sure that one party can or really intends to live up to what he or she is promising.
- When you feel like you're really losing your grasp of the facts, control of the process or emotional control.

In a Caucus

1. With each party, establish confidentiality of the session and general trust of the party (probably necessary only in the first caucus).

2. Get input from the party: "How do you feel about how it's going so far?"

3. Emphasize positive accomplishments such as areas of agreement, helpful behaviors or contributions of this party.

4. Allow venting of strong feelings and/or disclosure of sensitive information through active listening.

5. Explore hidden agenda and possible solutions.

6. Discuss what information the party may be willing to share in joint session and how it might happen.

–Ron Kraybill and Alice M. Price
© MCS 1989, 2000

Working With Power Imbalances

Mediators typically find themselves working with issues of power and with apparent power imbalances between disputants. At times, these imbalances may be addressed adequately through specific mediation interventions. At other times, you may determine that mediation is simply not an appropriate forum for particular parties and/or issues in dispute. Below are some ideas about recognizing and responding to power imbalances within the mediation process. Additional materials on the role of power dynamics in conflict can be found in Chapter Two.

Common Circumstances in Which Power Balance is an Issue

- Disparity of parties in access to information
- Disparity of parties in skill, experience, ability to negotiate (intellect, emotional difficulties, etc.)
- Emotionally abusive interpersonal dynamics between parties. Mental or physical intimidation that strains mediative process
- Disparities based on gender, class, age, position, etc.

Assessment and Analysis of Power Balance

- Assess nature and extent of apparent power imbalance
- Distinguish between value judgments of mediator about power imbalance and parties' judgment (e.g., parties want agreement mediator considers unfair)
- Can or should all power imbalances detected in the mediation process be confronted? How determine?
- When power imbalance between parties is not susceptible to realignment, when should mediation be terminated?

Strategies and Techniques for Minimizing and Realigning Power Imbalance

Resources outside the mediation process:

- attorneys
- financial planners
- reading material and videotapes
- counselors and support groups
- peer counseling

Resources within the mediation process:

- speculation (e.g., reframe the future—"I'm worried, what will happen if. . . .")
- caucus with parties
- reframe to address feelings about the issues
- set clear ground rules (e.g., full disclosure)
- communication interventions (e.g., inhibit control by one party)

Move away from difficult traps:

- mediator being "set up" by one or both parties
- fair in theory, not in practice (e.g., 50/50 splits)
- positional bargaining games (e.g., set the extreme and split the difference, to skew the outcome)
- party who controls by being extra *rational*, controls agenda (e.g., "I've already worked out the whole agreement that's fair to both of us.")

–Zena Zumeta and Robert Benjamin
© Zumeta/Benjamin 1986, from SPIDR conference workshop, October 1986. Used by permission of Z. Zumeta.

Handling Difficult Situations

Consider some situations that mediators may need to address during a mediation.

Receiving Critical Information in a Private Meeting

As discussed elsewhere, the use of separate or private meetings in mediation is a useful tool. A mediator may receive information from a party in private that makes it inappropriate to continue with the mediation.

- A party reveals they have not come to make agreements (perhaps they only want to get other party's information to prepare for a legal case, or they only agreed to come to oblige the other party's request to meet);
- a party reveals something that is a critical piece of the conflict situation, yet they insist that it not be shared with the other party;
- a party reveals physical or emotional threats or intimidation, abusive acts from other party or a non-present party which have impacted their willingness/ability to negotiate freely;
- a party reveals their grave emotional distress, thoughts of suicide, threats of violence towards the other party, etc.

When a mediator receives such information, it is important to consider the following:

- working with parties to consider their next steps if mediation does not resolve the issues at hand;
- the safety of all parties! It is unwise to go directly back to joint session, or even in private with the other party, and disclose that you now feel it would be inappropriate to continue. If you choose to end the session, do so in a way that does not imply private information has been revealed;
- any appropriate resources/referrals you can provide the party during the private meeting they may find helpful;
- if you are going to do anything other than keep the information confidential (e.g., if your mediation program asks you to report threats of harm toward anyone), let the party know what they can expect you to be doing.

Disruptive Behaviors

If a party continues to interrupt, yell, call names, etc. to the point that it has the effect of shutting down the other party, or negatively impacting on the dialogue or negotiations, the mediator has a range of interventions to consider.

- Remind party of ground rules, ask that they agree to stop the described behavior. Get a verbal "yes" from them before continuing.
- In a separate meeting with that party, confront them on their continued behavior, finding out if there is anything that needs to happen for it to stop and the mediation to continue. Let them know how it is negatively impacting the mediation and their chances for resolution.
- If the above steps do not succeed in ending the problem behavior, end the mediation and ask what each of their next steps will be.

Mediator Bias

You may feel in a mediation that you are having trouble maintaining your impartiality. Sometimes an attraction to or dislike for a party can be put back in check. Other times, a person or issue may trigger us in such a way that we cannot provide impartial service.

- Take a break and review in your mind/heart what has triggered you. Use any techniques you have found help center or rebalance you, reminding you of your role.
- If working with a co-mediator, tell them privately that you feel you are losing your impartiality. Negotiate a plan with them. Options may be for them to watch and be a reality check for you; for them to carry the speaking load of the work while you take notes or a lesser role; for them to continue alone; or for you to end the mediation and ask the parties to reschedule.

- If you decide to end the session, or leave and allow a co-mediator to continue, announce your inability to continue in a way that owns the problem as one *you* have, not that it is something about them or that you have a bias. It is best simply to state that you cannot continue as their mediator, that you realize you are not the best mediator for them right now, you cannot serve them in the way they deserve. Remember it is your problem that you cannot do your job here, not them.

One Party Does Not Show

If one of the parties fails to show up at the appointed time, the most important thing to remember is to NOT engage in conversation about the missing party or about the conflict situation with the party that is present.
- Call the missing party to see if there is a reason for the absence. Find out from both parties whether it is possible to wait for them to arrive, to reschedule, or if mediation is no longer an option.
- If there is no answer and the amount of time waited seems to indicate that they will not be coming, thank the other party for waiting and let them know they will be contacted (by you or mediation program staff) regarding follow-up once the other party has been contacted.

One Party Reveals a Major Piece of New, Upsetting Information

The growing comfort and safety one feels when discussing difficult issues with the help of a third party present often enables them to reveal information that they know will be new and upsetting to another. Often it can be a surprise to the mediator as well! Common examples include the announcement that legal action has begun or the involvement of some other party in the situation (e.g., "Your boss told me to do it because she doesn't trust you," "I'm involved with someone else and plan to move with them").
- Find out if the pronouncement is, in fact, a new piece of information for the other party. Name it as a big, new piece of information on the table. Don't pretend it wasn't said or try to put further down the list of issues to be discussed.
- If necessary, call for separate meetings and allow for venting privately in an attempt to keep the negotiations from disintegrating right there. Talk with upset party about what they may need at this point to continue.
- Discuss thoughts, feelings and ramifications of the disclosure, separately and/or jointly. Again, don't pretend it wasn't said or try to put it further down the list of issues to be discussed.

Disagreement with Co-mediator

Working with a co-mediator is the preferred model of mediating for this writer. That doesn't mean it is always easier. Each mediator has their own personality, strengths and weaknesses, approaches to the mediation process, comfort levels, and preferred intervention methods for the myriad of dynamics involved in mediation. In other words, you don't always agree. When you are struggling:
- speak privately with your co-mediator describing the behaviors that are causing you discomfort;
- while being mindful of the time, give each other a chance to identify the thoughts and hopes behind the behaviors, how they fit or do not fit with the role of the mediator, and/or how they may be negatively impacting the work of the negotiating parties;
- negotiate how to handle your differences so the parties can be best served. Options include agreeing that the behavior is not best suited in this situation, proceeding with one mediator's preferred method, trying one way and meeting privately again to assess progress, meeting separately with the parties if your co-mediator feels something s/he has been doing at the table is still important, yet you feel it is inappropriate to do in joint session (e.g., give resource information about one party's preferred solution, or counseling information). If the conflict between you is intractable, end the session using the "you own your problem" rule described under "mediator bias" above.

–Sandi Adams
© MCS 2000

Handling Difficult Situations Exercise

The caucus is one strategy for addressing touchy situations. During caucus, as well as at other times during mediation, you may be faced with the need to respond rather quickly and decisively to a variety of difficult situations. Your comfort level can be increased by roleplaying some of these "tough calls" in a training session, where you have the benefit of group feedback in a low-risk setting. You may find information elsewhere in this manual, as well as from other sources, helpful in assessing these scenarios.

"Tough Issues" Scenarios:

1. You are the mediator and you go into caucus in a family mediation case with a wife who has been very hesitant to talk in joint session. She reluctantly reveals to you that she thinks her husband has been sexually molesting their 10-year-old daughter.

2. You are the mediator and you go into caucus in a business partnership dissolution case with one partner, who reveals to you a secret asset which he has failed to disclose on the financial statement and which he resists disclosing to the other partner at this time.

3. You are involved in a landlord-tenant mediation in which the landlord has refused to return a security deposit. You know—and you think the landlord probably knows—that the tenant could get "triple damages" (three times the amount of the security deposit) for the unreturned security deposit from the small claims court. The tenant seems to be unaware of this and is bargaining in the hopes of getting something less than the complete deposit amount in trade for some other minor concessions by the landlord.

4. An irate husband in a marital separation case—after being called "good for nothing" by his wife—gets up and stomps out of the mediation session. On the way out, he yells, "I'll get you for this!"

5. Near the end of a mediation on a personal injury settlement between an individual and a large corporation, the corporate representative insists on a final condition to the agreement. The individual would be barred from discussing the fact of the injury or the nature of the settlement with anyone. You know that this individual is not the only person who has used this product and who may have been injured by it.

6. You are halfway through a mediation between a white man and a black woman, who have been having problems in the workplace. The black woman confronts you (or your male co-mediator), saying, "You're just like him! Because I'm black and female, I've already got two strikes against me in your book!"

7. You've met in several sessions with a divorcing couple. The husband has appeared to be extremely depressed, saying very little in the sessions, and generally agreeing to whatever the wife wants. The negotiations seem to be getting rather imbalanced, and the husband has resisted your suggestions to consult outside resources (attorney, accountant, etc.).

Directions

Option 1   Trainers quickly roleplay or explain the scenario to the group. Individuals volunteer to roleplay a response or suggest strategies, followed by group discussion.

Option 2   Trainers quickly roleplay or explain the scenario to the group or hand out the sheet to the group. People break into small groups and are given a limited time to come to consensus on a response. Report back to full group and discuss.

–Alice M. Price
© MCS 1990

Is It Time to Quit?

There are times when a wise mediator ends a mediation session. Ask yourself these two questions:

1: Can They Negotiate Fairly and Usefully?

Here are several warning flags:

- A key person seems incapable of participating productively:
  - The person persists in threatening or disrupting.
  - The person keeps repeating accusations and demands, even when the group has already agreed to accommodate them.
  - No amount of explanation resolves a person's confusion.

- A fair agreement is unlikely. For instance, the power differential may mean that one side is caving in to the other's demands.

- The main problems are not negotiable.

- A party who is a critical part of the dispute is absent. Or the person representing a group has not been authorized to make commitments.

2: Does Mediating Potentially Endanger Someone?

Occasionally, there are conflicts where a face-to-face negotiation session can be unfair or even dangerous for participants, other potential victims, for the organization, or for the community. You should stop the mediation if you have good reason to believe that:
- One party might react with violence, vengeance, or intimidation after the mediation.
- One party is covertly using mediation to elicit information that will be used against the other party (in court, to fire them, etc.) or as an opportunity for retaliation.
- Someone is using mediation as a way to keep illegal or unethical behavior under cover. By mediating, a person can avoid getting an official record or punishment. They don't have to admit fault in public. There may be future victims because a confidential mediation makes it harder to establish that there is a pattern of incidents going on.
- The agreement they are proposing is illegal or is harmful to people who aren't represented at the mediation.

Breaking Off the Mediation

Usually the parties break off the mediation before the mediators are ready to give up. When the mediator initiates, it can be hard to know when and how to draw the line. Consult with your co-mediator first and give yourselves a chance to think through what to do. It can be difficult to determine what is really going on and you will have to rely on your intuition.

Be sensitive to participants' interpretations of why you are ending a mediation. For instance, don't end the mediation abruptly following a separate meeting or one party's outburst, leaving others to imagine what was said privately, or that the mediator disapproved of one party's point of view.

Try to remain impartial as you withdraw from the mediation. (Remember too, that no matter how much they tell you, you are getting an incomplete and skewed picture from the participants.)

Try to end the session without blaming or discouraging the participants. You don't need to be explicit about the reasons, either.

I don't think we can get any further right now. I'm glad you were able to (have an honest discussion, reach agreement on X, give mediation a try).

Thank you all for coming. I don't think this is the right place for you to discuss this situation. If you would like some assistance on where to turn next, I'd be happy to meet with each of you privately for a few minutes now before you leave.

If you have information or concerns to convey, meet with each party separately at the end, or call them the following day.

You will want to evaluate in detail afterwards, of course, but don't be hard on yourselves. Good mediators know the limits of what they can deal with in a mediation process.

–Jennifer E. Beer and Eileen Stief

© Friends Conflict Resolution Programs 1997, from *The Mediator's Handbook*, 3rd ed. (British Columbia: New Society Publishers). Used by permission.

Resources for Further Study on Mediation

Adams, Sandi. *What the Fly Heard: What Mediators Say Behind Closed Doors.* Denver, CO: Queen of Hearts, 1998.
> Designed as a follow-up to trainings, gives clear idea of how a mediator may actually work and respond.

Beer, Jennifer E., and Eileen Stief. *The Mediator's Handbook*, 4th ed. Gabriola Island, BC: New Society Publishers, 1990.
> Developed as a reference manual for those taking basic mediation training.

Beer, Jennifer E. *Peacemaking in Your Neighborhood: Reflections on an Experiment in Community Mediation.* Philadelphia: New Society Publishers, 1986.
> A classic on community mediation, this is a provocative evaluation of the goals, objectives and results of the Community Dispute Settlement Project outside Philadelphia. Has four chapters on mediation skills.

Bush, Robert A. Baruch, and Joseph P. Folger. *The Promise of Mediation: Responding to Conflict Through Empowerment and Recognition.* San Francisco: Jossey-Bass, 1994.
> Explores and promotes the transformative potential of mediation as it critiques the field of mediation today. Very worth reading.

Duffy, Karen Grover, *et al.*, eds. *Community Mediation: A Handbook for Practitioners and Researchers.* New York: Guilford Press, 1991.
> A comprehensive volume on the nature of conflict, the state of the field of mediation, the process of mediation, useful methods for assessing and promoting mediation services, and a variety of other issues in community mediation.

Duryea, Michelle LeBaron. *Conflict Analysis and Resolution as Education: Culturally Sensitive Processes for Conflict Resolution (Training Materials)*, and, co-authored with Victor C. Robinson, *Conflict Analysis and Resolution as Education: Culturally Sensitive Processes for Conflict Resolution (Trainer Reference).* Victoria, BC: UVic Institute for Dispute Resolution, 1994.
> Designed to assist mediation trainers and mediators to address culture in a comprehensive way. Highly recommended.

Fisher, Roger, William Ury and Bruce Patton. *Getting to Yes: Negotiating Agreement Without Giving In*, 2nd ed. New York: Penguin Books, 1991.
> The best-selling, practical book on win-win negotiation using interest-based collaboration.

Folberg, Jay, and Alison Taylor. *Mediation: A Comprehensive Guide to Resolving Conflicts Without Litigation.* San Francisco: Jossey-Bass, 1984.
> A comprehensive guide to mediation, covering everything from interviewing clients and promoting good communication to keeping records and setting fees.

Kolb, Deborah M., *et al. When Talk Works: Profiles of Mediators.* San Francisco: Jossey-Bass, 1994.
> Interview-based profiles which show how mediators resolve conflicts in families, businesses and communities and between nations.

Leonard, Sam. *Mediation: The Book: A Step-By-Step Guide for Dispute Resolvers.* Evanston, IL: McDougall Littel Publishers, 1994.

Leviton, Sharon, and James Greenstone. *Elements of Mediation.* Pacific Grove, CA: Brooks/Cole Publishing, 1997.
> A practical book designed to be helpful to novices as well as to those with more experience resolving disputes.

Mayer, Bernard. *The Dynamics of Conflict Resolution: A Practitioner's Guide*. San Francisco: Jossey-Bass, 2000.
An essential guide that shows how successful mediators, facilitators and negotiators draw on their creative internal process to resolve conflict.

McKinney, Bruce, William Kimsey and Rex Fuller. *Mediator Communication Competencies: Interpersonal Communication and Alternative Dispute Resolution* (4th ed.). Minneapolis, MN: Burgess Publishing, 1995.

Merry, Sally Engle, and Neal Miler, eds. *The Possibility of Popular Justice: A Case Study of Community Mediation in the United States*. Ann Arbor: University of Michigan Press, 1993.
This in-depth study of one of the oldest community mediation programs, San Francisco Community Boards, highlights issues and challenges for mediation today.

Moore, Christopher W. *The Mediation Process: Practical Strategies for Resolving Conflict* (2nd ed.). San Francisco: Jossey-Bass, 1996.
Presents an in-depth, step-by-step account of how the mediation process works.

Slaikeu, Karl. *When Push Comes to Shove: A Practical Guide to Mediating Disputes*. San Francisco: Jossey-Bass, 1996.
A lucidly written guide with practical and wise advice for novices and seasoned mediators alike.

Yarbrough, Elaine, and William Wilmot. *Artful Mediation: Constructive Conflict at Work*. Boulder, CO: Cairns Publishing, 1995.
Offers a constructive framework for dealing with conflicts that inevitably arise in the workplace.

Chapter 5

Groups: Process, Conflict, Systemic Change

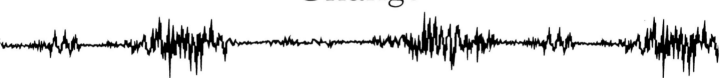

Now let me suggest . . . that if we are to have peace on earth, our loyalties must become ecumenical rather than sectional. Our loyalties must transcend our race, our tribe, our class and our nation, and this means we must develop a world perspective. No individual can live alone; no nation can live alone, and as long as we try, the more we are going to have war in this world. Now the judgement of God is upon us and we must learn to live together as brothers or we are all going to perish together as fools.

–Martin Luther King, Jr.

Introduction

Groups. From our initial introduction to this world, all of us are part of multiple groups. Beginning with the family and expanding to neighborhood friends and then to informal and formal associations at multiple levels, it is impossible to pass through this world without encountering and integrating into social groups. Many sociologists believe that it is in the context of this "Web of Group Affiliations" (Simmel) that personal identities are formed and reformed.

Organizations. Throughout recorded human history, organizations have increasingly defined the context in which human beings live, work, play and worship. Organizations dominate at the political level, pervade the business world, and also define the nonprofit and religious sector. From school age on, most of us spend up to half of our waking hours within the bounds of an organization. While organizations are simply formalized groups, their very structure allows them to assume a "life of their own" and to generally outlast the original founders.

Each group and organization represents a system, and each system's ability to function in healthy and creative ways is critical both to the individual members who comprise it and to the broader society. This chapter consists of two basic sections, one which proactively addresses healthy group functioning and the second which provides resources for managing conflict and change in systems. Because of the context in which MCS often functions, several resources specific to religious organizations are included throughout the chapter.

The chapter opens with a section on proactive approaches to *healthy group process*, divided into the following subsections:

1. distinctions between dialogue and debate,
2. process planning,
3. group facilitation, and
4. decision-making.

This section applies primarily to work and other associational groups where members desire to participate in decision-making, and where the leadership is committed to collaborative and inclusive processes. Despite the space in decision-making devoted to consensus, we do not presume that group consensus is the only (or even always the desired) form of decision-making. Participatory processes are, however, more likely to lead to outcomes that are broadly supported by those involved in the decision-making process.

The second major section addresses *conflict and systemic change*, and opens with a primer on a systems approach to organizational life and organizational culture and change. The following two subsections provide tips and guidelines both for internal processes for dealing with stress and for intervention by an outside mediator or consultant in organizational conflict. The importance of assessing the level (or intensity) of conflict and of planning a clear process for addressing it is underscored.

As you peruse the pieces which follow, you will note that most articles in the second section contain strategies and tools for dealing with times of high stress in an organization. However, the best time for organizational assessment and proactive change is not in the midst of a crisis, but during times of relative equanimity. Whether you work primarily as an internal change agent or function as an outside intervenor, I would encourage you to develop proactive strategies that build organizational health and capacity, and thus make crisis interventions less likely to be needed.

–David Brubaker
© MCS 2000

Part 1

Healthy Group Process

Dialogue vs. Debate

Dialogue	Debate
The goal of dialogue is increased understanding of myself and others.	The goal of debate is the successful argument of my position over that of my opponent.
I listen with a view toward understanding.	I listen with a view of countering what I hear.
I listen for strengths so as to affirm and learn.	I listen for weaknesses so as to discount and devalue.
I speak for myself from my own understanding and experience.	I speak based on assumptions made about others' positions and motivations.
I ask questions to increase understanding.	I ask questions to trip up or confuse.
I allow others to complete their communications.	I interrupt or change the subject.
I concentrate on others' words and feelings.	I focus on my own next point.
I accept others' experiences as real and valid for them.	I critique others' experiences as distorted or invalid.
I allow the expression of real feelings (in myself and others) for understanding and catharsis.	I express my feelings to manipulate others; I deny their feelings as legitimate.
I honor silence.	I use silence to gain advantage.

Questions to ask myself if I am having trouble staying with dialogue

Am I honoring my own experience as valid. . .	or am I feeling defensive about it?
Can I trust others to respect our differences. . .	or do I suspect others are trying to force me to change?
Can I trust myself to be permeable and still maintain integrity. . .	or do I fear that really hearing a different perspective will weaken my position?
Am I willing to open myself to the pain of others (and myself). . .	or am I resisting pain that I really have the strength to face?
Am I open to seeing God in others. . .	or am I viewing others as the enemy?

–Episcopal Church Center
from "Global Education for Mission," Episcopal Church Center, 815 Second Avenue, New York NY 10017. Permission to copy is granted.

Thoughts on Dialogue

Definitions of Dialogue

- The coming together of persons who desire to learn and grow in the truth through building on the insights and observations of another, particularly an adversary.

- An ongoing conversation between Christians of differing convictions who recognize their human limitations and who believe that God can use the various moral and theological conflicts to teach and reform the church for holy living.

What is Needed in Dialogue

- **Team work.** Personal convictions and assumptions are offered as resources or tools to be used by the entire team of dialogue participants . . . with the hope that new light and truth will come forth. At least for the duration of the dialogue adversaries become allies, working together to break new ground. Objections will still be raised; disagreement based on nonnegotiable convictions will still hold firm; but the tone is different. The goal is changed from conquering to growing; from silencing to knowing; from telling to asking. Questions are employed as tools for probing, not weapons for stabbing. New possibilities are considered.

- **Trust**
    - *In one's own position.* A confidence in one's personal worth that transcends the correctness of the position he or she holds. This trust is essentially an inner strength, or we may say, a basic trust in God who grants all people worth regardless of the coherence of their convictions on a given issue. Without self-trust, the questions and challenges posed by an adversary will create suspicion and defensiveness in ill-equipped participants.
    - *In the dialogue partner.* This is a new and startling experience, similar to Jesus' invitation to lose one's life in order to find it. In the process of dialogue, participants come out from behind the safety of carefully crafted defenses and diplomas in order to expose themselves and their ideas to the scrutiny of both self and the other, and to pledge to do the same for the other.
    - *In the process of dialogue.* We will subject ourselves to the work and vulnerability of dialogue only if we have some hope of its rewards. We take the risk because of the promise of growth that can come only by way of dialogue.

- **Desire for the Truth.** There is an awareness by participants that there is more truth than they can claim to know, that the truth of God and life and eternity are beyond any human knowing. We accept the possibility that God could choose to reveal truth through our adversary, or through a new self-discovery as we reveal ourselves before the other, or through the interchange of convictions.

- **A Place to Argue.** Dialogue depends on a kind of controlled argument in order to help analyze and clarify the issue at hand. Through argument, passion enters the conversation and is the catalyst for consistency and elaboration by both sides. Good arguments within dialogue are balanced between conviction and humility.

> Dialogue embodies the teachings of Jesus. It is loving, strong, intentional, risky, and redemptive. It is a hopeful tool in the hands of people of faith. It will not resolve differences. It does, however, give us a way to address them in the manner of our Lord. Ultimately, dialogue depends on a trust in Someone beyond ourselves.

A Few Relevant Biblical Passages

Matt. 18:15-16; 5:38-41, 43-44; Acts 15; Eph. 4:25-27, 29-32; Col. 2: 12-13; I Cor 13: 4-8; Rom. 12:16-21; 14:1-6, 19.

–Joseph Phelps
© Joseph Phelps 1999, excerpted from *More Light Less Heat: How Dialogue Can Transform Christian Conflicts into Growth*. Reprinted by permission of Jossey-Bass, Inc., a subsidiary of John Wiley & Sons, Inc.

Ground Rules for Useful Discussions

Talking about issues can bring out strong emotions because many of our beliefs are a large part of how we identify ourselves. Effective communication requires that you respect others and take ideas seriously—even when you think they're dead wrong. You can respect another's feelings without necessarily agreeing with their conclusions.

While there are no sure-fire rules, applying the basic principles below will make your discussions more productive, satisfying and enjoyable. Though many of these ground rules seem common-sensical, we all know that in practice they are not so commonly applied!

- Think together about what you want to get out of your discussions.

- Listen carefully to others in order to really understand what they are saying, especially when their ideas differ from your own.

- When disagreement occurs, keep talking. Stay curious, rather than judgmental. Explore the disagreement. Search for the common concerns beneath the surface.

- Try to avoid building your own arguments in your head while others are talking.

- Help to develop one another's ideas. Listen carefully and ask clarifying questions.

- Be open to changing your mind; ideally about the issue at hand, but minimally about the person(s) holding the opposing view.

- Value one another's experiences and think about how they have contributed to each person's thinking.

- Anecdotal stories have value because they describe our experience and can help us understand what others have gone through. But be careful not to overgeneralize from a story.

- Speak your mind freely but give others equal time.

- Above all, be civil.

–Study Circles Resource Center
© SCRC from "The Busy Citizen's Discussion Guides." SCRC has a variety of excellent discussion guides and facilitation resources, available from P.O. Box 203, Pomfret, CT 06258, 860-928-2616, scrc@neca.com. Used according to SCRC's broad permission guidelines.

"Fair Play": Guidelines for Church Dialogue on Inclusion

First, it seems significant to acknowledge that a truly "level playing field" is impossible to create in the current discussion about the inclusion or exclusion of gay, lesbian and bisexual people in the church. Whenever there is a power imbalance such as the one that exists in this current debate, the playing field is not and cannot be level. The risks taken by the parties involved are not even, the potential losses are not equal, and the privileges the parties experience are not the same. We believe that leaders are responsible for acknowledging this power imbalance and inequity whenever and wherever this debate is discussed. We also believe that it is the role of strong, effective leadership to protect the safety and dignity of those that are least powerful. It seems important to ask the question—where and with whom should the church stand when power is not bestowed equally? The following guidelines reflect our expectations of our church leaders in this debate.

Do not tolerate the use of weapons. Not all weapons are crafted out of metal, but all are crafted for battle. Do not tolerate spoken or written words whose purpose is to divide, scar or injure other people, other congregations or the dialogue process itself. Do not give consideration, time or energy to conversations that are initiated by an act of violence (i.e. an anonymous mailing, phone call or rumor that infringes on personal privacy or safety). Conversations or debates initiated by an unfair act are inherently unfair. Personal attacks and name-calling are also forms of weaponry. This includes the name "sinner," which is ultimately God's job to judge rather than our own.

Do not allow hostage-taking and threats. Individuals and congregations who issue ultimatums effectively grind to a halt any honest, productive conversation. It is disrespectful and unfair to those favoring the church's inclusion of gay/lesbian/bisexual people—those who have come to this conversation through the loss of personal privacy and risking total vulnerability—to have the conversation ended by their opponents' unwillingness to take reciprocal risks in honest, informed dialogue. More and more, churches are leaving or threatening to leave—and to take their dollars with them—unless the conference sees things their way. Name this as violence to the minority and to the process and be clear that threats are not an acceptable part of this dialogue. Hold hostage-takers accountable for their actions and for the harm that they do to the process. Have the courage to allow churches that issue ultimatums to leave if they insist. Do not allow yourselves or the conversation to be bullied into compliance with the loudest majority. This mode of functioning is always most harmful to the least powerful—clearly not a Christ-like model.

Do not allow an "easy way out." Our relationships and shared history are at stake. When churches are asked to leave or when churches choose to leave conferences, the fabric of our community's relationships and histories is torn. This should only be done intentionally, honestly and with clear accountability. Mail-in ballots allow us to rend the fabric of our history and relationships without taking accountability, without looking each other in the eyes, and without feeling the resulting wounds. This "easy way out" is nothing short of cowardice.

"Nothing about me without me!" This slogan from the disability rights movement is valid in the Church's conversation about the inclusion of gay/lesbian/bisexual members and their allies. It seems elementary that conversations geared at decision-making about a certain group of people should only happen with fair representation of the group in question. This is not only courteous and decent: it is a decision-making process that welcomes input. A closed decision-making process is not a process at all—it is a decision. However, a "nothing about us without us" policy within the church will prove to be difficult unless efforts are made to "level the playing field" in our conversations. This is not an ultimatum demanding that "we get our way or we'll leave." This is a request for decent, respectful treatment from others so that gay/lesbian/bisexual members can be part of the conversation without being abused spiritually or emotionally.

Insist on educated, informed, "responsible" dialogue. When education is needed, provide it and insist on it. Intervene with appropriate correction when comments are made that reflect inaccurate information (i.e., linking homosexuality to pedophilia, talking about homosexuality as a psychological disorder, citing AIDS as God's punishment for homosexuals, etc.). As in the case of any minority's relationship with its respective majority, gay/lesbian/bisexual Mennonites have much more information about and experience with straight

Mennonites than straight Mennonites have with them. Encourage reciprocation. Insist that those against the inclusion of gay/lesbian/bisexual Mennonites make efforts to acquaint themselves with such people prior to engaging in the conversation. Again, work to equalize the amount of risk individuals must take in having this debate.

Reframe the conversation to accurately reflect the issue. Do not tolerate the naming of the church's problem regarding inclusion as "the homosexual issue." Gay/lesbian/bisexual people are not issues, but people. And the real issue is the Mennonite Church's own inner conflict about whether it will include or exclude gay/lesbian/bisexual Mennonites and their allies within its congregations and conferences. Those gay/lesbian/bisexual Mennonites seeking membership within the Mennonite Church are not conflicted about whether they want to be included in the church. The church is conflicted about including them. By identifying this conflict as "the homosexual issue," responsibility for the conflict is placed squarely on the shoulders of gay/lesbian/bisexual Mennonites rather than on the shoulders of the church body as a whole.

We applaud the Mennonite Church's efforts in preparing and adopting documents geared toward helping the church "disagree in love." Our hope is that this letter might serve as a companion to these church documents and to other efforts the church has made to create a safe, respectful environment for this conversation.

–**Brethren/Mennonite Council for Lesbian and Gay Concerns**

Characteristics of Good Process

1. **Leaders or facilitators foster the attitude that conflict and disagreement are an opportunity, not a threat.**

2. **Planning begins with "*Who* is affected?", not "*What* will we do?"**
   Some questions to guide planning about whom to involve in the discussion process:
   - Who will view themselves as deeply affected by this negotiation, project or decision? (Almost always this group should be at the heart of the decision-making process.)
   - Who is in a position to block implementation if they are unhappy with decisions? (They should always at least be consulted; often they need to be an active part of the decision process.)
   - Whose approval will be required to enable this project to proceed? (Inform and consult.)
   - Whose advice or assistance will be valuable? (Call for consultation.)
   - What are the interests or motivations of each of the above groups?

3. **Involves representatives of affected people in the design and management of the process itself.**
   Consider establishing a "Process Committee" to plan, announce and oversee implementation of the process.

4. **Provides full information about the process** to those participating or affected: about the purpose of the process, about *what* will happen *when* (a time line is helpful here); about *who* will make the final decision and what kind of *decision rule* will apply (51% majority, 67% majority, consensus, modified consensus, unanimity, etc.). Of course, these things cannot usually all be decided at the beginning of the process, but they should be clarified as early as possible.

5. **Offers more than one kind of forum** for people affected to express ideas and opinions (e.g., in institutional settings, use large group discussion, small group discussion, polls or questionnaires, personal inquiry, etc.)

6. **Maintains trust through careful reports back to people affected.**
   - During the negotiation or discussion process, use open discussions, surveys, nonbinding votes, questionnaires, interim reports, etc., to keep people informed about the trend of the discussion before the decision is final. If people are shocked at the outcome of a decision-making process, the designers of that process have failed to build adequate report-back mechanisms into the process.
   - Give frequent opportunities for people to comment about how they feel about the process, whether it is fair, whether they understand next steps, etc.
   - Never conduct a formal query process (e.g., questionnaires, interviews or meetings designed to find out what people want) without reporting back to those queried about what information or preferences the query process revealed.
   - Follow-up at the end: report to people about the outcome/decision finally reached, solicit evaluation of the process used, report what monitoring or implementing process will be used.

–Ron Kraybill

Designing Good Meetings

Meetings are part of every organization's life. And in virtually every case people feel "meeting-ed out." Meetings are necessary but often seem inefficient, time-consuming and poorly managed. How to improve the lot of the modern-day committee member? Here are several suggestions.

Be Clear on the Purpose

Information Sharing, Planning and Reporting—These meetings are held to plan for, share information or report on upcoming events or projects and to permit a time for clarification. This may be better accomplished through memos unless there is need for input and task distribution.

Airing and Problem-Defining—There is often a need to face circumstances in which problems and conflicts are manifested in indirect ways, creating ineffective work patterns and poor follow-through on projects. The meeting provides a forum for exploring people's concerns and feelings in a more direct fashion, with the purpose of *documenting and defining*. It should not be confused with problem-solving or decision-making.

Problem-Solving—This meeting assumes the problem has been identified and defined clearly. The purpose is to produce options for change. This assumes that people coming to the meeting understand the need for the changes and are ready to work on them. Confusion emerges when the problem is not defined, or there is little commitment or felt need to change. This meeting will likely have a substantial component of brainstorming and will outline potential options. It should not be confused with making the final decision.

Decision-Making—Problem-solving discovers options, but decision-making meetings assume that the options are to be narrowed to a final solution. It is important to be clear about the procedure and authority by which decisions will be made before starting to make them.

Be Clear on the Roles

Facilitator—Of crucial importance to any meeting is the use of a facilitator who provides process guidance.
- Plan pre- and post-meeting logistics
- Clarify meeting type
- Prepare agenda
- Help to focus group energy on task
- Protect people from personal attack
- Encourage broad participation
- Do not enter into the substantive discussion

Public Recorder—For the majority of meetings we recommend a public recorder as opposed to a private recording secretary. Public recording serves many purposes which enhance the process:

- It provides a focus for the group
- It creates group memory, present and visible
- People can see what they said, it counts
- People can correct misinterpretations
- The visible nature facilitates the coordination of ideas

The recorder is responsible to capture basic ideas of what each person has said, in his or her own language, so that it can be recalled at any time. This permits them to keep pace with the group process and yet make visible what has transpired. Technique suggestions:
- Use newsprint taped on walls, starting with a taped stack that can easily be moved
- Use large markers in multiple colors (watercolor do not stain) and write in large, at least one and one-half inch letters

- Get the basic idea, try to catch key phrases or words
- Do not worry about spelling
- Ask the group for time when you need it
- Do not get defensive if someone challenges your phrase, just ask them how they want it and change it
- Support the facilitator

Plan and Follow an Agenda

The facilitator should work with leadership or a process planning group to plan the meeting agenda. Distribute to all participants in advance, if possible, indicating designated roles, presentations, etc. An agenda should include the following items, adjusted appropriately to the context and purpose of the meeting:

- *Gathering in*: Time for introductions, icebreakers, personal updates, networking, etc. May be structured or unstructured, depending on nature and length of personal relationships.
- *Centering time*: An opportunity to refocus from other activities to the mission of this group and the purpose of the meeting. May include readings, music, prayer, etc., as fits setting.
- *Agenda review*: An opportunity for both facilitator and group members to supplement prepared agenda with updates, additions, etc.
- *Ground rules*: Set or review meeting ground rules for communication (e.g., recognition of speakers, time limits, respect) and governance (e.g., constitutional guidelines, Roberts' Rules, decision rules, etc.).
- *Review of past actions/updates*: This may include minutes, committee reports, staff updates, etc., as needed and appropriate for meeting purpose.
- *Main items of business*: Based on meeting purpose.
- *Break-out sessions*: Depending on meeting purpose and context, executive sessions, small group discussions, or other break-out groups may be helpful to the agenda design.
- *Wrap-up*: This is often a combination of summarizing meeting content, identifying next steps, assigning tasks, and setting any needed meeting dates for the future.
- *Evaluation*: Oral feedback on how the meeting went is a helpful learning/planning tool for facilitators and other group leaders; written evaluations may also be appropriate.
- *Closure*: Some structure for group members to share a highlight, a commitment, an affirmation, etc., brings better closure than a simple adjournment. Many groups have their own closing rituals.

–John Paul Lederach and Alice M. Price
© MCS 1989, 1995

Stages of Decision-Making

Groups encountering difficulty with decisions are often skipping the first three stages.

Stage	Purpose	Typical General Activities	Helpful Leadership or Intervenor Activities
Plan	To agree on a fair process that is understood and supported by all	• Identify issues • Identify goals • Outline steps of process • Agree on decision rule If the issue is weighty or emotional, appoint a representative group to plan the above. After planning a process, ask the whole group, "Can you support this process?"	• Be sure issues are clear. • Make sure process planners are representative of or trusted by group. • Clarify goals. • Help plan process.
Generate	To generate a comprehensive list of available viewpoints/options	• List ideas • Brainstorm • Consult with outside resources to expand options	• Use newsprint! • Be firm about no evaluations yet. • Encourage diversity. The more diverse the ideas at this point the better!
Evaluate	To examine thoughtfully the strengths and limits of each option	• Identify criteria • List strengths and limits of each option • Anticipate impact of each option	• Use newsprint! • Be firm about evaluating one option at a time in first round of evaluation. Then allow comparisons of options in second round.
Negotiate	To formulate a proposal reflecting the best judgement of most of the group	• Dialogue • Debate/Persuade • Propose • Compromise • Find win/win solution	• Poll group, stressing nonbinding nature of poll. • Explore concerns and hesitations. • Stress areas of agreement. • Ask the key players to meet separately and develop a proposal.

Decide	To formally commit as a group to one proposal or plan	• Verbally review the proposal
		• Use agreed-upon decision rule to finalize agreement
			• Make sure minority is acknowledged and respected.
			  1) Do they feel heard?
			  2) Can they live with the majority's opinion?
			• Make sure details of implementation are addressed (who/what/when/etc.).
			• Clarify reporting, accountability and evaluation.

–MCS Staff

© MCS 1997, from *Conciliation Quarterly*, Vol. 6 No. 4

Agreement on Procedure

Groups facing major decisions or "hot issues" should have a clear agreement on process before substantive discussion begins. Someone, preferably a small group which represents a diversity of viewpoints, should be assigned the task of developing and proposing a decision-making process to the larger group. This group functions as *process advocates*, not outcome advocates. Once the process is approved, this committee can also coordinate its implementation.

In outlining a proposed process, four items deserve attention:

- The *issue* should be specified. Everyone should agree on what they are disagreeing about, before trying to seek solutions.

- A statement of *purpose* or goals should clarify what the group would like to happen, including whether a decision is to be made.

- A *process* section should outline what will happen and when.

- A *decision rule* should clarify how all decisions, if any, will be made (consensus, majority vote, etc.).

Sample Agreement on Procedure: A New Director

Issue: To define expectations/qualifications of, and to hire, a new director.

Purpose:
1. Provide opportunity for members of the organization to express views on this issue.
2. Develop a proposal regarding director qualifications acceptable to as many members as possible.
3. Undertake discussion openly.
4. Decide on a new director.

Process Time Line:

September 1:	Search committee presents proposed process to members for approval or modification.
September 1-30:	Avenues for membership input into director qualifications, including questionnaire.
September 19:	Panel discussion followed by small group discussions.
November 1:	Proposal from committee re director qualifications, based on earlier input, presented to members for approval/modification.
Nov.-Dec.:	Search committee conducts search for new director, based on approved qualifications.
January:	Applicants interviewed by exec. committee at its Jan. meeting.
February 1:	Candidate presented to members for approval.

Decision Rule: Consensus of the membership will be sought on all decisions; if consensus is not reached at any point, action may be taken by a two-thirds majority vote (by standing).

–adapted from Ron Kraybill and David Brubaker
© MCS 1987, 1992

The Decision Rule

An important factor in how groups make decisions is the "decision rule." The decision rule is the method by which a group makes and finalizes a particular decision. Decision rules can range from autocratic to consensus-making, with many variations in between. Some groups enter significant decision-making events without any predetermined decision rule. Other groups automatically apply their one traditional rule in every situation, regardless of the consequences. Good process planning includes awareness of the importance of the decision rule choice, in light of the nature of the group, its traditions, and the particular decisions a group is facing, and the need to make this choice *before* the decision-making process begins.

Types of Decision Rules

At what level and by whom is a decision to be made?
- **Single autocratic figure:** decisions handed down from "on high"; "no questions asked."
- **Authoritarian with consulting:** centralized power with consultative structures such as cabinets, advisory boards, study groups, etc.
- **Polling/ranking:** use of various statistical techniques (such as surveying, averaging, ranked responses) without discussion.
- **Minority rule:** hierarchical structures placing decisions with board of directors, executive committee, steering committee, etc.
- **Majority rule:** usually voting, by plurality, simple majority, etc.
- **Weighted voting:** various affirmative efforts at fairness by maximizing minority voices.
- **Consensus:** mutually acceptable agreement reached through discussion.

Evaluating Decision Rules

Following are some possible ways to evaluate the appropriateness of a particular decision rule for a decision-making process.

Quality of Outcome

Based on some set of objective criteria, will the decision be made on adequate information? Will it satisfactorily meet the principles, goals, standards, etc. necessary for a good substantive outcome in this situation? Will people be willing to implement it?

Any decision rule may result in a high quality outcome. However, the more authoritarian end of the spectrum often operates with less information and less support from those who may be needed to implement the decision.

Efficiency/consistency

Can the decision be made in a timely manner? Will the result be in keeping with group traditions, values?

Some decisions do not warrant extensive processing; others may call for an immediate response and a show of strong leadership. Some decisions need to be made within the constraints of group history, policy and structure; others do not. Some decisions can easily be made with written or representational input; others need face-to-face group processing.

Group Commitment

How will people feel about the decision and implement it, in light of its importance to them and their input into the decision?

How people feel about and support a given outcome is often dependent on how fair they found the decision-making process. A sense of fairness often depends on whether a person's views were represented and considered. The need for direct input will vary depending on the importance of the decision and its personal impact.

Growth/Learning

Will the decision-making process contribute to group understanding about itself and about the substance of the decision?

Some processes involve extensive exchange of information and dialogue and raise self-awareness, awareness of others' views and knowledge about the subject matter of the discussion. Relationship and team building, as well as equal distribution of information, are by-products. Other processes keep information in the hands of only one or a few people.

Decision Rules: A "Plus/Minus" Comparison

Type of Rule	Quality of Outcome	Efficiency/ Consistency	Group Commitment	Growth/ Learning
1. Autocratic	?	+ + +	– –	– –
2. Authoritarian w/consulting	+	+ +	–	–
3. Polling/ranking	+	+	+	–
4. Minority rule	+	+ +	+	+
5. Majority rule	+ +	+	+ +	+ +
6. Weighted voting	+ +	+	+ +	+ + +
7. Consensus	+ + +	– –	+ + +	+ + +

Note: Weighted voting, if designed to promote minority voices in an affirmative way, may be evaluated differently by majority and minority members of a group or community. The chart rates this approach by putting as positive a value on recognizing diverse voices as on majority rule, while recognizing that group commitment to the outcome may vary.

Resources: Center for Conflict Resolution, *Building United Judgment: A Handbook for Consensus Decision Making* (Madison, WI, 1981); Virginia Coover *et al.*, *Resource Manual for a Living Revolution* (New Society Publishers, 1985); Em Griffin, *Getting Together: A Guide for Good Groups* (IVP, 1982).

–Alice M. Price
© MCS 1989

Overview of Group Facilitation

Why Use a Facilitator?

Doyle and Strauss, in *How to Make Meetings Work*, recommend that people with authority and decision-making power should not typically run meetings. Their research indicates that leader/facilitators dominate the discussion and inhibit broader and more creative group input. One way to separate power roles from process roles is to turn the process role over to a designated facilitator.

Whether trained facilitators come from inside or outside the organization, and whether they are used on a regular or as-needed basis, will depend on an organization's make-up, resources and the issues it is facing at any given time. *What is key to organizational health, however, is that one or more members have an eye on process concerns.* And, as circumstances indicate, that adequate resources (human, time, money, etc.) be invested in designing and carrying out well-facilitated decision-making processes on matters of importance to group life.

The Facilitator Role

In a pure facilitation role, the individual facilitator or team is assumed to have no authority over outcome. The focus is on process only: setting ground rules, establishing trust, listening carefully and reflectively, identifying commonalities and differences, summarizing and framing issues, using a variety of problem-solving strategies, working with feelings, and defining settlement or other closure.

To work as a facilitator, you need to feel comfortable with yourself and your skills. You also need to feel comfortable with the particular context in which you are being asked to serve. This includes the ability to respond openly and sensitively to the full range of diversity in people and ideas which may emerge in a given setting. Knowing the group—or being coached in advance about key values and traditions—will add to your information about cultural and other dynamics which impact group members' experiences, perceptions and problem-solving approaches. Be aware of your own biases, hot buttons or other limitations. In some instances, such information may lead you to decide that a particular facilitation request is inappropriate for you.

Roger Schwarz, in *The Skilled Facilitator: Practical Wisdom for Developing Effective Groups*, identifies two levels or types of facilitation. The first he calls "basic facilitation." This involves helping a group on a temporary basis to discuss or solve a particular issue or achieve a particular goal. The second is "developmental facilitation." Here, attention is also given to helping the group improve its internal skills and processes to solve problems more effectively in the future. Opportunities to increase the long-term effectiveness of group functioning should rarely be passed up. Any well-conducted facilitation should provide some learning for the group, if only through facilitator modeling.

Facilitating in Your Own Groups

Strengths. An internal facilitator may have a "head start" in many areas.

- knowledge about the group's history and current issues
- shared values and traditions re culture, religion, community, etc.
- shared patterns of decision-making
- pre-existing relationships of trust/belonging
- track record of credibility
- easy access to and from group members
- insight into unwritten/unspoken rules and roles
- continuity and availability of service

Drawbacks. An internal facilitator may experience points of weakness or vulnerability.

- preconceived ideas about group issues
- part of a closed system, with limited world view
- limited objectivity/knowledge re new decision-making strategies & skills
- pre-existing relationship of non-trust/appearance of conflict of interest
- lack of credibility commanded by "outside experts"
- inappropriate contacts with group members
- blindness to or personal investment in implicit behaviors
- burn-out; vulnerability to job or group membership pressures

–Alice M. Price
© MCS 1995, 2000

Ten Commandments of Meeting Facilitation

I *Thou shalt begin with an agenda that establishes the purpose and structure of thy entire meeting.*
Post an agenda. The more information participants have about the "big picture," the better equipped they are to contribute constructively. The agenda is negotiable throughout, open to addition, deletion, and change of sequence. But it remains the backbone of effective meetings, providing a sense of order, clarity and fairness.

Ideally, planners prepare and post an agenda in advance so participants can reflect on issues. When this is not possible, the facilitator should list the agenda visibly before the group and invite comment or suggestions for change.

II *Thou shalt center thy discussion around one issue at a time; no other issue shalt thou consider.*
Like water, many group discussions quickly lap out to become dispersed and shallow rather than centered and deep. Constant vigilance by the facilitator is necessary to keep participants focused.

To a large extent the facilitator maintains focus with *punctuation skills* which clearly separate each issue from other issues. Punctuation should be so sharp that even lazy participants know when a new issue takes the floor and when it retires. This calls for a clear introduction of each issue and a conclusion summarizing what has been discussed or agreed upon. Punctuation also involves skillful use of emptiness; a five second pause between issues; a two minute stretch break; a transition phrase such as "Let's move to our next agenda item."

Facilitators also maintain focus with brief and gentle responses to individuals who inevitably drift from center stream. These phrases focus, like all gentle communication, on what the facilitator *wants*, not on what he or she does not want. "I'd like to stay focused for now on our current issue." "That's an item we need to discuss but for now I'd like to set it aside/add it to the agenda/etc."

III *Thou mayest covet ownership of thy meeting, but thou shalt not steal or even possess it.*
Don't dominate. Good facilitators know that more than anyone else present they will dip in and out of the limelight. They often enjoy the power they wield. Yet they recognize the continual temptation to abuse their role by lingering in the limelight or indulging their personal opinions.

If an issue arises on which the facilitator wishes to express personal opinions, he or she should ask someone else to facilitate for that issue. Alternatively, the facilitator may ask permission from the group to "take off the facilitation hat" occasionally to express personal preferences.

IV *Thou shalt exercise thy leadership through frequent summary of thy participants' contributions.*
Summaries of two kinds are effective. With *paraphrasing*, the facilitator establishes an atmosphere of respect and deep listening. "From your perspective. . . ." "As you see it. . . ." "So your suggestion would be. . . ." Especially when tension or confusion is present, this is a powerful skill. Used consistently after each speaker, paraphrasing alone is often adequate to maintain a sense of communication, even when emotion runs high.

With *group summary* the facilitator condenses the thrust of comments from numerous speakers. If comments seem to be moving in the same direction, the facilitator summarizes that direction. "It seems like there's been agreement among the last several speakers that. . . ." If comments diverge, the facilitator summarizes the differing viewpoints. "Some of us believe that. . . . Others say that. . . ." Usually the facilitator follows the summary by returning the focus to the group. "Are we in agreement on this?" "What do others have to say on this?" Summaries should occur frequently, always at the end of discussion of an issue, and often several times within each issue.

V *Thou shalt not allow vocal participants to dominate thy assembly. As many speakers as possible shalt thou hear.*
Encourage participation. Be prepared with phrases to gently muzzle the vocally agile and draw reticent members into discussion. "We'd like to hear especially from those who haven't yet had an opportunity to speak." "Let's go around the circle and give each person who wishes a chance to speak." If you feel they won't be uncomfortable with it, invite individuals to speak. "Bill, I'm curious what you have to say on this."

If necessary, interrupt the "speechmaker" by paraphrasing, and then state your desire to hear from as many people as possible.

VI *Thou shalt have more than one medium before thee to strengthen thy communication.*

People take in and work through information in diverse ways. Any communication which relies on only one of the six senses or a single discussion format is vulnerable to misunderstanding or blockage.

The easiest and most important medium to add is visuals. No group of more than five people should gather to make decisions without means to write on a wall or board. The agenda deserves visual prominence, of course. But differing viewpoints also become more manageable if summarized and listed before the group. This objectifies discussion; eyes go to the wall chart rather than to opponents. Further, participants can jointly and methodically create a written list of strengths and weaknesses for each viewpoint rather than argue back and forth from one idea to another.

The facilitator should also diversify forums for discussion. Not all people are equally comfortable with large group discussion. Small group discussions, written questionnaires, personal interviews or special listening sessions allow more participants to feel they have participated in a setting familiar and safe for them personally.

VII *Thou shalt not evaluate until thou hast first generated.*

Left to natural processes, most groups quickly fall into inefficient and bruising approaches to decision-making. The typical sequence is to generate an option, react; generate another one, react again. Individuals quickly become attached to their particular suggested solution, and conversation readily degenerates into hurt and antagonism.

Clear guidance from the facilitator establishes a more effective approach. The facilitator states: "Let's begin by just listing some options. We'll evaluate them in a few minutes." If someone challenges another person's idea, the facilitator responds: "Remember John, we'll evaluate these later. For now, ideas only. Tell us *your* idea, John." Once

the list contains numerous ideas, the facilitator guides in evaluating them: "OK, we've got several ideas; let's look at these one at a time. . . ."

VIII *Thou shalt value diversity; yea thou shalt invite disagreement, for in this lieth the strength of thy group and the purpose of thy calling.*

Groups require some basic sense of unity and in the end must reject certain options to make decisions. But paradoxically, groups which value diversity and welcome disagreement find unity easier to achieve on most decisions than groups which discourage differences. If dissidents feel truly heard and respected, they are more willing to set aside their preferences in recognition of the majority. Out of the disciplines of respect and occasional self-denial grow strength and great resilience.

By encouraging members to state their disagreements openly and making it safe to do so, the facilitator enables a group to find a unity which lies deeper than apparent differences. The facilitator who seeks a short-cut to unity by discouraging disagreement will end up in a wilderness of hostility.

IX *Thou shalt respect specifics, lest thou dash thy hard-earned agreements upon a wall of confusion.*

What specifically will happen next? Who will do what, when, where, and to whom will they report? Failure to work out specifics can easily derail things in the future.

X *Thou shalt not surprise thy group with any conclusions, rather thou shalt test conclusions before they are final.*

The final decision should never surprise participants. The facilitator's job is to enable members to inform others of their preferences and to get a sense of where the majority stands. If voting occurs, enough discussion should already have taken place so that all have a clear sense of group direction. Use a non-binding "straw vote" to test where the group stands and to set the stage for further negotiation. This gives opportunity for the minority to bring in any additional information or reasoning before the decision is final.

These "Ten Commandments" do not completely cover a facilitator's concerns. For example, a facilitator will also need to pay attention to the setting of the meeting and participants' physical comfort. Plan regular breaks and be alert to fidgeting or downcast eyes, suggesting the need for a change of pace.

–Ron Kraybill
© MCS 1987, from *Conciliation Quarterly*, Vol. 6 No. 4

Intercultural Facilitator Guidelines

Intercultural facilitation refers to the process of assisting and enabling an intercultural group to move forward together around common goals and values without allowing the dominant culture voices and values to dominate and control the movement. The intercultural facilitation process guarantees that the minority voices, values and skills are not subordinated or suppressed by the conditioning of racism, dominant control patterns or fear of minority anger. It ensures that the expression of minority anger does not become a barrier to the formulation of positive action. Forward movement is enhanced according to the degree of safety and trust which the facilitator can help create.

- A facilitator is really creating a sense of equality and community.

- Guarantee participation at the group level.

- The actual participation is what generates the cohesiveness and energy for commitment.

- Your audience is those participants in the group who are traditionally left out.

- Facilitate so that they speak more and dominant voices speak less. Goal: To quiet (not silence) the dominant voices by the strength of the formerly silent voices.

- If two or three people are talking and everybody else feels "covered" that is still not enough participation.

- Facilitate a balance where the normally silent voices are doing most of the talking and the dominant voices are adding their thoughts.

- There is a difference when a dominant culture person dominates than when an "excluded" person dominates.

- Conditioned privilege will cause some people to feel they can take all the time they want and give a patronizing lecture.

- Ground rules:
    - Only one person speaks at a time.
    - No side conversations; it triggers mistrust and feelings of not being taken seriously.
    - Do not let a person continue speaking without the group's attention.

- Have an agenda and stick to it, but allow for some immediate problem-solving.

- Validate feelings and allow limited expression. Use time structure to control the process not the participants; they need to feel constrained by the situation, not you.

- Provide ongoing feedback to the group about what is happening to them. Try to mediate conflicts as they evolve. Paraphrase and feedback.

- Explicitly connect what one person says to what another person has said and feedback the overall connecting or "voice" of the group as you integrate the sense of it.

- Important for participants to validate at the end what they learned: Bring to a focused closing.

–**Roberto Chené**

Dealing with Unhelpful Comments

Often a facilitator needs to deal with unhelpful or negative comments from participants. A facilitator can handle these constructively by recognizing them as they occur. In this list suggested facilitator responses follow in italics. While the responses below are often useful, sometimes simply ignoring unhelpful statements is the best way to discourage them.

Generalizing

"No one cares a bit about how I feel about things." *"Please tell us more specifically about who doesn't care about how you feel about things."*

"These people are always trying to get us off-track." *"Please give us a specific example so we can understand clearly what you are referring to."*

Blaming

Strong "they" or "you" focus: "They did this and they did that and they're always. . . ." *"Tell us what you would like to see happen in the future."* OR *"Tell us about the impact that these events had on you personally."*

Statements in Question Form

"Wouldn't you agree it's just downright irresponsible to do something like that without group approval?" *"Sounds like you felt it was inappropriate."* OR *"Tell us how you feel about it."* OR *"My job is to help you express your viewpoint to the others here. Please help us understand what your thinking on this is."*

Speaking for Others

"I happen to know that a lot of other people in the group feel the same way I do about this." *"Just speaking for yourself, tell us how you feel about these things."*

–Ron Kraybill
© MCS 1987, from *Conciliation Quarterly*, Vol. 6 No. 4

Poor Me

"I just get so depressed and discouraged when I see what they're doing to our fine group. They don't care what they do to the rest of us and I've lost all hope for change. We're too weak to stand up to them anyway." *"You really feel hopeless about things. Tell us about the point at which you began feeling the most discouraged. . . . Tell us about what you would like to see happen in the group in the next year."*

Super-Parenting

"I think what Mary's really trying to say is that the situation is just impossible to live in for anyone who really cares about the future of this church." *"I'd like to let Mary express for herself what she's trying to say to us."*

Interrupting

Leader ignores interrupter or simply says, "William, I'd like to hear your thoughts on this, but for now I'd rather not interrupt Mary's comments."

Withdrawing

Member sits silently without participating; sometimes orients body away from the group. *"I'd like to offer a special invitation to those who haven't yet had opportunity to speak."* OR *"___, are there any thoughts or comments you'd like to share with us?"*

Challenging the Facilitator

Stay cool, focus on hearing and understanding. "So your main concern is that I haven't. . . ." Then explain or clarify if appropriate, without defending. Recognize the urge to fight back and choose against it. Model self-disclosure: "I feel quite uncomfortable with your comments and I'm not sure exactly how to respond. I'd like to approach things in a way everyone respects so I don't wish to simply ignore your remarks. How do others feel about this?" Ask for input from others in the group.

Tools for Group Dialogue and Issue Formation

The following are tools to enable people to talk in a large group or small group setting about issues which they disagree on, when public disclosure and discussion are desired.

Conflict Spectrum

Identify one end of the room for people **strongly** convinced about one idea, the other end for those **strongly** convinced of the opposite. Ask everyone to take a position somewhere on or between these two points. Then invite individuals to share why they chose the spot they are standing in. This can be taken further by then dividing the spectrum into three groups—the two ends plus a middle group. Give each group 20 minutes to prepare a list of strengths and weaknesses of their position, and then report the list to the total group.

Interviews

Select and interview one to three individuals from each perspective in the presence of the entire group. Interviewer must be viewed as trustworthy and should relate warmly to each interviewee. Tone is that of a friendly, informal conversation with careful listening by the interviewer and lots of paraphrasing. Begin on a personal note ("Tell me a little about yourself," or, "Tell me what's been happening for you this week.") to establish rapport. Then move to the issues at hand. "How do you personally view these issues?" (Encourage people to speak only for themselves.) "Tell me what's been happening here from your own perspective." "In what ways have you personally felt misunderstood at times?" The key to making the interviews productive is for the interviewer to draw speakers out beyond their inclination to simply state their biases or simplistic analyses. "Explain that a little further. . . . Help me understand why that was so upsetting for you. . . . Tell me what your thoughts and feelings were as this was happening. . . ." Interviewer may wish to list views on newsprint or have an assistant do so.

When finished, interviewer may wish to turn to the listening audience and inquire if there are any views not yet heard that someone wishes to add. Interviewer should be firm that any speakers must come forward and be interviewed—this keeps discussion manageable.

Interviews with Listening Chair

A variation on the interview method is to add a "listening chair." Each person being interviewed is invited to pick someone from the group (ideally someone who has different views) to be their "listener." The listener comes forward and sits in a designated "listener's chair." The listener's task is to paraphrase everything that the speaker says. This requires the speaker to pause every few minutes to give the listener a chance to paraphrase. The facilitator may need to demonstrate this by serving as the "listener" for the first round. This addition is powerful in fostering a sense of respect and understanding.

Samoan Circle

Appoint one or two people to represent each of the views needing to be aired. Place enough chairs in a semi-circle to seat these people, plus 2-4 additional chairs. The representatives come forward, sit in the semi-circle and discuss the issues at hand. Anyone in the larger group who wishes to participate may do so by coming forward and taking one of the empty chairs. If those chairs are filled, others who come forward may stand behind one of the "extra" chairs until it becomes available. If the issues are volatile, a neutral moderator can be used. Key to success in tense setting: Facilitator announces at the beginning that all are welcome to participate, but stresses that *all* communication must occur *only* in the circle. A "listening chair" can be added to the Samoan Circle as with the Interview technique described above, with the same effect.

Small Group Discussion

Mixed Groups. Assign people to small groups in a way that assures that each small group has diverse members. Give small groups 15-30 minutes to create a list of the three to five most important issues facing the group. A spokesperson reports from each group to the large group, where the issues are tabulated. Useful when the issues and "factions" are not yet well-defined and greater clarity is needed about what the conflict is about.

As a general rule, groups with mixed members are less likely to get stuck if they are given assignments to simply identify a diversity of views or to seek clarification of viewpoints rather than to reach consensus. If tension is high and there are not enough skilled facilitators to place one in each group, the small groups can be asked to go around the circle and hear each person's views, with **no** discussion until everyone has spoken. Or use a small questionnaire for each person to fill out, and then to share with others in the small group.

Affinity Groups. An affinity group is made up of people with similar views. Use them when people are too timid to speak up in front of those with whom they disagree, when anger is very high, or at that stage in discussion when issues are fairly clearly defined but people need to check things out with those they agree with before being willing to commit to proposals for resolution. Ways to form affinity groups:
- Invite people to form groups (4-8) with people they feel comfortable sharing their feelings with.
- Assign people based on your knowledge of them.
- Use a spectrum, which quickly and easily identifies who stands where. After people have placed themselves on the spectrum, have them form an affinity group with 5-6 people closest to them on the spectrum. (The spectrum can be used to form mixed groups as well by numbering off down the line.)

Assignments that can be given to affinity groups to prepare for conversation with others:
- List the things that you are especially concerned about.
- Draw a vehicle (bus, train, car, steamroller, etc.) that reflects this organization or situation and the people in it.
- Prepare for dialogue about mutual perceptions. Each group develops a list for each of the following:
  1. All the adjectives that you think describe the other side.
  2. Adjectives you think the other side will use to describe you.
  3. Things done by people sharing your views that might have contributed to other side's impressions of you.

Normally, the next step in using any of these assignments would be for each affinity group to bring a summary of their discussion to the large group for presentation there in the context of carefully facilitated group discussion.

Role Reversal Presentations

Someone from each side is asked to spend time interviewing people from the other side and then give a presentation summarizing the things they have heard. Be sure to give each side a chance to respond to the summary of their views: Was the presentation of their views accurate? Would they like to clarify or expand on it in any way?

Role Reversal Interviews

This is a technique for work in front of an entire group of people. It requires a skilled facilitator who must select several persons to participate and explain in advance what will happen. These persons join the facilitator in front of the group. In the exercise they are asked to exchange roles and pretend they are the other person with opposite views.

Facilitator: "Mr. X, I'm going to ask you to pretend for a little that you're Mr. Y over here and to speak in first person as though you were him as I ask you some questions. Are you ready to try it? Well, now that you have your Mr. Y hat on, tell me a little about yourself, where you are from and what you do, Mr. Y. [The facilitator should always begin with a few personal questions to help the individual get into the role.] Now, as Mr. Y, tell me a little about your views on this issue. . . ." The facilitator should do much supportive paraphrasing as the speaker proceeds to help the speaker get into and stay in the role. When X is finished being Y, interviewer turns to the *real* Y and asks for evaluation. How well did X do in presenting Y's views? Any key points that he missed? Then reverse and have person Y be person X. This is a fairly high-risk intervention that may be perceived as "playing games." It should not be forced on participants too early or without careful advance preparation and support.

Fishbowl

One group sits in a circle surrounded by a larger circle of listeners. Only people in the inner circle may speak.

This can be used to give people on one side of an issue opportunity describe their feelings and perceptions uninterrupted by others. In this case probably each side should get their time in the middle.

The Fishbowl can also be used to give a small group of people from all sides a chance to dialogue uninterrupted in the presence of everyone, or to mediate a conflict between two persons that affects and has polarized a large number of other people (in this case the two sit in the fishbowl).

Tools to Balance Conversation in Group Discussion

Ground Rule—No one speaks twice before everyone has had chance to speak once.

Matchsticks—Everyone gets three matchsticks (or toothpicks, small stones, etc.). Every time they speak they must throw a matchstick into a dustbin. When the matchsticks are gone, no more talking! (or use M&M which must be eaten after one speaks)

High Talk/Low Talk—A variation on the Fishbowl. People who rate themselves High Talkers (in other words, likely to talk a great deal) sit in the outer circle; those rating themselves Low Talkers take the inner circle.

Comments

1. If people are timid to speak out in front of the group, the spectrum is a good technique for public disclosure of viewpoints *en masse*. It is often a good "ice breaker" for group dialogue. It cuts down on anxiety about what others may be thinking. Sometimes what people thought was an extremely polarizing issue actually brings the majority of the group to a "middle" position on the spectrum.

2. If the list of issues emerging in discussion is long, facilitators must guide in consolidating it into a few broad headings and then narrow it down to the most pressing issues. One easy way to select the key issues is to ask everyone to pick the three issues they see as most important. Go down the consolidated list and ask for a raise of hands on each issue: how many people had this as one of their top three issues? Issues with the highest number of votes are the ones people most want to discuss.

3. These techniques are primarily for the purpose of initial surfacing of issues in group settings or for enabling an open exchange of views. Often an additional step will be required: to make a decision that brings resolution to the issue. Facilitators should give some thought in advance as to how to enable this to happen. Often it is wise to devote a block of time at the end of an "issue surfacing" meeting to discussing what kind of process will be used to follow up on the issues identified.

   For example, a five-person process planning committee representing all key groups could be appointed at this meeting. This committee is then assigned to bring a process proposal to the group at a later date. Such a proposal should identify clearly:
   - what **issue/issues** need to be resolved
   - the **proposed activity** for addressing each issue (interpersonal mediation, referral to committee, group discussion and/or decision-making, etc.)
   - a **timeline for the activities proposed**
   - for issues requiring group decision-making, the **decision rule** should be stated explicitly early in that decision-making process, i.e., *who* will make the final decision and *how* (consensus, two-thirds majority vote, simple majority, etc.)

–Ron Kraybill
© MCS 2000

Guidelines for Brainstorming

Brainstorming is one method that can help a group in the process of generating creative ideas. A facilitator writes the topic or question to be brainstormed at the top of a large sheet of paper, then asks the group to call out their ideas in short phrases which can be written down quickly. To set a creative, high-energy tone, the following guidelines should be stated at the outset:

- **No judgments.** No idea or suggestion, no matter how wild, is to be shot down or edited. (There will be time to evaluate later.)

- **Anything goes.** Offbeat, unusual, humorous ideas are encouraged.

- **Go for quantity.** The more ideas, the better chance of a winner.

- **Collaborate.** Building on other people's ideas is fine.

The facilitator can help to keep things moving, if needed, by:

- Setting a time limit (commonly 3-10 minutes).

- Giving a few examples to start things off—a "hailstorm."

- Affirmative, gentle coaxing.

- Asking for different sorts of ideas, if "one track mind" occurs.

The conventional approach is to have one person record all ideas on newsprint. Sometimes two recorders can alternate, so the group won't have to wait. Another variation that is especially useful if you have several topics to brainstorm is to write each topic on a separate sheet of newsprint. Provide each participant with a marker, so they can go up and record items "graffiti-style." Or participants can write one idea per 8 by 11 piece of scrap paper and post them on a wall.

Recent research indicates that brainstorming is *not* necessarily the best technique to generate lots of creative ideas. Groups of people can go off on one tangent without exploring the full range of possibilities. Variations to counter this include:

Variation 1: Instruct each group member to brainstorm individually on a topic, writing down ideas on a small piece of paper. Share ideas by reading or compiling lists.

Variation 2: Divide the group into two or more teams. This "parallel groups" approach has some of the advantage of the first variation, plus the good side-effect of group cooperation.

Despite its limitations, brainstorming remains a popular technique. For many groups, it has provided a first chance to think creatively together and move in new directions. It also lets everyone know where ideas have come from, setting the stage for consensus action.

–Duane Dale and Nancy Mitiguy
© Citizen Involvement Training Project 1978, excerpted from *Planning for a Change: A Citizen's Guide to Creative Planning and Program Development.* CITP is a collaborative project of the Division of Continuing Education and the Cooperative Extension Service, University of Massachusetts, Amherst, funded by a grant from the W.K. Kellog Foundation. Used by permission.

Note: See also "Generating and Evaluating Options" on page 187.

Consensus Decision-Making

What is it?

Consensus is a process for making group decisions without voting. Agreement is reached through a process of gathering information and viewpoints, discussion, persuasion, synthesizing proposals and/or developing totally new ones. The consensus method is an effort to achieve a balance between task and maintenance needs in the decision-making process, and is most suitable for groups whose members value their association highly. *The goal of the consensus process is to reach a decision which everyone can agree on or live with.*

Blocking Consensus

Consensus does not necessarily mean unanimity. A group can proceed with an action without having total agreement. In the event that an individual or small group cannot agree with a given proposal and is blocking consensus, the facilitator may ask if the individual(s) are willing to "stand aside" and allow the group to act, or if they feel so strongly about the issue that they are unwilling for the group to act. If the individual(s) agree to stand aside, their disagreements can be noted in the minutes of the meeting, and the group is free to act on the decision. If the individual(s) are not willing to stand aside, action is blocked unless a compromise or substitute agreement can be found. The group may agree to postpone the decision until a later time so that more information can be gathered, people have a chance to discuss the issues in more detail, tempers can cool, participants have a chance to reflect on the options before them or a compromise can be worked out by the major disagreeing factions. Some large groups (with several hundred attending) use a modified consensus technique in which two or three people are not enough to block consensus unless they object strongly.

The Benefits

Consensus decision-making sometimes requires a great deal of patience. It is necessary to listen carefully to opposing viewpoints to reach the best decision. In spite of this drawback the consensus method has the following advantages over a voting method:

- It produces more intelligent decisions, by incorporating the best thinking of everyone.
- It keeps people from getting into adversary attitudes where individual egos are tied to a proposal that will win or lose.
- It increases the likelihood of new and better ideas being thought up.
- Everyone has a stake in implementing a decision, because all have participated in its formation. Participants have more energy for working on projects with which they are in full agreement.
- It lessens significantly the possibility that a minority will feel that an unacceptable decision has been imposed on them.

We have seen a single person, whose voice had not adequately been listened to at first by the group of fifty people, use the attention focused on him by the process of testing for consensus to persuade the whole group (which had been on the point of agreeing to a proposal) to decide differently. All agreed that the new decision was wiser. In a voting situation, a person outnumbered so heavily is more likely to feel that the situation is hopeless.

When Seeking Consensus

1. **Encourage presentation of viewpoints,** especially when they may be conflicting. Draw out those who do not speak. A real consensus comes only after the open facing of differences. When dealing with complex or controversial decisions, consider using the *Small Group to Large Group Consensus* process (page 231).

2. **Listen carefully for agreements and hesitations** within the group. When a decision-making process seems stalled, stating points of agreement helps group morale and may lead to agreement on new proposals.

Stating points of hesitation is clarifying and makes resolution possible. Often hesitations are based on misunderstandings and will quickly end when stated clearly.

3. Test for Agreement

- Test for agreement as soon as a decision seems to be emerging. Periodic testing will help clarify disagreements, making discussion more fruitful.
- State the tentative consensus in question form, and be specific: "Do we all agree that we'll meet on Tuesday evenings for the next two months, and that a facilitator will be found at each meeting for the next one?" rather than: "Do we all agree that we should do it the way it was just suggested?" If you are not clear how to phrase the decision, ask for help.
- Insist on a response from the group. Don't take silence for consent. The participants need to be conscious of making a contract with each other.
- Sometimes stating the perceived agreement in the negative helps to clarify group feeling: "Is there anyone who does not agree that. . .?" This method is especially useful for groups under time pressure or with a tendency for nit-picking, but it is also important for group members to be fully supportive of the decision. If you have doubts about their commitment, ask them.
- Be suspicious of agreements reached too easily—test to make sure that members really do agree on essential points.

4. When there is not agreement:

- Fully explore the concerns of those who disagree.
- Ask those who disagree to offer alternative proposals for discussion and decision.
- If agreement still cannot be reached people may need time to reflect on the feelings behind their opinions. Propose a break or period of silence, or postpone the decision.
- If postponing the decision, try to reach agreement on a process that will happen before the item is brought up again. It is often productive for representatives of opposing factions to work together to draft a compromise proposal during the interim.
- When one or two people are blocking consensus, ask if they are willing to stand aside, to allow the group to proceed with the proposed action. It may help them stand aside if the group assures them that (1) the lack of unity will be recorded in the minutes, (2) the decision is not precedent-setting, or (3) they are not expected to carry out the decision.

–**Virginia Coover** *et al.*

© New Society Publishers 1985, excerpted and adapted from *Resources Manual for a Living Revolution*. Used by permission.

Consensus Decision-Making In Congregations

In my work I have learned that people care almost as much about *how* a decision is made as they do about the issue itself. That is why it comes as no surprise to me when I hear people raise questions about congregational procedure in the midst of discussing difficult topics (such as sexuality). Having led my own congregation through many significant transitions and issues as chairperson of the leadership team, I offer the following observations about our collective use of a consensus decision-making model.

Consensus and "Sense of the Meeting"

One of the challenges in using consensus comes from our familiarity with other methods of decision-making, such as voting, which usually follows some kind of parliamentary procedure (e.g., *Robert's Rules of Order*). Voting, however, has its potential drawbacks:
- suppression of the individual,
- alienation of the minority,
- a propensity for destructive internal "politics."

Thus we have chosen consensus as an alternative.

There are different ideas about what consensus is and how it should be conducted. We might benefit from thinking about what consensus is NOT. First and foremost consensus should not be confused with unanimity. The expectation that every member should feel equally happy about decisions reached is unrealistic. As a starting point, it might be more helpful to think of *consensus in terms of something that everyone can live with rather than something that everyone must agree on.*

But Quakers (or Friends), who have been working at consensus for hundreds of years, suggest that this still falls short of the ideal decision-making process. It is not enough, they say, to seek a consensus of the membership. Rather, as Christians what we are seeking is the will of God in a particular matter. True spiritual guidance is found in the "sense of the meeting" through prayerful waiting upon the mind of Christ. It is not *our opinions*, but God's leading. Sense of the meeting is not compromise among differing factions; it is a holy gathering of obedient listeners. Sense of the meeting is the still small voice that tells us what we are to do in love. Consensus is people-made; sense of the meeting is created by God.

One of the implications for discerning God's will this way is that we may actually reach consensus on an issue but still not have a sense that it is the right thing to do. Thus no action might be taken, even after finding agreement, because there is a corporate sense that we have not yet found God's will in the matter.

How Do We Get There?

I have in the past suggested that our congregational meetings are a *continuation* of our worship. Consensus requires worshipful preparation. Just as the chairperson or facilitator must be prepared with agenda items and process tools, each member should endeavor to see him or herself and others with the eye of faith:
- to discern not only his or her own leading but the leading of others;
- to keep in mind that at any moment the most improbable person may be the prophet of God;
- to discern how the leading of the meeting may be different from the quite genuine leading of an individual.

The chairperson has many responsibilities, but the Friends say that "the clerk can best clerk the meeting only when everyone present is also clerking." That is, everyone present must be practicing spiritual discernment of themselves and others. It may be helpful then to think of congregational meetings as "worship focused on specific matters."

This means being attentive to one another and pausing between speakers to reflect, recollect and re-center. In this way we avoid quick retorts that substitute an attitude of debate in place of a group search for spiritual guidance. This lends itself to the slower pace of consensus, allowing ourselves and others to go more deeply into the matter while affirming that others' inward processes may be moving at a different pace. There must be time for change to take place inwardly—not just in the head but in the heart as well.

Then when we do speak, this slower pace prods us to cultivate the art of being relevant and concise, exercising self-discipline and sensitivity to the proper use of gifts, time and energy of others, as well as our own. Where another has stated a position satisfactorily, one need offer only a word or two expressing unity. This will allow time for others who are struggling to be encouraged to say what they can, giving consideration to all. Finally, this serious business recognizes that humor may have a rightful place, restoring perspective, lifting spirits and diminishing tensions.

Reaching Decisions

Each meeting does not need to culminate in some kind of decision. Experience has shown that matters of great emotional involvement should not be settled in the meeting at which they are first proposed. Frequent "straw polls" can lessen the tension involved in final decisions and give everyone an unfolding sense of the group along the way. Eventually decisions must be made. We must not succumb to the "paralysis of analysis."

At times, decisions seem nearly impossible when one member can block consensus. Friends suggest that the degree of unity necessary for a decision depends upon the importance of the question and the character and depth of feeling of those who oppose the general trend of opinion. After a community has labored faithfully over a period of time and most are in agreement, and when deferring the decision still further entails hardship and the diversion of energy and time that might better be used elsewhere, those who do not feel in unity may choose to:

- withdraw their objections, trusting that in time their understanding of the leading of the Spirit will be vindicated;
- stand aside, asking that their objections be recorded in the minutes, but expressing their unwillingness to block what the rest of those present see as the right way;
- maintain their opposition, asking that their names be so recorded, if they are unable in good conscience to proceed with the group's proposed action.

Feeling the pressure of time often erodes our patience, with others and with the process. It is easy to become annoyed with the member or members who are not ready to go along with what appears to many to be a sensible solution. But consensus is about ownership of a decision by everyone in the group. An old oil filter commercial used to say, "You can pay me now, or you can pay me later." Investing the time required by consensus decision-making may avert much costlier conflict later which has been buried under the surface of a short-cut process.

When I reflect on the range and sheer number of significant decisions in our congregation over the last two years alone, I am amazed at the quality of these decisions and support for them. And though our pace still feels slow at times, I believe that these have been relatively efficient decisions in light of their significance for our community. I would suggest that the number of major decisions we have faced is largely responsible for this feeling of never-ending processing, not the form of processing itself.

But the model must serve us, not the other way around. The form of decision-making is not nearly so important as the spirit and fruit of it. All decision-making must, in the end, foster relationships and community as we seek the will of God for our lives and life together.

–Larry Dunn
© MCS 1993

Small to Large Group Consensus

Purpose/Uses

To help a large group make a decision. To facilitate total membership participation in the decision-making process.

Description

1. Problem or issue is defined by the whole group.
2. Whole group *brainstorms* possible solutions to the problem.
3. Large group breaks into small groups of six to eight people to discuss the problem, review possible solutions and develop a proposal for a solution that they will present to the whole group.
4. Proposals from the small groups are presented to the large group and are recorded on flip charts.
5. Discussion by the large group. Facilitators should look for common conclusions in all the reports and call for a consensus decision on these points. Disagreements should be identified.
6. Small groups work on contested points and try to develop new proposals.
7. Small groups present new proposals to large group. Facilitators try to find a consensus. Steps 6. and 7. can be repeated as many times as necessary.
8. Once consensus is reached, facilitators need to help the group define the steps needed to implement the decision.

Note: It is very helpful for the group to set and abide by time limits for each step of this process. Groups will use all the time they are given but can work faster with a forceful facilitator and timekeeper. Holding to the time limits while solving a complex problem can increase the group's accomplishment and progress.

–**Virginia Coover** *et al.*
© New Society Publishers 1985, from *Resources Manual for a Living Revolution*. Used with permission.

Small to Large Group Consensus: Another Model

The following model can be used at various stages of discussion. For example, when a group is ready to begin looking forward at strategies, solutions or next steps, you might ask: "What do you think would be some helpful steps toward. . . ?" Then use the progression below:

1. People reflect individually and list their ideas.
2. People pair up and generate/merge one list of ideas on which they both agree.
3. Two pairs join and create a list all four agree on.
4. Two groups of four combine and do the same.

By the time eight people agree on some things, those ideas are well on the way to larger group consensus. At this point, ideas from each group of eight are presented to the whole group. If a decision needs to be made by the whole group at that time, these ideas give a good focus for discussion. If the whole group does not need to decide, or if final decision will come at some later point, the collection of ideas can be referred on to a smaller representative body for development of a consensus proposal.

This process has several helpful aspects:
- generates, tests and filters a large number of ideas fairly quickly (about one hour)
- moves from brainstorming toward group consensus in a manageable way
- gives group a positive sense of possibility and progress

–**Bob Gross**
© MCS 1995

Straw Poll: Testing for Consensus

The facilitator should remember that silence does not mean consent.

Several years ago Dee Kelsey demonstrated a method for quickly reading a group's responses to a question in working toward consensus. This approach is helpful in avoiding the trap of false consensus. I have used it with many groups, learning from them how to use it more effectively. Some people call it the "High Five" technique.

After general discussion, the facilitator clearly states the proposal and provides the scale below (it is helpful to post the scale on a flip chart before the meeting begins):

---

5. I can give an unqualified "yes" to the decision. I'm excited or enthusiastic about it.

4. I can live with the decision. It's OK with me.

3. I am concerned about this decision, but will not block the group.

2. I think there are major problems with the decision and choose to block the group's action.

1. It's too soon to make any decision. More work needs to be done before the question can be asked.

Each person in the group then responds to the question by indicating with a show of fingers his or her level of endorsement of the proposal. When the group responds with mostly 4s and 5s, the decision goes ahead. Two or three 3s indicate a need to discuss the question further, as do any 1s or 2s.

This scale has been very helpful in moving group processes along. Sometimes a group will continue to discuss a question exhaustively, simply because they haven't been asked if they agree. A quick show of hands can demonstrate that everyone is a 4 or 5 on the issue, allowing the group to move on.

The people who are concerned about the decision—the 1s and 2s and 3s—can be asked to help the group understand what problems they see with the proposed solution. This can shift the focus to solving the problems identified. A facilitator does need to use care in phrasing questions and encouraging group responses with this approach to guard against the possibility of group members being intimidated into agreement.

Consensus can be hard work for a group making a decision but it is very healthy work. It fosters understanding of and respect for each other within the group. It can produce creative and strong decisions. And group members walk away with an increased commitment to each other as well as to following through on decisions.

–**Susan H. Shearouse**
© MCS 1993, from *Conciliation Quarterly*, Vol. 12 No. 4

Training Exercises for Group Process Facilitators

Good Meetings/Bad Meetings

Tell the group they are going to have a chance to relive "meetings I have known and loved . . . " and "meetings I have known and hated. . . ." Elicit spontaneous memories of "unforgettable" meetings from group members. Identify and record *process-related* data on newsprint (e.g., long agendas never finished, unclear purpose, hostile exchanges/efficient use of time, well-structured dialogue, stretch breaks, etc.) People usually have many memories, especially of poor process experiences. Good way to "debrief" these memories with some humor and introduce the importance of good process planning and facilitation.

Zingers

Set up a short scenario of a meeting in a fishbowl format, with trainers or participants prompted to act as "unhelpful" speakers on a designated topic (e.g., "to build or not to build"). Use the training sheet, *Facilitation: Dealing with Unhelpful Comments*, as a guide. Have an empty *facilitator's chair*. Take volunteers from the large group, or have a rotation system, to give individuals an opportunity to try out one or more facilitation strategies in response to each unhelpful comment.

Agreement on Procedure

Divide into task groups of four to six members. Give each group a short case study of an intra-group decision which requires some process planning. Task: create a proposed *Agreement on Procedure*, with the underlying process principles/rationale. Use the *Agreement on Procedure* training sheet as a guide. Encourage small groups to be intentional about their *own* group process, using designated facilitators/recorders, a decision rule, etc. Have each small group present its proposal to the large group, as well as debrief its own group process.

Small Group Consensus-Building Exercise

Divide into task groups of four to six members. Give each group a common assignment. For example, tell each group they are a committee developing a proposal to improve conflict management skills and awareness in the congregation. The time-frame for the project is 6 months and the budget is $400. Have each group designate facilitation roles. Task: gather ideas, evaluate them, test for agreement and reach a consensus proposal. Limit the small group time to about 10 minutes.

Large Group Consensus-Building Exercise

Take the program proposal ideas reported by each small group in the exercise above. Demonstrate ways to move from small-group to large-group consensus. For example, use *story-boarding*. Put *each* discrete item (e.g., "monthly sermon on biblical reconciliation") on a separate card. Focus on commonalities by grouping cards with similar ideas together in subcategories. Allow additional brainstorming and evaluation to emerge from the story-boarding experience. Demonstrate other techniques, or elicit facilitation ideas from the participants, to move the whole group towards consensus on a program proposal.

Case Study

Miss Clark has been teaching the kindergarten Sunday School class at your church for the past 15 years. She loves the children and is much loved and respected by the congregation at large. But there have been some complaints from parents that her teaching methods are quite outdated. Similar complaints have been voiced about a few other old-time "regulars" on the Sunday School teaching team.

You are on the Christian Education committee. Some on the committee have suggested that you introduce a rotation system for Sunday School teachers, with a three-year maximum teaching term. This idea has been informally tested among the teaching team. Some support the rotation idea, but Miss Clark and others have indicated that they do not want to be subject to an arbitrary rotation system.

How do you decide, as a committee, to handle this situation?

Exercise A: Process Planning

Divide into small groups of four to six people. Each small group is the Christian Education committee, with the current assignment of determining who should be involved and how, in working at this current concern regarding Sunday School teacher performance and tenure. Give them approximately 15 minutes to reach consensus on a proposed Agreement on Procedure. Have small groups present their proposals to the larger group.

Exercise B: Brainstorming/Small Group Consensus-Building

Divide into small groups of four to six people. Instruct each small group to brainstorm a list of at least eight ideas or options which address one or more of the underlying concerns raised by this situation, in addition to the option of a three-year rotation system. After about five minutes of open brainstorming, give the small groups 10 minutes to evaluate and reach consensus on one or two options which the committee wants to support.

Alternative

If you wish, take the small group proposals from either or both of these exercises and work towards a large group consensus.

Elicited Roleplay

1. Divide into small groups of approximately 10 to 12 people, each with an assigned coach. Give approximately 30 minutes total for everyone in the small group to share an overview of an intra-group conflict with which they are/have been personally involved.

2. Have each small group select a two-person facilitation/recording team. Give these teams a few minutes to plan a group process to use for selecting *one* of the conflict stories for a group roleplay.

3. Have each small group implement their roleplay selection process. Give them no more than 30 to 45 minutes. Criteria for choosing a conflict story should include: 1) some clear-cut issues; 2) more than just two points of view; 3) easily assignable roles which can accommodate 8 to 10 people as individuals or "representatives"; 4) issues or conflict arena which will be of interest to the group members.

4. Once the roleplay story is selected, have small groups designate a new two-person facilitation/recorder team to facilitate the roleplay (other than the storyteller). Give these people, along with the coach, time to plan a strategy/process for a one-hour "facilitation" in the conflict story. Be clear about what stage in the process the "facilitation" is occurring and the purpose of the particular facilitation strategy.

5. While the facilitation team plans their strategy, have the storyteller meet with the remaining small group members to elaborate on the story and assign appropriate roles and cues.

6. Give each small group at least one hour to roleplay the "facilitation" by the facilitation team. Then debrief with the coach.

–compiled by Alice M. Price
© MCS 1991

Part 2

Conflict and Systemic Change

Systems Theory: A Brief Introduction

The universe consists of multiple, interdependent systems. Nature, for example, has many systems (e.g., vegetation, animal life and the atmosphere) that are dependent upon one another. Animals in the wild live in a world of interdependent systems that determine their survival. In addition each animal has its own body consisting of many systems (circulatory, muscular, nervous, etc) that are also interdependent. The survival of the animal world is dependent upon the well-being of these systems.

In human experience there are social systems with patterns of interaction (communication, rules of engagement, distribution of power, etc.) that are also essential for the nurture and survival of human life. Humans are relational beings, who live in bonded (attachment) relationships within the context of emotional-relational systems. The patterns of interaction in these emotional-relational systems help determine the well being of individuals, communities and society as a whole. Healthy relational systems nurture. Toxic relational systems destroy.

Emotional/relational systems are created by family, church, social groups, work groups, etc. Any group of persons in vital and continuous relationship becomes an emotional-relational system. As is true in nature these systems are interdependent with other emotional/relational systems in their world. Within such a system all its parts are interrelated. What happens to one impacts all. A biblical metaphor to describe this is the concept of the church being a "body," in which all parts are connected. What happens to one affects all. (1 Corinthians 12)

What are some of the particular characteristics of a relational-emotional interactive system? The following articles give brief descriptions of *key dynamics in systems theory* that may help provide awareness of how relational systems function in the context of organizational life and change.

–Marcus G. Smucker
© MCS 2000

Five Characteristics of a Relational System

Emotional Units

A relational system is an emotionally bonded unit, which functions as a single personality or entity. Families, institutions, churches or corporations are relational-emotional units in which each part is related to the whole. The relational and emotional bonding in any system may be healthy or unhealthy depending upon it patterns of interaction and relationships. Characteristics of a healthy system are described below.

Interdependence

Just as the human body is more then a collection of individual parts so a system is more then the sum of its parts. In a relational system, individual behavior must be viewed and examined as it relates to the system as a whole. Disturbance in one part influences all the other parts and weakens the whole; likewise health in any part strengthens the whole with all its parts. Just as codependent family members often enable the addiction of an individual, any behavior within a system must be viewed as being intertwined with the whole.

Members of a system have two paradoxical needs that affect all their relations and exist in continual tension: the need to be separate (differentiation) versus the need to be close (fusion)—also called the need to be "me" versus the need to be "we." How these needs are addressed and resolved helps determine the health of the system.

Intergenerational (Multigenerational Patterns and Problems)

The attitudes and behaviors of individuals are not only connected to the system as a whole but are also linked across the generations, and interlocked with other systems. For example, a person's behavior in a congregation often parallels behavior in his or her family of origin. A person who remains connected in unhealthy ways to their family of origin will likely try to connect with the congregation in a similar way. In any congregation there are numerous families interacting with, and influencing, one another. The health of a congregational system will be influenced by the health of the family systems within it.

In particular, the relationship of leaders with their own family of origin is a critical factor in their influence upon the organizational system. For example, the ability of any pastor to lead a congregation toward greater freedom and health will be significantly influenced by the freedom and connectedness experiences with his or her family of origin.

Rules and Boundaries

Rules are a dynamic and vital force in any system to guide or regulate action or conduct, and determine what should or should not be. They often become a powerful, invisible force that moves through the lives of all members of a system—family, church etc. They may govern the freedom to comment, i.e., what you can say, to whom, when and where. They may seek to regulate what you feel, think, see, hear, touch or taste. In a relational system rules are often implicit and even subtle. They may help or obstruct, facilitate or limit, nurture or destroy. In this sense rules help create health or dysfunction in a system.

Functional or Dysfunctional

A healthy system is an open system "in which the parts interconnect, are responsive and sensitive to one another and allow information to flow freely between the internal and external environments." Communication is direct, clear, specific and congruent. By contrast an unhealthy system is a closed system in which the parts are rigidly connected, or disconnected altogether. Communication is indirect, unclear, unspecific, incongruent and covert given to blaming or placating, or distracting. Roles are rigidly fixed and there is emotional isolation from the outside.

–Marcus G. Smucker
© MCS 2000

Four Points of Tension in a System

Stability and Change

Emotional systems mirror the balancing act that goes on within the body. Even as in a body, the interactions within a relational system may be deep, complex and often unconscious, whether expressed physically, verbally or emotionally. Communication in these systems is often "heart to heart" even as organs in the human body may interact in their own private way rather then openly and explicitly through the command center (the brain).

All systems need both stability and change to remain healthy. Yet a relational system tends to resist change because any change to a system is perceived as a threat, whether it be helping or healing, growing, modifying, crippling, destroying, or radically empowering. Individuals in the system may welcome or desire change, but it may still be resisted by the system as a whole. Patterns of interactions are created to help maintain stability. Whether healthy or not, if the patterns remain the same the system is experienced as stable. This is the principle of *homeostasis*, the survival dynamics inherent in a system that drives it to seek "to stay the same."

Change in a system leads to anxiety and provokes reactions to maintain the status quo. In order to maintain its status quo a system may "elect persons to contrive to fulfill roles (both good and bad roles), to maintain its present balance. Change may occur on two levels. *First order change*, seeks to simply rearrange things within the system. It may rewrite the rules or job descriptions, fire the "troublemaker," or replace the critic. Such change does not challenge the system. In contrast *second order change* seeks to transform the system. Change in a system creates anxiety because it is seems to be a threat to its stability.

Anxiety

Anxiety emerges when there is dysfunction in a relational/emotional system. Systemic anxiety is either *acute* (crisis generated) or *chronic* (habitual, cannot be put to rest). Tension, fear, anger, struggle for power, imbalance of power and toxic secrets (when covert and/or unaddressed) generate anxiety in a system and creates symptoms. When these symptoms are severe they become the focus of attention and the object of change. Typically a system will seek to alleviate its symptoms rather then address its deeper dysfunction and initiate genuine change. Often a system will resist dealing with its dysfunction and pain by trying to "kill the messenger" or finding a "*scapegoat*."

Scapegoating (Identified Patient—IP)

A relational system may seek to maintain balance (homeostasis) and reduces anxiety by creating a "scapegoat" (blame and causation) in terms of persons, issues, events or even other systems. This *identified patient* is the person (group, issue, symptom or situation) in whom the system's stress has surfaced or upon whom the stress is placed. In family life this is often a particular member of the family who exhibits symptoms on "behalf" of the whole. In larger systems, such as congregations, agencies, or neighborhoods the IP may be a person, a group of people or an issue, unconsciously delegated to display and carry the sins of the whole.

Triangulation

Triangulation occurs in systems to relieve anxiety of individuals or the system as a whole. Friedman says, "the basic law of emotional triangles is that when any two parts of a system become uncomfortable with one another, they will 'triangle in' or focus upon a third person, or issue, as a way of stabilizing their own relationship with one another."

This is most readily understood in interpersonal relationships. "When two people become anxious or uncomfortable with each other, one or both may 'triangle' a third party into the relationship" to help reduce their anxiety. For example when tension escalates between a married couple one or both may "triangle" one of their children, have an affair, bury themselves in their work, etc, Individuals may also triangle a minister or the church by "picking a fight" to displace their internal or relational pain.

Emotional triangles occur not only between individuals but also between a person and a group, between groups, or even events and objects. For example alcohol addiction may increase dramatically in a group that is severely oppressed as a way to relieve inner anxiety. Sometimes a subgroup within a neighborhood or congregation or company uses an issue or event to sabotage or snag (triangle) the leaders, thereby reducing their effectiveness and influence. In an anxious system "fighting" about particular concerns, issues or events may be a means of distracting the entire system from its deeper problems to avoid facing an even more profound anxiety. Such displacement may occur in families, neighborhoods, congregations, institutions, corporations or even nations.

–Marcus G. Smucker
© MCS 2000

Four Steps Toward a Healthy System

Self-differentiation

Differentiation occurs when each member of a system takes responsibility for his or her own life. To differentiate is to be able and willing to speak specifically and openly about what one thinks, believes, feels and values and about what one is willing or not willing to give, and it is to openly express one's hopes and/or disappointments while remaining in the system and connected with each other. It is to clearly define "me" in the presence of others, to say "I" when others are demanding "you" or "we." Differentiated persons speak for themselves, rather than for others. They describe, rather than blame, when addressing issues, problems or painful transactions.

Self-differentiation includes the capacity to remain a (relatively) nonanxious presence in the midst of an anxious system. In a dysfunctional system, the most difficult and challenging first step is for persons to openly define themselves in a clear and positive manner that is not in reaction to others. Often people wait for others to self-define first, then they define themselves in reaction to the other person. When persons in any group (family, institution, community) cannot, or will not, define themselves openly, the group has a sense of being stuck. When such emotional fusion occurs, both individuals and the group as a whole become reactive. Perceptions become skewed. Communication becomes ineffective. Emotions mount, and interactions become destructive.

Seeing Multiple Causation (Linking)

Whenever there is anxiety, tension or conflict in a relational system, people look for the "one" (person, group or issue) who is responsible. However, conflict within a system happens because it serves a function within the system. Most events in any system are multi-factorial with all factors coming together to create the result.

A system is like a suspended mobile. When one part is touched, moved, or shifted each of the other parts is set in motion. The interaction of the whole produces more energy then simply adding up the possibilities of the individuals themselves. This interrelatedness can also make it very difficult to sort out what is actually happening.

Systems thought recognizes that patterns of interaction are often multigenerational. This means that some problems in families, congregations, institutions, or larger entities will recur from "generation to generation."

Detriangulation

Detriangulation in interpersonal relationships can occur if the person or group being triangled (C) can gain some perspective on the anxiety in the relationship between A & B and help A & B take responsibility for their own process. If C can withstand the invitation to enter into the relationship as judge or messiah, keep enough emotional distance to stay connected with A & B while still maintaining a nonaligned stance, and as needed coach them, or find someone who can coach them, to deal constructively with their anxiety and conflict, the triangling will have been reversed. Self-definition, self-differentiation and being a nonanxious presence are essential to this process. (This paragraph is a restatement of Lyndon E. Whybrew, *Minister, Wife and Church: Unlocking the Triangles*, Alban Institute, 1984, page 17.)

Naming Reality versus Keeping Secrets

Secrets hold power in a relational system. For example in a family there may be secrets about past behaviors—suicide, sexual indiscretion, business failure, etc. Such secrets, sometimes maintained for generations, generate anxiety and have a negative power in the system. Virginia Satire says, "any rule that prevents family members from commenting on what is and what has been is a likely source for developing restricted, uncreative, and ignorant persons, and a family situation to match."

When secrets are brought to light they lose their power. Again, Satire says, "If on the other hand you are able to get in touch with all parts of your family life, your family life could change dramatically for the better. The family whose rules allow for freedom to comment on everything, whether it be painful, joyous, or sinful, has the best chance of being a nurturing family." Secrets hurt! Open communication brings greater health.

A secret in a relational system may be about the past or present. It may be related to events, or experiences, or any reality that "must" not be commented upon and addressed openly. When seeking the health of a system, it is often helpful to name things that are being avoided, to openly observe patterns that are destructive, to comment upon the cyclical nature of dysfunctional behaviors, and to identify those things which a family, congregation, institution or nation refuses to recognize and seeks to keep hidden.

–Marcus G. Smucker
© MCS 2000

Organizational Culture: An Overview

What is "Culture?"

"Socially constructed realities that provide learned ways of coping with experiences." (Thompson and Luthans, 1990)

"Culture is a property of a group. Wherever a group has enough common experience, a culture begins to form." (Schein, 1999)

Key Points
- Culture is not a historical given. At some point it was shaped or constructed and it is being continually reconstructed.
- Culture provides us with a "taken for grantedness"—the behavioral cues become so routine that we don't have to think about how to respond (unless the culture is foreign to us).
- Culture is learned. The process of learning a language usually accompanies the process of learning a culture—whether in a country or an organization.

How does Culture Operate in an Organization?

Organizational culture can be examined according to four "Rs":

Rules—ranging from "standard operating procedures" to unspoken taboos

Roles—ranging from the formal organizational chart to the informal "office gossip"

Rituals—ranging from lavish ceremonies to informal celebrations/punishments

Roots—ranging from our "official history" to deep but unspoken emotional ledgers

–Mitchell/Augsburger, 1988

These four Rs can be found operating at three levels:

Formal—The conscious, written level. Established procedures and titles.

Informal—The conscious but unwritten level. Established norms and informal roles.

Tacit—The unconscious and unexpressed level. Taboos, habits, and unspoken norms.

Why is Organizational Culture so Resistant to Change?

"Culture is so stable and difficult to change because it represents the accumulated learning of a group—the ways of thinking, feeling and perceiving the world that have made the group successful. For another thing . . . , the important parts of culture are essentially invisible." (Schein, 1999)

"Attitudes and behaviors are closely associated in organizational culture. . . . How can attitudes be changed? Through changes in behavior by those who wish to change the culture . . . management has to be consistent in its actions." (Thompson/Luthans, 1990)

–David Brubaker
© MCS 2000

Organizational Culture Grid Exercise

	Formal	Informal	Tacit
Rules			
Roles			
Rituals			
Roots			

This exercise can be a group builder. It can also be risky in that it begins to name the unconscious.

1. Divide a large group into smaller groups of four to eight people each.

2. Have each small group fill in the grid with specific examples from their organization/system.

3. Share small group examples back in the large group, and discuss the similarities and differences.

Variation: Do the small group work in affinity groups (management/support staff, women/men, whites/people of color, etc.). In the large group compare ways the system is experienced the same or differently by various groups.

© MCS 2000

Organizational Change: An Overview

Why Change?

- When the external *environment* changes
- When the basic purpose or *mission* changes
- When the organization's identity or *image* needs to change
- When the organization's relationships with key *stakeholders* changes
- When the way organizational members do their work (*process*) needs to change

What are the Components of a Successful Change Process?

- Vision-Driven—a positive, clear direction is set
- Leadership-Driven—support and articulation from all leaders in the organization
- Systemic/Holistic—takes account of all levels of the organization
- Planned—a deliberate process to go from the "current state" to the "desired state"
- Communicated—including opportunities for dialogue about the proposed changes
- Owned—generally supported across all levels

The change process involves "unfreezing" from the present state and "refreezing" at the desired state. (Lewin)

"During any transition, performance will inevitably decline before reaching the improved desired state. . . . Managing change is really about managing this transition. . . ." (Schneider and Goldwasser, 1998)

"Organizations that are highly successful with change take care both to plan change efforts and communicate the need for change." (Smith, 1998)

What are the Stages of a Successful Change Process?

> *Change isn't something you do by memo. You've got to involve people's bodies and souls if you want your change efforts to work.*
> *–Lou Gerstner, CEO of IBM*

1. Establishing a Sense of Urgency
    - Examine and reveal possible crises and/or opportunities.
2. Creating the Guiding Coalition
    - Gather a team with enough power to lead through the change.
3. Developing a Vision and Strategy
    - Decide where you want to go and how you can get there.
4. Communicating the Change Vision
    - Be in constant communication regarding the new vision with everyone affected.
5. Empowering Broad-Based Action
    - Encourage creative ideas that work at implementing the change vision.
6. Generating Short-Term Wins
    - Strive for and celebrate any steps made towards the goal.
7. Consolidating Gains and Producing More Change
    - Revitalize the process with new projects and more staff development while continuing the momentum forward.
8. Anchoring New Approaches in the Culture
    - Connect organizational success with new behaviors and ensure leadership development.

(Kotter, 1995)

"To change an organization's culture, you must first change people's behavior." (Trahant, Burke and Koonce, 1997)

–David Brubaker
© MCS 2000

- Retell the journey of your history openly and regularly, especially at times of transition.

- Hold a common vision for the future.

- Share core values.

- Embrace diversity and pluralism of viewpoints within core values.

- Clarify roles and expectations.

- Name and use clear, appropriate processes for decision-making and problem-solving.

- Value collaboration.

- Admit mistakes and deal openly with conflict.

- Share information freely among all levels.

- Empower and support each person in their work.

- Accept that all contribute to system dynamics, good and bad.

- Don't forget to have fun!

–summarized and adapted by Alice M. Price
© MCS 2000, from Sam Leonard workshop (Pueblo, Colo.) 1992

Powerlessness in Systems

A Key Assumption

Powerlessness is often key in understanding conflict and how to approach it. When people display symptoms of feeling powerless and invalidated, look at the whole organizational *system*. Ask what changes in the system will foster a sense of inclusion and empowerment. Look beyond individual antagonistic behaviors to typical systemic patterns and cycles. Individual responses often change if you improve the system.

Powerlessness

A. Of unfulfilled hopes

- Normal and inevitable.
- Most people can live with it.

B. Of invalidation

- Feelings of being unheard, disregarded, unrecognized.
- "I feel like they don't even *want* to hear my opinion. I don't always have to get *my* way, but I do need to feel that at least I count!"
- No one can function effectively for long when they feel this way.

Symptoms that Indicate People Are Feeling Powerless (Invalidated)

A. Passive Symptoms

- stony silence/clam up/sullenness
- boycott meetings
- leave organization or become marginal member
- indirect communication (talk *about* people, but not *with* them)
- gossip to larger community
- refuse to take part in decision-making processes
- withhold money

B. Active Symptoms

- walk out of meetings
- refuse to listen and interact thoughtfully with diverse views
- threats/angry outbursts/unreasonable ultimatums
- committee stacking or other manipulation of structures
- mystery voters; sudden reappearance of non-attenders at meetings
- belligerence, put-downs, personal attacks
- use of petitions, letters for personal agenda or attacks

Ways Organizational Systems Commonly Make People Feel Powerless and Invalidated

A. Historical Factors

1. An unspoken rule that "You cannot have conflict with someone you care about."
   - Thus people feel uncared-for and attacked whenever someone differs with them.
2. Within recent memory (up to 30 years), the group has experienced a lengthy period of highly authoritarian leadership.
   - Under stress, individuals begin to revert to former models.
   - People *assume* that others will employ this style, even when not the case.
3. When groups become too tolerant of individualized beliefs.
   - Trust and support in group life can't be taken at face value.
   - Group decisions become meaningless, too facile.

B. Structures—Unclearly Defined or Poorly Functioning

1. Job or committee assignments unclear. People don't know exactly what is expected or how to tell if they've done the job well.
2. Poor supervision and follow-through on assigned tasks: committees, teaching, etc. Good supervision is an important way of caring for people; it says, what you are doing is significant.
3. Poor systems of reward—honor, recognition, clear sense of accomplishment. People need these or they lose enthusiasm and refuse to accept responsibility.
4. Constitutions sometimes set up unclear relationships or lines of communication.
5. People—lay or leaders—sometimes go *around* key people or structures rather than work through them.

C. Decision-Making—Poor Planning or Facilitation of Discussion

1. Leaders don't foresee (or run from) significant decisions coming up and are unprepared or try to rush through the decision process
2. Leaders allow decisions to go too quickly to a vote. Results:
   - People don't feel heard.
   - What gets voted upon in a rush is usually a win/lose proposal, not a well-crafted one that reflects diverse interest. The minority goes home saying, "They didn't bend an inch for our concerns. They don't care about us."
3. Discussion leaders don't recognize that some people are uncomfortable talking in large groups and need a chance to respond in other ways to important issues (small group discussion, questionnaires, personal visits, key leaders available to meet with individuals, etc.).
4. People appreciate being asked for their opinion, especially if they feel somehow like a key person.
5. Facilitation of group discussion about important decisions is perhaps the most common weakness. People often feel unheard because of poor facilitation. Leaders of discussion should:
   - Slow things down.
   - Encourage disagreement as a way of inviting open discussion and helping people relax about differences.
   - Model good listening skills, especially paraphrasing.
   - Use newsprint to list various views so people know they've been heard.
6. Leaders sometimes take dogmatic stands and are unable to show personal caring or flexibility.

D. Communication—Lack of Information on Organizational Matters

1. Surprises destroy trust.
   - Make no important decisions without plenty of advance notice.
   - Prepare agendas for meetings and circulate them.
2. People assume the worst in the absence of information. Communicate more when things get tense, not less.
3. Many organizations get lazy on basic communication tasks. Thorough minutes from committees and other meetings are important! Report regularly from significant structures.
4. *Regular* evaluation is *crucial*. Otherwise people bottle up the feelings and resentment grows.
5. Organizational newsletters do more than provide news; they say to people: You *matter* enough to be informed.

–Ron Kraybill
© MCS 1992

Levels of Conflict: Assessment Guide

I. Problem to Solve

- There is a conflict of goals, values, needs, plans, information.

- Participants are problem-oriented rather than person-oriented; they seek rational solutions.

- Participants collaborate in seeking a resolution.

- Language is clear, specific, "here and now," descriptive.

Strategy
- Define problem together, gather information and seek mutual resolutions.

II. Disagreement

- Participants are concerned with self-protection; they become more shrewd and calculating.

- Language shifts from specific to general; rather than naming the persons with whom there is conflict one hears statements such as:
    "There is no trust."
    "We have a communication problem."
    "People should act more Christian around here."
  Behind each such statement is a specific factual happening.

- Participants are cautious about sharing all they know about the conflict; they tend to withhold information that might enhance the other or hurt themselves.

- Hostile humor is often present here.

Strategy
- Work to reduce fear and increase trust.
- Encourage broad participation of persons involved.
- Empower parties in their participation.
- Begin at lowest possible level of the organization.
- Help people to be open and to share freely.
- Teach communication skills.
- Seek ways to encourage a compromise of the differences.

III. Contest

- Participants move from concern for self-protection to that of **winning**; they engage in win/lose tactics without trying to get rid of the opponent.

- Factions often emerge and problems cluster into issues and causes; people take sides and seek to gain control over others.

- Language shifts and perceptions become distorted. These include:
    Magnification: Seeing self as benevolent and the other as evil.
    Dichotomization: Dividing everything and everyone into a neat dualism, leaving no alternatives.
    Overgeneralization: Seeing a particular behavior as example of all events.
    Assumption: Believing one knows the other's intentions, etc.

- There is resistance to making peace overtures because that appears to be losing. Parties hang back waiting for the other to show weakness.

- Personal attacks get mixed up with problem identification.

Strategy
- Seek to reduce the effects of fear on the group.
- Intervene so that distorted thinking will not be allowed to stand as truth.
- Encourage trust development in the group by:
  - . . . remembering past good experiences
  - . . . observing similar goals and interests
  - . . . increasing good communication.

IV. Fight/Flight

- Participants move from wanting to win to **wanting to hurt or to get rid of** others. Emphasis shifts from changing others to removing them, e.g., "get the pastor fired" or leaving them and getting others to go along; this is a fight/flight pattern. Being right and punishing become dominant themes.

- Factions solidify; strong leaders emerge and the welfare of the subgroup is more important than the health of the total organization.

- Language jells into ideology and members talk of principles more than issues.

- Parties become detached from one another; they become unforgiving, cold and self-righteous.

Strategy
- Get outside professional help
- Lay careful ground rules (somewhat arbitrarily)
- Appoint monitoring committee

V. Intractable Situations

- Participants wish to **destroy** one another. The goal is to remove the others from society.

- These persons see themselves as fighting for an eternal cause, for universal principles.

Strategy
Seek outside arbitration.

–summarized and arranged by Marcus G. Smucker

Conflict in Groups: The Cross-Stitching Effect

Effectiveness in groups begins with a remarkable paradox about conflict. Witness the contrasting experiences of conflict in the following accounts of two groups. In this illustration the groups are two congregations, but the same paradox applies to communities, organizations, businesses, etc.

Tale of Two Churches

River Corners congregation is experiencing conflict. Should they add a new wing to the sanctuary? Several sub-groups (A, B, C and D) say yes. They are spending time together, preparing a convincing case for why the group needs a new sanctuary. Other sub-groups (E, F, G and H) disagree. They are preparing reasons why the money should go to mission programs.

There's more conflict at this little outpost of the peaceable kingdom. Should they include contemporary music in worship? Some members (G, H, A and B) say yes. Others (C, D, E and F) have been working together to show that the old traditions are still best.

There's a third conflict. Local demonstrations against nuclear weapons have been controversial. Several members (A, B, E and F) recently asked the congregation to house the office of a local disarmament group. Other members (C, D, G and H) got red in the face just hearing about this request. They're meeting to outline reasons to shoot it down.

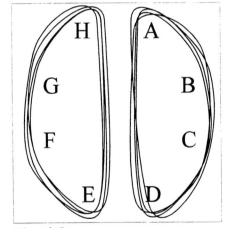

River Corners

There are other conflicts. Some love the pastor, others don't. Some support the local denominational college, others don't.

If you were looking for a place to worship, would you be interested?

Now look at another congregation, Placid Grove. This group also has conflict over a building program. Some members are for it (A, B, C and D); some against it (E, F, G and H). They have conflict over contemporary music—some support it but others are opposed. Some support the nuclear freeze; others are opposed. Some love the pastor, some do not. Some support the denominational college, others do not.

Now which congregation would you rather join?

From the standpoint of conflict management, the first congregation, River Corners, is healthy. No conflict could split this group. Rather, every issue provides opportunity for members to cooperate with different people. The result is a "cross-stitching" effect which binds the group together in diverse alliances. At Placid Grove, in contrast, conflict divides. Each issue only deepens the gulf between two groups who communicate rarely and poorly. Any emotional issue could paralyze and split the church.

Placid Grove

Attitude Towards Conflict

Why does conflict divide and weaken one group, but unite and strengthen another? The key is members' attitude towards conflict. What people expect in conflict happens.

Fear rules Placid Grove for the group *expects* chaos, polarization and destruction from conflict. Members view conflict as dangerous, even wrong. To disagree with someone immediately implies disrespect or malice. You don't do dangerous things to people you care about! Members thus have no choice but to shunt all disagreement underground. Rather than speak directly to those with whom they disagree, members simply avoid them. But they *do* voice their complaints to others and, of course, echoes of the whispering eventually reach those whispered about. Hard feelings, never openly dealt with, take root.

Group life consists of long periods of cottony apathy punctuated by intervals of pitched battle. In the apathy phase, chronic anxiety over stirring up differences causes members to withdraw from serious involvement with issues. Leaders genuinely seeking congregational participation in decision-making find it difficult to get responses. Members complain if asked to participate in small group discussions.

But things shift abruptly if an issue arises which arouses people emotionally, challenges long-held opinions or threatens to shift the balance of power in the group. The distant growl of anxiety, normally muffled by layers of apathy, suddenly becomes a paralyzing roar. Members prepare for, and experience, the worst. Bodies stiffen in fear, faces harden, voices rise. As anxiety escalates, fear leads to aggressiveness and defensiveness. Some members frantically build walls, others desperately throw bricks.

More concerned for shelter and comfort than for a joint quest for truth, individuals withdraw to the safety of old alliances. From the sidelines they cheer on a small handful of vocal people who spoke for them in the past. Conflict becomes a matter of strategic battles for numbers rather than thoughtful testing of the issues. In the end, the church gets precisely what everyone was desperately wishing to avoid—a nasty split.

At River Corners conflict unfolds differently. Members know conflict is inevitable, even necessary to healthy group life. To disagree is evidence of caring and involvement. When issues arise, members move towards each other, not away, and they enjoy the vigorous exchange of views that follows. Relationships flourish, for disagreement alienates no one. People who disagree on one issue join forces on others.

To learn how to accomplish this, compare group meetings at the two congregations. Picture congregational meeting at River Corners. Significant issues are on the agenda and viewpoints differ. As members speak, others lean forward and listen intently. Viewpoints emerge without bluster, for the atmosphere is receptive and inviting. At Placid Grove, in contrast, congregational meetings over significant issues are an intimidating experience. Bodies are stiff, arms folded, eyes are down, faces hard. A nonverbal message reverberates throughout the room, "Something terrible is about to happen!"

Invite Disagreement

Ironic! The group able to tolerate, even enjoy, conflict often finds the experience constructive. The group trying the hardest not to have conflict suffers grave damage when it occurs. This suggests the remarkable paradox: *to have less conflict in a group we must try to have more!*

But be careful! This does *not* mean trying to get people angry and upset, intentionally roiling the flock. More precisely—to have less conflict, *invite disagreement.*

We hear strength and respect in her voice as a woman at River Corners speaks. "I've spent a great deal of time thinking and praying about this and I feel that there are three important things to keep in mind here." She lists her reasons, then adds, "I know not everyone sees this as I do and I'm eager to hear how others feel about this." She's inviting disagreement!

At Placid Grove, a speaker rises and also offers a viewpoint. Along with the words, however, another message goes forth. In tone of voice and body language, this speaker says to fellow members, "I speak the Truth. Don't even *think* of disagreeing with me!"

Contrast the chairpersons in the two groups. At River Corners energy and involvement rise as the discussion leader invites open sharing of viewpoints, thanks each speaker for his or her thoughts and then welcomes new ideas and opinions. She's inviting disagreement! Further, she underscores the invitation to openly express viewpoints from time to time, listing the range of perspectives on newsprint in front of the group. You almost get the feeling she's enjoying herself!

At Placid Grove, the chairperson is visibly tense and his anxiety feeds polarization in the group. He fears open discussion and relies heavily on parliamentary procedure to structure the meeting. He scarcely acknowledges the content of comments that are made and twice urges the group to "remember we are Christians" and to "please be charitable with each other." For some reason, the remonstrances seem to have no effect.

At River Corners members shake hands warmly at the end of the meeting, even those who disagreed sharply. They know that exchanging differing viewpoints is an important part of healthy church life, and tonight was a vigorous but respectful discussion.

To be sure, a minority at this church goes home feeling disappointed. The final decision was not their preference. But they are not bitter and they will support the group's decision. Why? They feel good about the discussion *process*. Others invited them to share their views, even encouraged them to state their disagreement! The majority listened thoughtfully and weighed their ideas. They even modified the final proposal to reflect several minority concerns. The minority feels disappointed, but not squelched or silenced or manipulated. The church will remain as one.

Inviting disagreement doesn't solve all problems. Hard work remains. Further skills are necessary to translate this invitation into effective decision-making. But most groups already have these skills. The key is changing the attitudes that prevent groups from using the skills they possess. Doing the opposite of what anxious leaders and group members *feel* like doing often enables a group to break loose from destructive habits of conflict resolution.

–Ron Kraybill
© MCS 1987, from *Conciliation Quarterly*, Vol. 6 No. 4

Note: The video *Conflict in the Church* (1999), available from MCS, can be used to present these ideas in group settings.

Habits in Conflict: *Divided By* vs. *Bound Together By* Conflict

Divided By Conflict

1. **Conflict viewed as:**
   - wrong
   - dangerous
   - sign of not caring
   - something to avoid at all costs

   Typical Quote:
   - "If he disagrees with me, that proves he's a dangerous, untrustworthy and uncaring person. I'll tell my friends to pray that he repents. . . ."

2. **Members blur issues and people.**

   Nice Guys
   - soft on people
   - also soft on issues

   Typical Nice Guy Quote:
   - "Fine, I'm sure you're right. I have nothing to contribute on this issue. See you later. . . ."

   Tough Guys
   - hard on issues
   - also hard on people

   Typical Tough Guy Quote:
   - "That's a stupid idea! How could a Christian even think something like that! Now as I was saying. . . ."

3. **Indirect communication flourishes.**
   - Members talk **about** others, but not **with** them.

   Typical Quotes:
   - "Yes, it's that one over there. Did you ever. . . ."
   - "Don't tell anyone I told you this, but that pastor of ours. . . ."

4. **Long ledgers, never balanced**

   Typical Quotes:
   - "His grandfather never treated my grandfather right, so I always. . . ."
   - "Conflict is **wrong**, so I'll just keep my distance. That way we'll never have any problems. It's just a part of my cross. . . ."

Bound Together By Conflict

1. **Conflict viewed as:**
   - inevitable, neither right nor wrong
   - opportunity
   - evidence of involvement and concern

   Typical Quotes:
   - "It's going to take some work to talk this one through, but I can see she cares a lot about our church and me."
   - "I can tell I'm nervous about disagreements, but I know it's an important part of being brothers and sisters to each other!"

2. **Members separate issues and people.**

   Skillful people
   - hard on issues
   - soft on people

   Typical Quotes:
   - "As I see it. . . . I'm also very eager to understand **your** views on this."
   - "I agree with you that. . . . Where I personally disagree is. . . . Help me understand your reasoning on that."

3. **Direct communication reigns, even when difficult.**

   Typical Quotes:
   - "I'm feeling confused about our discussion last night. I'd really like to sit down and talk with you."
   - "Great! Let's go out for coffee. I've felt pretty upset myself. . . ."

4. **Short ledgers, balanced promptly.**

   Typical Quote:
   - "I guess I was pretty hurt by his comments. I want to have good relations with him, so I'd better sit down and talk with him about it.

Divided By Conflict

5. **Members spiritualize conflict in order to avoid it and diminish others.**

   - equate personal opinion with God's will
   - call for others to get their hearts right with God, a substitute for the rigorous discipline of listening.
   - fear and laziness expressed in reluctance to exercise human skills and saying that "God will work this out for us."

6. **Atmosphere is reactive.**

   - each side reacts to and attacks others

   Typical Quotes:
   - "How can any sensible person say **that**!"
   - "**That**'s ridiculous!"

7. **Leaders discourage disagreements and ignore problems.**

   Typical Quote:
   - "Please, try to be peaceful. We **must** be harmonious, brothers and sisters!"

8. **Group discussion is solution-focused.**

   Typical Quotes:
   - "**X** is the answer!"
   - "No, **Y** is best!"
   - "Come on, **Z** is the only sensible way!"

9. **Low tolerance of uncertainty.**

   Typical Quote:
   - "Look, let's just put this to a vote now and be done with it."

Bound Together By Conflict

5. **Members draw strength from spiritual depth to enter into conflict maintaining a gentle spirit.**

   - Members state opinions and invite testing self to listen, initiate pray for openness.
   - Deep spirituality enables members to overcome fear of self and others; enables trust that "God will speak and work through us if we each do our part."

6. **Atmosphere is interactive.**

   - careful listening acknowledges others
   - I-messages
   - clear, thoughtful statements

   Typical Quotes:
   "So the way you see it, it would be best to. . . ."
   - "Thanks! I feel confident now you understand my concerns. Now I want to make sure I understand *yours*."

7. **Leaders invite disagreement.**

   Typical Quote:
   - "Let's have as many different perspectives on this as we can. Before we can agree on anything meaningful, we have to take some time to **disagree** and look at all sides of this!"

8. **Group discussion is problem- and process-centered.**

   Typical Quotes:
   - "Let's begin by agreeing on how we'll go about reaching a decision on this."
   - "Maybe we could first define what the **problem** is."
   - "After that, let's list as many different solutions as we can come up with."
   - "Then we can evaluate the pluses and minuses of each."
   - "Let's make sure everyone gets a chance to participate."

9. **Calmness and confidence enable members to tolerate periods of uncertainty necessary in all good decision-making.**

   Typical Quote:
   - "It took some time, but looking at all sides thoughtfully paid off in the long run!"

–Ron Kraybill
© MCS 1986, 1988

How to Move from *Divided By* to *Bound Together By* Conflict

1. **Identify** *destructive* habits and agree on *constructive* habits to replace them. During what situations do these divisive habits become most apparent? What should be done differently to be "bound together" by conflict?

2. **Examine** different examples of *conflict in Scripture*, noting not only those that stress harmony, but also those that assume the presence of diverse gifts and views in church life. Discuss how disagreement is an integral part of life in the early church.

3. **Model** effective conflict management skills.
   • Invite disagreement. Move towards disagreement, not away from it.
   • Confront. Demonstrate loving confrontation of others. Be confrontable.
   • Talk *with* others, not *about* them.

4. **Empower and encourage** both sides when issues arise. Do not do this by saying, "I think you're right," but by saying, "You have perspectives that need to be heard," and "I think it is important that the church hears your views."

5. **Foresee and plan** for major decisions.
   • Plan the process with all key groups involved before getting too far into major decisions.
   • Provide several forums for input by members, in addition to large group discussions, such as small groups, questionnaires, Sunday School classes and having leaders available at special times.
   • Be prepared to go after and initiate conversation with habitual withdrawers. Avoid having the same few individuals always make the final decision for the whole group.

6. **Strengthen** relationships, especially by nourishing respect for and involvement of diverse individuals.
   • Celebrate diversity by acknowledging individuals for their unique accomplishments, contributions, activities and gifts.
   • Encourage small fellowship groups.
   • Plan work projects/retreats/fellowship meals.

7. **Strengthen** reporting and communication mechanisms.
   • Make public reports and minutes of committees.
   • Share regularly reports from decision-making or leadership groups.
   • Regularly solicit comments from church members on key issues and decisions.
   • Test whether your structure really supports good decisions and representation.

8. **Reflect** together on your history. Give opportunities to grieve (by honoring, recollecting, acknowledging) for "great leaders" or "golden eras" past.

9. **Prepare** carefully for leadership evaluation and transition, especially for ministers.
   • Use outside counsel unless your church has a good history in leadership evaluations.

10. **Provide skills training** opportunities for lay leaders.

–Ron Kraybill
© MCS 1986, 1988

Conflict Management for Leaders: Some Principles

• **Build an atmosphere of trust**
Trust is the single most important element in healthy conflict management. Building an open, respectful and safe system is the foundation for constructive rather than destructive conflict.

• **Establish conflict as normal**
Expect it. Don't let it catch you off guard. It's as much a part of life as food. Be open about its presence. Name it. Explore it.

Invite it. Welcome and explore differences. Be wary of a decision that seems to be "flying through" without dissent. Create ongoing structures that invite dialogue, feedback and evaluation.

Exploit it. Conflict is the stuff of growth and change and progress. Learn from it and help others learn from it. Use it to learn new truths about yourself, each other and God.

• **Equip yourself with skills, especially listening**
Careful, deep listening is a tangible sign of respect and is the most important element in conflict transformation. It includes temporarily setting aside your own agenda in order to understand what the other person is trying to communicate.

• **Be a non-anxious presence and stay connected**
Conflict often produces fear and anxiety. Your ability as a leader to move toward the point of anxiety and be a calm, non-judgmental and sensitive presence is critical. It means staying engaged with people, their emotions and their issues rather than retreating or attacking.

• **Invite and model self-definition**
Model the capacity to openly state your feelings, goals, values, preferences and roles. This clarity opens the way for others to define themselves as well rather than waiting to simply react to others.

• **Good process prevents unnecessary conflict**
"Go slow to go fast." Carefully planning problem-solving and decision-making processes and being clear about the steps involved saves much time and frustration in the long run. The process is not only as important as the outcome but actually helps determine the outcome.

• **Keep your eye on the system**
Your congregation/organization is a system with rules and patterns and habits. Every interaction and every conflict is affected by the system and visa versa. Ask yourself what meaning specific things have for the larger system.

• **Keep conflict manageable**
Be proactive. Listen constantly and deal with issues as soon as they emerge. Sorting through differences of opinion early is much easier than dealing with antagonism and escalated conflict later.

• **Feelings are an important part of the process**
Invite, acknowledge and validate the presence and expression of emotions. Explore their meaning. They are key to transformation.

• **Keep the process mutual**
Invite feedback, suggestions and criticism from others. Receive it non-defensively, listen carefully and accurately paraphrase the concerns before responding.

Work to remove problems from a competitive framework. Frame it as a problem to be solved together.

Validate the other and the relationship and your commitment to both.

• **Ask for help**
Know when you need to ask for help and where you can find that help. Seeking outside help is a strength not a weakness.

• **You can only change yourself**
Resist the temptation to focus on changing others. Edwin Friedman (*Generation to Generation*), says that the success of a leader is more related to how he or she functions as an individual than on managing the members. In his words, "the key to successful coaches is less a matter of how they 'handle' the players than how they handle themselves."

–Carolyn Schrock-Shenk
©MCS 1995

What Does Facilitation Have to Do with Social Change?

Dimensions of Conflict in Group and Intergroup Settings

More immediate, obvious, at the
surface of relationships

Issues	the immediate focus of conflict
Micro process	the moment-by-moment nature of people's interaction
Macro process	the overall process of interacting and making decisions—how a decision-making process gets established, who "owns" and gets credit for it, who decides what the "issues" are, who actually makes decisions in the end, how participants relate to their own constituencies, etc.
Structures	the institutions and mechanisms which allocate and manage resources
Values	usually unstated beliefs and assumptions people hold about "what really matters"

More long-term, perhaps
obscure, but ultimately more
influential; at "the root" of
conflict

Some proposals

- The facilitator's point of entry is usually in response to trouble at the level of issues. Parties often expect facilitators' primary contribution to be at that level (i.e., to help them find a solution).

- Facilitators' primary contribution is usually at the level of micro and macro process. Good processes enable the parties to come up with their own solutions.

- A key goal for facilitators should be to inject values of respect (for self and for others), equality, equity, empowerment and human development into human processes of interaction (i.e., we seek to influence the processes through which people interact with each other and make decisions so that these values are served).

- If processes informed by these values are set up, the outcomes of interaction will eventually come to reflect them as well (i.e., good process, as defined by the values in item above, will over time lead to structural change, justice and changed social values).

–Ron Kraybill
© Eastern Mennonite University 1999. Used by permission.

Making Interventions Appropriate

When considering an outside intervention, it is important to be as clear as possible between the organization and the potential consultant about what is needed. This will vary, depending on the level and sources of conflict. For guidance, see "Levels of Conflict: Assessment Guide" on page 245. Many organizations today are needing to respond to extremely difficult dynamics. For example, groups which have experienced inappropriate sexual conduct by leaders require specialized help. A good consultant will use assessment tools at the outset, as well as along the way, to guide interventions in an appropriate and safe way. At times, this may mean incorporating or referring the group on to more specialized resources, interdisciplinary teams, etc. The resource list at end of chapter includes additional information such as resources to deal with sexual misconduct by professionals.

The organizational context and cultural expressions are also key in selecting consultants and designing interventions. The following experience from the Alban Institute is included to underscore the importance of cultural appropriateness in designing outside intervention. It is excerpted from interviews by Leslie Buhler with three participants in the Institute's work to form an Asian American team for conflict interventions, Virstan Choy, Bert Tom and Ben Wu:

> At the start there was an assumption that The Alban Institute conflict-resolution process was a universal process, applicable to all congregations. There was a sense that we just needed to figure out how to translate—through language or culture—that universal applicable process to different congregational settings. We started out bringing together Asian Americans, Native Americans and African Americans from different denominations. The trainer said "we need your help in translating the Alban approach for conflict resolution." At that meeting, most of the participants saw that none of us thinks about or responds to conflict in the way the Alban folks talk about it—or how predominantly white churches do. Those distinctions necessitated separate teams (from each cultural group) working on culturally sensitive responses.

> There was a growing awareness among our team that Asian American congregations have peculiar ways of dealing with conflict and that the Alban process would only exacerbate the conflict in a congregation or provide fuel to a conflict that had not exploded. Culturally, across different Asian nationality groups, we share a unique and distinctive posture and predisposition. Folks discovered their commonalities and, after those moments, creative images emerged, images like "acupuncture instead of surgery, and ginseng before aspirin." The denominational staff really wanted techniques and this blinded some folks to our plea to begin with an understanding of our Asian cultures. This desire for technique reminded us of the "Alban map": All you have to do is just follow the map. It might work in white congregations, but it doesn't work for us. This parallels what David Augsburger is doing in his *Conflict Mediation Across Cultures* book. He talks about pathways, not processes.

> I think some folks who came to our consultations assumed that there would be a *process* to resolving intercultural tensions—even though it might not be the traditional Alban process. We don't give people processes. We work with images and creative problem-solving. As some folks have said, we use non-invasive, non-surgical ways of working with congregations. If you play with the acupuncture image, you can see: Whether it is a denominational task force or an outside consultant who works with that church, they need to work in a way that is not invasive and injurious to the individuals or, more important, to the relationships between individuals in the church. This paradigm for understanding relationships represents not so much a psychological or sociological paradigm but one based on cultural anthropology.

See also the articles on structural and cultural dimensions of conflict transformation in Chapter Two.

–Alice M. Price
1995, 2000

Potential Roles for the Consultant

The clarification of the consultant's role is particularly important, especially when the consultant is an official or representative from within the larger system to which a group belongs. **Every effort should be made during the contracting phase to prevent role confusion.**

Within the broader arena of conflict management, a consultant may play a variety of roles, including:

Support to Leadership

- Counselor, coach, supportive colleague.
- Anticipate the difficulty of being both a "counselor to leadership" and a mediator to resolve differences in the group.
- May be used exclusively when the group rejects intervention attempts.

Fact-Finder

- Identify issues and parties involved, separate rumors from facts, etc.
- Identify destructive patterns within the organization system.
- Particularly important when people are accused of a breach of trust—stealing or sexual misconduct.

Educator

- Trainer for leaders and/or members in conflict management skills and strategies.
- Reporting on destructive patterns within the system and other learnings acquired when gathering information.

Process Consultant

- Recommend process for collaborative decision-making.
- Focus on structures of conflict management rather than recommend outcomes.

Facilitator

- Facilitate a meeting or series of meetings, without preliminary data-gathering.
- Invited when a difficult meeting is anticipated.

Mediator

- Facilitate healing of relationships.
- Facilitate problem-solving on substantive issues.

Arbitrator

- When the conflict becomes unmanageable for the group.
- Make decision for disputants after thoroughly hearing all views.

–Lombard Mennonite Peace Center
© LMPC 1991, adapted from George Parsons, "Intervening In a Church Fight" (Alban Institute, 1989). Used by permission.

Diagnostic Flow Chart for Intragroup Intervention

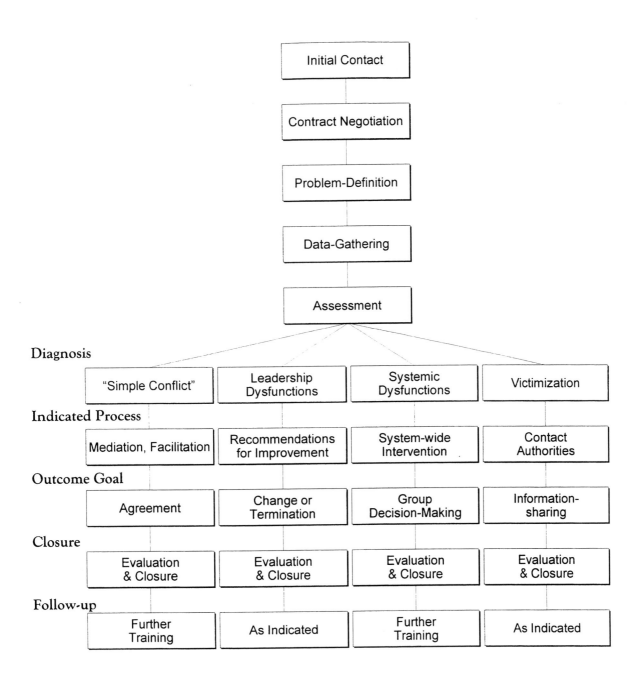

Diagnosis

Indicated Process

Outcome Goal

Closure

Follow-up

–David Brubaker
© David Brubaker 1992. Used by permission.

Organizational Intervention: One Model

1. Contracting Phase

    a.   Clarify consultant's purposes and roles.
    b.   Outline goals and describe steps in the intervention.
    c.   Clarify terms of the contract: fees, scheduling, etc.

2. Education Phase

    a.   Training workshop.
    b.   Ongoing equipping of members and coaching of leaders.

3. Information-Gathering Phase

    a.   Constitution, past minutes, other relevant documents.
    b.   Questionnaire.
    c.   Telephone interviews.
    d.   Small groups—structured dialogue.

4. Healing Phase

    a.   Large group—structured dialogue.
    b.   Large group—neutralizing history.
        • Distant past
        • More distant past
    c.   Interpersonal mediation.

5. Problem-Solving Phase

    a.   Reflection on interests.
    b.   Brainstorm ideas.
    c.   Evaluate ideas.
    d.   Build agreement for the future
    e.   Obtain agreement of those not present.

6. Bringing Closure to the Intervention

    a.   Written report.
    b.   Closing reconciliation ritual, as appropriate.
    c.   Follow-up contracts

–Lombard Mennonite Peace Center
© LMPC 1991. Used by permission.

Facing Difficult Issues in the Congregation

A. Assess the significance of this issue in the life of the congregation.

1. Scope: Identify the circles of involvement and concern.
- Who are the person(s) directly involved with the issue? Is leadership involved or enmeshed?
- Who are the persons in primary or significant relationship with those most directly involved?
- Who are the persons most likely to call for defending values?
- Who are the persons most likely to call for compassion?

2. Impact: Observe the nature and severity of the issue in its potential for tension.
- Is this issue to be addressed primarily on a personal or a congregational level? Is this primarily a concern for pastoral care or also discernment by a larger group?
- Is this primarily a crisis requiring immediate resolution or an issue that will require long-term attention?
- On a scale of 1-5, what is the severity of the conflict potential of this issue in the congregation? (See "Levels of Conflict" on page 245)
- What is the current level of conflict and polarization in the congregation around this issue?

3. Priorities: Consider the scope and impact of this issue for ministry and management.
- What will be the time demands for congregational process? (How many meetings over what period of time?)
- What will be the time and personnel demands for pastoral care?
- What limitations of time and energy apply?
- What boundaries are needed to enable a process to be effective in this congregation at this time?

4. Questions: Write a clear, concise statement of the question(s) to be addressed.

When a congregation faces a difficult issue which needs discernment, it is essential to assess the scope and impact of the issue on the life of the congregation and establish priorities for action. The *Scope* is concerned with how deeply and broadly the issue is rooted in the experience of the congregation. This will help indicate the time and energy needed to address the issue. *Impact* seeks to identify the extent to which polarization is occurring and the level of conflict resolution needed. Severity is determined by the nature of the issue in context. For example, the issue of abortion is likely to be much more severe than whether or not to change the time of the Sunday worship service. The more severe the issue the greater the potential for escalated conflict. This has implications for the extent to which pastoral care will be needed by various persons within the church during the process of discernment.

Often conflict is multidimensional and messy. Many things beg for attention at once. Congregational leaders need to ask what the *priorities* are for management and ministry in this situation. If it is a short-term but intense crisis, how will the intensity be paced and managed? If it is likely to take longer to resolve and discern, how will the congregation be helped to engage in a sustained process? What will be the pastoral care needs during this time? How can the congregation maintain a sense of order? What are the personnel and time limits?

Finally, it will help everyone if the issue can be stated in a sentence or two. Often it is most helpful to put it in terms of a *question*: "Is it essential for our mission to enlarge our building?" Such a question may have several subsidiary questions, but a primary one serves to clarify discussion and focus the congregation's prayer and discernment.

B. Clarify the locus of responsibility for discernment and decision-making.

Does responsibility for decision-making on this issue rest with:
- The congregation as a whole?
- Leaders of the congregation? If so, which leaders?

- The district or conference?
- The denomination?
- A combination of the above?

It is essential at the outset to establish who is ultimately responsible for making a decision about the issue. If it is congregational leaders then the congregational process needs to include information dissemination and education about the issue. If the decision truly rests with the congregation, then it is essential to design a process that includes adequate study, discussion and prayer. If the decision is both congregational and denominational then the congregation must be led to the clearest discernment possible in order to be prepared to engage in dialogue with the conference, district or denomination.

C. Develop a plan for the process.

1. Leadership: Identify, appoint and prepare leadership for the process.

- Appoint specific persons to provide leadership for the process. (Leadership may include the pastor, elders or deacons, the church moderator, a committee of persons assigned to this, a facilitator, etc.).
- Assign clear roles and responsibilities to the leaders; it must be clear to all who is responsible for what.
- Provide essential preparation (training) for leadership. This may include giving attention to:

Attitude:	To be able to accept tension and conflict as normal in congregational life. To be able to tolerate ambiguity.
Self Awareness:	To know one's own conflict style. To know one's own strengths and limits in facing conflict
Skill Development:	To learn basic group process and mediation skills.

2. Schedule: Create a tentative time line for the process, making sure it is clear to everyone.

3. Discernment and Decision-Making: Design a process for discernment and decision-making.

Such a process may include the following steps:
   a. Listen to the story or experience of those involved. Invite conversation between members.
   b. Reflect upon the implications of these stories or experiences. Clarify concerns. Note commonalities and differences.
   c. Study Scripture and theology relevant to the issue at hand. Examine various understandings.
   d. Relate stories and Scripture to relevant conventional wisdom. (Sciences, culture, tradition).
   e. Seek the face of God together through prayer, reflection, fasting, etc.
   f. Identify the mind of the congregation to make the needed decisions.
   g. Apply the decision with mercy and grace.

4. Pastoral Care: Develop a plan for congregational and individual pastoral care.

- Plan worship services, sermons, teachings with the discernment process in mind.
- Encourage a spirit of mutual care (I Corinthians 12), forgiveness and hope; teach people to release fear, anger, power struggles, self-centeredness.
- When difficult meetings occur, reassure the people of God's care, acceptance and guidance; reflect openly with the congregation about the struggle that is occurring.
- Identify persons and groups for whom the process will most likely be difficult.
- Assign persons to provide pastoral care during the process, e.g., visits and conversations.
- Those who care for persons must: 1) be willing to stay in touch; 2) be clear about the care procedures (expectations, confidentiality, accountability); 3) be able to listen well and stay in dialogue; 4) help person(s) reflect on their own life as well as on the issue within the congregation; 5) help identify a network of support: family, friends, professional persons, etc.

The significance of the steps in this phase are self-evident. It is important to have clearly designated and prepared *leadership* not only for the effectiveness of the process but also so congregational members know who is responsible for what and to whom they can communicate their concerns. The greater the conflict the more leaders need to be prepared to listen and dialogue between sessions for a sense of inclusion and fairness. In severe conflict it is important that leaders hold their own convictions while respecting those who disagree. Members need to know that the leader of the process is able to fairly guide the process whatever the spectrum of opinions and convictions.

The process for *discernment and decision-making* is the heart of this outline. The process begins with the story of those most immediately affected; it encourages broad expression of concerns and opinions in a context of openness and safety. In times of severe conflict there need to be several sessions, without the threat of a decision, in order for people to dialogue openly and respectfully. Leaders must at all times model this respect and openness.

This process is designed to create dialogue between personal experience, the Scriptures, theology and ethics, conventional wisdom and the Christian community. People need to pray throughout and keep holding the issue and the congregation before God. *It is absolutely essential to create a climate of openness and yieldedness to God, with a sense of spiritual responsibility beyond individuals and the congregation itself. People need to have a keen sense of God's ultimate authority in the life and decisions of the congregation.*

In this process it is essential that all members know what to expect. Will the decision be by majority voice, consensus or some other form? Likewise it will be important that all know when the decision is to be made and the process leading up to the decision.

The second most important element in this plan is *pastoral care*. The ability of a congregation to engage in genuine dialogue and prayerful searching in the face of differences will be significantly influenced by the care that is provided for individuals and the congregation. At the core of such care is listening, understanding, encouraging, providing safe dialogue. These are ways to validate and value those who are most concerned, fearful or threatened.

D. Prepare a climate for discernment and decision-making.

1. **Provide biblical perspectives on dealing with differences in the life of the church.**
   - God working through diversity within the Body of Christ (I Corinthians 12)
   - Resolution of conflict in the early church (Acts 15)
   - God's love and care for the people of God (Romans 8:28-38).
   - The call for Christians to accept and forgive one another (Ephesians 4-5)

2. **Teach basic skills for discernment and decision-making.**
   - *Listening*: How to do active listening and/or give feedback
   - *Speaking*: How to speak for self; I-statements vs. you-statements
   - *Dialogue*: How to engage in respectful give and take
   - *Praying*: How to hold issues/people before God
   - *Discernment*: How to be receptive to God; how to listen to God together
   - *Decision-making*: How to ascertain direction and act on options

3. **Identify negative effects of unresolved conflict on relationships and congregational life.**

4. **Create awareness of different styles of conflict resolution and their consequences.**

5. **Practice dealing with "more manageable" issues to help people learn these skills.**

Here it is evident that the means for discernment is dependent upon Christian relationship. The nature of human interactions has much to do with the freedom of the Spirit to work in the hearts of the people. A divided, hostile congregation is not in a position to discern truth together. Congregational discernment is dependent upon the ability of people to work toward resolution of destructive interpersonal elements: misunderstandings, power struggles, resentments, polarization. While spiritual and moral discernment must go beyond mediation, the use of mediation in the process of discernment is often essential. Leaders are encouraged to use the excellent materials provided in this manual as well as elsewhere. Even though we believe in peacemaking, the attitudes and skills for conflict resolution are not natural to most people. These must be learned and practiced if they are to be of use in difficult and tense moments. To this end we do well to create a culture of peacemaking in our congregations.

E. Facilitate the congregation in a process of discernment and decision-making.

1. **Report the issue/concern/problem at hand to the congregation.**
   - Provide a clear description of the issue, the question(s) to be answered and the decision(s) to be made.
   - Describe the plan that is being recommended to help the congregation to address the issue.
   - Allow ample time for congregational reaction and response.

2. **Negotiate with the congregation to engage in a process of discernment and decision-making.**
   - Provide information about specific leadership roles and responsibility.
   - Explain the process to be pursued. There should be no surprises.
   - When scheduling meetings, be clear about time, length and number of sessions.

3. **Lead the congregation in the process for discernment and decision-making.**
   - Lead the congregation through the steps of discernment.
   - Allow ample time for study and reflection.
   - Structure each session with clear goals and adequate time for the agenda.
   - Facilitate open, discerning communication in congregational conversations.
   - Encourage an attitude of inclusion and care as members address their differences.
   - Create a safe environment for all to speak.
   - Maintain a spirit of discernment: (reflection, prayer, encouragement)

4. **Monitor the process by meeting regularly with leaders to reflect and seek direction for the future.**

5. **When the time is right, facilitate a decision by the congregation using the agreed-upon method.**

6. **Implement pastoral care procedures for individuals and the congregation.**

7. **Assign a listening committee to draft a formal statement of any action taken by the congregation.**

There are essentially four parts to this step: contract, implement the process, implement pastoral care, and confirm the decision. The more clear and agreed upon the question to be answered and the process for answering it, the more potential for an effective process. Discernment will be facilitated by a gentle interplay between discussion, dialogue, debate, etc. on the one hand, and times of reflection and prayer on the other.

–Marcus G. Smucker
© MCS 2000

Healthy Expression of Conflict in Group Settings

A difficult time in the life of any group occurs when serious conflicts emerge between individuals and sub-groups. Often in group life the meetings and events where these conflicts are publicly and overtly expressed create uneasiness at best and outright attack and counterattack at worst. The presence of the mediator creates a new and hopefully safer environment for exploring the differences and conflicts. Family systems theory suggests at least three essential elements, and we have added a fourth, for the healthy public expression of conflict. These are useful for mediators, and leaders in general, to keep in mind in group settings where emotions and anxiety are high.

Invite Self-Definition

The most difficult and challenging first step is to help people openly define themselves in a clear, positive way and not in reaction to others. Often we wait for others to define first, then define ourselves in reaction to them. In groups, waiting to define and being unable to define self openly create a sense of being stuck, and feeling lost. You simply are not sure how others feel. Healthy self-definition occurs when you openly address what you feel and believe, what you need and can give, what you hope for and where you feel disillusioned.

Foster a Non-anxious Presence

This is the opposite of "uptightness," of being upset and tense. Good self-definition by members in a group means different definitions and perspectives will emerge. The open expression of conflict tends to produce anxiety. Anxiety makes us feel like we "have to respond," or "have to get out." The goal here is to create a relationship and/or a forum where differences, hurts, feelings, and issues can be expressed and explored from diverse viewpoints in a pro-active rather than reactive way. Non-anxious presence is not detachment from emotions or issues, but engagement of them without retreat or attack. The mediator, in particular, is a living example, engaging fully with one perspective and then another.

Maintain Emotional Contact

Expression of conflict tends to separate. When anxious, angry or hurt, people move away from the source of their anxiety by moving away from each other. Distance takes both physical and emotional forms. To restore a relationship, or make good decisions, emotional contact with others whom we perceive as blocking, disagreeing with, or rejecting us is essential for constructive conflict management. As a general rule, mediators should note anxiety and move toward it, but maintain emotional contact with the participants and help them maintain it with each other.

Offer Collaborative Options

Although not developed in family systems theory, as such, we would add a fourth way to model the healthy expression of conflict in group settings. This is to offer collaborative options such as those outlined more fully in the earlier sections on group dialogue and discernment. Although these may initially be resisted in a system which is experiencing high anxiety and reactivity, they provide the possibility for de-escalation of tensions and re-establishment of more direct communication and trust.

–John Paul Lederach, expanded by Alice M. Price
© MCS 1989, 1995

Opening Up Systems Issues

What follows is a collection of intervention strategies and exercises, with brief descriptions, collected from a variety of sources. These activities may be used to collect important systems information for leaders and consultants. They also are avenues for group members in general to become more conscious overall of how the system is functioning and to identify unhealthy or undesirable patterns which need change. Many are suited for use in fairly routine leadership or membership retreats, staff meetings or annual planning events. Others are particularly appropriate for significant times of group transition or as part of an extended intervention in a more acute conflict situation.

Group History

Have group members recollect the essential history of the group, chart it on butcher paper and hang it up around the wall. If there are keystone events in the organization's history (e.g., the death of a beloved leader), you might arrange for an appropriate old-timer to do some animated storytelling or lead the group in some impromptu dramatic skits related to that period. Use the butcher paper and any related storytelling as a jumping off point for identifying long-term patterns in group life such as leadership transitions, the role of conflict, etc. History-telling has been used successfully in congregational interventions, as well as for celebrating important turning points or orienting newly arrived leaders.

Variations: If there is a large group and/or a long history, start the process in small groups first—perhaps giving each an assigned focus or time period. Then have small groups share/debrief together in the large group. Form small groups to maximize mixes which are multigenerational, old members/new members, liberals/conservatives, or whatever will cut across and broaden typical lines of communication or perspective.

Corporate Character

Have individuals or small groups describe the organization as if it were a single human personality. This can include both verbal and pictorial images. Include the character's gender, age, favorite activities and interests, habits, etc. Some use this exercise to do congregational interviews focusing on "family" language, e.g., how often the "person" has been married, have there been any divorces or deaths, are there children, etc. Gets quickly at relational patterns. Can be used as jumping off point for system-focused discussions, as in #1. above.

Corporate Puzzle Game

This exercise is adapted from a published version designed for local congregations by Energize Associates. The group is divided into teams. Each team is given an hour to create its own "puzzle" or organizational chart to hang on the wall and share with the larger group. Instructions are to describe *all* the functional components or roles in the organization, place these into some type of organizational format and then add relevant connecting lines of authority and communication. Stress that formal, informal and tacit roles and connectors should all be included, but perhaps designated by different colors, shapes or other codes to distinguish them.

Use the posted charts to discuss similarities and differences in the different puzzles and their implications for group life. What can be learned about the roles and rules in this system? Do any of the puzzles look like the official organizational chart of the organization? What do people *wish* the official organizational chart looked like?

Variations: Depending on whether your goal is to surface differences in perceptions or to create opportunities for cross-stitching, these can be either intentionally mixed teams or teams which each represent a distinct department, facet or vantage point from within the group's structure (e.g., ordained/lay, staff/board, men/women). If there are particular dynamics you want to explore, teams can be given specific questions to explore (e.g., how many people over and under certain ages form a certain committee, etc.).

Conflict Habits

How groups handle conflict is often a good window into systems issues. Design a group activity to create a comprehensive list of organizational habits or norms related to how conflict is handled in the group (e.g., conflict viewed as wrong/normal, communication mainly indirect/direct, use of personal attacks/separating people from issues). Discuss which of these rules are constructive and which are not. Consider what norms the group *wishes* to have regarding conflict and how the group might work to achieve changes in its conflict patterns (e.g., conflict skills workshops, clearer decision-making processes, improved communication channels, accountability structures, etc.).

Variations: Begin the exercise by having individuals identify and share the conflict norms in their **own** families of origin. In religious settings, surface the early theological teachings underlying these norms and how helpful these teachings were or continue to be. Discuss how these affect them in the new system.

Fables, Parables

Storytelling of all kinds, particularly of stories which embody classic dilemmas, can be used with groups to break loose insights about their own group dynamics. Stories can be selected which are suited to the group's needed area of focus. *Friedman's Fables* and its study guide provide a wonderful storehouse of such stories. Stories and parables from the Bible also provide excellent materials for religious settings.

Variations: Less literary-minded groups can be encouraged to think of popular stories, movies, TV dramas, comic strips, etc., which remind them of something the group is experiencing. Or take a well-known fable or fairy tale and let the group rewrite it as it wishes.

Metaphors

Keep your ears open for metaphors which will free a group or individual to move to a new level of understanding of their situation. Many conflict resolution trainers use metaphor to engage people in looking at conflict styles and habits by asking people to come up with verbal or picture images to finish the phrase, "We do conflict like . . . ."

Metaphor can also be an intervention tool. Someone says, "Look at us. We're jumping ship for a more glamorous yacht." Metaphoric responses for facilitator to explore: "Is the boat sinking?" (grief, loss, anxiety). "Are we getting on the wrong ship?" (loss of direction, purpose). "Are we leaving people behind?" (separation, loss of relationship).

Paradoxes

Use of paradox is one of the most potent interventions available. Fables, noted above, often rotate around paradox. This technique also includes use of the *paradoxical injunction* such as telling a group that is really stuck or ardently holding on to old grievances that you do not think it would be good for them to move ahead or let go of their strong feelings too quickly.

Having identified key paradoxes or tensions in a group or conflict, create helpful exercises for playing with these ideas. In congregations experiencing tensions related to growth, for example, group movement exercises expressing the identified tension between growth and intimacy can be designed. In organizations facing significant retrenchment, one can explore the tension between what may be the strong institutional tradition of a secure "family" and the fact that people are walking around feeling highly unsafe.

Variations: One exercise which addresses polar tensions—and can begin to lift up paradoxes—is the *human spectrum.* Group members are all asked to get up and place themselves where each one is personally along any designated line (e.g., openness to conflict at one end and conflict avoidance at the other). This clear naming of what may be unspoken or confusing tensions not only promotes healthy self-differentiation, but provides a lot of good group information quickly. It can break through rigid coalitions and communication patterns—and at times dispel the myth that the group *is* polarized. Dialogue about what the spectrum means for people individually and for group life can follow.

The human spectrum idea can be taken out of its purely linear format and used quite successfully to explore more than two interlocking tensions or paradoxes in systems through movement exercises involving triangles, wheel spokes, four corners, etc.

"Family" Sculpting

Sculpting is a technique used commonly in some family therapy settings. Someone is asked to "sculpt" his or her system's roles and relationships. Actual system members or volunteers stand at designated places and distances, relative to one another. They then assume assigned facial expressions and body poses to illustrate their role's typical physical and emotional posture in the group "scene." The sculptor and others may then be asked to respond to the finished tableau from their perspective.

Variations: This technique can be used effectively with simple props, role-designating placards and costuming, if one wants to add a bit of drama and perhaps even some levity to the discussion. I have also seen it include someone with a ball of string—perhaps the sculptor—wandering among the people and intertwining them in appropriate linkages, to demonstrate coalitions, fusion, triangling, etc.

Systems Inventory

When there is an adequate time-frame, groups can commit to a comprehensive systems inventory of some type. This entails having each group member or member of a leadership team fill out a questionnaire designed to elicit a broad range of systems information. This information is then given to someone to collate and analyze and/or shared in the group for analysis.

Some inventories are in a guided exploration format in which individuals are given a set of topics and/or thought-provoking questions to which open-ended responses and reflections are then recorded (e.g., what triangles operate in this group?). Other inventories are in a forced-choice format (e.g., mark one: "We tend to business first" "We tend to people first") and may result in a specific score or profile sheet. The Alban Institute has one which explores systems dynamics related to seven key aspects of group life and leadership.

Breaking the Rules

This is often more of an overall strategy or attitude assumed by a leader or consultant than a single intervention. It can also be incorporated into group activities or group life more generally. It involves deliberate breaches of rules, especially informal or tacit rules, in the system. One fruitful area for rule-breaking in many systems is communication patterns: Refuse to talk about or insist on talking about certain things, subvert normal lines of communication, resist being triangled into issues and relationships, be "unconfidential" about secrets and sacred cows, etc.

Many of the intervention options listed above provide ripe avenues for this kind of breaking down of rigid or dysfunctional communication patterns. Keep this goal in mind by maximizing healthy rule-breaking in your design of group exercises, mixers, etc.

–compiled by Alice M. Price
© MCS 1991

Letting Go of the Past

A major problem in almost in every situation of conflict is the past. Lies have been told, damage has been done, pain has been inflicted, resentments have been aroused, injustice has been perpetrated. How can peacemakers contribute to the necessary task of letting go of this history?

An important reality for any discussion about healing from the wounds of the past is that reconciliation is a journey, not an event. It is not just a matter of saying nice words and having pleasant feelings. Reconciliation requires facing the damage and hurt of the past, hearing the anger and resentment of those who are injured, and helping to undo, wherever possible, the damage that has been done. Some of the steps in the journey of reconciliation are scary and painful, and appear to be a step backward. But often there is no way to continue with the journey unless the parties are prepared to take these steps in faith that they will lead ultimately to a good outcome.

Positive Attitude Toward Anger

One of the most important moments in determining whether mediators and facilitators contribute towards movement in the journey of reconciliation is when people express anger, hurt, and resentment. If we block people from expressing these emotions, we may "freeze" them in the healing process and make it difficult to move on. On the other hand, uncontrolled expressions of anger may lead to a breakdown in all communication.

Often it is effective to maintain a positive attitude towards anger as it surfaces in parties to conflict, acknowledging anger without judgement and looking for ways to enable further expression of it in "safe" ways.

Tell and Retell

The most important step towards healing is telling the story of hurt to an attentive listener. Despite what many people believe, telling stories of hurt does not reinjure old hurts. On the contrary, it is the story never told that holds people in secret bondage to old and festering wounds. By telling stories, people reassert ownership over their lives. Thus giving an angry or traumatized person oppor-

tunity to tell the whole story about his or her trauma is a major contribution to that person's healing. However, storytelling is healing only if it is accompanied by careful, nonjudgmental listening by someone else. Peacemakers need to cultivate the ability to listen with great attentiveness, setting aside all judgement, as a fundamental skill in contributing to healing.

Stories of deep trauma often need to be told many times in order to achieve healing. In normal daily life, someone who has been in a car accident, for example, will recount the experience again and again to sympathetic family and friends in response to queries about a bandaged arm. Such retelling serves an important emotional purpose in gaining release from the trauma of the experience.

Neutralizing History

A powerful exercise for letting go of old hurt is called "Neutralizing History." It is based on a procedure developed by Barbara Daté and her colleagues in Eugene, Ore., in the early 1980s. In one bitter conflict, after several fruitless hours of seeking solutions to the issues, the mediators announced to the two groups involved that bitterness about the past seemed to block all possibility of progress. They suggested that the parties set aside efforts to negotiate for a time and instead take some time to express their resentments to each other. The groups agreed to this proposal.

The mediators asked Group A to come to the next meeting with a list of all the things they were angry about, and to appoint a spokesperson for each item. During that meeting, the appointed spokespersons came forward one at a time to talk about the events on Group A's list. Each spokesperson chose a "listener," which could be anyone whom they wished to choose from the opposing group, whose job was to simply hear the speaker, and briefly summarize what he understood the speaker to be saying without responses or challenges.

By the end of the first meeting, the people from Group A were feeling wonderful; those from Group B were deeply discouraged. But in the next meeting the process was reversed. This time, Group B got the lift. At the end of this meeting the facilitators asked each group to come to the third meeting prepared to assess the situation.

At the third meeting, surprising things happened. One group read a written statement of apology. Individuals from the other group not only accepted this statement, but added their own apologies. Over a two-hour period, many statements of a desire to forgive and move on were made. The logjam had broken and the parties were now able to quickly agree on next steps to resolve a series of practical decisions.

Neutralizing History is an extremely powerful intervention, effective both in group and inter-personal conflicts. The purpose of Neutralizing History is to provide emotional release from past destructive events. The exercise is incomplete on its own and needs to be followed up with joint plan-ning and decision-making about the kind of relationship participants would like to have in the future. Failure to do this is likely to lead to the parties' falling back into old resentments.

This intervention requires clear, confident facili-tation. It is important that facilitators provide con-stant emotional support to both sides. This is espe-cially important for the person who is listening.

Keeping with the focus on "letting go," facilitators can ask parties to put each issue on a card. When the speaker has described an incident and been paraphrased, the facilitator can ask the speaker, "In a minute I'd like to ask you to toss this card in the

–Ron Kraybill
© MCS 2000

trash can. Is there anything else you want to say about this experience before you do that?"

A Useful Question

A simple question facilitators can ask of people who are stuck in old hurt: "What, specifically, do you need to do and what could others do that would enable you to move on from the past?" Responding to the question moves people out of the role of passive, blaming "victim," a role which makes them permanently dependent at an emo-tional level on the people they resent the most. By describing these two things, people begin to exercise some mastery over their own lives.

Rituals of Healing

Ritual can be a powerful resource in assisting people to move through healing processes. At its best, ritual provides a pathway for people to safely channel negative emotions and open themselves up to new possibilities. Traditional societies of course were often rich in ritual, but under the influences of urbanization and modernization many of these rituals are now falling into disuse. Peacemakers do well to explore the literature, dance, drama, song, poetry, liturgies, folk sayings, ceremonies of cleans-ing and healing, etc., that lie within the cultural traditions of people in conflict. The wisdom and ways of the elders sometimes offer important re-sources for healing the wounds of their children and grandchildren.

Some Not-So-Tongue-in-Cheek Principles for Intervenors

- Each side of the conflict will judge your competence as an intervenor on whether you are able to see the obvious truth that they are right and the other side is wrong.

- Everyone involved in the conflict already knows what should be done about it. The problem is simply making the other side do it.

- By the time you are contacted everyone has already done everything humanly possible to resolve the problem. Now it's up to the other side to make the next move.

- Everyone wants a change, as long as they don't have to change.

- Nine times out of ten, people conceive of "resolution" as getting back something they feel they have lost in the conflict. Though often unspoken, and perhaps unconscious, this hidden expectation can undermine the best-laid plans.

- People ask for help in conflict not because they can envision a successful outcome or because they feel capable of being constructive (in fact, just the opposite), but because the pain has become unbearable.

- As soon as the pain of the conflict has been slightly relieved, people will want to end the process. In general, people will be looking for a quick fix.

- People will acknowledge your expertise or impart authority to you, not so you can work more effectively, but so they will have an expert authority on their side.

- People will go to great lengths to misunderstand others and to make sure others misunderstand them. Most commonly this is second-guessing others (I know you better than you know yourself) and misrepresenting themselves (you couldn't possibly understand my true feelings or treat them with respect).

- Most people in a church conflict will not purposely hurt others, unless they feel threatened or cornered, and in a church conflict, everyone feels threatened or cornered.

- People will try to put their conflict in the best light in order to save face, and will resent you later after the front has crumbled and you have seen them at their worst.

- When people are too quick to agree with you, they're trying to get rid of you. Generally, resistance is healthy.

- What people tell you is the problem is usually not the problem.

- People will be most resistant when you are closest to the real problem.

- When the actual conflict becomes too threatening to deal with, people will sometimes try to make your relationship with them as intervenor the issue.

- People are usually willing to listen to a new perspective on themselves, as long as it agrees with their own.

- Sometimes you just have to know when to let go and let God.

- If things go well, you can either successfully be an agent to bring healing to a conflictual situation, or take credit for bringing the healing. But not both.

–Jim Yaussy Albright
© Ministry of Reconciliation (Church of the Brethren) 1995, from *Discipleship and Reconciliation Committee Handbook*. Used by permission.

Resources for Further Study on Systems and Groups

Group Process

Auvine, Brian, *et al. A Manual for Group Facilitators.* Madison, WI: Center for Conflict Resolution, 1978.
> A good, inexpensive resource for group facilitators and trainers.

Avery, Michel, *et al. Building United Judgment: A Handbook for Consensus Decision-making.* Madison, WI: Center for Conflict Resolution, 1981.
> The best overall guide to consensus process we know.

Bertcher, Harvey. *Group Participation: Techniques for Leaders and Members.* Thousand Oaks, CA: Sage, 1979.
> An excellent source of ideas for specific techniques that leaders can use in working with groups.

Butler, C.T., and Amy Rothstein. *On Conflict and Consensus: A Handbook on Formal Consensus Decision-making.* Portland, ME: Food Not Bombs Publishing, 1991.
> Specific advice on planning and conducting consensus-based meetings.

Coover, Virginia, *et al. Resource Manual for a Living Revolution.* Santa Cruz, CA: New Society, 1977.
> An early, still valuable resource for working at social change from a nonviolent orientation. Good sections on group process.

Creighton, James L. *Involving Citizens in Community Decision Making.* Washington, DC: Program for Community Problem-Solving, 1992.
> Ways to incorporate a broad base of citizens into collaborative processes.

Doyle, Michael, and David Straus. *How to Make Meetings Work.* New York: Berkley, 1976.
> An inexpensive paperback chock full of good ideas about planning, running and evaluating meetings; clear on role delineation.

Harder, Leland. *Doors to Lock and Doors to Open.* Scottdale, PA: Herald Press, 1993.
> The meaning and process of discernment; how to make decisions as people of faith.

Hart, Lois B. *Faultless Facilitation: A Resource Guide for Group and Team Leaders.* Amherst, MA: HRD Press, 1992.
> A ring-bound "how-to," also available with an instructor's manual for training settings.

Hutcheson, Richard G., Jr., and Peggy Shriver. *The Divided Church: Moving Liberals and Conservatives from Diatribe to Dialogue.* Downers Grove, IL: InterVarsity Press, 1999.
> The two authors, coming from very different theological perspectives, offer hope for constructive dialogue in our own Christian circles.

Johnson, Luke T. *Scripture and Discernment: Decision-making in the Church.* Nashville: Abingdon Press, 1996.
> Good biblical study of the opportunity and challenge of making decisions in the church.

Kayser, Thomas. *Mining Group Gold: How to Cash in on the Collaborative Brain Power of a Group.* Blue Ridge Summit, PA: McGraw-Hill, 1995.
> Written for a corporate audience, but contains so much good material on facilitation that it is probably the single best book on the topic.

Kelsey, Dee, and Pam Plumb. *Great Meetings! How to Facilitate Like a Pro.* Portland, ME: Hanson Park Press, 1997.
> User-friendly book that gives readers skills and confidence to facilitate successful meetings.

Lakey, Berit. "Meeting Facilitation: The No Magic Method." Santa Cruz, CA: New Society (undated).
    An inexpensive pamphlet outlining basic rules for good meetings.

McCoy, Martha, et al. Planning Community-wide Study Circle Programs: A Step-By-Step Guide. Pomfret, CT: Study Circles Resource Center, 1996.
    This is a guide for setting up "study circles" as a response to racism, but the concept could be used in any setting where there is tension and need for dialogue among a large number of people.

Morris, Danny, and Charles Olsen. Discerning God's Will Together: A Spiritual Practice for the Church. Nashville: Alban Institute with Upper Room Books, 1997.
    Proposes a clear series of practical steps in decision-making which could easily be adapted to nonreligious settings as well. Excellent integration of faith and practical approaches.

Phelps, Joseph. More Light, Less Heat: How Dialogue Can Transform Christian Conflicts Into Growth. San Francisco: Jossey-Bass, 1998.
    Offers hope and practical tools for healing the deep and painful wounds that divide members of the Christian family.

Schwarz, Roger M. The Skilled Facilitator: Practical Wisdom for Developing Effective Groups. San Francisco: Jossey-Bass, 1994.
    A comprehensive text for outside and internal facilitators.

Stoesz, Edgar, and Chester Raber. Doing Good Better: How to be an Effective Board Member of a Nonprofit Organization. Intercourse, PA: Good Books, 1994.
    Includes a good guide to planning and running efficient meetings.

Tagliere, Daniel A. How to Meet, Think and Work to Consensus. San Diego, CA: Pfeifer and Co., 1993.
    Good resource for team leaders in business or organizational settings looking for ideas on how to address specific problems.

Conflict and Systemic Change

Boers, Arthur Paul. Never Call Them Jerks. Washington, DC: Alban Institute, 1999.
    Shows how a better understanding of difficult behavior can help congregational leaders avoid the trap of negatively labeling parishioners.

Bossart, Donald E. Creative Conflict in Religious Education and Church Administration. Birmingham, AL: Religious Education Press, 1980.
    A good book for trainers on conflict dynamics in religious settings.

Carpenter, Susan L., and W.J.D. Kennedy. Managing Public Disputes. San Francisco: Jossey-Bass, 1988.
    Provides step-by-step guidelines for designing workable strategies to deal with organizational conflicts.

Cosgrove, Charles H., Church Conflict: The Hidden Systems Behind the Fights. Nashville: Abingdon Press, 1994.
    A practical book that applies family systems theory to church conflicts.

Diamond, Louise, and John McDonald. Multi-Track Diplomacy: A Systems Guide and Analysis. West Hartford, CT: Kumerian Press, 1993.
    An overview of systems and multitrack diplomacy.

Friedman, Edwin H. Generation to Generation: Family Process in Church and Synagogue. New York: Guilford, 1985.
    The best book on family systems thinking in religious systems.

Gray, Barbara. *Collaborating: Finding Common Ground for Multiparty Problems.* San Francisco: Jossey-Bass, 1989.
   Collaborative problem-solving strategies for complex disputes.

Halverstadt, Hugh F. *Managing Church Conflict.* Louisville, KY: Westminster/John Knox, 1991.
   An excellent resource.

Jacksteit, Mary, and Adrienne Kaufmann. *Finding Common Ground: A Manual,* 2nd ed. Washington, DC: Search for Common Ground, 1995.
   Outlines a model for dialogue which could be easily used with many different topics, although the main focus of this manual is the abortion issue.

Johnson, Barry. *Polarity Management: Identifying and Managing Unsolvable Problems.* Amherst, MA: HRD Press, 1992.
   Distinguishes between problems to solve and ongoing polarities or dilemmas which organizations must manage and cannot resolve.

Kliewer, Stephen. *How to Live with Diversity in the Local Church.* Washington, DC: Alban Institute, 1987.
   Working with diversity and conflict at the congregational level.

Landis, Susan Mark. "Conflict in the Congregation: A Beginning Resource Guide for Congregational Leaders of the Ohio Conference of the Mennonite Church." Kidron, OH: Ohio Conferences PJSC, 1994.
   A paper designed to help congregational leaders begin to recognize and deal with conflicts.

Leas, Speed. *Moving Your Church Through Conflict.* Washington, DC: Alban Institute, 1985.
   Assessment and intervention tools for conflicted congregations. A good first book for those interested in church conflict.

McKinney, Mary Benet. *Sharing Wisdom: A Process for Group Decision-making.* Allen, TX: Tabor, 1987.
   An excellent resource for faith groups wanting to move from more authoritarian or majoritarian processes to group discernment.

Mennonite Conciliation Service. *Conflict in the Church.* Akron, PA: Mennonite Central Committee, 1999.
   A two-part, 40-minute video with discussion guide offers alternative ways of viewing and dealing with conflicts in congregations.

Mindell, Arnold. *Sitting in the Fire: Large Group Transformation Using Conflict and Diversity.* Portland, OR: Lao Tse Press, 1995.
   Thought-provoking reflections on facilitation in groups, particularly settings of racial, ethnic, economic conflict. Limited in some settings due to its urban/Western perspective.

Mitchell, Kenneth. *Multiple Staff Ministries.* Philadelphia: Westminster, 1988.
   A clear description of systems theory in religious organizations.

Parsons, George, and Speed Leas. *Congregational Systems Inventory.* Washington, DC: Alban Institute.
   Assumes "controlled tension" in a church. Makes recommendations about how to balance some perennial issues.

Qualben, James D. *Peace in the Parish: How to Use Conflict Resolution Principles and Process.* San Antonio, TX: LangMarc Publishing, 1992.
   Presents a system of principles, analytical steps and how-tos for moving conflicted situations toward vitality.

Rendle, Gilbert R. *Leading Change in the Congregation: Spiritual and Organization Tools for Leaders.* Washington, DC: Alban Institute, 1998.
  Provides church leaders and others with practical diagnostic models and tools.

Richardson, Ronald W. *Creating a Healthier Church: Family Systems Theory, Leadership and Congregational Life.* Minneapolis, MN: Fortress, 1996
  A good summary of systems theory and practical set of leadership ideas and behaviors.

Schoene, Lester, Jr., and Marcelle E. DuPraw. *Facing Racial and Cultural Conflict: Tools for Rebuilding Community.* Washington, DC: Program for Community Problem-Solving, 1994.
  Valuable guide and source of innovative ideas.

Steinke, Peter L. *Healthy Congregations: A Systems Approach.* Washington, DC: Alban Institute, 1996.
  A deeper exploration of the congregation as an emotional system than *How Your Church Family Works* (see below).

Steinke, Peter L. *How Your Church Family Works: Understanding Congregations as Emotional Systems.* Washington, DC: Alban Institute, 1993.
  Teaches new and effective ways to deal with such as issues as the roots of church conflict and dealing with change in the congregation.

Thomas, Marlin E. *Resolving Disputes in Christian Groups.* Winnipeg, MB: Windflower Communications, 1994.
  Articulates in practical terms a biblical approach to interpersonal and group relations, facilitation and problem-solving.

Ury, William, *et al. Getting Disputes Resolved: Designing Systems to Cut the Costs of Conflict.* San Francisco: Jossey-Bass, 1988.
  Diagnosing/creating organizational systems for conflict prevention/resolution.

Special Issues

Eiland, Millard, and LeDayne McLeese Polaski, eds. *Rightly Dividing the Word of Truth: A Resource for Congregations in Dialogue on Sexual Orientation.* Charlotte, NC: Baptist Peace Fellowship, 1999.
  This looseleaf binder of 260 pages divided into ten sections draws on the wisdom of more than 30 writers and tells the stories of 13 congregations who carried out study processes.

Fortune, Marie M. *Is Nothing Sacred? When Sex Invades the Pastoral Relationship.* San Francisco: Harper and Row, 1989.
  In case study format, the book details the events that led up to six women confronting their pastor and the congregation's response.

Gaede, Beth Ann, ed. *Congregations Talking About Homosexuality.* Bethesda, MD: Alban Institute, 1998.
  Helpful reflections on how to enter into the conversation, as well as several case studies.

Geiss, Sally, and Donald Messer. *Caught in the Crossfire: Helping Christians Debate Homosexuality.* Nashville, TX: Abingdon, 1994.
  Offers diverse perspectives on the issues of the debate but is exclusively content oriented with no input on the dialogue process.

Hartman, Keith. *Congregations in Conflict: The Battle Over Homosexuality.* New Brunswick, NJ: Rutgers University Press, 1996.
  Nine detailed studies of congregational struggles over homosexuality documenting the struggles and the costs.

Heggen, Carolyn Holderread. *Sexual Abuse in Christian Homes and Churches*. Scottdale, PA: Herald Press, 1993.
An examination of the many difficult issues surrounding sexual abuse, including a look at congregational response and the possibilities for healing.

Holben, L.R. *What Christians Think About Homosexuality: Six Representative Viewpoints*. North Richland Hills, TX: Bibal Press, 1999.
The clearest definition of the issues available in print. Challenges the idea that there is only one Christian view on "homosexuality."

Hopkins, Nancy Myer, and Mark Lasser, eds. *Restoring the Soul of a Church: Healing Congregations Wounded by Clergy Sexual Misconduct*. Collegeville, MN: The Liturgical Press, 1995.
A book about crises and long-term healing strategies for damaged congregations that will restore them to being healthy communities of faith.

Miller, Melissa A. *Family Violence: The Compassionate Church Responds*. Scottdale, PA: Herald Press, 1994.
A look at issues such as survivor's healing, power dynamics in the family, congregational response and hard faith questions for those seeking to understand and address family violence.

Rutter, Peter. *Sex in the Forbidden Zone*. Los Angeles: Tarcher, 1986.
In this landmark study, Rutter exposes the pattern of men in positions of power using that power to sexually exploit those under their care or tutelage.

Organization

Program for Community Problem Solving, 915 15th St. NW, Ste. 610, Washington DC 20005; 202-783-2961; dcpcps@aol.com; www.ncl.org/ncl/pcps.htm
This organization has case studies and other resources on building consensus in large-scale disputes.

Chapter 6

Standards and Ethics for Practice

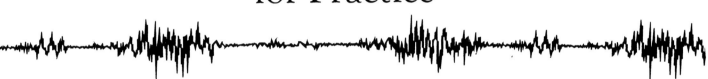

The concept of qualification from an intrusive outside entity for grassroots, community-based programs is contrary to the fundamental empowerment principle from which these programs sprang. . . . Our experience and proven track record give us as legitimate a claim to the crown of "expert" mediator as anyone.

–Daniel P. Joyce

Introduction

This chapter provides background and discussion on standards to guide and evaluate the training and performance of people providing mediation, facilitation and group intervention services. Also included are questions of ethics.

Various standards and codes have been developed over the years from different sectors and professional groups within the conflict resolution field. These standards and codes continue to evolve as the field evolves. Also, there is not consensus within the field at large on all aspects of practice. Some of these differences represent the spectrum of approaches from grassroots voluntary programs to highly professionalized or institutionalized models of practice. Other differences represent the many streams of practice, each with their own practice codes and certification standards, from which countless mediators have migrated: social work, psychology, law, education, ministry, community activism, labor-management relations, etc. And still others represent differences based on context and perspective related to culture, ethnicity, theology, gender, class, etc.

The materials we have included here are not comprehensive. They are a sampling to 1) introduce you to various streams of thought, 2) alert you to some of the key questions and dilemmas in the field, and 3) give you greater self-awareness and some reference points for your own journey as a peacemaker. Other information touching on these topics is found throughout the manual. A number of these questions are addressed in the Summer 1992 issue of *Conciliation Quarterly*, "Promises and Pitfalls of Professionalization" (Vol. 11 No. 2), as well as in ongoing dialogue on the web sites of national mediation organizations such as SPIDR, NAFCM, ABA Dispute Resolution Section and others.

–Alice M. Price
© MCS 1995

MCS Mission and Philosophy of Practice

Mission Statement

The mission of Mennonite Conciliation Service is to equip and resource individuals and groups in the United States to respond redemptively to the conflicts in our homes, churches, communities and broader society.

The MCS Philosophy of Practice

Imbedded within our understanding of the ministry of reconciliation is a series of paradoxes which guide our practice and can be summarized as follows:

We ground our work in a call to, and theology of, both community *and* personal transformation. Our work in peacemaking arises from a commitment to building community because God calls us to live in relationships of justice, mutuality and love. At the same time, we believe that personal repentance and faithfulness are essential to reconciliation and healing.

We are a constituency-based, faith-based network *and* seek relationships beyond ourselves. As one of the peace and justice ministries of Mennonite Central Committee U.S., MCS operates within the theological framework of the Anabaptist understanding of faith and life. We seek to provide conciliation services to the diverse constituency we represent (Mennonite Church, General Conference Mennonite Church, Mennonite Brethren, Brethren in Christ) as well as being open to others who provide and seek conciliation services.

We value technical proficiency in dispute resolution *and* emotional and spiritual sensitivity. MCS embraces procedural skill and proficiency as well as emotional and spiritual integrity.

We pursue negotiation *and* forgiveness. To forgive too quickly may deny participants opportunities for healthy conflict resolution and change. We support open acknowledgment about the past and negotiation about the future, while simultaneously calling participants to the possibility of forgiveness.

We seek harmony *and* justice. The skills we use and teach are intended to transform conflict, yet they can also be used by advocates seeking empowerment of the voiceless. We support the judicious use of nonviolent confrontation and ethical conflict escalation in the pursuit of just peace.

We support the pursuit of dispute resolution as both a career *and* lifestyle. We seek to empower both professionals and lay people. Everyone is called to seek peace and pursue it. We support adequate financial income for professional dispute resolvers *and* believe that services should be provided whenever possible regardless of ability to pay.

We honor knowledge and skills already acquired *and* seek to learn and impart new approaches and strategies. People in all cultures know how to do peacemaking. We acknowledge and learn from the diversity of peacemaking styles while sharing what we have found effective.

–MCS Staff
© MCS 1995

Values We Bring to Intervention

What are the values we bring to intervention in conflict?

We bring the value of working with, of sharing power with others.

We bring curiosity and a genuine interest in working as a catalyst for the fulfillment of the parties' desires where those desires are legal, fundamentally fair, and not harmful to others or self.

We bring an awareness that much of our work involves healing.

We bring an attitude of inquiry, realizing that the parties are the experts on their conflict, and have given us the privilege of witnessing their attempts to find resolution.

We bring an awareness of the importance of culture, not only culture as ethnicity, but culture as gender, class, sexual orientation, organizational affiliation, age, generation, country of origin, and many other things.

We bring an interest in learning, as those who seek to help always do.

We bring some skills in communication, in perceiving where communication between others is not effective, and some ways of going around the impasses.

We bring a respect for the stories of others.

We bring an attitude of acceptance, seeking to facilitate the creation of a climate of respect among all those present.

We bring a willingness to secure a safe environment in which to work, through agreement on ground rules and the creation of an atmosphere of shared respect for all assembled.

We bring hope, for those in conflict who have tried and not found the way through may have lost it, but only temporarily.

We bring tools, an understanding of human systems of interaction, and the experiences of negotiating through others' conflicts and our own.

We bring theoretical understandings that convert to practice and inform our interventions.

We bring a deep faith in the resilience of the human spirit.

–Michelle LeBaron
© UVic Institute for Dispute Resolution 1994, from *Conflict Resolution and Analysis as Education*. Used by permission.

Thoughts on Practitioner Integrity

Several years ago during a particularly rough time in my marriage I was invited to do a workshop at a major denominational gathering. The workshop was called, coincidentally of course, "Peacemaking With Those We Love Most." The closer it got, the more internally conflicted I became. I was not at peace with the one I loved most. How could I stand before several hundred people and pretend to be something I wasn't? I talked about my inclination to cancel with my husband. While he understood my dilemma (all too well!), he convinced me not to cancel.

I don't remember the specifics of the conversation, but I got in touch with two critical elements that made it possible for me to lead that workshop. One was my fundamental commitment to my marriage and to bettering it. The other was a willingness to be transparent with my audience.

I stood before them several months later and, with a shaky voice, said simply that I was struggling unsuccessfully to put into practice the very things we were about to discuss that morning. It was a most humbling experience, one I've had to repeat in different forms several times over the years.

....

Sometime ago I was en route to an intervention in a highly visible conflict. I sat on the plane fiercely willing and, yes, praying for a specific outcome of that intervention. I knew the direction I wanted it to go. In the midst of my praying I realized that part of my focus was on what this "success" might mean for me. I thought about the write-up. I thought about proving something to several people who seem uncertain about my competency. And slowly, sitting in that plane seat, I felt my face begin to burn. "Why am I doing this?" I asked myself. "For whom?"

The reality is that we are all packages of mixed motives. We have ego needs, legitimate ones of acknowledgment and affirmation and less legitimate ones of wanting the credit and being *the* best. I don't believe it is possible or desirable to get rid of all ego needs. I do believe we need to cleanse ourselves of the competitive and destructive ones. And we need to examine whether there are broader, "beyond ego" kinds of motives leading the way.

Mixed in with my need to prove myself in this intervention and gain recognition was the deep, more altruistic desire for grace to burst into this complex, painful situation that I was asked to join. I wanted the best: God's "will on earth as it is in Heaven" for all those involved.

I sat back in my seat and literally opened my hands. This is what I am bringing. Here are my motives, my ego needs. Empty me of the damaging, grasping ones. Put the natural self-worth ones into perspective. Fill me with the healing, other-serving ones.

I began to relax. This was not my situation. It was not mine to claim victory or defeat. It was not even mine to chart the course.

....

Over the years I have served on the boards of various kinds of peacemaking organizations, as have many of my friends and colleagues. We have lamented, with no small dose of irony, the conflict and tension that often bubbles below the surface, sometimes going unnamed, sometimes named but poorly handled.

How is it, I wonder, that we who promote "a better way" seem to have so much difficulty living it ourselves? Does that compromise our integrity, personal or professional? Indeed, what does it take to be practitioners of integrity? I'd like to venture several interconnected ideas.

A personal, spiritual transformation. Effective peacemaking starts with me and cannot be separated from me. In all of our conflict work, we must be aware of what we personally bring: our personality style, our strengths and vulnerabilities, our temptations to abuse our power, our potential for violence. Adam Curle made this point as convincingly as anyone when he wrote that we need to "dig out the roots of unpeacefulness" within ourselves in order to "have any real effect on others."

It is not enough to do good work, to master the skills and processes, to be self-defined and clear. We are called to personal transformation that is deeply spiritual. We are on holy ground when we walk with those in conflict and that holiness needs to seep up through the soles of our feet and transform us as practitioners, from the inside out. Until we deal with the anger, fear and violence within, we cannot be free and effective without.

This is a spiritual journey, but it is a spirituality of being rather than doing. This is not a call to perfection or even total consistency, which is neither possible nor desirable. Rather it is a call to humility and transparency. To commitment and accountability.

Humility. We practitioners are great at generalities. "We all have conflict." "None of us can apply these skills all the time." "Everyone gets stymied in their relationships sometimes."

But the specifics are tough for us to acknowledge. "I am struggling in my marriage." "I am a church leader in a mess and stuck." "I just completely blew that exchange with my boss." These specific admissions are tough for us because they require vulnerability and because we in the conflict field like to think we're closer to that "arrived" state. Not perfect, but closer.

In reality, we are like the disputants with whom we work. They are petty, self-centered, unreasonable and mean-spirited at their worst. And they are wonderfully tolerant, charitable and forgiving at their best. So are we. We are not a separate category of people, no matter what our calling and no matter how much we have grown. We are only different in the roles we play in a particular situation.

Remembering this is critical. It makes all the difference in how I view those with whom I work. It will keep me humble as I attempt to walk with them.

Transparency. This is very connected to humility but takes it one step further. It means we share with our community, and sometimes even minimally with our clients, our doubts and questions, our missteps and inadequacies. It means we are honest, at least to ourselves, about our various motives. We don't have it all together. We shouldn't pretend that we do.

Commitment. I need to be clear about who I am, about what values I am committed to, about what drives me. While I believe that it is more important to be transparent than to be perfect, transparency in my actions does not give me licence to mistreat people. It *does* matter how I treat people, professionally and personally. If I am not committed to "doing right" in my relationships at all levels and committed to growth and change in these areas, I do not believe I can practice with integrity. This does not mean that practitioners with integrity will never get divorced or have unresolved agenda with a colleague or a church committee. But it does mean these things matter, that we will not shut the door on progress and more transformation, that we will continue trying to walk the talk in all of these relationships.

Accountability. We can't do this alone. The path is too rocky, too tiring, too fraught with temptation to go solo. We need to connect with those who share our values and commitments. We need to set up accountability and support systems. This needs to come in many forms. One of the best forms, I believe, is to work in pairs or teams for intervention and training. It is in cotraining/mediating/facilitating that I have had to directly confront my competitiveness, my need to be seen as competent and expert, my desire to get the credit.

There are other forms of accountability. We can surround ourselves with people who will challenge us on issues of racism, sexism, classism, etc. We must continually invite and welcome critical feedback from those with whom we work. We can make ourselves vulnerable to our faith community or small group, admitting our doubts, our mistakes, our inadequacies, and ask for wisdom and counsel when we encounter the temptations.

Clearly there are expectations upon us as conciliation practitioners that are different than many other professions. Not only do we espouse a set of values antithetical to society, we call people and systems to transformation. We address relationships and people's psyche and their fundamental need for intimacy and connectedness. We are messing with "where people live." This is power.

It is no wonder, then, that we are expected to follow suit, that we are called to treat our own lives and relationships and intimacy needs with the same reverence to which we call others.

It is a daunting reality, one which I both embrace and resist.

–Carolyn Schrock-Shenk
© MCS 1999, from *Conciliation Quarterly*, Vol. 18 No. 1

Assuring Quality

Mediation programs have proliferated in many sectors and a number of organizations have wrestled in recent years with how to assure mediator quality. What *are* the most effective ways to develop and measure mediator competency? What role does mediator certification play? Is there a difference if the process is voluntary or mandatory? . . . if the mediators are community members who donate their time or paid professionals? The recommendations below are excerpted and adapted from a 1995 report by the Society of Professionals in Dispute Resolution (SPIDR) entitled "Ensuring Competence and Quality in Dispute Resolution Practices." On the following page is an earlier SPIDR report excerpt on performance-based standards.

1. The multiple paths to becoming a competent practitioner ought to be recognized, maintained and expanded. Some combination of natural aptitude, skills, knowledge and attributes acquired through an appropriate combination of dispute resolution training, education and experience is the best route to ensuring practitioner competence.

2. Context is a critical factor in determining the type and amount of training required. Where dispute resolution is mandated, programs have a higher responsibility to ensure that the training is thorough and that the competency of practitioners is assured through supervised practice.

3. Education and training programs must incorporate the core theories in addition to practical skills that underlie the basic steps or stages in the dispute resolution process being taught. Training programs should engage trainees in role plays and provide them with direct supervision and feedback during the role plays.

4. Practitioners have an ongoing obligation to upgrade their skills and knowledge and to work within their areas of competence. Competency includes understanding issues related to social justice, equity and diversity.

5. Practitioners should determine whether they possess the necessary skills, knowledge, attributes and cultural awareness required to be effective in a given context.

6. Substantive knowledge is important in some kinds of disputes, and in others is necessary for acceptability to the parties.

7. Institutional policies related to competencies should guarantee diverse panels.

8. Consumers should participate in evaluating the performance of practitioners and programs.

–adapted by Alice M. Price
1995, recommendations adapted with permission of SPIDR

Performance-Based Standards for Mediators

The Society of Professionals in Dispute Resolution (SPIDR) believes that performance criteria (such as neutrality, demonstrated knowledge of relevant practices and procedures, the ability to listen and understand and the ability to write a considered opinion for arbitrators) are more useful and appropriate in setting qualifications to practice than is the manner in which one achieves those criteria (such as formal degrees, training or experience).

Policy makers setting standards for those who may practice as a neutral, programs developing their own criteria for the neutrals they employ or include on rosters and organizations determining relevant information to disclose to parties should consider the following performance criteria:

I. **Skills necessary for competent performance as a neutral [third-party intervenor] include:**
   A. General
      1. Ability to listen actively;
      2. Ability to analyze problems, identify and separate the issues involved and frame these issues for resolution or decision-making;
      3. Ability to use clear, neutral language in speaking and (if written opinions are required) in writing;
      4. Sensitivity to strongly felt values of the disputants, including gender, ethnic and cultural differences;
      5. Ability to deal with complex factual materials;
      6. Presence and persistence, i.e., an overt commitment to honesty, dignified behavior, respect for the parties and an ability to create and maintain control of a diverse group of disputants;
      7. Ability to identify and to separate the neutral's personal values from issues under consideration;
      8. Ability to understand power imbalances.
   B. For mediation
      1. Ability to understand the negotiating process and the role of advocacy;
      2. Ability to earn trust and maintain acceptability;
      3. Ability to convert parties' positions into needs and interests;
      4. Ability to screen out nonmediatable issues;
      5. Ability to help parties to invent creative options;
      6. Ability to help the parties identify principles and criteria that will guide their decision making;
      7. Ability to help parties assess their non-settlement alternatives;
      8. Ability to help the parties make their own informed choices;
      9. Ability to help parties assess whether their agreement can be implemented.

II. **Knowledge of the particular dispute resolution process being used includes:**
   A. Familiarity with existing standards of practice covering the dispute resolution process;
   B. Familiarity with commonly encountered ethical dilemmas;
III. **Knowledge of the range of available dispute resolution processes, so that, where appropriate, cases can be referred to a more suitable process;**
IV. **Knowledge of the institutional context in which the dispute arose and will be settled;**
V. **In mediation, knowledge of the process that will be used to resolve the dispute if no agreement is reached, such as judicial or administrative adjudication or arbitration;**
VI. **Where parties' legal rights and remedies are involved, awareness of the legal standards that would be applicable if the case were taken to a court or other legal forum;**
VII. **Adherence to ethical standards.**

–SPIDR Commission on Qualifications
© SPIDR 1989, excerpted from "The Report of the Commission on Qualifications." Used by permission.

Evaluating Mediators

Evaluation of mediators is difficult. Often there is no good way to get objective feedback. The clients usually do not know enough to offer feedback on the mediator's skills. Bringing in an outside observer may be awkward and, sometimes, makes the mediators more nervous than usual. The simplest way to evaluate a mediator is to evaluate yourself and, if you had a co-mediator, to evaluate your partner.

A word of caution about *evaluation*. For many people evaluation is synonymous with grading and leads to the old anxiety of not passing. I am using evaluation here to mean only this: giving yourself and/or your partner feedback on what worked and did not work in a mediation so that your skills improve. Good evaluation will be reaffirming of all of the successful things you did. Only in this context can most of us be open to hear what we might need to change. The risk of mediating without the discipline of constant evaluation is that one can fail to appreciate the good work one has done, as well as fall into habits which do not help the client.

Here is an outline to guide evaluations. Use it as soon after a mediation as possible so the information will be fresh. Build in fifteen minutes after each mediation to evaluate what happened. This outline has as a premise my belief that disputants need three things to occur in mediation: they need to feel reasonably safe, they need to believe they have been understood and they need to believe that the outcome is reasonably fair. I also think of mediations as having four stages: an introduction; a time to discuss what happened, how people felt and identify the issues which need resolution; a time for creating a solution; and an ending.

Following is an outline for self- or partner-evaluation. Use it to improve the services you provide.

Mediation Assessment Inventory

Introduction
- Did you help the disputants feel comfortable and safe? How?
- Did you clearly explain your role as mediator?
- Did you get each disputant to agree to the rules or expectations for the mediation?

- During the mediation, did you help disputants meet these expectations without becoming too bossy?

What happened
- Did you make sure each disputant said all he or she wanted to say? How did you make sure of this?
- Did disputants say how they felt? Did you have to help them with the expression of feelings? If so, what worked?
- Did you make sure that you understood, and disputants knew you understood, what they said?
- Did you clearly identify what issues needed to be resolved? Did you check this out with the disputants?

Solutions
- Did you refrain from offering suggestions?
- Did you help draw out each disputant's interests when this was necessary?
- Did you help the disputants assess the agreement to insure that all disputants believed that it was fair, workable and specific enough?
- If you became stuck, what skills did you use to help overcome the problem?

Conclusion
- Did you do a good job writing up the agreement? What criteria do you use in assessing the agreement?
- Anything apparently left unsaid as the session ended, and what might you have done about this?

Skills in general
- Did you use active listening skills well, including paraphrasing and summarizing what was said, mirroring feelings and reframing?
- How did you feel during the mediation? How did this affect your ability to mediate?
- If disputants reached impasse, what skills did you use to help them?
- Did you take notes and did this help or hurt you as you mediated?

What else might the mediators have done that would have helped the disputants?

–John Conbere & Associates, Inc.

© John Conbere & Associates, Inc., from *Minnesota Mediator*, March 1995. Used by permission.

Grassroots Qualifications

I am compelled to write this as a response to all this folderol about licensing, credentials and certification of mediators. As the director of a grassroots, community-based mediation center, I generally do not concern myself with the machinations of the "professional" dispute resolution community. However, I have learned that the "professional" community has been discussing matters that could have a profound effect on every grassroots, community-based mediation program in the country.

I am confident though that this is just talk because I am sure the "professionals" would not violate the fundamental principle of conflict resolution which is that all parties with an interest must be included in the discussions. In case I am overlooked, here are my two cents' worth.

Violates Fundamental Principles

The concept of qualification from an intrusive outside entity for grassroots, community-based programs is contrary to the fundamental empowerment principle from which these programs sprang. The thought behind community-based programs is that everyone could and should mediate. The goal of a community-based program is to offer a viable alternative to court. Our belief is that through the management of the program (the board of directors) and the community members acting as mediators, the community becomes empowered.

The community that we service is racially, culturally, socially and economically diverse. Our volunteers come from all walks of life from people who are homeless to an accountant. They are high school dropouts to graduate degree people. Their age range is from 16 to 76. We have devised a mediation process that transcends educational and written skill level. Our mediators resolve interpersonal, intra-family and intra-community disputes.

Training

Mediators attend 16 hours of basic mediation training. Before actual mediation, they receive an additional 4 hours of role play supervised by skilled mediators. Then mediators are required to observe a live mediation. Mediators are evaluated by staff and experienced mediators who make a mutual decision about the new mediator's readiness to mediate. Experienced mediators serve on a panel. Also the panel is balanced along gender, race and age lines.

We have a system that has worked for 11 years. Our initial response to anyone who would try to tell us who could mediate for us, or what disputes we could mediate, would be to challenge their moral right to do so. Our experience and proven track record gives us as legitimate a claim to the crown of "expert" mediator as anyone.

Those of us who have been in this field for longer than it takes to get a J.D. or Ph.D. are very familiar with this dispute. I have ignored it because: 1) there is room for everyone; 2) "professionals" don't want our clients; and 3) I do not have the resources, time or energy to do much about it. I took time to write because of the following incident.

At a recent workshop a young lawyer with her freshly minted cards cornered me and said, "I have a lawyer friend from another city. He said that they let people who are barely literate mediate. Don't you think that gives the field a bad name?" This person was taking her first mediation course.

I do not know who is going to decide what for whom. When it is decided, I will be here working with the community volunteer mediators who in the past week:

1. Convened and facilitated a meeting with representatives from six social service agencies whose client was an elderly widow in danger of being evicted from her public housing apartment;
2. Mediated an inter-family dispute involving a "feud" between two Appalachian families. Both families threatened to resolve the feud by shotgun;
3. Mediated an inter-family dispute where racism was identified as the underlying cause by both parties;
4. Mediated a dispute between a primary school teacher and 50 parents. Physical and emotional abuse were alleged;
5. Began to mediate an intra-family dispute between a terminally ill woman and her ex-husband whom she has not spoken to in 11 years. She wants to plan their son's future collaboratively.

Who other than the parties themselves has a right to judge the effectiveness of the mediations?

My fervent hope is that any "professional" credentiallers whom this article reaches realize that there are many of us who toil in this field and have no desire to be part of your "profession." You are presumptuous to make decisions that will have a dramatic effect on grassroots, community-based programs, either in the short or long term. I challenge your moral and ethical right to do so.

–Daniel P. Joyce

© Conflict Resolution Center International, Inc. 1993, from *Conflict Resolution Notes*, January 1993. Used by permission.

Model Standards of Conduct for Mediators

I. **Self-Determination:** *A Mediator Shall Recognize that Mediation is Based on the Principle of Self-Determination by the Parties.* Self-determination is the fundamental principle of mediation. It requires that the mediation process rely upon the ability of the parties to reach a voluntary, uncoerced agreement. Any party may withdraw from mediation at any time.

II. **Impartiality:** *A Mediator Shall Conduct the Mediation in an Impartial Manner.* The concept of mediator impartiality is central to the mediation process. A mediator shall mediate only those matters in which she or he can remain impartial and evenhanded. If at any time the mediator is unable to conduct the process in an impartial manner, the mediator is obligated to withdraw.

III. **Conflicts of Interest:** *A Mediator Shall Disclose all Actual and Potential Conflicts of Interest Reasonably Known to the Mediator.* After disclosure, the mediator shall decline to mediate unless all parties choose to retain the mediator. If, however, the conflict of interest casts serious doubt on the integrity of the process, the mediator shall decline to proceed. The need to protect against conflicts of interest also governs conduct that occurs during and after the mediation.

IV. **Competence:** *A Mediator Shall Mediate Only When the Mediator Has the Necessary Qualifications to Satisfy the Reasonable Expectations of the Parties.* Any person may be selected as a mediator, provided that the parties are satisfied with the mediator's qualifications. Training and experience in mediation, however, are often necessary for effective mediation. A person who offers herself or himself as available to serve as a mediator gives parties and the public the expectation that she or he has the competency to mediate effectively. In court-connected or other forms of mandated mediation, it is essential that mediators assigned to the parties have the requisite training and experience.

V. **Confidentiality:** *A Mediator Shall Maintain the Reasonable Expectations of the Parties with Regard to Confidentiality.* The parties' expectations of confidentiality depend on the circumstances of the mediation and any agreements they may make. The mediator shall not disclose any matter that a party expects to be confidential unless given permission by all parties or unless required by law or other public policy.

VI. **Quality of the Process:** *A Mediator Shall Conduct the Mediation Fairly, Diligently, and in a Manner Consistent with the Principles of Self-Determination by the Parties.* A mediator shall work to ensure a quality process and to encourage mutual respect among the parties. A quality process requires a commitment by the mediator to diligence and procedural fairness. There should be adequate opportunity for each party in the mediation to participate in the discussions. The parties decide when and under what conditions they will reach an agreement or terminate a mediation.

VII. **Advertising and Solicitation:** *A Mediator Shall be Truthful in Advertising and Solicitation for Mediation.* Advertising or any other communication with the public concerning services offered or regarding the education, training, and expertise of the mediator shall be truthful. Mediators shall refrain from promises and guarantees of results.

VIII. **Fees:** *A Mediator Shall Fully Disclose and Explain the Basis of Compensation, Fees, and Charges to the Parties.* The parties should be provided sufficient information about fees at the outset of the mediation to determine if they wish to retain the services of a mediator. Fees shall be reasonable, considering, among other things, the mediation service, the type and complexity of the matter, the expertise of the mediator, the time required, and the rates customary in the community. The better practice in reaching an understanding about fees is to set down the arrangements in a written agreement.

IX. **Obligations to the Mediation Process:** *Mediators Have a Duty to Improve the Practice of Mediation.* Mediators are regarded as knowledgeable in the process of mediation. They have an obligation to use their knowledge to help educate the public about mediation; to make mediation accessible to those who would like to use it; to correct abuses; and to improve their professional skills and abilities.

—Adopted by ABA, AAA, and Society of Professionals in Dispute Resolution (1995)

A "Code of Professional Conduct," based on these same nine principles, was also adopted by the Colorado Council of Mediators and Mediation Organizations in 1995.

–summarized by Alice M. Price

Confidentiality

Sample Confidentiality Guidelines

Mediation often reveals private information about the disputants. In order to protect the privacy of disputants, all details of the intake or mediation session are kept confidential. Information will not be revealed to anyone other than staff and volunteer mediators without the consent of the parties.

During the opening statement, the mediators reassure the parties that their case will not be discussed with anyone outside of Good Shepherd Neighborhood House. Mediators may find it helpful to take notes during the mediation session; however, all notes should be destroyed at the end of the session. The disputants may discuss the case with whomever they choose unless they agree to do otherwise.

There are a few, limited cases where confidentiality must be broken. These include situations where information regarding child abuse and other serious crimes comes up. These issues are not suitable for mediation and such cases will not be referred to Good Shepherd Neighborhood House. However, information regarding child abuse or felonies may surface during mediation sessions. If this happens, the mediator should:

- Inform the disputants that these issues cannot be mediated.
- As soon as the mediation session is over, tell the mediator supervisor what occurred.
- Contact the appropriate agency (as instructed by the mediation supervisor).

While discussing confidentiality during the opening statement, many mediators include the following statement: "Everything which is said during mediation is confidential, except those areas which by law I would be required to report, i.e., child abuse, serious crimes."

–Good Shepherd Neighborhood House
© GSNH (Philadelphia, PA), from *Mediator's Manual*. Used by permission.

Confidentiality Rules in Flux

With the widespread use of mediation to settle—or attempt to settle—many state and federal court cases in the United States, the once accepted notion of mediator confidentiality has begun to be eroded by judicial mandates to open up mediation processes to court scrutiny. A similar move has been seen within federal regulatory agencies which utilize mediation for both internal and public disputes.

Currently, these issues are being debated and guidelines of various types being proposed. In particular, by 2001, a Uniform Mediation Act (UMA) is expected to be forwarded to all 50 states for possible adoption. The UMA proposes a variety of practice-related rules and ethical standards, including a list of potential confidentiality exceptions. The draft proposal can be found at www.pon.harvard.edu/guests/uma.

–Alice M. Price
© MCS 2000

Intervention from the Inside

"But what you are teaching us doesn't make sense in our organization. As managers we know the individuals in the conflict, and we *do* have power over them," she said. The comment left me groping for a response in a workshop on mediating conflict in the workplace. My initial reaction was to feel slightly irritated—why did she have to complicate my presentation?

I no longer remember the woman's name, or even her face, but I am deeply grateful for her comment. Her words stuck with me and eventually prompted a path of discovery and re-examination in my work. In retrospect, her insight was so obvious. Why did it take me so long to see the pattern that was before my eyes?

I had long known that the way I practiced mediation was a somewhat peculiar artifact of Western society. Sally Engle Merry and other anthropologists have described in detail the dispute resolution customs in traditional societies that inspired North American legal and social reformers as they developed a movement for community mediation in the 1970s.

Merry has done a particularly good job of exposing just how different the North American practices are from the tribal moots upon which they were supposedly built.[1] She points out that traditional mediators in "nonindustrial" societies often occupied positions of power in the community and wielded significant clout (physical, familial, economic, or military) over those in dispute. Moreover, the mediator was not a detached observer from another community but a village or clan member who frequently had an investment in the outcome.

John Paul Lederach has neatly laid out the distinctions between what he calls "insider-partial" and "outsider-neutral" mediators. I found that I did not need to lecture on the differences, that students and workshop participants could easily generate the two columns of the chart once I explained the headings.

When I worked with Native Canadian groups, they could readily identify where the traditional ways of their elders differed from the emphases of white society. The aboriginal uses of talking sticks, circles, elders and the role of clans dovetailed well with Lederach's description of insider-partial peacemaking practices.

After all of this I thought I understood the differences between insiders and outsiders as mediators, and the cultural determinants of when each was appropriate or inappropriate. Then five years ago I was confronted by the woman in the workshop. As I reflected on what she said, I began to understand in a new way that the vast majority of mediation or peacemaking that takes place in Canada and the U.S. on a daily basis fits closely with the insider-partial definition. In the home, the school, the congregation and the workplace, the third-party problem-solvers are often parents, teachers, elders, pastors and supervisors.

These "interveners" have an ongoing relationship with the disputants. Many times they are affected directly by the outcome of the dispute. Often they have influence over the parties or bear some responsibility for the conduct or performance of the people in the dispute.

Why had I been so quick to buy into the outsider-neutral concept of mediation? Was it possible that in fact a great portion of my culture was more in tune with using internal peacemakers than external interveners? I nearly choked one day on the irony when I realized that I had elicited cultural assumptions about handling conflict from Aboriginal peoples, but I had *prescribed* them for my own culture. And why not? After all, I know and

Insider-partial mediator	Outsider-neutral mediator
• Enters dispute through trust	• Enters dispute through functional role
• Legitimacy based on tradition and connections	• Legitimacy based on neutrality, efficiency, and effectiveness
• Qualifications are station in life or role in community	• Qualifications are specialized or academic training, certificates, etc.
• Allows participation of primary and secondary parties	• Limits participation to primary parties
• Process can be public or semi-public	• Privacy and confidentiality seen as essential to success
• Focus is on relationships enabling the social group to function	• Focus is on outcome or settlement

understand my own culture, don't I? No need to use an elicitive approach when with my own people.

As the scales gradually fell away from my eyes, several things came into focus for me. I looked in a new way at the resistance community mediation programs commonly encounter in persuading people who desperately need help to use the program's free services. Maybe the resistance is not just a matter of people's aversion to dealing with conflict or of not understanding mediation. Maybe it has something to do with trying to sell stressed people a model of mediation that does not fit their own intuitions about how a situation should be handled.

I looked again at the hesitation of church groups to invite an outsider into their midst to see and hear the grindings of their internal machinery. Even when they want someone who can stand outside their immediate dispute, they want someone who stands within their experience of faith, and who brings recognizable spiritual resources to the task.

I remembered the times when people asked me to work with their conflict *because* they knew me and trusted me. I thought of the leadership group in the congregation where I worship, the friends whose joint house purchase and intentional community had soured and the roommates who felt they could no longer live together. These were people who had invited me into their pain and confusion because they had a relationship with me and who might never have sought help from a stranger.

Not for a moment would I suggest that all peacemaking should be done by insiders. There are many occasions, particularly when the conflict has escalated to a high level of intensity and groups have become rigidly fixed into either/or camps that outside intervention is essential. I have seen congregational leaders and workplace supervisors become badly wounded when their attempts to mediate foundered. I am still gripped with caution when two friends call and ask if I can mediate the dispute in their business partnership.

But I am beginning to wonder how much of our contemporary penchant for the outsider model has resulted from the self-interested need to create a market for our own services. As the coordinator of a community mediation program for a number of years, I certainly participated in selling an outsider

model. And as someone operating a conflict mediation and consulting business today, I continue to have a vested interest in promoting that model. It is, after all, a model that pays my mortgage.

How do we blend old and new, and provide ways for those who are close to the people caught in a web of conflict to have a valued role? A married couple has come to me recently to discuss an overwhelming conflict in their family. As an outsider I cannot come close to resolving the myriad issues, and they can ill afford to pay for all the time that would be required even if I could. So, I am thinking of convening a circle, comprised of family members, pastor, lawyer, financial advisor, therapist and friends to encourage and enable the people already involved with this family to work together on a resolution to the conflict.

It takes time for a middle-aged dog to learn new ways, but I am excited and energized by my current quest to understand better the roles that insiders can play. I have been talking to friends and colleagues, collecting stories and reading the literature with new eyes.

When I started this quest, a key question for me was, "When is insider mediation appropriate, and when is it not?" As I continued, a series of other questions and observations came to the fore.

Can we learn to view relationship with the parties as a resource rather than as an impediment or something to be minimized?

In one situation, a pastor described how he struggled to figure out what his role should be when he met with two disputing members of the congregation he served. Finally he knew the answer. "I would be their pastor," he writes. Eureka! He is being true to his relationship, maximizing it, not trying to contort it into being anything less or more than what it is.

Trying to work at conflict when we are connected to the people in conflict is fraught with danger.

If conflict is a danger zone, the mediator is a ready target. "The hardest blow of the fight falls on the one who steps between," observes a Scottish proverb. People in conflict can and will engage in hurtful, fighting behavior. When I am an outside mediator, I can suffer attack and humiliation, but after a night or two of sleep and tender words from my wife, the knot in my stomach will unwind and I will be no worse for experience. But if that attack comes from people connected to me, it is a different matter.

It is easy to understand why in some settings the internal mediator represents a powerful position. Such power can be essential if the mediator is to avoid being pummeled.

Moving from a triangle to a circle changes a lot more than geometry.

Interaction in a mediation is frequently depicted in a triangle comprised of a mediator and two individual parties. Bringing in other people such as church or community elders, family members or others affected by the conflict moves the configuration into a circle. The extra people in the circle provide safety, both to the primary parties and to the mediator. The circle shares responsibility for making things right.

Finally and foremost, building peace in one's own setting involves a lot more than skill, strategy and technique.

–Dean Peachey
© MCS 1998, from *Conciliation Quarterly*, Vol. 17 No. 2

It requires having enough self-knowledge and awareness to be a *presence* that helps hurting protagonists transform their relationships without getting sucked into their morass.

Cultivating and working from a spiritual center, and putting as much emphasis on *who we are* as we place on *what we do* is essential. Ron Kraybill wrote in an e-mail conversation, "distinctions between skill and being make modest sense only in Western-ized settings where people are accustomed to focusing on skills and professional status rather than identity." He continued, "In much of the world, who you are, who you are identified with, and what values you represent have vast impact on what you will be able to accomplish."

I now suspect that Ron's statement rings true in *every* part of the world.

[1] A good example is Merry's article "Mediation in Nonindustrial Societies," which has been reprinted in Ken Kressel and Dean Pruitt (Eds.) *Mediation Research*. San Francisco: Jossey-Bass, 1989.

The Illusion of Neutrality

What the parties decide to do is their responsibility. Be entirely neutral at all times.
                                               –labor mediator's advice to an intern

The duty of the churches is to be agents of reconciliation. We must avoid taking sides and be neutral.
                                               –church leader commenting on a community conflict

Yes, one side has launched most of the attacks. . . . But we are trying to make peace here and must maintain our neutrality.
                                               –mediator responding to concerns of negotiating party

Is "neutrality" ever a constructive goal in conflict? I believe the answer is no. Were I able, I would remove the word neutrality from the English language, for it has caused much injury to the cause of peacemaking. It confuses many mediators with a false understanding of their task; it blocks many sincere leaders from acting on their own deeply held principles of justice; it damages the credibility of the entire enterprise of peacemaking in the larger community.

People who try to be "neutral" do so, I believe, because they think that if they want to work for peace they have no alternative. There are alternatives and we shall propose several. But first, consider two objections to the concept of neutrality.

Problems with Neutrality

Neutrality is an illusion: there is no such thing as a detached or objective observer. Natural and social scientists have in recent years come to recognize this as a given. Even if I sit in a corner in complete silence while two people fight, I communicate assumptions or values which influence the situation such as "screaming is acceptable" or "this conflict and the things being agreed upon here are of no concern to others," etc. Rather than pretend to have no values or to be neutral, people seeking to be a constructive presence in any conflict should learn to be reflective about what values motivate them and be open about those values with others.

Another objection to neutrality is that, in the words of Father Albert Nolan of the Institute for Contextual Theology in Johannesburg, "it makes reconciliation an absolute principle that must be applied in all cases of conflict." Neutrality, says Nolan, assumes that all conflicts are based on misunderstandings, that blame lies equally on both sides and that all that is needed is to bring the two parties together and the misunderstanding will be rectified. In truth, Nolan points out, these assumptions are wrong in some conflicts. Sometimes "one side is right and the other wrong, one side is being unjust and oppressive and the other is suffering injustice and oppression. In such a case . . . not taking sides would be quite wrong."

Alternatives to Neutrality

Rather than hiding our values, peacemakers can be explicit about them. After all, we are the ones who call for unusual responses from others. We, more than anyone else, need to be clear and articulate about what motivates us and what others must do if they are to participate in the peace we seek to support.

In a seminal 1974 essay, American conflict practitioners James Laue and Gerald Cormick suggest that any social intervention should be guided by core values of freedom, justice and empowerment. Of these criteria, justice is the primary one since freedom and empowerment are actually pathway values leading to the creation of justice. For Laue and Cormick, "the single ethical question that must be asked of every intervenor in community disputes at every decision-making point in the intervention is: Does the intervention contribute to the ability of relatively powerless individuals and groups in the situation to determine their own destinies to the greatest extent consistent with the common good?"

Thus intervenors must first analyze the conflict in its context and then choose an appropriate response. Laue and Cormick identify five roles commonly played by intervenors:

1. The activist works closely with the powerless or non-establishment party in a conflict. He or she is usually either a member of the non-establishment group or closely aligned with that group.
2. The advocate plays a similar role to the activist and promotes the interests of a particular side. But the advocate remains more detached, serving as an advisor or consultant to the group, rather than identifying with it personally.

3. Mediators "do not have their base in any of the disputing parties and thus have a more general, less party-parochial view of the conflict." The mediator is also "acceptable at some level of confidence to all of the disputing parties."
4. The researcher may be "a social scientist, a policy analyst, a media representative or a trained lay observer who provides an independent evaluation of a given conflict situation. The researcher perceives the conflict in its broadest context and is able to empathize with all positions."
5. The enforcer brings formal coercive power to the conflict. The enforcer is often "a formal agency of social control in the larger system within which the conflict is set—the police or the courts—or perhaps . . . a funding agency or an arbitrator." Though elements of this role appear in many conflicts, one rarely sees it in pure form.

Advocacy as an Alternative to Neutrality

Another alternative to neutrality begins by broadening the definition of advocacy and recognizing that we are advocates of something all of the time, whether we are conscious of it or not. The question is not if we are advocates, but rather of what. From this perspective we can identify at least four kinds of advocacy.

A party advocate takes the side of one party and pushes loyally for its advantage. "My country/my party/my friends—right or wrong." An outcome advocate works for an outcome he or she deems desirable, without regard as to who happens to benefit from this outcome. A process advocate promotes neither party nor outcome, but rather a particular way of deciding things or getting things done. A values advocate champions concepts or principles: democracy, fair play, the rule of law, human rights, etc. Thus peacemakers can choose forms of advocacy that enable them to define a clear perspective without falling into the blind partisanship of party advocacy.

Mediator as Process & Values Advocate

Mediators should view themselves as passionate process advocates. As process advocates we should be clear within ourselves and articulate in describing to others the nature of the processes we facilitate. We should be prepared to walk away decisively, if necessary, from any situation which does not support the values we stand for. Our commitment to justice, freedom, and empowerment will enable us to take a clear and explicit stand on a variety of principles regarding any process which we facilitate:

• *Conduct of participants*: Should respect the dignity and equality of all persons in the negotiations as well as those affected by the negotiations.
• *Parties represented at the table*: No negotiations should proceed without serious effort to involve all parties with a legitimate interest at stake.
• *Negotiator mandates*: Negotiators must hold a genuine mandate to negotiate on behalf of the people they claim to represent.
• *Access of constituencies to decision-making*: Final decision-making power must be in the hands of the people most affected by decisions taken at the mediation table, either directly or through legitimate representation.
• *Access of negotiators to constituencies*: Negotiators must have free access to the people they are representing.
• *Power*: Must be relatively equal if conflicts are to be genuinely resolved rather than merely temporarily suppressed. Mediators must acknowledge the realities of power and recognize that power is a relative and constantly changing phenomenon deriving from many sources. Mediators should analyze carefully the timing of their efforts so as to ensure relatively equal power. They should also recognize and support the necessary role of activists and advocates and be ready to decline to mediate if power imbalances are too high.
• *Problem-solving approaches*: Mediators should be articulate and persuasive in advocating processes of negotiation and decision-making that shift the dynamics of interaction between the parties from simple positional power maneuvering (which only postpone real resolution) to genuine grappling with the legitimate needs of each side.
• *Information*: All parties should have equal access to critical information.
• *Accountability*: A mediator should hold all parties accountable: to other parties at the table in living up to agreements and in being honest about the extent to which they can make binding commitments; also to their own constituencies in accurately and competently representing constituency concerns and interests and in keeping constituencies informed and appropriately involved in the decision-making process.

The challenge for all mature human beings, and peacemakers in particular, is to stand for something, to have opinions and goals and to work constructively for their implementation. We are not neutral, but then what are we? Impartial, fair, principled, committed to the legitimate needs of all. Many words will do, but let us never accept a description that robs us of the heart of our humanity: our identity and our values.

–**Ron Kraybill**

© Centre for Conflict Resolution 1992, from *Track Two*, November 1992. Used by permission.

Questions of Appropriateness

A variety of concerns related to assessing the appropriateness of mediation or other intervention approaches have been addressed throughout this manual. What follows is a typical checklist of "flags" which third parties should seriously consider in evaluating specific cases:

- Do the parties fully understand the process? Have they agreed with all arrangements and ground rules before the process begins?

- Is there information indicating that any of the parties or their family members are in threat of physical danger? If so, has this been reported to appropriate authorities?

- Has there been physical, emotional, sexual or other abuse of power in the relationship? Are any court actions pending involving abuse or other criminal actions between the parties?

- Are there issues of legal competency in decision-making involving any party?

- Is abuse of drugs or alcohol a concern? Other significant mental health problems?

- Do extremes of power imbalance exist which would prevent legitimate negotiation?

- Does a party express fear or intimidation from emotional dynamics?

- Does either party appear to be totally inflexible or otherwise demonstrate bad faith or manipulation of the process?

- Are there issues of accessibility to the process—such as language fluency, developmental limitations, etc.—which cannot be adequately addressed to ensure full and fair participation?

- Are cultural differences so significant between the parties, or between the mediator and the parties, as to challenge the appropriateness of the intervention?

–compiled by Alice M. Price
© MCS 1995

Mediation and Domestic Violence: Two Views

Is mediation ever appropriate to resolve any of the issues between persons where domestic violence has been perpetrated? What follows is two contrasting views.

"No"

There are many who believe that mediation is a viable and reasonable tool for resolving disputes, and who include domestic violence cases as "disputes" which can and should be addressed with mediation. Many practitioners believe that while they cannot mediate the violence, they can mediate other issues, such as custody, visitation and property settlement. Proponents of using mediation say that mediation is "one tool among many" that may be used, that mediation encourages cooperation instead of litigation, community building instead of adversarial proceedings, empowerment instead of being made spectators in a court process—in short, that it is "restorative justice" instead of "retributive justice."

Mediating any situation between partners where abuse has been perpetrated is mediating violence. The victim of abuse walks in fear through every day, even when appearing to be calm and safe. The continual threat of the repetition of abuse functions to keep a victim controlled, as do "reminder" incidents such as smashing a wall, threatening a relative or child, breaking a victim's possessions or talking about suicide, all while invalidating the victim in dozens of subtle and overt ways. Domestic violence is a pattern of behavior in a relationship, not a single act.

An abuser's behavior is, despite common misunderstandings to the contrary, very controlled and calculated to get him exactly the results he wants. Abusers are very different from what they appear to be, and we cannot safely deal with them based upon appearances. They lie, deny, minimize and hide their abusive behavior very creatively.

To use mediation is to subscribe to the mistaken idea that abuse is related to "misunderstandings" or lack of communication. If discussion and compromise, the mainstay of mediation, could help in any way, most domestic violence situations would be resolved long ago because victims of abuse "discuss and compromise" constantly. Mediation assumes both parties will cooperate to make agreements work; the victim has always "cooperated" with the abuser; the abuser never cooperates. A person who has been terrorized by an abuser is not free to participate in a mediation process with him, even if the mediator(s) assume or believe that they "understand." Being truthful about any of her needs or experiences in the abuser's presence or proximity practically ensures that she is in more danger later.

The mediator is left with a no win situation: either the victim's danger is increased, or she is not fully or truthfully participating or both. The well-meaning mediator may actually encourage the victim to feel safe enough to share information that could seriously compromise her safety. In any case the whole intent of mediation is lost. To engage an abuser and a victim in a process that implies equal responsibility is damaging to both. The victim is once again made to feel responsible for the abuser's behavior, and the abuser is allowed to continue to not accept full responsibility for his behavior choices. Any mediated agreement that addresses abuse or other issues when abuse is also present risks supporting abuse: if a contract is predicated upon an abuser's agreement to not abuse or control it must be countered against the victim's agreement to do or not do something. If she "fails" to live up to her agreement he then, in effect, has permission to abuse her.

Helpful and safe domestic violence interventions look to expand the victim's locus of control. When we impose a course of action that we own, be it mediation, couples counseling or other endangering interventions that collude with the abuser, we contribute to her abuse. The mediation or dispute resolution program that cares about justice, fairness and safety will carefully avoid mediating any issue between parties where domestic violence has been perpetrated.

–Rose Garrity
with thanks to Barbara Hart along with Susan Schechter, Beth Richie, Ellen Pence and other foremothers of the movement on furthering understanding of battered women's realities
© Rose Garrity 1998. Used by permission.

"Yes"

The issue of whether mediation is appropriate in cases where there has been spousal abuse is of great concern to mediators, advocates, and policy makers. Historically, women's advocates have deplored mediation and the preferred policy is to excuse domestic violence cases from mediation. The protocol developed by the Oregon Domestic Violence Council states: "Mediation is not an appropriate process for all cases and an agreement is not necessarily the appropriate outcome of all mediation." The State Justice Institute policy holds that (1) where domestic violence is present, past, or feared, the case should be presumed inappropriate for mediation, (2) the screener should recommend the victim against mediating, and (3) mediation shall occur only if requested by the victim, and then only with specially trained mediators and with the option of having an advocate present.

The prevailing concerns are that a cavalier attitude exists regarding domestic violence, that mediators may be mediating the abuse (no hitting if dinner is ready on time), that mediation (and not just an orientation) is being mandated in cases where there is not equal bargaining power, that mediators are not screening for domestic violence issues, that mediators are unaware of the dynamics, and that mediators are not adequately protecting victims. There is additional concern that mediation is too brief to adequately address and counteract the effects of long-term abuse and the socially sanctioned domination of men over women which results in submission, placating, obliging, and accommodating behavior on the woman's part. Finally, there is a strong belief that batterers must be punished and not allowed off the hook in mediation.

In any consideration of whether mediation is appropriate, it is useful to consider the efficacy of the existing options. Any action which automatically denies victims access to mediation, necessarily imposes the legal system which has historically failed battered spouses. Women who leave abusive relationships without their children have been accused of abandoning the children. Women who leave abusive relationships with the children have been accused of hiding the children. Until recently, restraining order requests and violations have not been taken seriously. And women often report feeling revictimized by the harshness of the system. The traditional adversarial process increases hostility and threat as demonstrated in the case of Allen McGuire in Springfield, Oregon who, in November of 1993, killed himself and his daughter after his wife returned home from an appointment with her attorney and told him that her lawyer said he'd never get custody of the child. The legal system has not been shown to be significant in ending the cycle of violence, learning anger management techniques, increasing communication skills, or otherwise empowering both parties of abusive relationships. Batterers' treatment and mediation have been found to make a contribution toward violence reduction. In a study involving over 250 separating and divorcing parents, Desmond Ellis (1995) found mediation makes a greater contribution toward preventing post separation abuse of women by their ex-partners than lawyer assisted negotiations. In addition, the study found women in the mediation sample were more successful in obtaining the amount of child support they wanted than the female clients of the lawyers in the study. Mediation clients made more informed choices than the lawyer clients.

In any consideration of mediation where there has been a history of domestic violence, mediators are asked to consider a triage approach: there are cases which can be mediated with no special considerations, there are cases which should not be mediated, and there are cases which can be mediated with special considerations given to safety and negotiating ability.

–Kathleen O'Connell Corcoran

From the Inside

An Aboriginal Community Responds to Sexual Abuse

The Community Holistic Circle Healing (CHCH) Program, a small First Nations program in the central Manitoba community of Hollow Water, has developed a powerful "insider-partial" process to deal with a deeply painful issue in their own community.

Community leader Berma Bushie and Elder Lawrence Houle describe how, over several generations, the small community of Hollow Water has suffered the dismantling of most of their cultural, governmental and familial traditions by the surrounding dominant culture. About 15 years ago, a group of community leaders gathered to discuss their community problems including patterns of violence such as substance abuse, suicide, property damage, etc. Through a unique community process, they decided to confront the pervasive problem of sexual abuse.

As they began to address this problem, the community leaders worked intensively at healthy team functioning. During the nearly two dozen team training programs, they came to the dramatic realization that most of the team members had silently suffered from sexual abuse themselves.

The breakthrough for the team was to recognize that in order to help their community find justice and healing, they themselves needed to participate in a healing process. Only then could they offer a program to others caught in the cycle of abuse.

The process they initiated uses traditional Aboriginal sharing circles. When a situation of sexual abuse is disclosed, the abuser is confronted in an intense process. There are many people who take part in the sharing circles, sometimes up to 200 or 250. They include the victim, the offender, their families, their support workers, clergy, teachers, professional helpers, elders and a judge representing the legal system. Members from the victim and offender teams facilitate the process.

A feather is passed around the circle as each person speaks. In the first round, people state why they are present. In the second round they speak to the victim, in the third round they speak to the offender, and in the fourth round they make recommendations to the judge about what should happen to the offender. Usually that recommendation includes keeping the offender in the community in order to continue being part of the healing process.

Since the beginning of the project, the CHCH has met with more than 48 abusers and has successfully guided them through the process of healing. Less than five offenders have been handled through the routine adversarial court process which usually results in a prison sentence.

The unique aspect about Hollow Water is that the community itself recognized that need for healing and they realized that for true healing to occur, community members had to find their own solutions to the problem instead of relying on the outside system who were mostly dominant culture folks. This system historically had not provided healing solutions but rather incarceration and a continuation of the cycle of oppression and abuse.

Bushie observes, "The main difference in Hollow Water now is that we can't blame the system, our white brothers, the residential schools. The quality of life in my community is my responsibility. It is a hard message to come to grips with."

"Before you bring in any outside people," she continues, "you first have to make sure the process is controlled by the community and that there is help for the victim and the offender from within. You have to educate the outside system that they are invited to participate but that it is not OK to take over."

The experience of the Hollow Water community has been helpful to us in other settings. When we form a response team, whether it is for training or intervention, we include people who have previous and current relationships with all parties. When such relationships exist, we are better able to develop rapport, assess the situation, design and implement helpful processes and build healthy communities.

–**Barbara Daté and Lorna Monkman**
© MCS 1998, from *Conciliation Quarterly*, Vol. 17 No. 2

Tough Stuff

This is tough stuff—this notion of culture. I'm not sure I have anything to say. Or perhaps more accurately, I don't know how to articulate what I think I'd like to say. It reminds me of my attempts to explain concepts like air and nerves to my three-year-old son, Caleb. They are concepts so fundamental, so encompassing and yet so very hard to grasp. Caleb looks at me with that quizzical, "yeah, right" look and I resort to "When you get bigger, you'll understand better."

Yeah, right.

As I think about my "getting bigger" journey in cultural awareness, many pictures flood my mind. I remember what began as an internal conflict while I was working with a health team during my three years in the Philippines. I had entered that culture with a very well-developed sense of what made a good worker: productivity and efficiency. Both of those elements, however, seemed to completely elude me in the midst of a new language and culture. I concluded that I was therefore not contributing and was likely a burden. Finally I brought up the issue at a staff meeting. I was set straight as forthrightly as their culture allowed and I found myself feeling a bit chagrined when it was over. Of course I had been told that how I related to my teammates and interacted with our clients was what mattered most in Philippine culture. But I didn't really believe it. Surely they wanted my all important work. . . .

Right.

And I remember a memorable argument between an African American woman and an Anglo woman. The presenting conflictual content got lost in the first two minutes and the essence of the argument became process. I finally realized that what the Anglo woman was trying to say was, "I can't hear you if you yell at me." The African American woman was saying, "I can only express myself if I do it with passion" and "Don't you have any feelings about this?" It was an enlightening moment in my cross-cultural learning journey.

Then there is the painful memory of the night Tykie got shot across the street from our house. It was during a shoot-out between an African American gang and a Hispanic gang. I'll never forget the feelings I had those two hours on our front sidewalk while we waited for the body to be taken away. As the tension among those gathered would ebb and flow, I felt completely impotent. I was a trained mediator but my skills and knowledge felt worthless, not only in the face of physical violence but also in the face of two cultures that were still strange to me. My white, middle-class, educated expertise felt like a monkey on my back.

Then, more recently, there was my experience of co-training with John Paul Lederach in the Philippines this last February. By that time I was convinced that culture is foundational to conflict and I was committed to the notion that our role as trainers is to facilitate the process of mining the gold from within that foundation. Aside from dabbling on my own, this was my first real emersion into the elicitive process of training. I came away impressed with the importance of this approach, both in training and in one's approach to all human interactions, especially in multi-cultural settings. It is congruent with one of my mottos: "Our first task in approaching another people, another culture, another religion, is to take off our shoes, for the place we are approaching is holy. Else we may find ourselves treading on someone's dreams; more serious still, we may forget that God was there before our arrival" (Max Warren, Maryknoll 1987). The respect inherent in this approach is absolutely critical.

I also came away impressed with the difficulty of doing elicitive training. Prescriptive training is much easier. Doing elicitive training well means knowing how to helpfully frame the questions, how to listen with a third ear and what to listen for, how to affirm authentically and elicit deeper sharing, how to pull disparate pieces together into an understandable whole, how to identify patterns and models, how to facilitate analysis and evaluation, how to think on your feet and extemporaneously draw on your knowledge, etc. Being convinced about the value of an approach does not make one skillful in using it. It is not easy.

But there seems to be no way around the difficult challenges. As we are moving from the melting-pot concept to one of multiculturalism, our options seem to be finding our way through creatively or blowing up. The choice is ours. And it seems clear to me that we in the conciliation field must help lead the way. It would be a disgrace if the very field that emerged to deal creatively with diversity and to focus on the unique needs and interests of each individual, would not live up to its reason for existing in the whole arena of multiculturalism. Or even worse, if its tight grasp on specific tools, strategies and models would actually serve to further alienate one culture from another.

So we must continue. First and foremost we must examine the cultural makeup of those in the field and begin to address the blatant gaps in diversity. We must each become more aware of our own culture and all that it brings. We must learn to view each of our interactions through the lens of culture, to be aware that there are cultural elements waiting to be noticed and dealt with. We must break out of our homogeneity and learn all we can about cultures different from our own. We must normalize talking to each other about culture and its implications for our interactions.

This is exciting stuff. Yet I am finding that my increasing commitment to explore the role of culture in my conciliation work is exceedingly difficult to operationalize.

One final example reaffirms that. A while ago I was contacted by "Sara" who was interested in pursuing mediation with her supervisors because she believed she had been wrongly treated by them. The supervisors (all men) and most of the staff in this religious organization were from a theologically conservative tradition. The highest position held by a female was Sara's, and she was clear that her gender was the cause of much of the mistreatment.

I worked very hard to bring that case to mediation. An immediate challenge to my commitment to be culturally sensitive was their approach to conflict. It simply should not happen. Traditionally, their desire for peace at almost any cost has seemed to result in sanctioned conflict avoidance and denial.

It was a tedious process that included much listening, empathizing and affirming—as well as biblical principles, moral imperatives, persuasion, and an open examination of their resistance. Finally we began talking about how we might structure the mediation.

The challenge continued however. I had already violated their sense of propriety by bringing the situation into the open and beyond their own circles. It then became clear that I was not a suitable option for a mediator. My gender was problematic. In their theology, leadership was for men and they were not comfortable with a woman at the mediation helm—even with a man as a co-mediator. I expressed my respect for that value as well as my commitment to find suitable mediators.

That commitment became increasingly difficult for me to sustain. Clearly there was already an imbalance of power between the parties. The men were more powerful due to their gender and their positions in the organization. Having a woman mediator who could help empower Sara seemed like a minimum requirement. How, then, could I respond to their need to have only men involved without violating my own commitment to a just process? Additionally, how could I honor their desire to have a "known insider" rather than a "neutral outsider" serve as a third party when their choices were men who shared both their theological views on gender and their approach to conflict?

Somehow, what began as a sincere attempt to be a skillful cross-cultural intervenor, began to feel more and more like coopted justice-seeking. It was not that I knew how justice would look if the situation were to be resolved but it was that I was committed to a process that would allow for the possibility of justice. The longer I worked at it the more muddled it became and I began to feel like I was selling out. Yet who was I to think that I could define a just process for their culture?

I found myself returning to questions I have asked numerous times in other situations: Are there universal values that transcend culture and upon which we in conciliation circles can base our work? Are there norms to which we can hold each other no matter what our class, race, gender, age or other sociological categories happen to be? Is respect a value that transcends culture? Many say that it is. If so, what would respect mean practically in this situation? For Sara? For her supervisors?

I continue to believe that culturally inappropriate interventions in many disputes, even combined with the best of intentions, may actually maintain an unjust situation. Or it may cause even more degeneration. But is it also possible that a culturally appropriate intervention may do the same? What is my responsibility if I believe that being culturally appropriate violates what I believe to be just? Do I just wash my hands of the situation?

I don't know the answers to these and many other culture-related questions. Obviously, I need to continue "getting bigger." It is a prospect that I relish.

–Carolyn Schrock-Shenk
© MCS 1994, from *Conciliation Quarterly*, Vol. 13 No. 3

Chapter 7

Pedagogy

As good teachers weave the fabric that joins them with students and subjects, the heart is the loom on which the threads are tied, the tension is held, the shuttle flies, and the fabric is stretched tight. Small wonder, then, that teaching tugs at the heart, opens the heart, even breaks the heart—and the more one loves teaching, the more heartbreaking it can be. The courage to teach is the courage to keep one's heart open in those very moments when the heart is asked to hold more than it is able so that teacher and students and subject can be woven into the fabric of community that learning, and living, require.

–Parker Palmer

People are resources, not recipients.

–Paulo Freire

The Art and Science of Training: Critical Assumptions

Back in my regular jogging days I occasionally experienced that "runner's high" we've all heard about. I would collapse onto the floor, my exhaustion mixed with a remarkable sense of accomplishment. I would know with complete certainty at that moment that running was what I was meant to do.

I occasionally get a similar trainer's high—a powerful sense of being alive and doing what I know I have been called to do. When I get that high it is always in conjunction with complete emotional and physical exhaustion that is, paradoxically, part of the high.

The occasional highs of post-training however, just as in running, do not substantially affect my pre-training feelings. I often wish the next training were over and occasionally find myself dreading it. I think about all the energy it will take and wonder if I have it to give. I second-guess myself. I harbor a variety of fears, from the minor "Have I over-planned?" to the more unsettling "What if I'm discovered as the impostor I really am?"

Training is hard work and requires heavy doses of passion and compassion. It is both an art and a science. It is a high calling.

Recently, I got a "help, I'm desperate" call from a friend and colleague. Mostly she needed an attentive ear as she talked her way through a tough situation with a co-trainer. As she recounted the events of the first of those sessions, it became clear that she and her co-trainer did not bring the same assumptions or basic values to the training process. Understanding that reality led her to rethink how she would address the problem with him. As we talked, I found myself jotting down some of my deeply held training assumptions:

Transformation. Ultimately, a good trainer is one who understands the significance of the task, both delighting in and treating it with seriousness—even reverence. Within each training event lies the potential for another step in the transformation journey of every person and system represented. The task, then, is to create the space for transformation. Space that invites and blesses both the gifts and vulnerabilities of each person. Space that invites transcendence, light and new truth. Space that invites and celebrates that sense of "ah-ha" we've all had when we've walked away from an experience knowing that we have or are turning a corner. We can never impose or orchestrate change or transformation or even learning. But we can be a catalyst.

Empowerment. Very early in my job here at MCS, I was a participant at a training that was jam-packed with excellent material and facilitated by a very experienced intervenor and trainer. I spent much of that week trying not to drown. I left feeling tired and insecure. Months later I was in another training with a focus similar to the first one. There was a lot of material but the effect on me was very different. I left with a sense of excitement and confidence. This was work I could do if given the chance. I began to assess how I evaluate learning experiences. I began to realize that my unconscious rating of these experiences is directly proportional to the sense of personal validation and affirmation that I experience. If a training draws me out, builds on the best that I am and have, if it somehow validates who I am and what I know, I find it much more successful and beneficial than one that doesn't, no matter how good the input. These elements serve as the glue that allows the new material to stick.

I have realized that this is the basis for John Paul Lederach's elicitive approach and Paulo Freire's belief that "people are resources, not recipients" (*Pedagogy of the Oppressed*, 1970). Truly effective learning builds on the belief that each person both possesses unique, useful truth and has the ability to discover new truth. I smile to myself because I realize that even the process of understanding the importance of elicitive learning had to be learned elicitively.

This realization profoundly affects my training. I do much more participatory and experiential teaching and much less concentrated theory input. The input I do is often built around, or fills in the gaps, of a discussion or the debriefing of an exercise.

I feel less pressure to be the expert. I am working at "learning to learn" in my sessions and to enter in as a partner with the participants rather than setting myself apart. When I can do that it allows me to listen to expertise and knowledge that exceeds mine without feeling threatened. It allows me to hear and learn from negative feedback with much less defensiveness. It allows me to be flexible, to let go of my need to tightly control the agenda, to not fear questions to which I may not know the answer.

I am learning the importance of a positive response to participants' comments and building small pieces of my input on their contribution. This also means some letting go at times. At a recent workshop, one participant several times made a key point I was just about to make. I forced myself to exchange the "I was just going to say that" to "That's a really good point." I was gratified by the observation during the evaluation that I was able to draw much of my "presentation" from them and weave it together in a useful way. I think "weaving" is an appropriate metaphor for training.

Validation is especially important if I disagree with a comment and want to present an alternative view. Just as in interpersonal conflict, I am learning that it is often helpful to invite the person to elaborate. In so doing I find that my initial disagreement is generally less strong and there are pieces that I can affirm and build on before adding something like "one danger that comes to mind is. . . ." Sometimes "just" accurately paraphrasing a comment is enough for the speaker to feel heard and affirmed before I proceed to share an alternative view. Body language that is inviting and responsive is also important in a training just as in interpersonal relationships.

Community Building. Michelle LeBaron notes (see the following article) that "conflict resolution processes function in community and need to be experienced in community." Not only do they "need" to happen there, but the most enduring learning happens in community where a high level of trust and safety has been built, where risk and vulnerability are both expected and respected.

Building community is important because of what it models. The fact that an element of community can be built among diverse people in the space of hours or days is itself both a microcosm and a symbol of the kind of world we hope we are helping to build "on the outside." This means that intentional community building is not tangential but central to the training experience. It can include a host of things, from the general "invitational atmosphere" to specific experiences such as structured sharing times, worship, playing or eating together and small group work. Community-building is also a natural result of the "right brain" kinds of activities such as storytelling, roleplays, sociodramas, sculpture, graphics and drawing, light-and-livelies, songs, metaphors and the use of humor.

Modeling. This may be the most critical and most difficult value. Again LeBaron says it well: "Nothing can enhance the impact of well-conceived and delivered training more than a trainer whose life is clearly lived in accordance with the espoused values of conflict resolution. Nothing can detract

more than one who is not." This does not mean that the call of a practitioner is to a kind of syrupy perfection—a robot lit up with holy lights. Rather the call to "being" and "modeling" is a call to sincerity and transparency. It means being in touch with my emotions, embracing them and seeking to understand them. It means recognizing my inadequacies, doubts and fears, and being honest about them. It means being ready to admit when I've "blown it" and then picking myself up with grace and humility. It means being able to laugh at myself.

It is also a call to reverence deeply the personhood of the other, their gifts, needs and vulnerabilities. It means that I try to listen deeply and seek to find "that of God" in the other, even in those who lash out with ferocity or seem completely unlovable.

Co-training is an important symbol in and of itself. Additionally it presents perhaps the best opportunity for modeling collaboration and other values foundational to our work. It gives opportunity for openly supporting, affirming and building on each other and even working through disagreements together. In short co-training is an opportunity to model power sharing rather than competition, granting credibility to the message of the training.

One memorable co-training experience found me and "Allan" becoming increasingly competitive as the training progressed. Rather than deal with it, either privately or publicly, we both found passive-aggressive ways to gain the "upper hand," to prove that each of us knew more and was more competent than the other. We were "good"—both sharp and subtle—but we didn't fool the participants. They named it openly during the evaluation (we had the good sense to own it) and, in hindsight, I'm clear that it interfered with both the learning and the sense of community, possibly more dramatically than we can know. We have worked together since and have put lots of hard work into openness, mutuality and accountability. It has unquestionably increased our effectiveness and we have grown in the process.

As conflict resolution trainers, we have both training expertise and knowledge of our field. We need to continue developing both. Lederach says it well, "The key issue . . . from the perspective of popular education is how to create a process that is consistent with the outcome goals of empowerment and transformation that the educational project purports to achieve" (*Preparing for Peace*, page 27).

–Carolyn Schrock-Shenk
© MCS 1995, from *Conciliation Quarterly*, Vol. 14 No. 4

Trainers as Tools for Transformation

The plain fact is that the planet does not need more successful people. But it does desperately need more peacemakers, healers, restorers, storytellers, and lovers of every kind. It needs people who live well in their places. It needs people of moral courage willing to join the fight to make the world habitable and humane. And these qualities have little to do with success as our culture has defined it.

–David Orr, *Earth in Mind*

Successful Trainers

The qualities Orr lists have a great deal to do with success in the world of conflict resolution training. We engage in a dance of change with participants as we explore those patterns that keep us at a distance and determine what we can do to close the gap. As conflict resolution trainers, we are tools for transformation, engaging the deepest part of ourselves in the enterprise. Our brothers and our sisters are those who work toward similar or related ends: the diversity and anti-racism trainers, those who help build communities, those who create zones of peace through advocacy and multi-track diplomacy. Together, we bring passion, faith, respect, experience and an understanding of the importance of congruence, of "walking our talk," to our work. It is these elements that I see woven through the diverse approaches of the trainers who have touched me most deeply and influenced my work.

This article draws from real and imagined conversations among us as conflict resolution trainers about what moves us to do this work, about how we image it and what meaning we attach to it. It is about commonality. For the curious, there are countless articles about differences in approaches to training in journals devoted to training methodology and philosophy. This exploration peeks beneath this literature to the stuff of which the friendships and respect that connect us as trainers are made. It is an inductive exploration of where the shining trainer goes for inspiration and ignition; of the vision that sustains us. I offer it in the hope that these words will speak to the cleric and the humanist among us, for good trainers cover the spectrum of spiritual beliefs.

Agents of Change

Often, we see our work as more than a job; it is our passion, a focus that encompasses the personal and professional in our lives. We are motivated by the desire to create and sustain a better world through conveying skills and hope, and we are children-of-the-sixties-in-spirit, believing that we can make a difference. Our work brings us inevitably into contact with the profound; it has to do with the construction of meaning, with relationship and with the too-often unplumbed human capacity for change and transformation.

Training is about change. It is about the acquisition of knowledge and skills, but it is more than that. We invite participants in our training to examine their conflict-related behavior and to entertain a paradigmatic shift from an adversarial, competitive mode to a cooperative, problem-solving mode. We offer the vehicle of authentic and safe exploration within the training setting. We offer a chance to change the flow of the river; to challenge the destructive effects of conflict. In countless conversations, I have heard trainers, teachers and consultants in conflict resolution remark on the way that this work turns the heads of participants, and ultimately touches hearts.

The best conflict resolution training is never the one-way dissemination of information. It envelopes everyone involved, and draws on the best that everyone involved can bring. One metaphor we can use for our training role is midwifery. Like the midwife, we are bridging worlds. To do this well, it is essential to cultivate self awareness, without which sensitivity to cultural and world view differences is impossible. This self awareness involves asking ourselves questions about the roots of our commitment to this work, how we define success in training, what values we model in training, which personal interests we seek to fulfill in training, and how we can devise frameworks for training that will become crucibles for the emergence of authentic voice, both our own and the participants'. It is through exploring and knowing the answers to these questions that we can engage freely with participants. Knowing and trusting ourselves and others allows us to let go of the need to control, of the ego-involvement that stands as a barrier to authentic dialogue.

Dialogue

The best training invites dynamic dialogue, for only through dialogue can the ideas presented be tested, adopted and integrated. Conflict resolution processes function in community and need to be experienced in community. As trainers, we seek to create a safe community within the training setting where vulnerability, risk-taking and reality-testing can coexist. We seek to create an environment for critical analysis, described by Freire this way: "Born of a critical matrix, dialogue creates a critical attitude. It is nourished by love, humility, hope, faith and trust. When the two poles of the dialogue are thus linked by love, hope and mutual trust, they can join in a critical search for something. Only dialogue truly communicates" (*Education for Critical Consciousness*).

When the threads of dialogue and faith run through our work, we know that there is no one formula that will work for all people in all settings. We seek to embody flexibility and the facility to smoothly modulate ideas into different contexts. Many of us are deeply concerned with tracing the natural course of resolution efforts in the cultural and/or professional setting of our participants, jointly examining old maps and creating new maps. It is this marriage of the resources and experience we bring with the wisdom and insight of the participants that makes our work so exciting. It is the integration of the synthesis into lived experience that makes it real.

Trainers who have ongoing practices in the area in which they train bring a richness to the process that cannot be brought any other way. It is not just the stories that can be told and the connections that can be drawn from theory to practice, from research to application that make this true. Trainers who use the skills and the knowledge they seek to convey bring a unique depth and appreciation for the skills in the often messy and unruly reality in which we live. Because they live the skills, they know the blind alleys, the pitfalls and the pinnacles along the way. In short, there is congruence between the material they present and what they do as professionals.

We are best able to act as effective midwives when we are congruent in all facets of our lives. Congru-

ence in this sense refers to modeling the values and the skills espoused within the training setting. But the importance of congruence extends beyond the boundaries of the training setting and even the professional setting. It relates to the alignment of our thoughts, beliefs, values and actions. Nothing can enhance the impact of well-conceived and delivered training more than a trainer whose life is clearly lived in accordance with the espoused values of conflict resolution. Nothing can detract more than one who is not.

This can be seen clearly in co-training situations. Participants in training pick up both the messages conveyed through lecture, demonstration and exercises and the meta-messages. If the trainers are not seen to be working together with faith in each other and in the participants, if there is tension between them or within them, this will negatively affect the training experience. In some cases, it will interfere so powerfully that the intended message is significantly undermined.

I am reminded of a training I observed where the differential treatment of male and female participants by the male presenter became such a preoccupation for the women in the class that they stopped listening to the substance of lectures. Women felt minimized and objectified in class discussions and interactions, and gradually began to participate less and less. At breaks, a pattern developed of several women clustering together to discuss the latest instances of differential treatment and how to respond. These women began to speculate about the nature of the trainer's relationships with women outside the training setting. Like it or not, we do not leave ourselves at the door when we don our training hats. And neither do participants. In this case, the value of respect for all participants, though espoused, was undermined by the presenter's behavior. The lack of congruence between the presenter's expressed views and his behavior made it unsafe to risk engaging in real dialogue.

Beyond Dialogue

Engaging in authentic dialogue is a process that uses more than our rational selves and longs for more than our words. We engage our creative and visioning capacities when we focus high quality attention on our partners in dialogue. To honor and "ground" the experience of dialogue, ritual and the use of nonverbal media are helpful. Music is one form that is particularly potent. Music, a powerful metaphor for both conflict and harmony, can be used to "frame" and set a climate for reflective time; it can be used to mark transitions, to enliven or to diffuse. It can be a vehicle for sharing and appreciating cultural difference. Silence, too, is a powerful tool for grounding and integrating.

It is with the idea of authentic dialogue in mind that I have moved away from the use of pre-devised roleplays in my training. Increasingly, I am convinced that the power and authenticity of lived experience is a far richer ground for sharing than the scenarios I can devise, however clever. In multicultural environments (and all environments are multicultural in one respect or another), this has the added advantage of not inviting participants to share their stereotypes of other groups through uncomfortable portrayals of characters.

This relates to the significance of using the whole self in the training enterprise. Activities such as sculpting (where participants physically arrange themselves to show relationships and patterns of conflict behavior, allowing for experimentation and "trying on change" when the arrangements are shifted) and the third chair technique from counseling (where the participants actually change chairs as part of an activity, signifying becoming another and truly "sitting in their chair") have extraordinary impact. Shifting out of the focus on the verbal, overwhelmingly the medium of choice for U.S. American trainers, can facilitate the engagement of other resources of the self including the creative energy that flows when pain or long-held patterns are released.

Ripples

There are times when as a trainer I have been nervous. There are times when I have been acutely aware of being on stage. But it is when I lose myself in the process, when I work with the higher energy that guides me to a true joining with the participants that the real potential is tapped. The focus becomes reciprocal curiosity and respect for the indigenous wisdom, intuitive common sense and experience of all participants. It is when the balls in which are wrapped our world views are rolled together through dialogue that this joining can occur.

But even with all of the idealism we carry, we still pause to ask why do we do what we do. Picture the conflict resolution trainer: logging many hours on airplanes; eating at irregular intervals; missing her or his family; preoccupied with unreliable photocopiers and computers that crash with the latest version of the training materials, not backed up. We stand before the participants in all of our humanness, knowing often that we are setting out together to accomplish a six month job in six days. We draw on our experience, on the powerful connections of research and theory to practice, and we draw on our hearts. The secret we will never fully know in its entirety keeps us doing what we do: the secret of where and how far the ripples of the impact of the training extend.

–Michelle LeBaron
©MCS 1994, from *Conciliation Quarterly*, Vol. 14 No. 4

Prescriptive/Elicitive Training

John Paul Lederach has articulated the distinction between training approaches which impose (prescribe) a conciliation model and the trainer/mediator's knowledge, and approaches which draw out (elicit) the common sense knowledge of the trainees/disputants in order to facilitate the creation of new, culturally appropriate models.

This diagram contrasts the "pure" prescriptive and "pure" elicitive approaches. As Lederach stresses, all training and intervention falls somewhere between the two extremes, and much of the efforts at the prescriptive end of the spectrum would be more empowering—helpful in the long-term—if they had a more elicitive orientation.

–MCS Staff

Prescriptive   Elicitive

←——————————————————————————————————————→

Prescriptive	Elicitive
Training as transfer	Training as discovery and creation
Resource: Model and knowledge of trainer	Resource: Within-setting knowledge
Training as content-oriented: Master approach & technique	Training as process-oriented: Participate in model creation
Empowerment as learning new ways and strategies	Empowerment as validating/ building from context
Trainer as expert, model and facilitator	Trainer as catalyst and facilitator
Culture as technique	Culture as foundation and seed bed

–John Paul Lederach
From *Preparing for Peace: Conflict Transformation Across Cultures* (Syracuse UP, 1995). Used by permission.

I hear, I forget.
I see, I remember.
I do, I understand.
–Chinese proverb

Conflict management trainers face two very different challenges. First, they must understand both how people learn *and* how learning is transferred to "real life" application, i.e., how do people *remember under stress*. Second, trainers serve in the vanguard of a paradigm shift: nurturing fundamental change in how people handle conflict, manage difference, and accommodate diversity. Reversion to old methods for handling conflict exerts an enormous pull even for experienced conflict managers, let alone for new trainees. To ensure maximum transference and minimum reversion, training content and structure need thoughtful design.

Developing the Training

Experiential Training Theory. Developmental learning theories hypothesize that learning follows a sequence: *experience→reflection→new understanding→new experience.* The principal task of the trainer is to provide opportunities for experience, reflection and new experience to ensure that understanding emerges and "locks in" before the workshop ends. The best training offers both theory *and* practice ("experiential activities"), followed by *equal* time for reflection and feedback.

Matching the Training to the Client. John Paul Lederach suggests that trainers become students of those they will train. In other words, the ideal workshop should reflect the needs, culture, and conflict management traditions of the individual client. During the design phase, trainers are responsible for familiarizing themselves with participants' culture(s). Key questions to ask include:

For all conflict management trainings:
- Who are the participants (e.g., religious; professionals; adults, youth, or intergenerational)?
- What are participants looking for (e.g., professional development, introductory overview, skill development, help resolving actual disputes)?
- What are the dominant values/culture/gender of participants?
- What is the education/experience/skill level of participants?

Additional questions for a specific group or organization:
- Who will or needs to be at the training?
- Why will participants be present (voluntary, mandatory, continuing education)?
- History of resolving conflict (church/business splits, forced resignations of top leaders, employee discipline/transfers)?
- Level of participation at primary organizational meetings (e.g., congregational meetings, shareholders meetings, faculty or staff meetings)?
- History of making decisions (hierarchical, collective, identified or hidden leadership)?

Once the information has been elicited, analyze and USE IT! Even general training "blueprints" can be customized. Pattern roleplays to reflect the client's circumstances (but be careful about using existing conflicts in training). Alter emphasis or language. (See the elicitive/prescriptive spectrum on the previous page.)

Organizing the Training

Physical Set-up. Great workshop content can rarely overcome poor facilities, lousy set-up, and inattention to basic comfort. Treat participants as invited guests. As host, the trainer is responsible for assuring a welcoming and comfortable place of work. Consider:
- Privacy (noise levels from adjoining areas; ability to work without interruption)

- Space size and flexibility (break-out areas for small group work; walls for hanging charts; smoking area; places to relax during breaks; movable chairs and tables)
- Environmental comfort (lighting and sound; heating and cooling; access to outdoors and fresh air; comfortable chairs and writing space; accessibility for the disabled; restrooms)
- Refreshments (don't skimp and be creative—try fresh fruit and vegetables, tart and tangy hard candies, good-quality coffees/teas/juices, fresh-baked cookies and pastries; water)
- Maintenance (rules on smoking and eating; daily outside or participant clean-up crew)
- Seating arrangements (circle or U-shape; single or double rows; maintain good sight-lines)
- Equipment (availability and technical support; set up and test-run equipment ahead of time)
- Supplies (name tags, paper, pens, markers, manuals, handouts)

Using Co-Trainers or Going Solo. Determine whether or not the use of a co-trainer would be appropriate. Financial considerations, group size and length of the training will be key factors, but also consider the added value that a co-trainer brings to the process:
- Balance (gender, ethnicity, race, age)
- Variety of working/teaching styles
- Sharing of tasks, mutual support
- Better observation and work with individual participants and small groups
- Model cooperative problem-solving, teamwork and conflict management

Group Size. Determine optimum group size for the type of training to be provided. Be firm in setting limits on numbers of participants. Groups of 15-20 are ideal for highly interactive trainings. Groups of 50-100 allow for far less experiential learning opportunities. Groups of 20-50 can be more or less experiential depending on the number of co-trainers and the facilities.

Publicity. Well-designed and thoughtfully-distributed publicity goes a long way toward ensuring a successful workshop. Let knowledge of the potential participant pool guide both design and distribution. Use quality materials and attractive graphics. Give clear information on:
- The nature and scope of the training (what, when, where, how long; identity and qualification of trainers)
- What participants can expect and what is expected of them (agenda or objectives; methodology to be used, e.g., lecture, role plays, multimedia, interactive techniques)
- How to prepare for the training (what to wear; what to bring; advance readings)
- Cost (training and materials; scholarships or sliding fee scale; deposits and refunds)
- Application requirements (minimum prerequisites; deadlines; contact persons)

Role of the Trainer

Learning new conflict management skills is emotionally demanding work, requiring trial and error in the arena of interpersonal relations. Consequently, the primary task of the trainer is to establish an environment within which participants feel safe to work. While content expertise is important, no trainer has all the answers in conflict management. When trainers are open about personal challenges in managing conflict, participants are more likely to risk trying new skills. Thus, the trainer's goal is not so much to impart knowledge as to empower participants to risk change. For such purposes, experience and skill in facilitating groups is essential. Key tasks include:
- *Managing the Agenda.* Honor the agenda; if more time is needed, negotiate changes with co-trainers and participants. Use time limits to generate necessary pressure for exercise objectives; short time limits often produce the most meaningful training work.
- *Giving Clear Instructions.* Make sure all participants understand purpose, guidelines, and directions for all activities and exercises.
- *Guiding the Reflection Process.* The skillful facilitator uses thoughtful questions to highlight, understand and build on the unique experiences of each participant.
- *Recording Group Work.* Recording key events and concepts on wall charts provides a common lens through which to view the training, producing group memory for all to share.

- *Monitoring Group Dynamics.* Trainers must be keenly attuned to the group, and be able to adjust and improvise as the situation demands. Modeling good conflict management by openly acknowledging process or participant problems and dealing with them nondefensively is critical.
- *Dealing with Difficult Participants.* Prepare *in advance* for participants who monopolize discussions, refuse to participate, or heckle and disrupt. Responding with confidence and grace provides security for the group, and helps ensure that everyone participates fully.

See also, "Overview of Group Facilitation" (p. 218) and "Dealing with Unhelpful Comments" (p. 222).

Training Tools and Techniques

Audiovisual. As the Chinese proverb suggests, seeing is foundational to remembering. Audiovisual aids help participants "see" what they are learning. By varying the pace and tone of the training, such aids also help maintain group energy. Commonly-used audiovisual techniques include: overhead transparencies, newsprint, handouts, slides, videos, charts, and music. To make visual aids effective:
- Keep text simple and readable; writing on flip charts should be 1" tall for every 15' from audience; for overheads use 24-point type or larger and limit text to 6 lines of 6 words.
- Reduce information to visual images, e.g., flow charts, graphs, tables, models, diagrams.
- Use pictorial images to enhance written text.
- Have equipment completely cued and in place before the training starts.
- Use overheads for larger groups and flip charts for smaller groups.
- Alternate marker colors when writing on flip charts or overheads.
- Preview videos and break every 10-15 minutes for discussion. Give viewers something to look for as they watch. Use a large screen or several monitors.

Interactive. Experiential activities teach in "real time" rather than through the condensed learning of lecture or reading. Commonly-used techniques include: roleplay, skill practice exercises, tableau/sculpting, and games. Be clear on the goal of each interactive exercise and assure that it fits a particular group. For example, activities or games requiring physical contact may not be appropriate, especially early in a workshop. Always allow participants to opt out of an exercise. Remember that when participants rehearse new skills and strategies, the mind does not distinguish between artificial and real-life experience. In both, participants must take risks, use intuition, and draw on prior experience and knowledge. In both, participants emerge changed.

The primary learning in experiential activities is not so much in the "doing" as in the debriefing *after* the exercise concludes. Reflection allows participants to examine their behavior during the activity, obtain immediate feedback, pinpoint lessons, and then try alternative approaches a short time later in another exercise. Successful debriefing requires trainers to:
- Set aside between one-quarter and one-third of total training time for reflection and debriefing.
- Select the appropriate feedback method, e.g., Q&A, round robin (brief comments from everyone), whip around (one-word "feeling" responses from everyone), small group sharing.
- Thank participants for taking part in the activity.
- Focus assessment by reminding the group of the exercise's original purpose.
- Encourage participants to ask questions and acknowledge personal feelings about the exercise, support others, and suggest improvements in the activity.
- Affirm good effort while gently suggesting challenges raised by the exercise.
- Keep the group process moving and on task while still monitoring individual coping.

For discussion and sampling of particular techniques, see the following articles in this chapter and "Practice Cooperation Skills" (p. 136), "Anger and Conflict" (p. 142), "Practice Exercises for Reframing" (p. 186), "Handling Difficult Situations Exercise" (p. 198), and "Training Exercises for Group Process Facilitators" (p. 233).

Training Structure and Pace

Sequencing. Sequencing and pacing can make or break a workshop. Pay close attention to the following when developing the training agenda:

- Vary presentation style (spoken, written, audiovisual, interactive, musical, dramatic), length (intersperse short and longer pieces, use breaks and hands-on activities to vary pace) and intensity (follow complex or emotionally draining work with light 'n livelies or breaks).
- Repeat key points; integrate the training by frequently referencing previous segments.
- Structure components to progress from easiest to most difficult, from general to specific, and from content lecture to experiential activity (although it may sometimes be more effective to use an activity *first* followed by discussion of relevant theory).
- Use breaks or light 'n livelies to avoid the mental fatigue and information overload that are real dangers in the intensive learning environment of a workshop.
- Pace interactive activities from less to more intense. Early exercises should concentrate on team-building and communication. Allow time for group trust and cohesion to develop.

Basic Building Blocks of a Training Agenda. Certain components should be part of every training agenda. Be *realistic* about the time each segment will take. Plan ways to make up time if a particular segment runs long.

- *Welcome*. Set the tone with a strong introduction. Welcome participants and give them a brief preview of objectives and anticipated benefits. Assure them of confidentiality. Encourage participants to help shape the workshop through questions and dialogue. Encourage them to avoid post-training "brain drain"—loss of 64% of what is learned within 24 hours and 98% within one week—by reviewing written materials at least 6 times post-training to internalize the information.
- *Introductions/Ice-Breaker*. Select a method to have participants introduce themselves and "break the ice." Glean samples of participant expectations, and suggest how they will be addressed.
- *Meditation/Warm-Up*. Gather and focus group energy. In shorter trainings, meditations can be incorporated into the "Welcome." In multi-day workshops, participants can be asked to provide a meditation or warm-up.
- *Light 'n Livelies*. Plan activities to enliven the group and create *esprit de corps*, especially after lunch or following an intense interactive exercise. In a multi-day training, participants can be responsible for selecting and leading such activities.
- *Evaluation*. Solicit overall workshop evaluations. Try written forms, an oral round-robin "check-out," a "graffiti" sheet for informal comments/moans/cheers, or a "sounding board" (small group chosen to provide feedback for the group). For multi-day trainings, short daily evaluation is an invaluable tool for staying on top of group dynamics.
- *Wrap-Up/Conclusion*. Don't skimp on the wrap-up! Prepare a short conclusion to ready participants for closure and departure. Create a training capstone through participants' brief sharing of "memorable moments" or challenges for future growth.

Follow-up and Support. Training value is enhanced and learning transference maximized by good follow-up. One or two months after the workshop, contact participants or the client to find out if the workshop is making a difference, if further training is desired, or if other support is necessary. Personal follow-up is particularly critical after a private training, such as for a congregation, school or business entity. Mailings can be used effectively after public workshops.

–Kirsten Zerger
© MCS 2000

The Power of Games

From the age-old "Follow the Leader" to complex simulation games like Star Power, games are powerful tools for transforming a group. Left-brain instruction gives way to right-brain experiential learning as participants see, feel and move through activities that bring out valuable lessons.

The Power to Energize

My first experiences with games in a training setting consisted of physical activities designed to keep participants awake in a warm room after too big of a lunch. We would do stretching exercises or play Upset the Fruit Basket as a diversion from the more tedious training session. Begrudgingly, the facilitator would then call us back to work, which meant sitting down again to take notes based on more formal input.

In this sense, games have the potential to enliven a group, to break the monotony of other teaching forms. Just as recess does for children, games in a training both allow participants to physically sit longer and increase their concentration on a given subject. In addition to getting the juices flowing, games can draw a group together through spontaneous laughter and play. A heavy debate takes on less weight as everyone freely dashes across the room seeking an empty chair. People invariably express themselves freely in these games, allowing others to see parts of their personality previously unknown.

While strengthening a training workshop, this type of play has limited application, in that it is primarily a diversion or energizer for the group, not a teaching tool in itself.

The Power to Teach

Gradually I began to see how games could have a teaching quality to them. This came by coincidence at first, as participants would jokingly draw a connection between a silly game and the topic of the session. For example, "If only we could move as quickly through conflict as we did in Upset the Fruit Basket."

I am indebted to the Alternatives to Violence Project (AVP) for opening my eyes to the world of play as a powerful tool for teaching. In cold dark New York prisons I felt barriers drop as educated and illiterate inmates came together on the level playing field of games. Posturing over who was the most eloquent disappeared as people lost themselves in play. Learning became a joy, not a task. Standing shoulder to shoulder with inmates, I clasped the hands of my partner across from me as we together braced for 250-pound Charles to come flying off the end of a picnic table. As twelve of us simultaneously cradled Charles to a safe landing, we inadvertently screamed at our accomplishment.

The games allowed each of us to return to the innocent child within, the playful side free of inhibitions and prejudices. From these enjoyable activities valuable insights naturally came into our consciousness as we returned to our seats. Losing (or gaining) ourselves in play pulled us together. We came as strangers; we left as committed friends. The transforming power of AVP workshops is tied to the strategic use of games and play.

But it was only as we began to debrief and reflect on a game did the power to teach come alive. Facilitators carefully helped participants link an activity to a previous discussion, for example, on violence and nonviolence. As people commented, a scribe would summarize the point on the flip chart, "It doesn't matter if one person is stronger than another when we all work together to share the load." Natural observations from a game evolved into profound concepts for deep reflection. Rather than limited head knowledge, participants walked away with strengthened values, greater confidence in themselves and the group, and practical principles for daily living.

Games also provide the opportunity to practice communication and conflict resolution skills without the sense of performing that comes with roleplays. Touchy subjects too difficult to confront head-on can be brought out through a game. AVP trainers often assess a group during a break and introduce a game to work on a problem facing the group.

In one workshop, different colored dots were placed on the foreheads of each participant while they kept their eyes closed. As they opened their eyes and silently grouped themselves according to color, people became keenly aware of what it feels like to be in the majority, minority or a token. The discussion that followed included persons sharing about their feelings of rejection from the rest of the group.

The danger of using games to teach is that some participants may want to extrapolate too much out of one activity. Stretching conclusions to fit one's former prejudices can also happen. These drawbacks are often overcome through the frank dialogue that accompanies the reflection period.

The Power to Heal

In addition to teaching salient points, games can be powerful tools for healing and reconciliation among persons in conflict with one another. Increasingly, I see the need to bring opposing groups together in such a training setting to encourage the transformative process.

Participation in games by members of both sides of the conflict broke an impasse in post-war El Salvador. Under the United Nations brokered peace plan, former guerrillas and right-wing government councils had to arrive at a unified plan before their municipality could receive reconstruction funds. On their own they could not even meet together, due to the resentment and hatred resulting from twelve years of war.

In highly structured workshops facilitated by Salvadoran training teams, these polarized groups came together at a neutral site. From the opening name game to the final working session, playful games provided the oil that lessened the friction between them. Weeping and laughter filled the same session as serious reflection took place over what had seemed simply a silly game.

In these workshops, musical chairs soon became one of the most popular and most healing games. Played first in the traditional competitive way, eliminated players watched on the sides as a few aggressive players fought to be the player in the single chair at the end. Without debriefing, players reassembled the chairs and played again, only this time eliminating chairs but not people. The first time the music stopped, 20 players pushed and shoved to sit on 19 chairs. They could not go on until everyone was seated. Throughout successive rounds, as more and more chairs were removed,

the players gradually learned to hold one another rather than push to find a seat. Competition gave way to cooperation. They burst into laughter as everyone tried to pile on laps with two people straddling the last chair.

Reflection on this exercise evoked strong emotions about the limits of competition and the value of cooperation. Participants compared the two rounds to two earlier brainstorming sessions about what is violence and what is nonviolence. A turning point occurred as one former guerrilla said, "We just went through 12 years of the first way with no winners. What would it be like to go through 12 years of cooperation?"

By the end of the three-day seminar, one could no longer distinguish between participants from the right and the left. Whereas in the first few games they consciously tried only to interact with those from the same side of the war, in the end they actively engaged themselves without a second thought about the person with whom they were matched. They came to the training saying, "We can't talk to them." They left committed, saying, "The only way to a peaceful future is together with them."

While games provided the tools for breaking through thick walls of hatred, there are clear dangers to using them with polarized groups. A poorly selected game may be too risky, driving participants away. An exercise can also trigger deep personal losses that might be difficult to process in the group setting. Play can also bring out personality traits that might reinforce negative stereotypes. Likewise, the feel-good experience of a workshop does not translate into resolution of real conflicts over land, legal rights and development priorities.

Despite the drawbacks, I can think of no alternative that provides the opportunity for safely bringing opposite sides together to achieve such a degree of healing in a short time.

–**Mark Chupp**
© MCS 1994, from *Conciliation Quarterly*, Vol. 14 No. 4

How to Make Games Work

- Select appropriate games, bearing in mind the principles and skills you want to focus on in that particular session and the trust level of the group. Be sure that the game will not put down any individual or group. I never pick a game I would not be willing to do myself.

- Present the game as a continuation of the training, pointing to the theme you wish to address through the activity. At the same time, be careful not to overly influence the players by saying too much ahead of time about the conclusions you hope to draw out of the game.

- Give clear instructions before getting people out of their seats and moving around. It is also important to lay down some ground rules ahead of time, including that participation is voluntary. "Challenge by choice" is a standard phrase to let participants know they will be challenged and have the choice to not take part.

- Stay in the facilitator role, modeling the appropriate levels of abandonment and seriousness. I also monitor participants to be sure they clearly understand the rules of the game and to curb any inappropriate behavior. Improper touch or humor can quickly erode the trust in a group.

- Clearly identify the end of the game or activity, taking people out of any roles assigned to them. Thanking and affirming people for risks they have taken can help increase the groups capacity to take on later challenges.

- Open the reflection time, guiding participants through a progression that begins with the activity and ends with practical application. I use a few basic questions to guide me:

    a. What happened in the game?
    b. How did you feel when. . . ? (Point to key transitions in game.)
    c. How does this game relate to your life?
    d. What can we learn from this game? How could we apply it to ourselves?

- During the reflection time, use active listening to validate participants' contributions and be mindful of where you want to take the discussion. The same activity, such as the human knot, can be used to bring out diverse themes, like the nature of conflict, communication patterns, community organizing strategies, etc. Do not be afraid to build on participants' observations to crystallize key points related to the theme.

–**Mark Chupp**
© MCS 1994, from *Conciliation Quarterly*, Vol. 14 No. 4

Mediation Roleplay Tips

A roleplay is a simulation of a real-life situation played by training participants for the expressed purpose of learning specific concepts. It is a powerful learning tool because it forces us to put into action the skills and processes we have read and heard and seen.

Roleplaying isn't always comfortable. It requires a momentary suspension of our own reality to take on another's reality. At times that may feel contrived or forced. At times discomfort may come from feeling the pain of the character because it has touched something deep in our own experience. Being aware of and naming the discomfort, whatever its source, can help free us from it.

Begin the roleplay process by deciding who will play which role. You may want to refrain from playing a role that you identify with too closely. Each participant reads only the information pertinent to her/his role.

Tips for Disputants

- Read through the description of your character. Put yourself into her/his shoes and try to imagine what this person would feel and think and do. Be creative in adding details, but stay consistent with those provided since they were written in conjunction with the other character(s). It is often helpful to wear a name tag bearing your character's name.

- Your task is to play the role realistically and naturally. Find a balance between being totally passive and agreeable and being aggressive and unmanageable. The goal is to make it a good learning experience for all of you, not to give your mediators a hard time!

Tips for Mediators

- As co-mediators, decide who will take responsibility for the various steps. You may want to talk about your styles of working. For example, do you appreciate a "back and forth" style where each is free to contribute to the leading? Or do you prefer more clarity about who leads when?

- Set up your environment. Make the setting as safe and process-ready as possible. Think about seating, table, temperature, newsprint, markers, paper and pencils.

- During the roleplay, remember that experiencing confusion and frustration is expected and is an important part of the learning process. If one approach doesn't seem to be working, try another.

- The collaborative effort with your co-mediator is a critical part of the learning. Co-mediating can be terribly frustrating if you're not working well together, it can be a joy when you're in sync and it can be a relief when you're stuck. Keep checking signals with each other.

Tips for Both

- Before the roleplay, take a moment to center yourselves and get into your roles. You are about to enter a learning process which, even in role play, is potentially transformative. Your attitude, much more than your acting ability, will make it good learning.

- Stay in role, through confusion, tiredness and even absurdity. If there is a role break—everyone bursts out laughing, for example—get back into role as quickly as possible and continue.

- There may be a trainer or coach present to observe the process and help provide feedback. Ignore them. They will not intervene—except in extenuating circumstances, such as a complete impasse.

–Carolyn Schrock-Shenk
© MCS 1995

Suggestions for Coaching Mediation Roleplays

(This sheet is designed to guide roleplay coaches, not necessarily trainers, in a mediation training.)

Over the years we have consistently received comments that having coaches present during the roleplay practice times is much appreciated. Below are just a few ideas for giving verbal and written feedback in your role as a coach. Feel free to use ideas gained from your own experience and context with participants.

During the Roleplay

Generally it is best to allow participants to work through things without comment or intervention. Part of the value of the experience comes from feeling confusion, frustration, uncertainty or discomfort and then finding resolution on one's own. However, there are some situations when a sensitive coach can enhance a role play through a timely intervention:

- Sometimes a key comment or event (or absence of it) will have a major impact on the course of the mediation.

- Calling a time out might be helpful if participants are losing touch with the feelings called for by their role or if either disputants or mediators seem to be losing track of the role play.

- On occasion coaches may suggest techniques or behaviors to try out, especially where the role play would otherwise reach a dead end.

Any intervention should be as brief and unobtrusive as possible to prevent the coach from taking over the role play or the practicing mediators depending too much on the coach's advice. Encourage participants to "learn by doing."

Verbal Debriefing

Groups vary in how much structure they need/desire from coaches. In many cases, participants effectively debrief themselves. Where you sense a need for more structure, the outline on the previous page may be helpful.

It is helpful to refer to characters by the name used in the role play so the individual participant does not feel hostility, anger or criticism directed at him/her personally. Also, it is best to avoid language which indicates what participants should have done, instead using language such as: "Another option you might try is. . . ." or "From the response you got, what might be used in the future?"

Depending on how the role play goes, there will be varying amounts of time to debrief in the small group setting. Sometimes we will debrief in the large group also, and individuals tend to do additional processing at breaks and mealtimes.

Written Feedback

Many of the comments above also apply to written feedback. Even if you've had enough time to voice all of your comments, participants may still find a written sheet helpful so they can mull over it later on their own. Be sure to include observations about room set-up, use of flip chart/chalkboard, body language, tone of voice, "presence" skills, etc., in addition to specific mediation skills in your feedback. Try to balance negative and positive feedback. Or, better yet, make the list of "positives" longer than the "ideas for change." "Coaching forms" are often provided for giving feedback. Use a separate sheet for each mediator.

–MCS Staff
© MCS

Debriefing Mediation Roleplays

At the end of the set roleplaying time, stop the roleplay. Relax, take several deep breaths and slowly let yourself out of your role. Just as importantly, let the other participants out of their roles as well.

Debriefing is the most important part of the roleplay. It involves discussing together, for the sake of learning, the process of the role play, not the content of it. Resist the temptation to revisit the problem and continue trying to solve it. In debriefing, the more specific your feedback on the process, the more helpful the learning.

Begin With Feelings

- As disputants, describe how you felt in your role. Did your feelings change through the process? How and why?

- As mediators, describe how you felt in your role. Did your feelings change through the process? How and why?

What Went Well?

- As disputants, describe what the mediators did or said that helped you feel safe and engaged. What was helpful in moving the process along in a positive direction? Describe any key turning or movement points.

- As mediators, describe what you did or said that helped set a positive tone. What strategies seemed to work particularly well and why? How were you able to use your natural strengths in the roleplay? What things worked well in collaborating with your co-mediator?

What Could Be Changed?

- As disputants, what things could the mediators have done differently to increase your trust and sense of safety? What would have moved you more readily toward a constructive response to the conflict?

- As mediators, what didn't go so well? What things did you do or say or what strategies did you try that seemed unhelpful, inappropriate, or even neutral? What things do you wish you would have tried? What was frustrating or difficult about working with your co-mediator?

After the debriefing a coach or trainer may give you a few written observations about the process and your role as a mediator. Reflect on the comments. Ask questions if you don't agree.

Roleplays are important learning opportunities—both for learning skills and processes and learning about yourself as a person. It may be helpful to spend some time journaling after a role play. What things do you want and need to learn? What things were touched in you personally through the process? What do these tell you about yourself?

–Carolyn Schrock-Shenk
© MCS 1995

Power Tableau

One of the richest and most powerful training exercises I have led is a power tableau. It is a kind of human sculpture that was first used by Kip Hargrave, a Maryknoll lay missioner in Central America. It is powerful because each participant can apply it usefully to their unique situation, because it can accommodate a host of goals and because it draws on both right brain and left brain thinking. I am amazed each time at the variety of situations it elicits; from individual families and interpersonal relationships, to congregations and work places, to race, gender and economic oppression, to revolutionary settings.

You can use the tableau to accomplish a variety of goals depending on the direction you want to go, the questions you choose and how much time you have. You cannot do justice to it in much less than an hour. Most commonly I have used it during mediation training to help participants situate the role of mediation within the context of broader conflict transformation. Using the tableau can:

- help underscore in a tangible way our fundamental goals of justice and right relationships in peacemaking

- help participants recognize the limitations of mediation and ways it can undermine our deeper goals

- help examine the elements needed for mediation to be an appropriate intervention

- provide a practical tool for analysis of power, kinds of power and methods for power balancing

- provide a practical tool for analyzing situations where a significant power imbalance exists, including both structural conflict and interpersonal conflict that has systemic roots

- facilitate the discussion of various nonviolent responses that are required (education, conscientization, advocacy, confrontation, negotiation) and when each of these is appropriate for nonviolent change and conflict transformation.

Setting Up the Tableau

1. Person A lies flat on the floor, face up.

2. Person B stands beside Person A with one foot resting lightly on the stomach of Person A.

3. Person C stands on a chair which is placed directly behind Person B. Person C puts both hands on the shoulders of Person B.

Application and Reflection

4. After a moment of silence ask the group to think about what is happening. What situations in their lives, or about which they are familiar, does this configuration resemble?

5. In groups of three, ask them to share the situations and identify who each person in the tableau represents for each particular situation.

6. In the whole group, elicit and list a variety of situations.

7. Ask each person in the sculpture how they feel. Encourage them to talk about their physical feelings as well as their emotions in their particular role. Other questions, if time, can include:
   - What can you see from your vantage point?
   - How do you feel about the other two tableau members?
   - What messages are you getting from society?

8. Moving back to the larger group begin a discussion about the situation. You can select one of the situations listed to focus on or you can keep it general. I have found the latter more helpful because it allows each person to interact with the situation of their choice. Depending on your direction, questions can include:
   • Is this a conflict? Why or why not?
   • Is it a good situation and are you comfortable leaving it like this? Why or why not?
   • What would it take to transform this situation?

9. As ideas for transformation begin to emerge, invite one or more volunteers to implement their suggested change to the tableau. Possible questions:
   • What happens to the level of conflict with this intervention?
   • What are the positive and negative results of this intervention?
   • How would each tableau member respond?
   • What else can you do?
   • What are the options for a collective response?
   • What sources of power does each member of the tableau have? How can power become more balanced?
   • What role does mediation play in this kind of situation? What would have happened if someone had tried to mediate between the three persons at the beginning?
   • What are the various nonviolent responses that may be needed to transform this situation?

Input

10. Much of the input I do happens in small pieces throughout the discussion. You can provide input on power, power balancing, conflict analysis, nonviolent strategies, etc. I frequently end with an emphasis on the importance of looking for, recognizing and responding appropriately to power imbalances.

–Carolyn Schrock-Shenk
© MCS 1995, from *Conciliation Quarterly*, Vol. 14 No. 4

Warm-Ups, Trust-Builders, Light 'n Livelies, Wrap-Ups

Warm-Ups

Memory Monikers

It's surprising how adding a "moniker" like an adjective, rhyme, or other word association helps us remember another person's name.

Have participants sit or stand in a circle so everyone can see one another. Ask each person to think of a moniker, like an adjective or rhyming word, to associate with their name (or the first letter or sound of their name). For example, "Mighty Monica" or "Chill Bill." Start by having one participant introduce him or herself ("My name is "Mad Max.") Continue around the circle with each participant introducing him or herself, and then repeating the names and monikers of ALL preceding persons. The game ends when the first person repeats all names around the circle.

My Three Symbols

Best with no more than 25-30 people. Supplies: white paper and bright water-based markers.

Give everyone a sheet of blank white paper; have them fold the paper into thirds. Using markers, have each person draw 3 symbols or symbolic pictures, one per folded panel, showing: 1) who they are, 2) what they do, and 3) what they like to do. The first often elicits something about family (of origin or current), the second is work-related, and the third is usually a hobby (often interesting and fun). Go around the room and have each person share their 3 symbols and explain briefly why each was selected. To avoid monotony, have the sharing start at a mid-point in the group and work from side-to-side outward.

Trust-Builders

Folding Hands

This is an easy way to normalize the anxiety everyone feels at trying new techniques like active listening and assertive speaking.

Ask participants to shake out and then clasp their hands in their laps. Notice which thumb is on top. Now ask them to shift all their fingers so the other thumb is on top. Ask how it feels now? Replies will include "unnatural, weird, uncomfortable." Have them clasp and hold their hands in this position for five minutes, then ask how it feels. Most will say it feels less odd. Explain that a neuronal shift takes place as the body and mind become comfortable with the new way. The same thing happens with learning any new skill, including conflict management. That neuronal shift can't happen, however, if one doesn't practice and give the neurons a chance to shift!

Variation

Have people stretch their arms out wide, and then fold them across their chests. Notice which arm is on top and refold with the other arm on top. Follow same instructions as for folding hands.

Blind Trust Walk

An excellent activity to experience giving and receiving trust; can symbolize the mediator's role in helping mediation participants understand and move through the mediation process. Supplies: bandanas.

Have group pair up with someone they don't know well, or don't usually work with. Each person will take a turn being "blind" while a "seeing" partner leads them around the room, building and outside. The blind partner can simply keep eyes closed or wear a bandana, and hold an arm or hand or shoulder of the "seeing" partner, who leads the blind partner to a variety of places (corners, steps, chairs), textures (water, carpet, brick, grass) and other physical experiences (darkness, sunlight, cool, heat). Each partner takes about 10 minutes being "blind."

To Debrief

Ask what it felt like to be "blind," what the seeing partner did well or could have done to add more security; ask the seeing partner what it felt like for them. Make connections to the training, e.g., how critical it is to go slow and give careful explanations for those entering a frightening or unknown situation like mediation or dealing with conflict.

Light 'n Livelies

Energy Surge

Good pepper-upper! You will need a prepared leader in each circuit.

Create "energy circuits" with up to 25 players in each circle holding hands. The energy starts flowing when the leader gives a hand squeeze which is passed from person to person. Wait about ten seconds, and then send another squeeze the same direction or around the opposite way. Send squeezes both ways at once or try a double squeeze! Hardest of all: eyes closed. Send squeezes, each time waiting less between pulses. Usually within a minute or two (when you hear lots of laughter) you know there's enough energy to return to the training.

Three Positions

This exercise can serve both as an energy booster, and also as a way to explore group dynamics. Plan to debrief about each group's decision-making process: who each group's "leaders" were, how they were chosen and what their leadership qualities were; each individual's personal influence; how disagreement was handled. Best with no more than 50 players.

Divide into three groups, facing center. Everyone starts with hands at side in the "neutral" position. Ask someone to model a variation on "neutral." This will be First Position; have everyone try it. Return to neutral. Continue until the entire group has three different positions, and everyone knows how to do them. Ask each group to huddle privately and decide which of the three positions everyone in the group will present. The point is to have all groups presenting the same position without prior consultation, and as quickly as possible. Give the groups 30 seconds to huddle. Call time, and ask each group to face center in the neutral position. At the count of 1-2-3, each group reveals its chosen position at the same time, without talking. Rehuddle for 30 seconds, and reveal again. Continue until all groups take the same position.

Hokey-Pokey

No kidding! This is a great way to wake up a group with the 2 p.m. "sleepies." It works well with international groups too!

Gather the group into a circle; ask for a volunteer to lead the Hokey-Pokey song. Sing it through once so everyone gets the tune and routine. Everyone sings and acts out: "You put your right hand in, you put your right hand out, you put your right hand in and you shake it all about. You do the hokey-pokey [waving or wiggling your hands above your head] and you turn yourself about, and [clap] that's what it's all about." Continue with left hand, right-left leg, elbows, hips, backside, and end with putting your "whole self" in and out! It's fun to have folks hold on to each other at the shoulders a la NY Rockettes when doing feet and legs.

My Bonnie Lies Over the Ocean

You gotta have good knees for this one.

You need a leader on a chair in front of the group. Have everyone sing "My Bonnie Lies Over the Ocean." Each time a word starts with "B," have them stand (if they are sitting) and sit (if they are standing). It gets tricky in the chorus. Once they've got it, speed it up.

Nonverbal Lineup

A good way to mix things up before numbering off a group.

Have participants line up nonverbally by height. This one is easy. If you want a real challenge, have them line up by the month and day of their birthday, nonverbally as well, of course. When they're done, go down the line and have each say their month and day. If a group is very comfortable with each other, you can try age!

Build a Machine

Uses participants' creativity. And their bodies. And it's fun besides.

One person goes to the middle of a large open space and begins some kind of movement that resembles a machine, real or imaginary. Others come up and connect, making up their own kind of movement. Appropriate sounds can be added. The only rule is that you have to be physically connected or touching someone else. When all are connected, the leader can ask the machine to speed up, go full steam, slow down, then stop.

A Big Wind Blows

"Big" people's musical chairs.

Everyone sits in a circle. The leader begins with, "A big wind blows on all who are an only child." (Or "are wearing a belt" or "have never roleplayed" or "love chocolate," etc.) Those who fit the category have to change seats. The leader finds an empty one and the "seatless" person is the new leader and calls out a new category.

Knots

A wonderful metaphor for conflict. Can be just for fun or debriefed with discussing the many ways the experience was like a group conflict they have been in.

Have participants stand in a circle in groups of 8-12. Everyone reaches in their right hand and grabs the right hand of someone else, then reaches in their left hand and grabs the left hand of someone else. The tangled group now tries to untangle. The only rule is no dropping hands. Many groups are able to do it. Some you simply need to call time after while because they are "stuck." That can become part of the debriefing and learning.

Wrap-Ups

Different Strokes for Different Folks

This works best after a multi-day training with no more than 25-30 participants, when certificates of completion are being handed out.

Give the group five minutes to think of a brief positive "stroke" to give each other person in the training. Suggest that "strokes" can be comments about a particularly nice physical feature, a personality trait which is unusually pleasant, a talent or skill that is noteworthy, or something about that person which really enhanced the training experience. Then call each participant's name, ask them to come forward to receive their certificate of completion, and have other group members call out their "strokes" for that individual.

Variation for a training of a week or longer

Sometime during the last half day of the training, put up pieces of large white paper for each participant, noting his or her name at the top. Make colorful markers available and ask everyone to take time to write positive "strokes" or comments on each sheet. Make sure enough time is given, even if extra break time needs to be set aside for writing. Participants take the finished sheets home for "instant strokes" on those "down" days we all experience.

Endgame Toss

A fun ending for trainings of any length. Supplies: a Nerf ball.

Ask participants to sit or stand in a circle to share highlights of the training session. Ask for a volunteer to start the process and toss him or her the Nerf ball to start. Each person should give his or her first name and then briefly share a training highlight. When finished, that person tosses the ball to someone in the circle, who gives his or her name and highlight, and so on until everyone has had a chance to share. If the ball is tossed to someone who has already shared, they simply toss it on to another person who hasn't.

Variation

Participants can say whatever they'd like to say—a highlight, something they've learned, a blessing, words of appreciation, a new commitment, etc. Can be done with the Nerf ball or simply go around the circle.

Texas Hug (or Tennessee Squeeze)

Works great at the very end, after a final song or prayer or other ritual/exercise.

Have participants stand in a circle and link arms around the next person's waist. Ask everyone to take one large step backward. Then take three steps forward.

–Kirsten Zerger, David Brubaker and Carolyn Schrock-Shenk
© MCS 2000

Resources for Further Study on Pedagogy

Lederach, John Paul. *Preparing for Peace: Conflict Transformation Across Cultures*. Syracuse, NY: Syracuse University Press, 1995.
  Note especially Chapter 6 on an elicitive approach to training development.

Lederach, John Paul, and Mark Chupp, *¿Conflicto y Violencia? ¡Busquemos Alternativas Creativas!* Guatemala City: SEMILLA, 1995.
  A practical trainers' manual in Spanish on workshop planning, participatory education techniques, training exercises and role plays.

Macbeth, Fiona, and Nic Fine. *Playing With Fire: Creative Conflict Resolution for Young Adults*. Philadelphia: New Society Publishers, 1995.
  A curriculum and guide for a *completely experiential* training on conflict management; geared for youth but with many ideas adaptable for other settings.

Mock, Ron, ed. *The Roleplay Book: 41 Hypothetical Situations*. Akron, PA: Mennonite Conciliation Service, 1997.
  Roleplays, case studies, sociodramas and one scripted mediation for classroom and workshop use.

Newstrom, John W., and Edward E. Scannell. *Games Trainers Play: Experiential Learning Exercises*. New York City, NY: McGraw-Hill, 1989.
  This is the first of four widely-used books by the same authors full of low-cost, short- to mid-length interactive training activities, complete with instructions for implementation.

Ruth-Heffelbower, Duane. *Conflict and Peacemaking Across Cultures: Training for Trainers*. Fresno, CA: Center for Peacemaking and Conflict Studies, Fresno Pacific University, 1998.
  Helpful resource designed to be used by resettlement agencies that want to train staff to work with conflicts in a culturally competent manner.

Stoesz, Gary. *Meditations for Meetings: Thoughtful Meditations for Board Meetings and for Leaders*. Intercourse, PA: Good Books, 1999.
  A good, basic resource for workshop meditations. Many can be easily adjusted to reflect training concerns.

Walter, Gordon A., and Stephen E. Marks. *Experiential Learning and Change: Theory, Design and Practice*. New York: John Wiley & Sons, 1981.
  A scholarly resource on experiential training.

Journal

Simulation and Gaming: An International Journal of Theory, Practice and Research. David Crookall, ed. Sage Publications.
  Features theoretical papers about simulations in research and teaching, empirical studies, and technical papers on new gaming techniques.

Internet Resources

sg.comp.nus.edu.sg (Simulation/Gaming Internet Exchange)
  This is an indispensable site for access to national and international simulation and gaming professional associations, publications and Internet resources in the area of experiential training, including training tips, industry-specific games, debriefing concepts and learning theory.

www.infoteam.com/nonprofit/nica/meeting.html
  An excellent resource for facilitation techniques and tools; lots of web-based links and online materials.

Permission for Copying

MCS publishes this manual so that it will be used. We strive to maintain a responsible balance between sharing our material and retaining the rights to it. If you find this manual useful and would like to reprint or copy portions of it, please observe the following considerations. If you have further questions about the appropriate use of this material, please contact MCS at PO Box 500, Akron, PA 17501, 717-859-3889, mcs@mccus.org. Most importantly, we trust that your life and work will be enhanced through interaction with this manual.

To reproduce for occasional use in group settings (classes, workshops, seminars, etc.):

1. Material for which MCS gives permission (marked with "© MCS" and listed in the Occasional Copy Reporting Chart which follows):
   - A fee of $.10 a page, per copy, is requested for use in religious, academic and other nonprofit settings.
   - A fee of $.20 a page, per copy, is requested for use in other settings (business, government, etc.).
   - Payment should be made payable to "MCC" and earmarked for "MCS copyright payments," and sent to the above address. A report of which pages you used is helpful for our records. The Occasional Copy Reporting Chart on the next pages can be copied for use as a reporting sheet.
   - Please be sure that proper credit is given to both MCS and the author.
2. Material for which MCS cannot give permission (anything that we have "used by permission"):
   - Contact the author or publisher directly to obtain permission to reproduce these pages. We will gladly assist in providing contact information.

To reprint in a publication (training manual, newsletter, journal, book, etc.):

Please contact the indicated copyright holder. In no case may any of the materials in this training manual be reprinted in any publication without the express written permission of the copyright holder. Again, we can assist with contact information for non-MCS materials.

When asking permission to reprint MCS materials, please include in your request:
- the title and nature of the publication (e.g., *Conciliation Quarterly*, newsletter)
- organization, contact person, address, phone number, e-mail address
- which article(s) you would like to reprint (feel free to adapt the Occasional Copy Reporting Chart for this purpose)
- the anticipated number of copies of the publication
- the anticipated price of the publication

Use of material from this manual does not constitute recognition or designation as an MCS trainer. MCS is not responsible for how material from this manual is used.

Occasional Copy Reporting Chart

MCS does not require you to report your occasional use of material from this manual. However, it is helpful for us to know what pieces are most helpful to our colleagues. A simple note with your payment indicating which articles you used is sufficiently helpful. The chart on the next two pages can also be used, particularly if you are copying a number of articles. This chart lists all articles that MCS gives permission for (as noted in #1 above), so if it is not listed here, please secure permission from the copyright holder before you make copies.

Occasional Copy Reporting Chart

Your Name/address: _____ Date: _____

Page	Title	# of pages	x	# of copies	=	Total sheets
181	Positions vs. Interests (MCS Staff)	2	x		=	
183	Positions and Interests Exercise (Sandi Adams)	1	x		=	
184	Reframing a Conflict (John Paul Lederach)	1	x		=	
185	Reframing Opportunities (Carolyn Schrock-Shenk)	1	x		=	
186	Practice Exercises for Reframing (MCS Staff)	1	x		=	
187	Generating and Evaluating Options (Ron Kraybill and Alice M. Price)	1	x		=	
188	Summarize Points of Agreement (Ron Kraybill)	1	x		=	
190	Some Sample Agreements: Sample Partnership Dissolution (first page only) (Alice M. Price)	1	x		=	
192	Tools for Breaking Impasse (Ron Kraybill)	2	x		=	
194	Calling a Caucus (Ron Kraybill and Alice M. Price)	1	x		=	
196	Handling Difficult Situations (Sandi Adams)	2	x		=	
198	Handling Difficult Situations Exercise (Alice M. Price)	1	x		=	
201	Resources for Further Study on Mediation	2	x		=	
205	Groups: Process, Conflict, Systemic Change: Introduction (David Brubaker)	1	x		=	
212	Designing Good Meetings (John Paul Lederach and Alice M. Price)	2	x		=	
214	Stages of Decision-Making (MCS Staff)	1	x		=	
215	Agreement on Procedure (adapted from Ron Kraybill and David Brubaker)	1	x		=	
216	The Decision Rule (Alice M. Price)	2	x		=	
218	Overview of Group Facilitation (Alice M. Price)	1	x		=	
219	Ten Commandments of Meeting Facilitation (Ron Kraybill)	2	x		=	
222	Dealing with Unhelpful Comments (Ron Kraybill)	1	x		=	
223	Tools for Group Dialogue and Issue Formation (Ron Kraybill)	3	x		=	
229	Consensus Decision-Making In Congregations (Larry Dunn)	2	x		=	
231b	Small to Large Group Consensus: Another Model (bottom of page only) (Bob Gross)	1	x		=	
232	Straw Poll: Testing for Consensus (Susan H. Shearouse)	1	x		=	
233	Training Exercises for Group Process Facilitators (compiled by Alice M. Price)	2	x		=	
235	Systems Theory: A Brief Introduction (Marcus G. Smucker)	1	x		=	
236	Five Characteristics of a Relational System (Marcus G. Smucker)	1	x		=	
237	Four Points of Tension in a System (Marcus G. Smucker)	1	x		=	
238	Four Steps Toward a Healthy System (Marcus G. Smucker)	1	x		=	
239	Organizational Culture: An Overview (David Brubaker)	1	x		=	
240	Organizational Culture Grid Exercise (MCS Staff)	1	x		=	
241	Organizational Change: An Overview (David Brubaker)	1	x		=	
242	Toward Organizational Health (summarized and adapted by Alice M. Price)	1	x		=	
243	Powerlessness in Systems (Ron Kraybill)	2	x		=	
247	Conflict in Groups: The Cross-Stitching Effect (Ron Kraybill)	3	x		=	
250	Habits in Conflict: *Divided By* vs. *Bound Together By* Conflict (Ron Kraybill)	2	x		=	
252	How to Move from *Divided By* to *Bound Together By* Conflict (Ron Kraybill)	1	x		=	
253	Conflict Management for Leaders: Some Principles (Carolyn Schrock-Shenk)	1	x		=	
259	Facing Difficult Issues in the Congregation (Marcus G. Smucker)	4	x		=	
263	Healthy Expression of Conflict in Group Settings (John Paul Lederach, expanded by Alice M. Price)	1	x		=	
264	Opening Up Systems Issues (compiled by Alice M. Price)	3	x		=	
267	Letting Go of the Past (Ron Kraybill)	2	x		=	
270	Resources for Further Study on Systems and Groups	5	x		=	
277	Standards and Ethics for Practice: Introduction (Alice M. Price)	1	x		=	
278	MCS Mission and Philosophy of Practice (MCS Staff)	1	x		=	
280	Thoughts on Practitioner Integrity (Carolyn Schrock-Shenk)	2	x		=	
288	Intervention from the Inside (Dean Peachey)	3	x		=	
293	Questions of Appropriateness (compiled by Alice M. Price)	1	x		=	
296	From the Inside (Barbara Daté and Lorna Monkman)	1	x		=	
297	Tough Stuff (Carolyn Schrock-Shenk)	2	x		=	
301	The Art and Science of Training: Critical Assumptions (Carolyn Schrock-Shenk)	2	x		=	
303	Trainers as Tools for Transformation (Michelle LeBaron)	3	x		=	
307	Overview of Training (Kirsten Zerger)	4	x		=	
311	The Power of Games (Mark Chupp)	2	x		=	
313	How to Make Games Work (Mark Chupp)	2	x		=	
314	Mediation Roleplay Tips (Carolyn Schrock-Shenk)	1	x		=	
315	Suggestions for Coaching Mediation Roleplays (MCS Staff)	1	x		=	
316	Debriefing Mediation Roleplays (Carolyn Schrock-Shenk)	1	x		=	
317	Power Tableau (Carolyn Schrock-Shenk)	2	x		=	
319	Warm-Ups, Trust-Builders, Light 'n Livelies, Wrap-Ups (Zerger, Brubaker and Schrock-Shenk)	3	x		=	
322	Resources for Further Study on Pedagogy	1	x		=	

Total number of sheets	
Nonprofit use, x $0.10; other use, x $0.20	$
Total fee	$